Phyllis Fiarotta's

NOSTALGIA CRAFTS BOOK

Phyllis Fiarotta's
NOSTALGIA

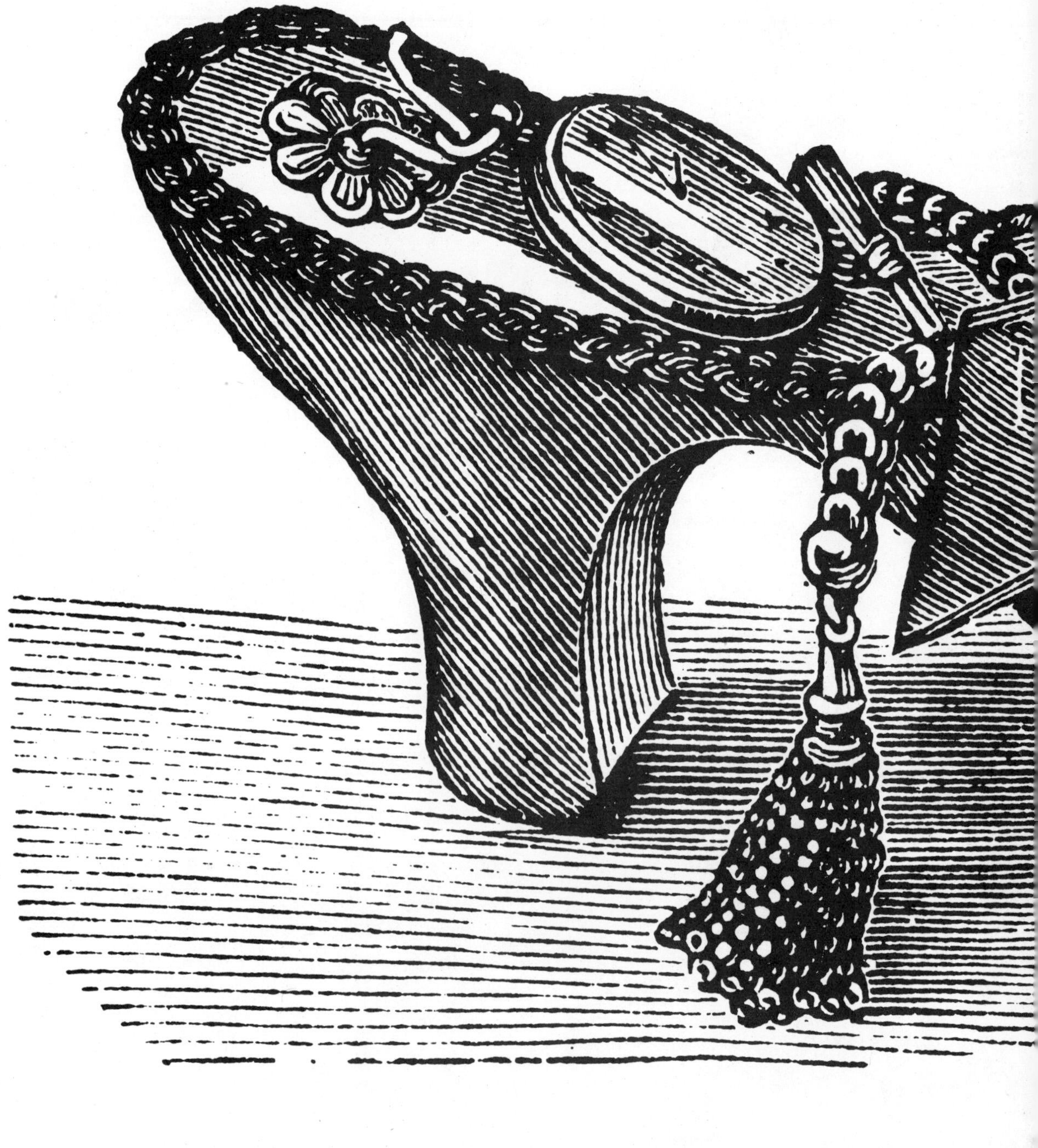

CRAFTS BOOK

Workman Publishing Company, New York City

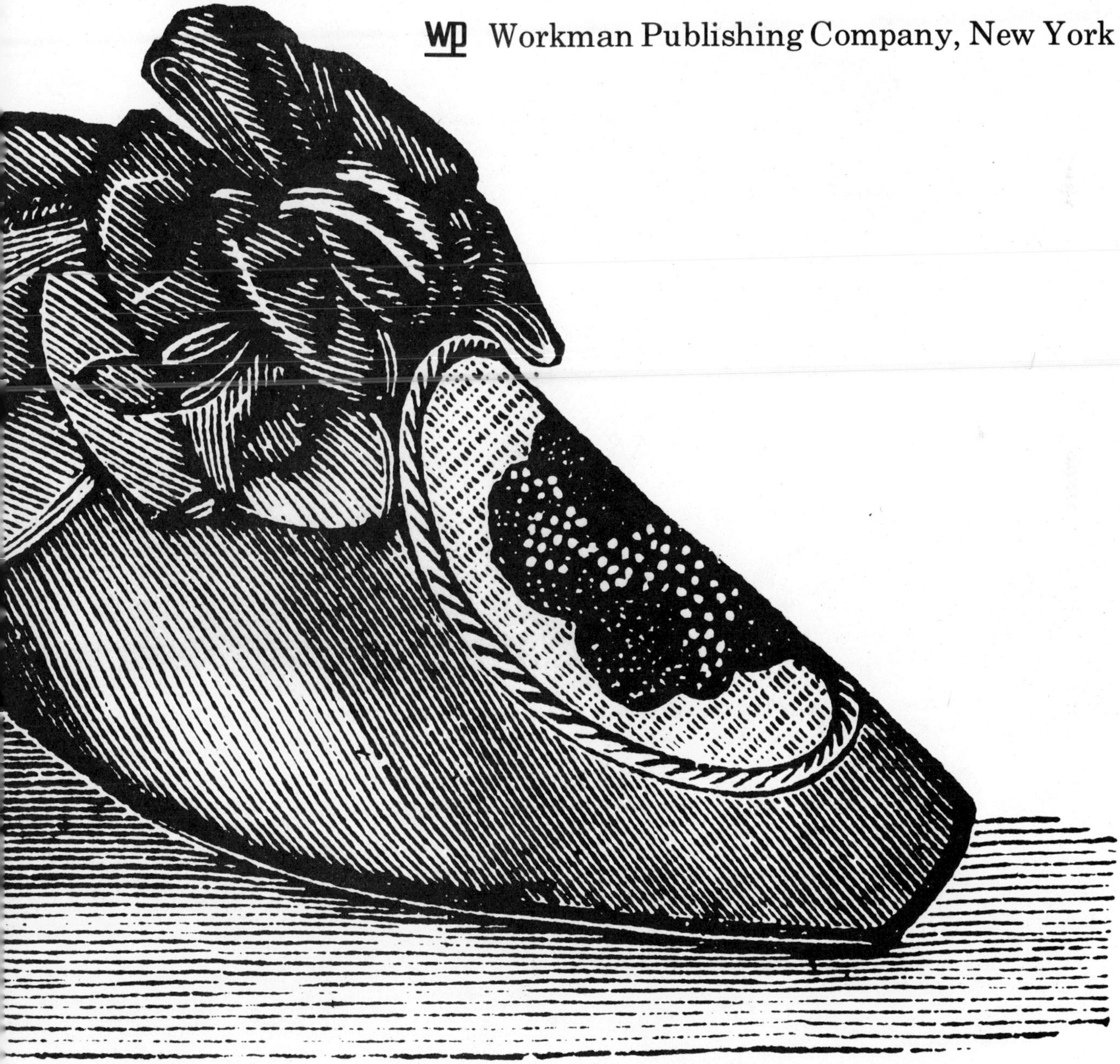

ALSO BY PHYLLIS FIAROTTA
Sticks & Stones & Ice Cream Cones

Illustrations by Phyllis Fiarotta

Cover and color photography by Will Rousseau
Black and white photography by Gustavo Francisco and Allan Baillie
Typeset by Vermont Photo-Tape
Color work by Scala Fine Arts
Printed and bound by the George Banta Co.

Workman Publishing Company
231 East 51st Street
New York, New York 10022

ISBN:
Hardcover—0-911104-43-7
Softcover—0-911104-44-5

First printing, September 1974
Second printing, December 1974

To Mom, the most beautiful lady to have ever touched my life

Written with
the invaluable help
of
Noel J. Fiarotta

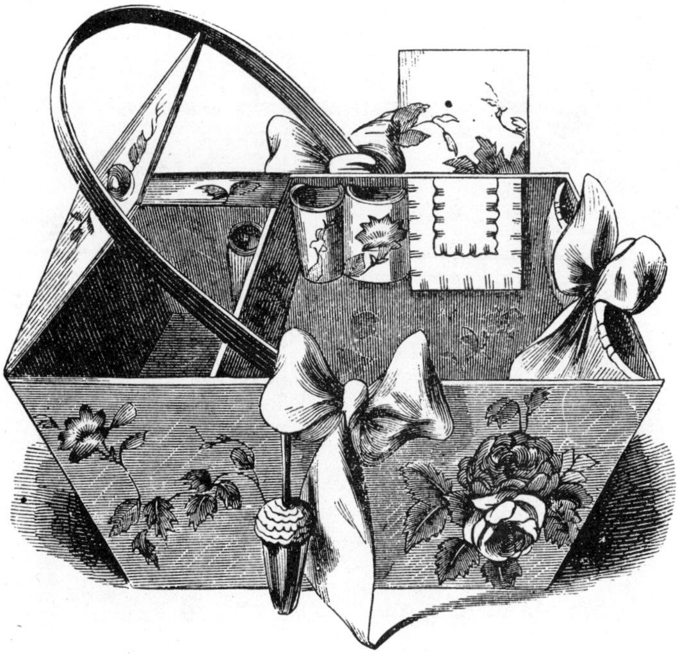

ACKNOWLEDGMENTS

Mom, for your gingham curtains, the endless granny square pillows and afghans, and for all your chocolate covered "Cheerios." Thanks for a house filled with "The joy of making it yourself."

Esta Ginsberg, for dragging me out of bed at six in the morning to go shopping for nostalgia at flea markets. For all the items you found in jam-packed heaps I was too sleepy to even see. Also to her mother for saving *her* mother's incredible quilts.

Lee Lulu, for letting me pull the Bonnet Baby Quilt right off sleeping Jonathan even though he started to shiver in his sleep.

To Giavana LaMarca, the most talented human being I know. Thanks for all those needlepoint creations you whipped up for this book in less time than it takes to roll a ball of yarn.

To Barbara Poulsen, for coming in at the last minute with a few items too good to pass by.

And thanks to those nameless craftsmen whose priceless handmade creations I've stumbled upon while putting together this book. Their work will live on through it.

CONTENTS

REFLECTING

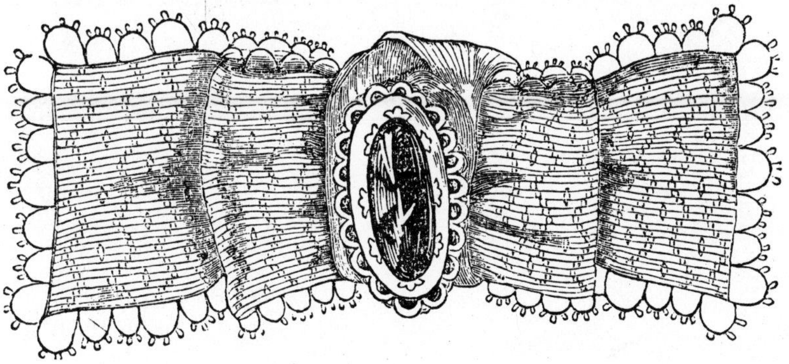

Somehow, it always seems that things were better when you were younger. (It doesn't really matter how old or young you may actually be.) There was something about the style of life, the sweetness of the peaches, the quality of the products that once were.

Technology has improved our living standards. Anything and everything a person needs is just a walk or car ride away. At the super shopping centers you can find it all: bolts of fabric, aisles of furniture, racks of clothing and shelves of kitchenware in every style and size imaginable. It's not the material goods that we're missing. What you can't find is the handcrafted quality of a grandfather clock made by J. Hetzel, a set of dishes cast by Jim Garah or a lace tablecloth made by Grandma. Though we all live with mass-produced goods, many of us feel a loss, something missing, an instinctive yearning for the imperfect and unique, for the primitive world of the handmade.

Let's go back in time: it's early nineteenth century and you happen to be a person who enjoys weaving your own lace. Along comes a chap by the name of Jacquard who has just invented a bobbin net machine. It can produce lace by the mile in a fraction of the time you can produce several inches. Now you don't have to spend hours weaving lace, you can purchase as much as you want. Great, isn't it? But now you sacrifice the satisfaction you got in your own work, and the quality and originality of your lace. That's not so great.

The need for handwork diminishes as technology provides us with machine-made, perfectly stamped replicas. They tell us we now have more leisure time. They are right. Can you imagine if you had to weave your own material after spending weeks just making and dying thread, just to produce one garment for your wardrobe? In most cases the machine has helped people live better. But be that as it may, there remains something that was better before.

Everything handmade has a special quality about it. You want to run your fingers across it. It is softer, more intricate, more pleasing to look at. Even an old car, when it was waxed to its most brilliant luster, provoked a tactile experience: you just had to add that last extra buff to the shine with your shirtsleeve.

It is because there's such pleasure in that feel, in the pride of a creator and in the uniqueness and integrity of something homespun that we have all gone back to crafts. No home should be without the glow and warmth of things handmade. It is amusing to think that the craft techniques we work today will be considered nostalgia art by someone of another generation, reflecting on the good old days—the days we are living now.

BASIC CRAFT INFORMATION

THE GRID

The most important tool the craftsman will ever have to master is the grid. The grid enables the "I-can't-draw-a-straight line" artist to re-create a drawn design to perfect scale.

There are two parts to the grid. The first, the horizontal and vertical lines that form a network of squares called the graph. The second, the line drawing placed on the graph. The carriage design will serve as an example.

Study the grid. The key to the grid is the scale given in the instructions; in this case, 1 square equals 1 inch. This means that each square of the final drawn graph will measure exactly one inch.

A quick study of the grid's graph will help you select paper large enough to accommodate the design. The carriage's graph is 8 squares wide. Since each square is one inch, the width of the completed design will measure 8 inches. Some designs will call for paper patterns while others will require the design to be drawn directly on the intended surface. Brown wrapping paper is ideal for large projects. Use indelible felt-tipped markers for drawing.

If you feel uneasy about projects that call for a design drawn directly on a surface, try this trick. Draw the design first on lightweight paper. Place a sheet of carbon paper between the paper design and the intended surface, carbon facing down; drawing facing up. Follow the design's lines with a straight pin. The design will transfer in pin dots.

How to plot the horizontal lines. To start the graph, draw the first horizontal line (left to right) close to the top of the paper. Measure one inch down from each end of the line and mark.

Connect both marks with a ruled line. Continue to plot one inch horizontal lines until you match the same amount of lines shown in the graph.

How to plot vertical lines. Draw the first vertical line close to the left edge, perpendicular to the horizontals (at right angles). Plot the vertical lines in the same manner as the horizontal lines.

If a design should call for a scale of one square equals 3 inches, follow the same procedure as above using a 3-inch measurement.

How to place the line drawing. Placing the drawing on the graph is just a matter of concentration. Study how the line passes from square to square. Does it cut a corner, pass diagonally or curlicue through the center? Re-create the exact path of the line as it moves through each square.

How to rescale the grid. The grid can be adjusted, larger or smaller, to fit your particular need. Suppose you wish to make a needlepoint carriage to fit in a 10-inch wide frame. To enlarge the design you must establish a new scale. This is done by dividing the number of squares on the width of the carriage's graph into the desired measurement. In this case, 8 (squares) divided into 10 inches). The new scale will then be one square equals 1¼ inches.

How to grid an ungridded drawing. Several drawings in this book are not placed on a grid because they are drawn exact size for the intended craft. These drawings can be rescaled larger or smaller to suit your particular needs. To rescale any exact-size drawing, trace the drawing from the book on tracing paper. Draw a grid over the design with a ¼-inch box network. If you use a scale one square equals ½ inch, you will be doubling the design, and so on. Using this method, any drawing or photo from books, posters, magazines, greeting cards and so on can be gridded and then enlarged or reduced to suit your needs.

SEWING NEEDS

Felt. A non-woven wool and synthetic fabric. It is ideal for many craft projects because it does not require hemming. This is especially convenient for appliqué work. Felt shrinks slightly when washed.

Stuffing. Cotton is sold by the roll and is best suited for quilted or patchwork spreads because it can unroll in large flat sheets. Polyester is a synthetic stuffing sold in one-pound packages. It is lightweight, washable, and it does not shift or bunch. It is non-allergenic. Chip foam is sold by the bag and is used to stuff heavy fabric items.

Threads. Embroidery thread is sold in small packages and is used primarily for embroidery. Nylon thread or plastic threads are extra strong and are used where transparent threads are desired.

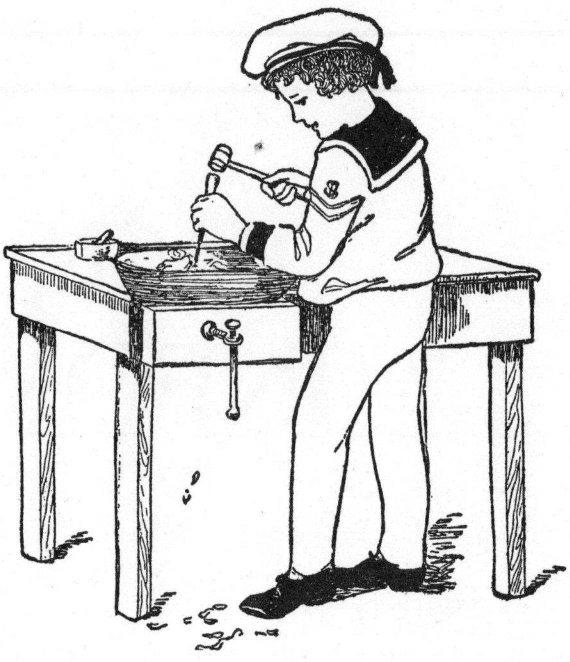

ADHESIVES

White glue. Water-base glue sold in applicator-tip plastic bottles. This glue is ideal for most craft projects. It dries clear.

Bond Cement. A clear cement in a tube. It is a quick drying cement used in heavy duty projects. Do not use bond cement on foam balls, back of mirrors or painted surfaces.

Epoxy. A super-strong glue. It comes in a five minute variety which dries in five to eight minutes, or in the regular formula which dries overnight.

Rubber Cement. A rubber-base cement sold in a bottle with a brush-lid applicator. Excess rubber cement can be rubbed away with your fingers. This is not a permanent glue and can stain through paper.

PAPER

Tracing paper. Transparent paper sold in pads at stationery and art supply counters. For. extra large tracing paper, check art supply stores.

Oaktag. Lightweight cardboard sheets with a sheen finish, sold in large inexpensive sheets in a wide variety of colors at five-and-dime stores or stationery counters.

Mat board. Heavy cardboard with a pebble finish sold in large sheets. Stationery stores carry white boards and art supply stores stock a wide variety of colored mat boards.

Origami paper. Small square packages of lightweight paper. One side is colored and the other side is white.

Tissue paper. Tissue is sold in packages of multicolored sheets. Art supply stores carry different size packages.

Construction paper. Basic colored craft paper sold in packages at five-and-dime stores.

Wrapping tissue. Gift tissue is sold in five-and-dime stores and is a good substitute for tracing paper which is used in many craft projects.

Bond. Basic drawing paper sold in spiral pads at any counter selling paper goods.

FOAM

Hard foam shapes. Craft foam is sold in many different shapes. Balls are available from ½ inch to 8 inches in diameter. There also are cones, egg shapes, a 12-inch wreath shape, square blocks and sheets that come ½ inch thick. Craft foam can be carved with a sharp knife.

Soft pillow shapes. Upholstery foam comes in 12-inch round or square pillow shapes and in large sheets in various widths that can be used for chairs and couches.

Soft chip foam. This foam is used for stuffing pillows or soft toys and it is sold in large bags.

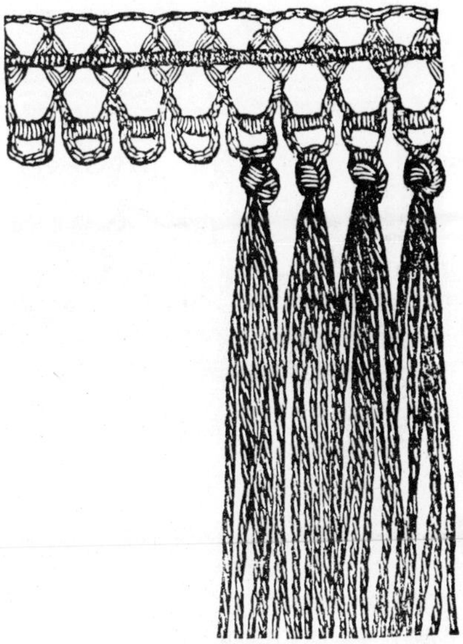

BEADS

Seed beads. These are tiny glass beads that are sometimes referred to as Indian beads. Seed beads are sold in small packets at your five-and-dime store and are used to make beaded flowers, woven bags and detailed designs on clothing.

Tube beads. Also known as rectangular beads. These beads have a wide hole and are available in glass and plastic. Avoid using plastic beads in projects that may involve heat.

Decorative beads. Crystal beads are faceted glass beads. Pearl beads are coated in a soft pearl-like finish. Donkey beads are large ceramic beads that have been fired and glazed. Buy old necklaces for a wide variety of these special beads.

Wooden beads. A wide variety of round, square, tube and decorative shapes are available in wood in all sizes and colors. Some beads are heavily painted while others are just lightly stained allowing the natural grain to show. Wood beads can be used in all crafts.

Sequins. Sequins are available in many sizes and textures—small, large, faceted, smooth—and in a variety of special shapes such as leaves and hearts. All can be bought at the five-and-dime store sewing counter.

Jewels. Sew-on jewels, flat on one side and faceted on the other, are round or diamond shaped and come in several decorative colors.

WIRE

Beading wire is sold in small packets wherever beads are sold. Picture wire can also be used in some crafts that require a heavier structure.

RIBBONS AND OLD LACE

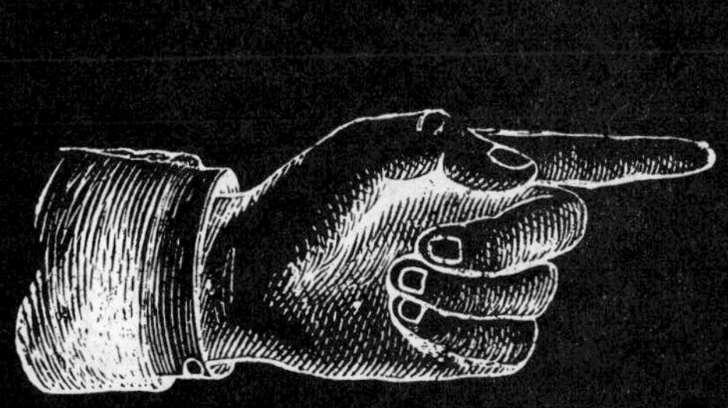

RIBBONS AND OLD LACE

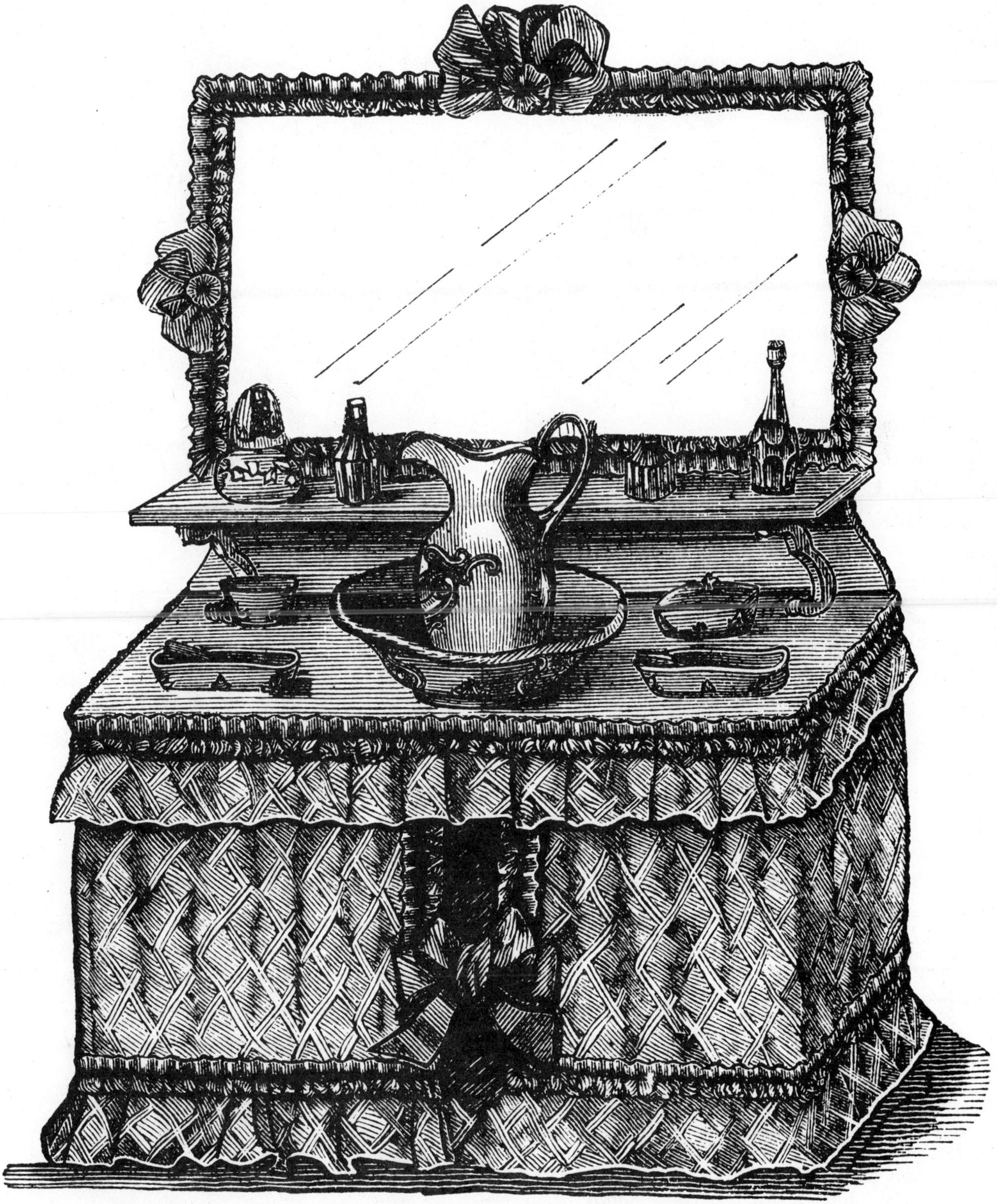

In 1867, at the Paris Exhibition, a dress of filmy handmade lace was valued at $17,000. It took forty women seven years to complete. Handmade lace was quite popular a hundred years ago—doilies, collars, tablecloths and other household items were made or trimmed with this most delicate of cloths. To this day, some people still make their own.

It is hard to say when and how lace had its origin. Although swatches of lace-like fabric have been found in ancient tombs, it is generally agreed that lace, as we know it today, blossomed when Europe emerged from the Middle Ages and took to bedecking itself with grace and splendor. For some two centuries, men wore more lace than women. It was used for ruffs, cuffs, collars, scarfs and ties. Boots, too, were adorned with ruffles of lace.

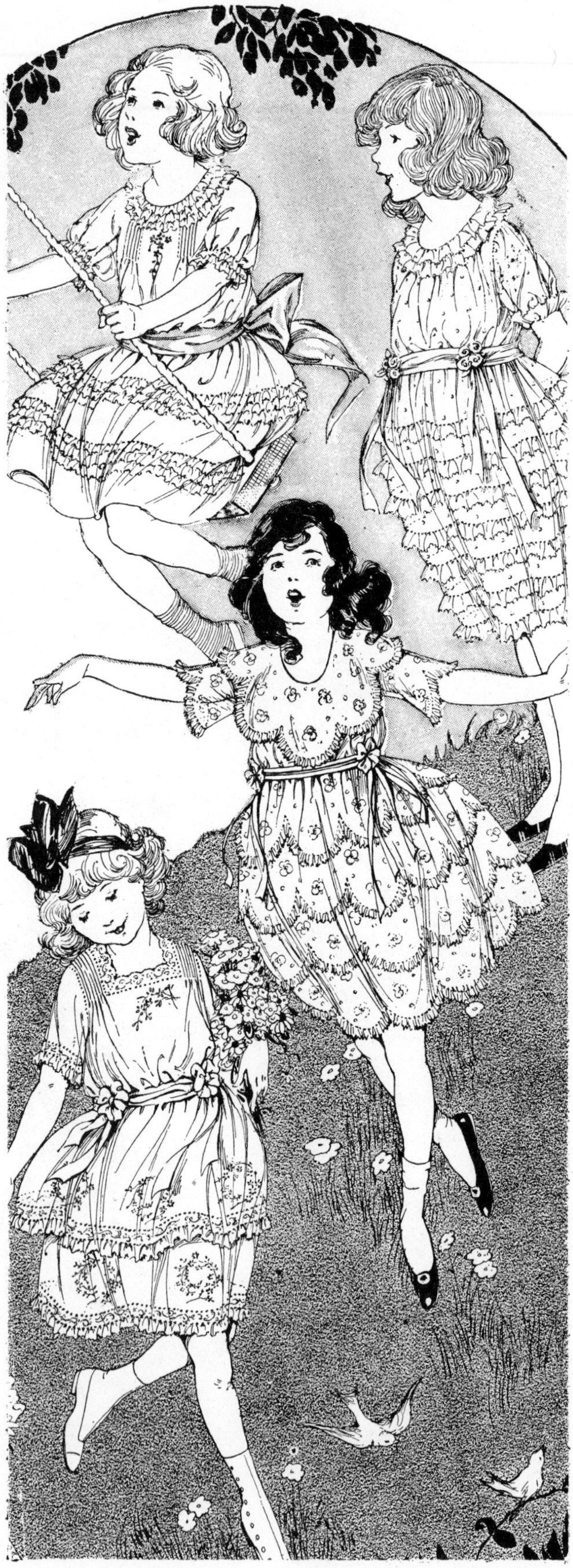

Handmade lace is of two types: needlepoint lace and bobbin (or pillow) lace. Needlepoint is made with a needle and a single thread. The pattern is drawn on parchment and is stitched to a piece of heavy linen for the purpose of holding it straight. Threads, sometimes three or four in number, are placed on the many lines of the pattern, and are lightly fastened through to the lin-

en. The entire figure is then worked, filling and open work, mesh by mesh, and when it is completed, the stitches holding it to the linen are cut and the lace comes free.

In bobbin lace, the design is drawn off on stiff paper which is carefully stretched over a pillow—a round or oval board padded to form a cushion—and placed on the knees of the worker. The pattern is picked out along the outline of the draw-

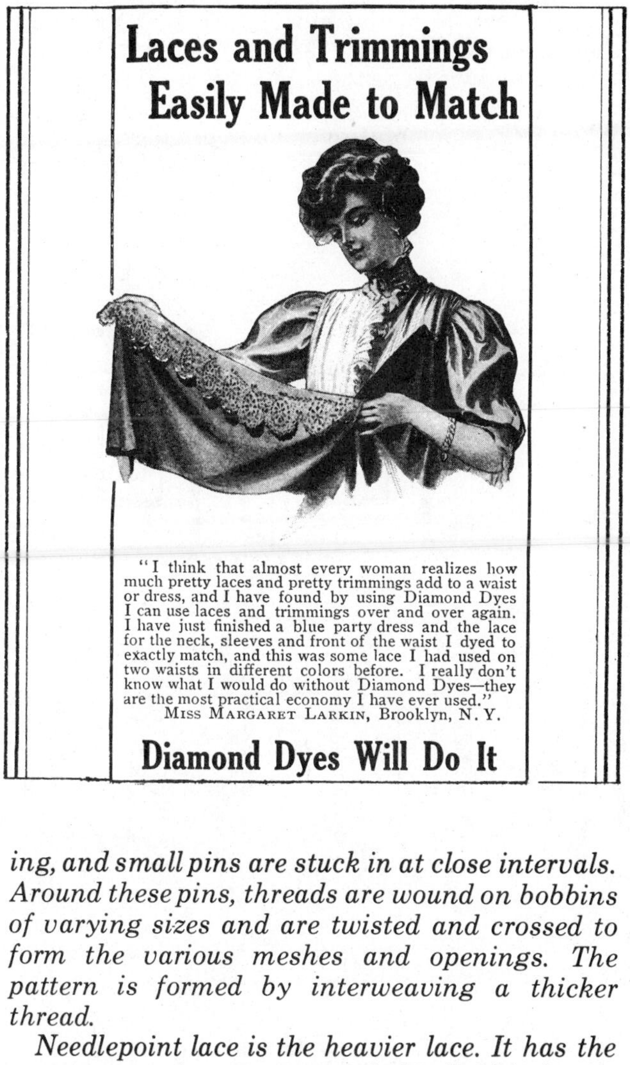

ing, and small pins are stuck in at close intervals. Around these pins, threads are wound on bobbins of varying sizes and are twisted and crossed to form the various meshes and openings. The pattern is formed by interweaving a thicker thread.

Needlepoint lace is the heavier lace. It has the appearance of greater strength, but bobbin lace is very supple and is prized for the way it can be draped.

The development of the lace machine to its present perfection was a slow process. In 1760, a stocking weaver of Nottingham examined the lace on his wife's cap. He believed he could produce this fabric on his stocking machine, and he did produce an open-weave fabric, but it unravelled if the thread broke. This process was improved by the invention of the bobbin net machine in 1809. Since then, nearly every design and mesh of handmade lace has been mechanically produced. It takes machines seconds to produce what women have worked years to make.

This chapter is not about how to make lace. To the initiate that would be quite an undertaking. What follows are projects made with machine-made, store-bought lace—all different types of lace. Frilly, soft, delicate items that sentimentalists will adore.

LACE FRAMES

The least one can do for a treasured family portrait is coddle it behind a delicate, lacy frame.

1. Purchase an inexpensive frame or recycle an old frame. A wide, flat frame is recommended.
2. Buy pre-gathered lace (sold by the yard at sewing counters). To figure how much you need, measure the sides of the frame.
3. Steam-press the gathered edge of the lace.
4. Glue the lace to the frame, about ¼ inch from the inside edge, with white glue. Begin at the bottom center of the frame and continue all the way around, slackening the lace as you round the corners. Allow the ends to meet and overlap slightly. Trim.

5. Finish the frame with one-inch ribbon. Choose a pastel color. Glue the ribbon so that half of it covers the gathered portion of the lace. Fold the other half into the inside opening of the frame. Fit the ribbon into right angles when rounding the corners. The ribbon should begin and end at the same point as the lace.

6. A finishing touch—glue a satin bow over the spot where the ends of the ribbon meet.

7. For a fancy mat like the one shown in the illustration, follow the instructions for the next project.

BROCADE MATS

Nowadays mats are usually made of plain cardboard, but one covered in lace or brocade—or really any fabric—is easy to make and much the nicer. The mat is placed between the picture and the frame to provide a border.

1. Measure the frame opening on the underside. Cut a piece of cardboard to this measurement.

2. To map out the mat, measure 1½ or 2 inches (depending on the size of the frame or the picture you want to mat) in from all sides of the cardboard. Mark in two places on each side and connect the marks with ruler-drawn lines. This should give you an inside rectangle or square.

3. Use a mat knife or a single-edge razor blade and a ruler to cut out the inside rectangle (Fig. 1).

4. Place the mat on the wrong side of your fabric. Trim the fabric to within one inch of the mat.

5. Snip off the corners of the fabric up to the corners of the mat. Then cut away the fabric in the center opening to within ½ inch of the mat's inner edges. (See Fig. 2. The striped areas show which fabric should be cut away.)

6. Cut slits from the corners of the fabric in the center of the mat to the inside corners of the mat (Fig. 3).

7. Fold over the four sections of fabric in the mat's opening and glue them to the underside of the mat (Fig. 4).

8. When the glue on the inside fabric has set, pull the two pieces of side fabric taut and fold them over the mat. Glue (Fig. 5).

9. Repeat with the top and bottom fabric. Fig. 6 is what the back of your mat should look like. When dry, place mat over your photograph and frame. Try a brocade mat in a lace frame (see preceding project).

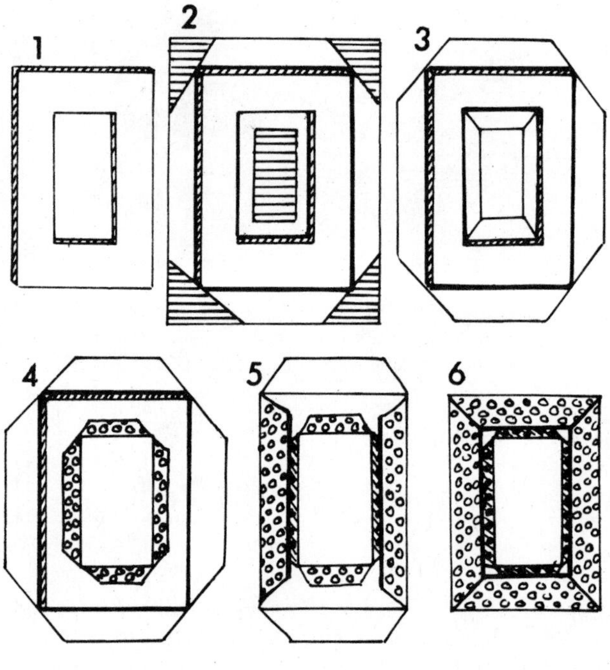

RIBBON MATS

These ribbon mats are actually free-standing frames. Riffle through your old papers, and pick out something memorable to display on a ribbon mat.

1. Cut a piece of cardboard larger than the item you intend to frame. It should be more or less the same shape.

2. Place the cardboard on the wrong side of a piece of fabric, lace or otherwise, and trim it to within one inch of the cardboard.

3. Snip off the corners of the fabric (See Fig. 2 of Brocade Mat).
4. Fold over the four fabric sides and glue them to the underside of the frame. Allow to dry.
5. Lay decorative ribbon across the right and bottom sides of the mat's face.
6. Tuck the ends of the ribbon under, and glue them to the back of the mat.
7. Cut out a piece of colored paper or gift-wrapping paper slightly smaller than the mat.
8. Glue the paper to the back side of the mat.
9. Cut a rectangle of shirting cardboard as shown by the dotted line in Fig. 1.
10. Fold the cardboard and glue it to the back of the mat as shown in Fig. 2.
11. Tuck your keepsake into the crisscrossed ribbon, and tack it down with an embroidered flower patch.

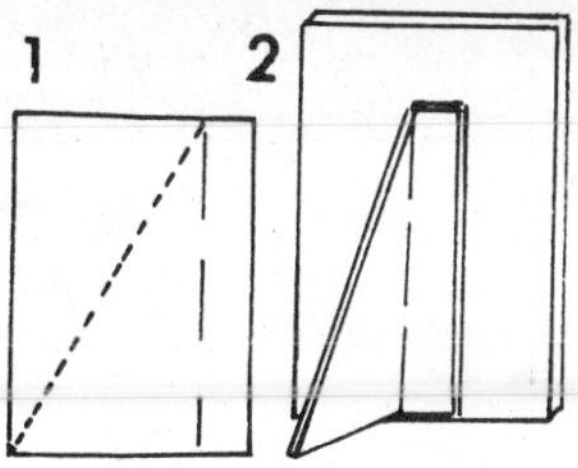

PORCELAIN LACE MIRROR

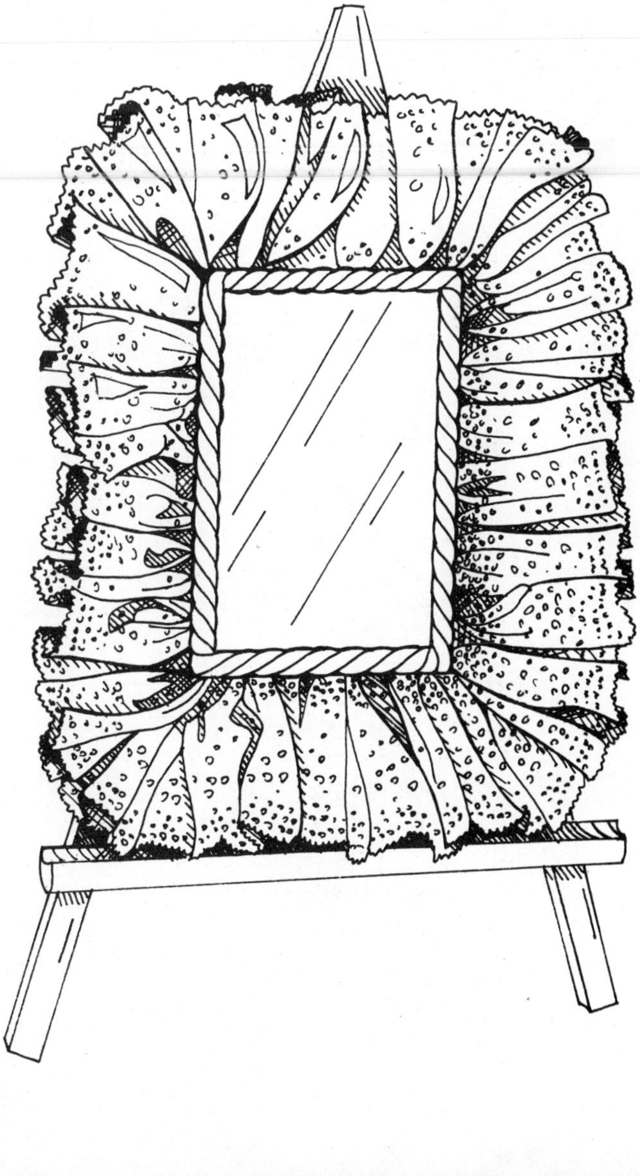

This little mirror has the delicate look of a porcelain doll and is so ingeniously simple in design that you might want to make several.

1. Buy a small 5-inch x 7-inch framed mirror at the five-and-ten.
2. Buy a wide piece of pre-gathered lace, at least six inches longer than the four sides of the frame.
3. Saturate the lace in a cup of liquid white glue.
4. Place the mirror right side up on wax paper. Brush extra glue on the frame.
5. Lay the gathered edge of the lace along the frame, overlapping the mirror slightly. Start at one corner and go all the way around, adding extra lace at the corners. Cut off any excess lace.
6. Arrange the lace in smooth folds, and allow it to dry thoroughly.
7. When dry, brush on high-gloss varnish, liquid plastic, or a découpage finish.
8. Glue a wide decorative cord or ribbon over the gathered edge of the lace.
9. Hang the mirror, or stand it on an easel.
10. Note that with this same method, you can transform an ordinary picture frame into a porcelainized-lace confection.

MEMORABILIA SHADOW BOX

You see a lot of these around today—it's the latest craze. Bits and pieces of memorabilia tacked to the back of fancily lined boxes. The effect is unusual—rather like having a miniature hutch on your wall.

1. Any box can be transformed into a shadow

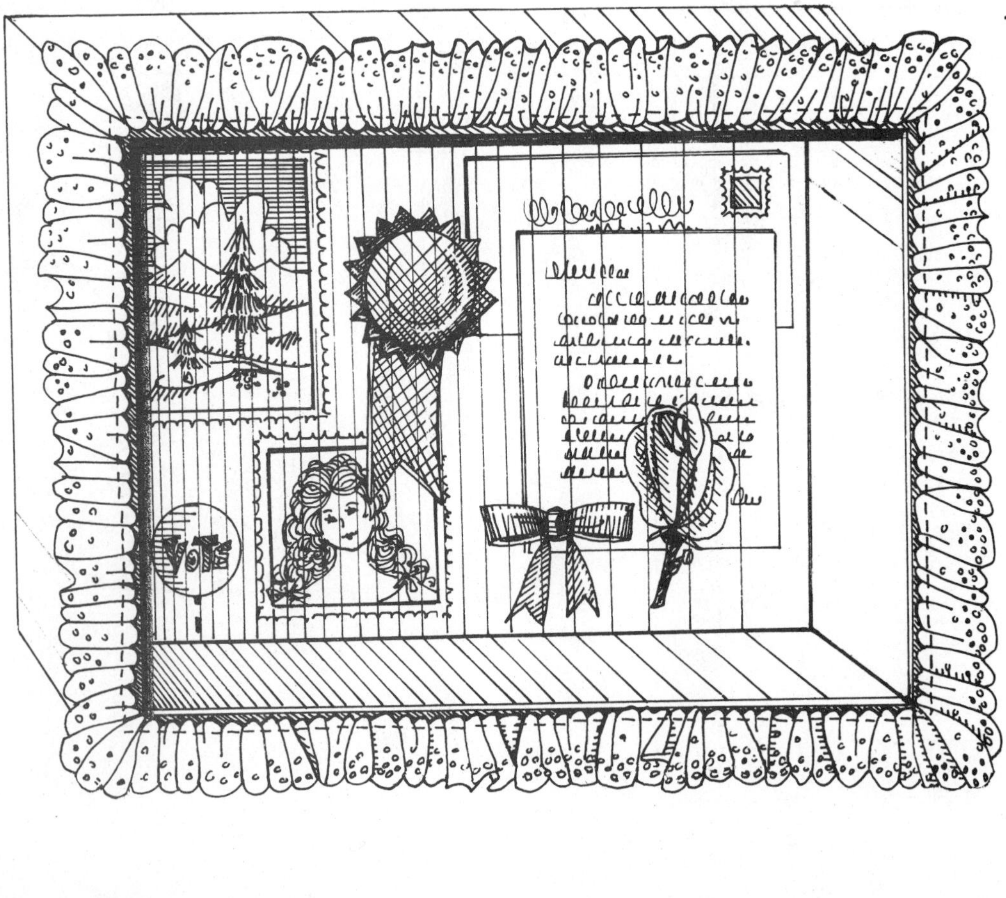

1

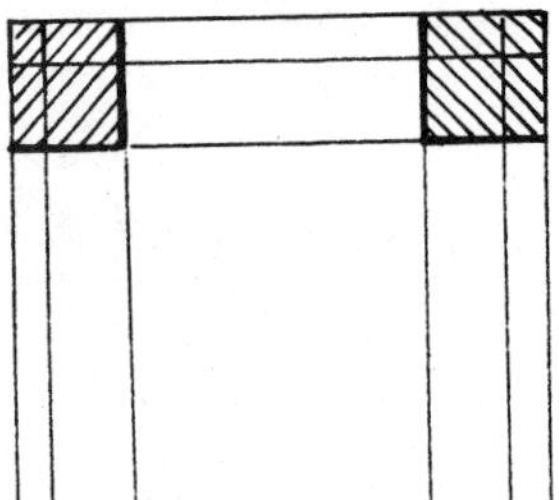

2

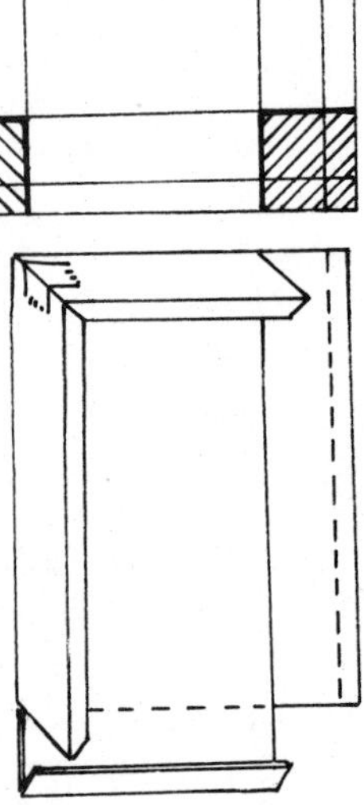

box. Food, soap, or gift boxes are all ideal.

2. To make your own box from a piece of oaktag, see Fig. 1. First, draw a rectangle or a square the size of the desired box in the center of the oaktag. Next, measure about 4 inches out from each side of the rectangle. Mark with a soft pencil line and cut away all excess outside of that line. Now take one-inch measurements in from each edge and mark with lines.

3. Cut away the corners as shown in Fig. 1.

4. Fold toward the center along all pencil lines.

5. Tape the sides together as shown in Fig. 2, and then tape the top edges.

6. If you choose a ready-made box, you will have to add a ledge on the rim. Cut one-inch strips of lightweight cardboard the length of the four sides. Tape or glue the four strips onto the top rim of the box.

7. You cover the outside of the box by gluing on fabric, gift wrap or colored paper. Precut the fabric, making each piece ¼ inch longer than each side, so it can extend slightly around the corners. Pour liquid white glue into a small paper cup, and using a wide brush, cover one side of the box at a time. Stretch the fabric over the glued surface and let dry. Cover the four sides.

8. Paint the inside of the box in a pastel shade.

9. Glue pre-gathered lace along the top edge. For a smoother finish, glue a decorative ribbon over the gathered portion of the lace.

10. Use paste or photo corners to attach your keepsakes to the inside of the box.

11. Either stand the shadow box up (you can make a cardboard stand following the directions given earlier in this chapter for Ribbon Mats) or hang it on the wall.

LACE TRINKET BOX

A popular pastime on which much attention was once lavished was the making of decorative boxes to store hairpins, jewelry, or trinkets, to send gifts in, or to send as gifts.

1. Choose a small gift box with a cover, or an empty candy, cracker or soap box.

2. If you are using a gift box, remove the sides of the cover. If you are using a food box, remove the face of the box with a single-edge razor blade. Tape shut any side that may have been opened in use.

3. Paint or paper the inside of the box. If you paper it, choose a colorful gift wrap. Cut the paper to fit the individual sides and glue it to the inside of the box by applying white liquid glue with a wide flat brush.

4. Glue pre-gathered lace to the four exterior sides of the box. Start with wide lace on the lower

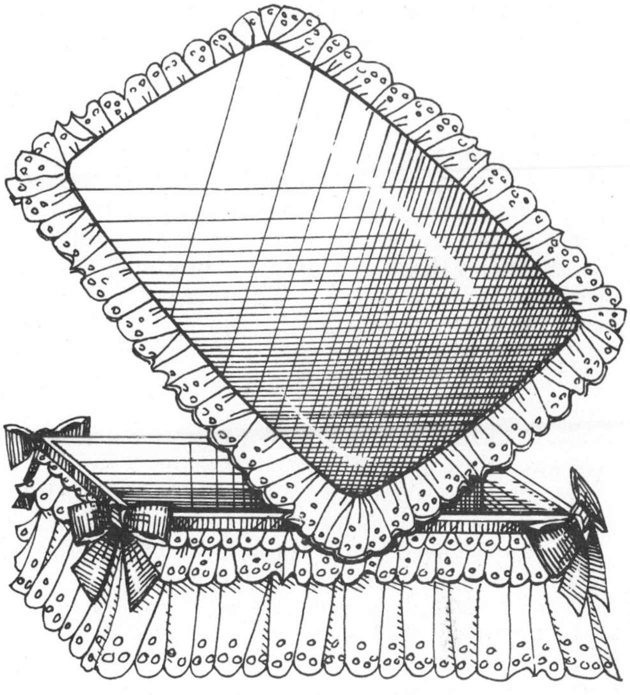

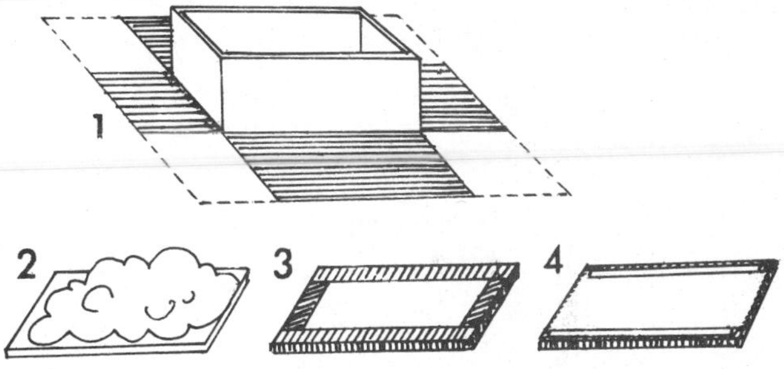

part and add one or more layers of narrow lace above it, overlapping each slightly. The top of the last layer should be flush with the rim of the box.

5. Fold over and glue a wide pastel colored satin ribbon along the rim to hide the gathered edges of the lace. Paste small bows of the same ribbon to the four corners of the box.

6. If you prefer to cover the box with cloth before you add the lace, place the box in the center of a piece of fabric. The extending fabric should

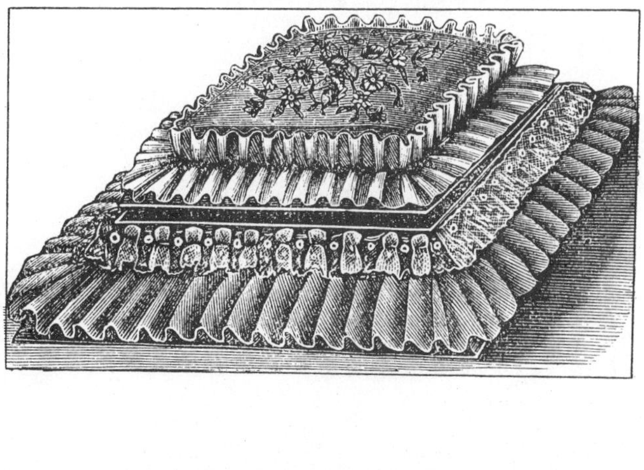

be one inch greater than the height of the box on all sides. Cut away the corners as shown in Fig. 1. Paint the sides and rim of the box with white glue, bring the fabric up on the sides, and fold it over into the box.

7. Choose a piece of velvet or bridal satin for the lid. Again, cut the fabric so that it is one inch larger on all sides than the area to be covered.

8. Place a generous wad of cotton or polyester on the cover (Fig. 2). Top this lining with the fabric (right side facing out). Then invert the layered cover so that its bottom faces up.

9. Fold over the fabric that extends beyond each edge and tape or glue it to the underside of the lid, as shown in Fig. 3.

10. Cut out a piece of colored construction paper slightly smaller than the cover.

11. Paste the paper on the underside of the lid.

12. To keep the cover from sliding, glue two drinking straws along the long sides of the lid, about ¼ inch in from the edge (Fig. 4).

VANITY TRAY

Arrayed with perfume and apothecary bottles, the graceful vanity tray added a touch of elegance to the Victorian lady's dresser.

1. Select a wide wooden frame, preferably one that has some depth.

2. If the frame you choose does not have its own glass, have a piece cut to size at your local glazier or hardware store.

3. Paint the frame with an oil-base paint or a semi-gloss latex paint in a soft pastel shade.

4. When the paint is dry, brush on a furniture stain. Before the stain dries, wipe it off, leaving whatever gets trapped in the frame's recesses and in the imperfections in the wood. This will give the frame an antique look.

5. Cut a piece of heavy cardboard to fit the inside of the frame.

6. Paint the cardboard the same color as the frame.

7. Cover the entire top of the cardboard with lace. You can use individual lace motifs pieced together, lengths of lace ribbon or a piece of the lace fabric that is sold by the yard. Use small dabs of glue to keep the lace in place.

8. Insert the lace-covered cardboard and the glass into the frame. Tack both securely to the inside ledge of the frame.

9. Screw decorative handles (available at fancy houseware and hardware stores) onto each end.

RIBBON PILLOWS

In the old days, throw pillows were heavily bedecked; even the simplest would have a decora-

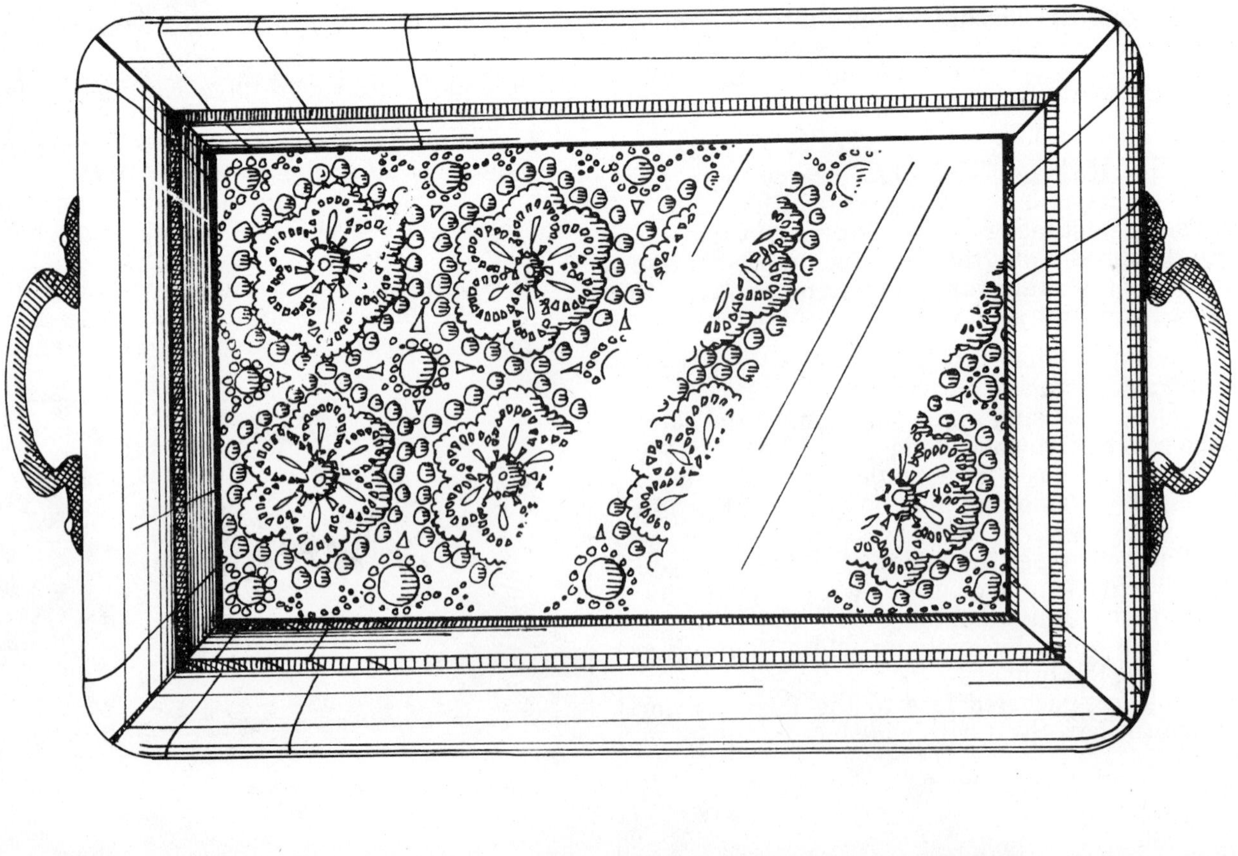

1

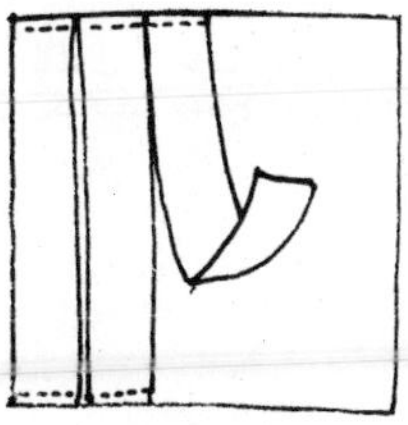

2

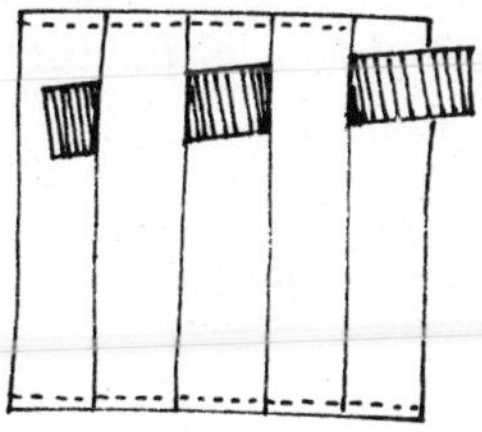

tive fringe. Today, plainer pillows are the common favorite. These ribbon pillows are a compromise between the two—combining modern simplicity and a little charm of the old.

1. Ribbons can be the same width or can vary in width. The pillow shown is made with contrasting-colored ribbons of the same width.
2. Cut two base pillow shapes any size you desire. The base shape should be ½-inch wider than the pillow on all sides to allow for seams.
3. Place the first vertical ribbon ¼ inch from the left side of one base shape. Sew it down at top and bottom, starting not quite at the edge of the fabric. Trim any extending ribbon (Fig. 1).
4. Continue to sew vertical ribbons side by side and flush with each other, but leaving the ¼-inch margins above and below, until the entire base is covered.
5. Weave the first horizontal ribbon in and out of the base ribbons. Slide the ribbon to the top of the pillow. Sew the ends of the ribbon to the sides of the pillow, ¼ inch from the two side edges (Fig. 2).
6. Continue weaving the cross ribbons, alternating each row so that one ribbon begins beneath a vertical strip, the next begins above, and so on. Keep the weave fairly tight.
7. Place the two pillow sides together, right sides facing.
8. Sew the pillow together on three sides and half of the fourth side, stitching ½ inch in from the edge.
9. Turn the pillow right side out.
10. Stuff with cotton, chip foam, polyester or worn stockings.
11. Hand sew the open seam closed.

LACE DÉCOUPAGE

Découpage is a method of sinking something under a layer of varnish or finish. It is an excellent way to preserve old mementos that are in need of restoration, and an opportunity for some of those old photos and papers to emerge from their storage and into your life again. You don't have to choose a document for your découpage —it could be matchbook covers from romantic

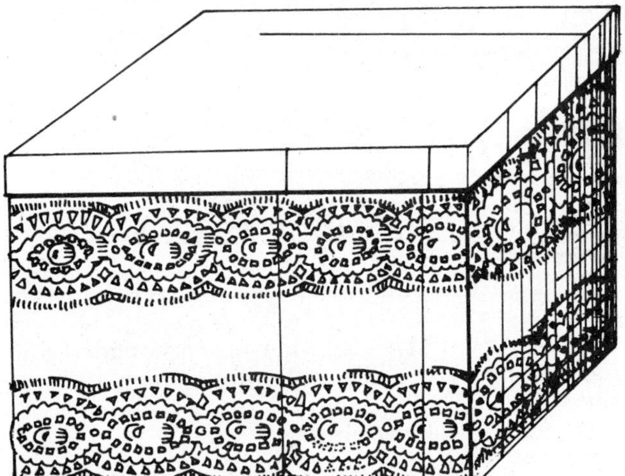

places, a dried flower picked on some memorable day, or, as in the illustrations, some pretty lace.

1. Give a fresh coat of paint to a frame, box—jewelry or otherwise—or any other item you wish to découpage.
2. Select lace to fit the item or items to be decorated. The frame shown uses a strand of connected lace vignettes of the type which is sold by the yard. The box below it is bordered with two rows of embroidered lace ribbon.
3. Apply white glue to the intended découpage area with a wide brush.
4. Stretch the lace over the glued surface and press down. Overlap the connecting ends slightly.
5. Brush a liquid finish over the entire item. You can purchase commercial découpage finish or just use white glue (which dries clear). Liquid plastic or varnish are less satisfactory choices as they both have a yellowish cast when dry.
6. Apply at least five coats of finish, allowing each one to dry thoroughly before applying the next. The finished découpage item can be antiqued by sanding with steel wool or by brushing on a wood stain and wiping off the excess with a soft rag.

BUCKLES AND BOWS

No fashionable lady at the turn of the century failed to sport at least one bow on her attire. Bows adorned hats, bodices, skirts and sleeves; they did duty as buckles and bounced on the toes of dancing shoes.

1. Make six loops of ribbon using 3-inch lengths.
2. Sew three loops together so that the ends overlap slightly, as in Fig. 1. Sew the other three together.
3. Gather two lengths of lace, each 2 inches long and 4 inches wide.

SHOE ROSETTE

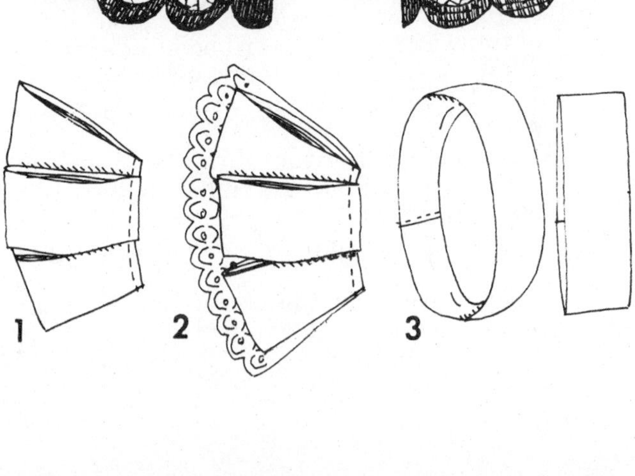

4. Sew the gathered lace to the underside of each loop unit, ends together (Fig. 2).
5. Sew the two units together so they overlap by ¼ inch.
6. Make a second lace bow that is identical to the first but smaller. The loops should be made from 2½-inch lengths of ribbon and the lace should be 1½ inches long.
7. Sew the two constructed bow units together.
8. Sew the ends of a 4-inch length of ribbon together to form a circle (Fig. 3). Fold the circle to form two loops, keeping the sewn ends on the underside.
9. Slip the loop through a buckle form (available at sewing counters). Sew this buckled loop to the center of the constructed bow.
10. If you wish to camouflage the raw ends on the underside of the bow, sew on a small lace or flower patch.

THE PETTI-SKIRT

The petti-skirt is fashioned after the delicate petticoats women wore so many years ago. In those days, the intimate apparel was so intricately designed, so beautiful; what a shame to have been hidden under so many layers of clothes. One of these ruffled creations would make an elegant skirt—soft as an era past, yet chic as the latest in the fashion magazines.

1. To make a dressy skirt, choose a fabric like bridal satin, lace or velveteen. For more casual wear, you might use a bright calico, denim or gingham.
2. Choose a flare, semi-circle, A-line or any other full skirt pattern for the base of the petti-skirt. Follow the pattern's instructions for completing a knee-length skirt. Do not hem.
3. Cut a length of the skirt fabric 5 inches wide and twice as long as the circumference of the skirt's bottom hem. You may have to sew several lengths of fabric together to make a long enough piece.
4. Gather one side of the strip to make a ruffle

Ladies' Fine Silk Finished Petticoat

Given Free for a Club of Only Six Yearly Subscribers at Fifty Cents Each, or Twelve at Forty Cents Each

The well-bred, dainty woman loves pretty gowns and furbelows of all sorts—it is her nature to admire the beautiful and to wish to please those about her by the garments she wears. But no matter how handsome her dress and accessories are, she cannot appear genteel and up-to-date if, when she lifts her dress skirt, she shows a shabby petticoat. The petticoat we offer as a premium this year, and which is shown to good advantage in the accompanying illustration, is one that will delight the feminine heart, because it is one of the most attractive styles shown in New York this season. It is strictly tailor-made, of a fine quality of mercerized silk finished sateen, and has no raw surfaces, all the seams being French made. The 15-inch flounce around the bottom has twelve rows of shirring, and has strapping at the top and bottom of the flounce. It is finished at the bottom with a dust ruffle. Heretofore we have sent the petticoat at the receiver's expense, but this year we are able to send a petticoat of the same quality free and post-paid for the same number of subscribers as formerly. Petticoat manufacturers assure us that colors will be fashionable again this fall, and with that fact in mind we have decided to offer a selection. We therefore will supply this petticoat in black, or in a fashionable shade of either green or brown, these latter colors being the most popular at the present time. We will send the Ladies' Fine Silk Finished Petticoat by mail post-paid, also THE LADIES' WORLD for one year, upon receipt of **$1.85**; or we will give the Petticoat *free* to any one sending us a club of **Six** subscribers for one year at 50 cents each, or **Twelve** subscribers at 40 cents each; or for **Seven** subscribers at 40 cents each and 60 cents extra in cash. Or we will send the Petticoat post-paid, without subscription to the magazine, upon receipt of $1.45.

that will fit the skirt's hem. Leave an extra ½ inch at each end for seam allowance.

5. Sew the two ends together, right sides facing, to form a continuous band.

6. Pin the ruffle to the hem of the skirt, right sides facing, and sew together.

7. The next layer of flounce should be a band of lace between 3 and 5 inches wide. Its length should be twice the circumference of the gathered ruffle's hem.

8. Gather this second flounce and sew it—right sides facing—to the hem of the first ruffle on the skirt.

9. Continue to add ruffles in this way, alternating lace with fabric, until the skirt reaches the desired length. Each flounce should be twice as wide as the preceding one to create a full sweep of ruffled skirt.

10. Hem the final row of ruffle. If you'd like to, you can use the eyelet lace that is scalloped on the bottom and requires no hemming.

11. For an added touch, sew thin satin ribbons over the seams above the first and last ruffles.

DOLL COLLAGES

This quaint doll collage—made from colored paper, lace and fabric, and once a common sight on nursery walls—makes a perfect present for a young child.

1. You can use a paper doll, a cut-out figure from a magazine, or an old-fashioned print for your doll form. Or you can make your own; in fact, a head is all you need. Cut a circle from colored construction paper with some kind of protuberance that will pass for a nose.

2. For the background, glue a piece of colored construction paper to a piece of cardboard that has been cut to fit your frame.

3. Paste the figure in the center of the background. If you are using only a head shape, glue it near the top.

4. Make the hat from an oval piece of colored paper. Glue thin gathered lace along one side to make a brim. Then glue the hat to the head.

5. The skirt is made from several layers of thin gathered lace. Start at the feet and work up to the waist. If you are working with a head shape, judge where the feet and waist would fall.

6. For the cape, cut a largish triangular piece of fabric and then round the top side.

7. Sew center-gathered lace on the bottom and side of the cape.

8. Glue the cape in place and add a small bow under the neck.

9. To suggest a basket or bag, paste small fabric flowers to a circle of felt and glue to the completed doll.

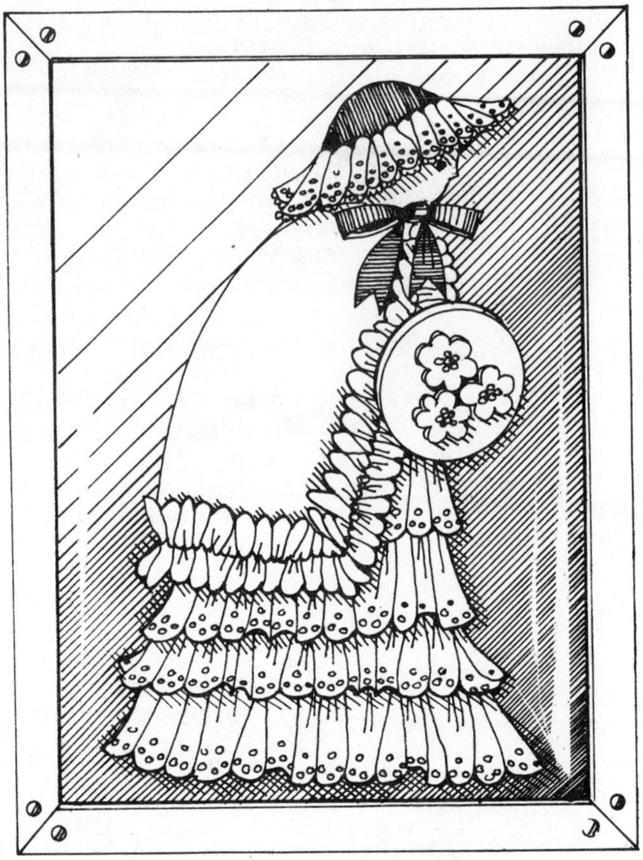

LACE COLLARS

Of the lovely things elegant women have worn about their necklines—necklaces, chokers, delicate chains—one of the most charming was lace. Intricate lace collars circled the necks of the fanciest dresses, softening those demure, high-necked gowns. Make one for yourself or for some good little girl.

1. The numbered figures on the grid represent the front and back of the corresponding collars in the old illustration. *Note:* on the old illustration, the figures on the left are the *backs* of the collars.

2. To make a pattern for the collar of your choice, enlarge the grid on a sheet of paper (preferably brown wrapping paper) so that one square equals 1½ inches. Then draw the collar parts on the enlarged grid. (See page 13 for detailed directions on how to enlarge patterns from a grid.)

3. Once you've drawn your patterns, cut them out and pin to the fabric. Then cut your fabric. Note that with the exception of the back of collar 3, the back-collar shapes make only one-half of the back collars. When cutting out the fabric for

4062. FOUR ATTRACTIVE COLLARS FOR A GIRL, 4 sizes, 4 to 16 years; price 10 cents. It requires ⅝ of a yard of material either 18 or 27 inches wide.

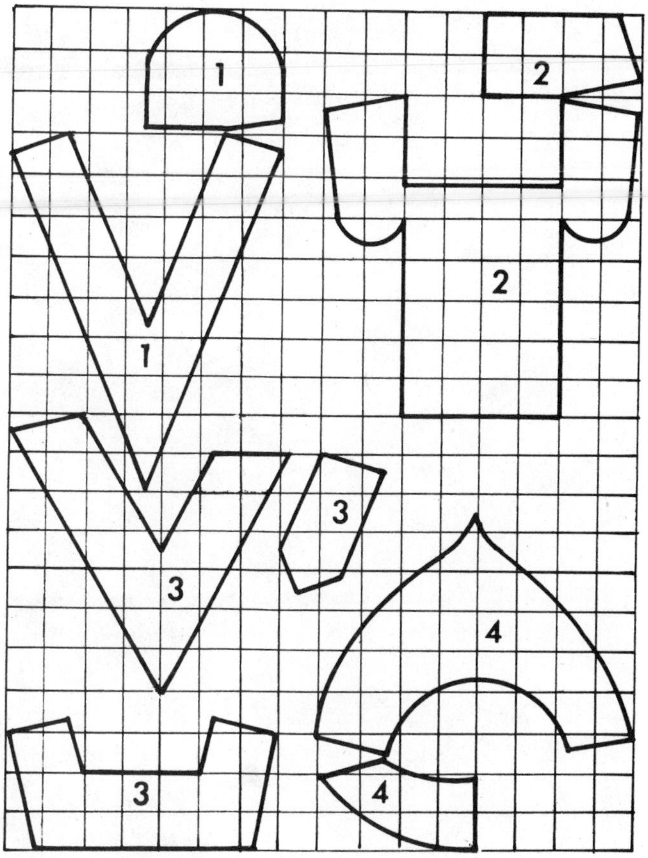

back collars 1, 2 and 4, you have to cut out two of each shape. You can just flip the pattern over to cut out the second half.

4. Construct the collar by pinning the two back collar shapes to the shoulder line of the front collar. Sew each together, right sides facing, with ½-inch seams.

5. For unlined collars, make a ¼-inch hem around all unfinished edges. Sew pre-gathered lace to the underside of the collar all the way around. Hand-stitch bias tape on the underside to cover the raw edges of the lace.

6. For lined collars, you have to cut out *two complete* collar shapes (front and back). Sew the lace along the rim of one collar shape, ¼ inch in from the edge, right sides facing. Then place the two collar shapes together (right sides facing, lace tucked between the two), and sew along all edges, ½ inch in from the edge. Leave two inches of collar unsewn on the back edge. Turn the collar inside out and hand-sew the open seam closed.

7. To fasten the collar, use hooks and eyes, buttons and loops, snaps or a frog.

Collar 1 has ribbon trimming sewn to the front. Angle the ribbon as you sew around the corners.

Collar 2 is made from a bright floral print.

Collar 3 has no lace trim but is bordered on all sides with decorative cord or piping. The extra tab closes the collar on one side with a buttonhole and button.

Collar 4 has embroidered borders.

RIBBON ROPE

This simple technique can be used with any material, and the end product has as many uses as you can think of. Today, children braid vinyl strips into lanyards to wear around the neck. In the nineteenth century, leather was braided into handles. A ribbon rope might be used as a decorative handle for a handbag, a Christmas ornament, gift wrapping, as a window-shade pull . . . anything.

1. To start the rope, take four long lengths of thin grograin ribbon and loop the ends of each length. Stitch the loops in place.
2. Slip the unlooped ends of the ribbons into the loops in a clockwise pinwheel (Fig. 1).
3. Stitch the four interlocking ribbons secure on the underside (Fig. 2).
4. Fold the top and bottom ribbons (letter b in the diagrams) over the center of the locked loops so that they now face in the opposite directions.
5. Fold the side ribbons (letter a) over then under the b ribbons (Fig. 3). Continue to fold as above.
6. Sew on added ribbons to lengthen the rope.

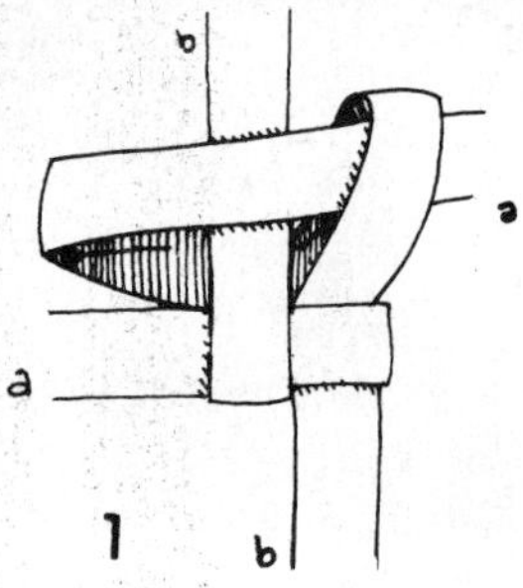

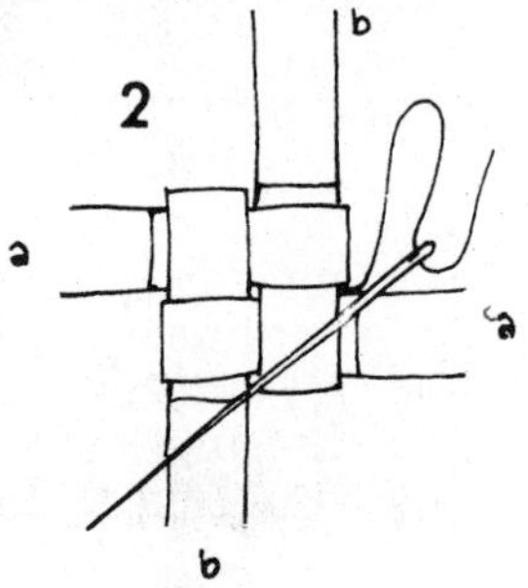

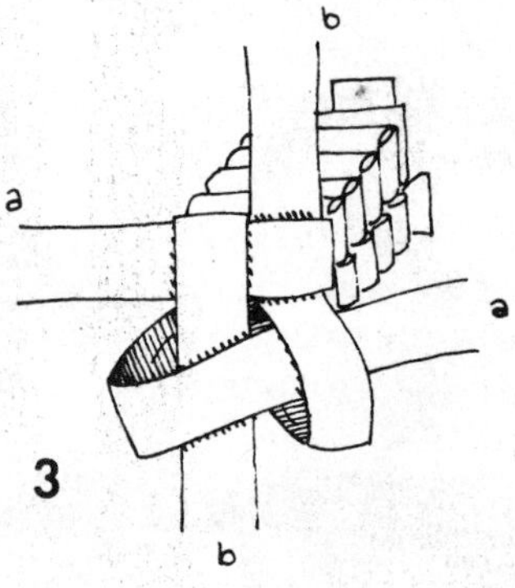

Baubles, Bangles and Beads

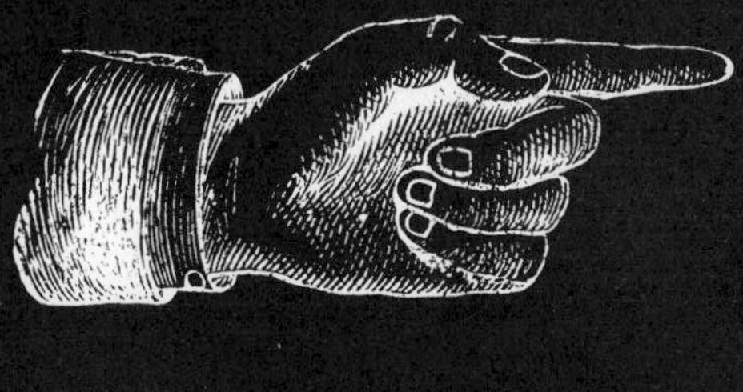

Baubles, Bangles and Beads

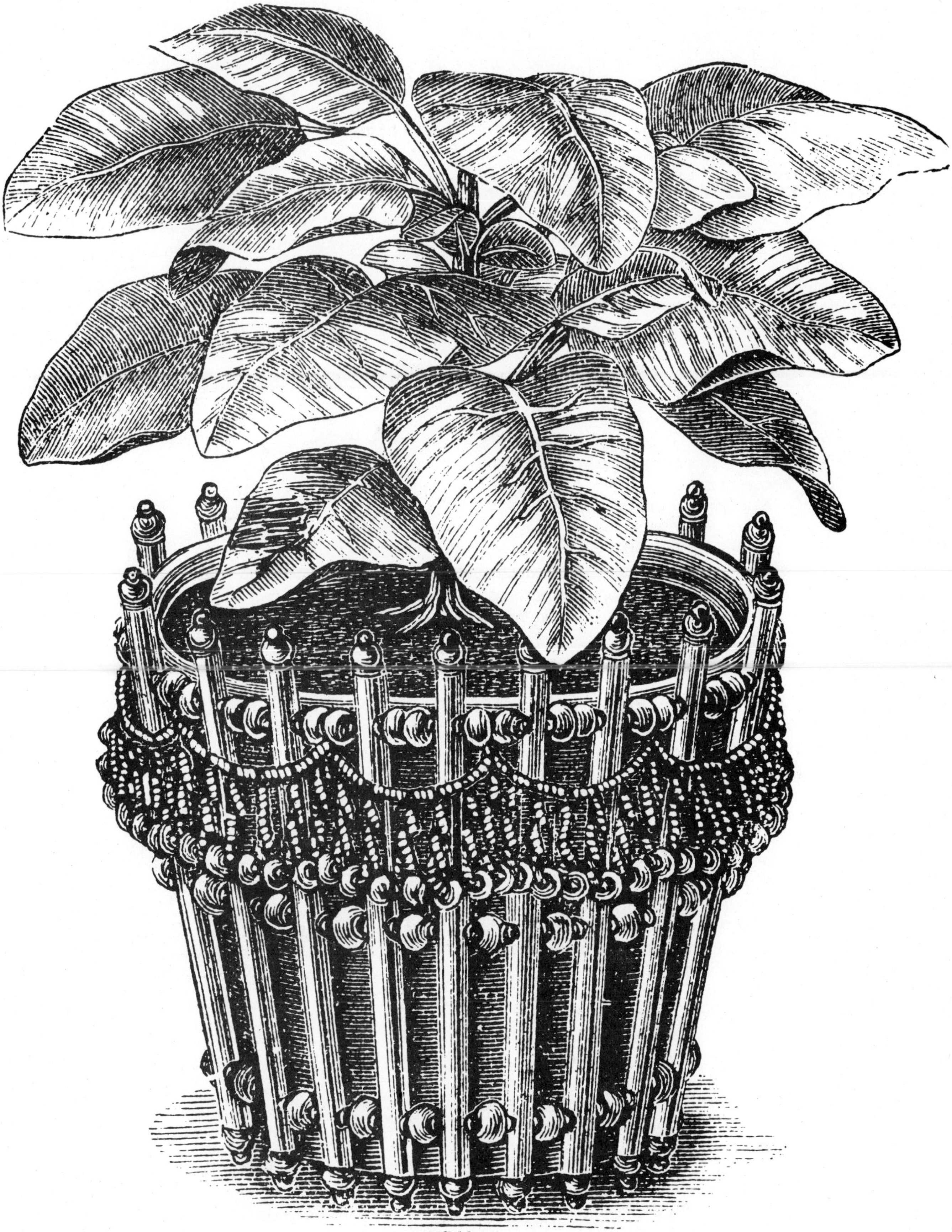

Beads have been worn by the rich and poor from the earliest times. They have been used as currency, as talismans, as jewelry.

Archaeological discoveries in Egypt have uncovered ancient glass beads that were beautifully shaped. Medieval women wore elaborate bead ornaments in their hair. American Indians brought beading to a major art form. Their bold designs have influenced many of today's fashions. In the nineteenth century, Victorian ladies made small beaded accessories as a home craft. Bead jewelry or some form of decoration made from beads has always been a part of fashion, whether it is a string of cultured pearls or a Victorian beaded purse.

Almost anything through which a hole can be bored can be used as a bead. This makes the craft supply rather staggering. Shells, seeds, fruit pits, sweet smelling spices (cloves and cardamom), nut shells, food kernels, dried berries, animal and fish teeth, pieces of bone, scraps of leather, pieces of wood and twists of paper have all been successfully used for decorative jewelry. The more conventional beads are usually round, oval, square, raindrop or baton shaped. Some of the materials they are made from are precious and semiprecious stones, mineral substances, coral and jet, glass and crystal, porcelain, pottery, plastics and resins.

You will need several important accessories in order to work with beads. A variety of different threads and string: strong twist thread, bead silk, Perlon and Trevira thread, various weights of nylon thread, thin cords and wire are among the most commonly used. There are other materials used, such as leather thongs, thick cords and macramé twine, dental floss and sometimes florist's wire. Wire for jewelry making is available in soft copper, brass or silver.

Long thin beading needles are helpful for threading beads with small holes. Needles of different gauges can be used as long as they can pass through the bead. Some threads are stiff enough to pass through a bead without a needle. You can also dip threads in glue or twist them with soap to stiffen the ends. When working with wire, a pair of pointed, half-round pliers is a must. For finishing off a necklace or bracelet buy a selection of clasps and fastenings. A trip to your local craft center will acquaint you with all of the tools of the bead trade.

There are many other techniques in bead-jewelry making, some requiring more skill and patience than others. But the charm of beads makes it worth all.

SIMPLE BEAD DESIGNS

The simple bead designs shown here come from a 1915 magazine. They were used to border and embellish women's fine clothing.

1. Trace the designs you wish to use on tracing paper.
2. Pin the designs on the area to be beaded—a neckline, sleeve cuff, skirt hem.
3. Pass thread from under the fabric up through a line on the tracing. Thread a bead and sew it firmly to the line. Continue to sew on beads until you have covered all the lines. The beads can be sewn in tight formation or with small spaces between them.
4. When the beading is completed, tear away the tracing.

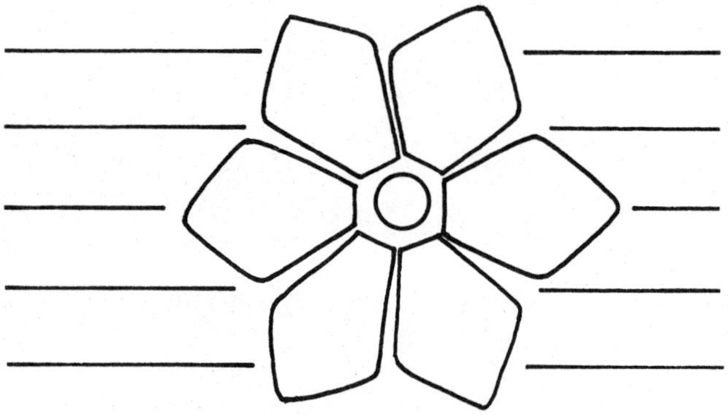

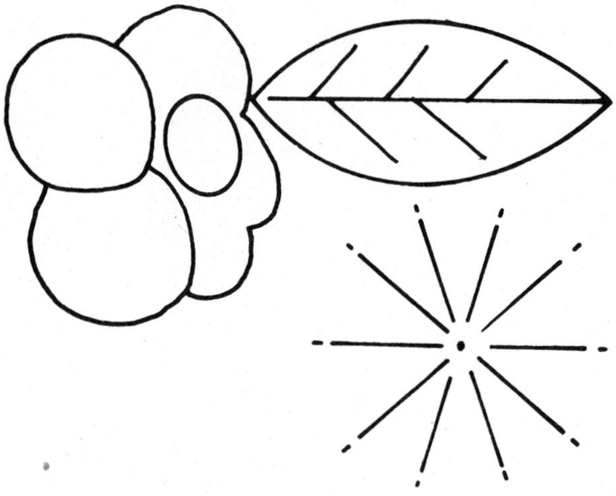

EMBROIDERY WITH BEADS

Bead embroidery dates back to the days when embroidery itself, as a new art form, was much in vogue. In Tudor times, the covers of manuscripts

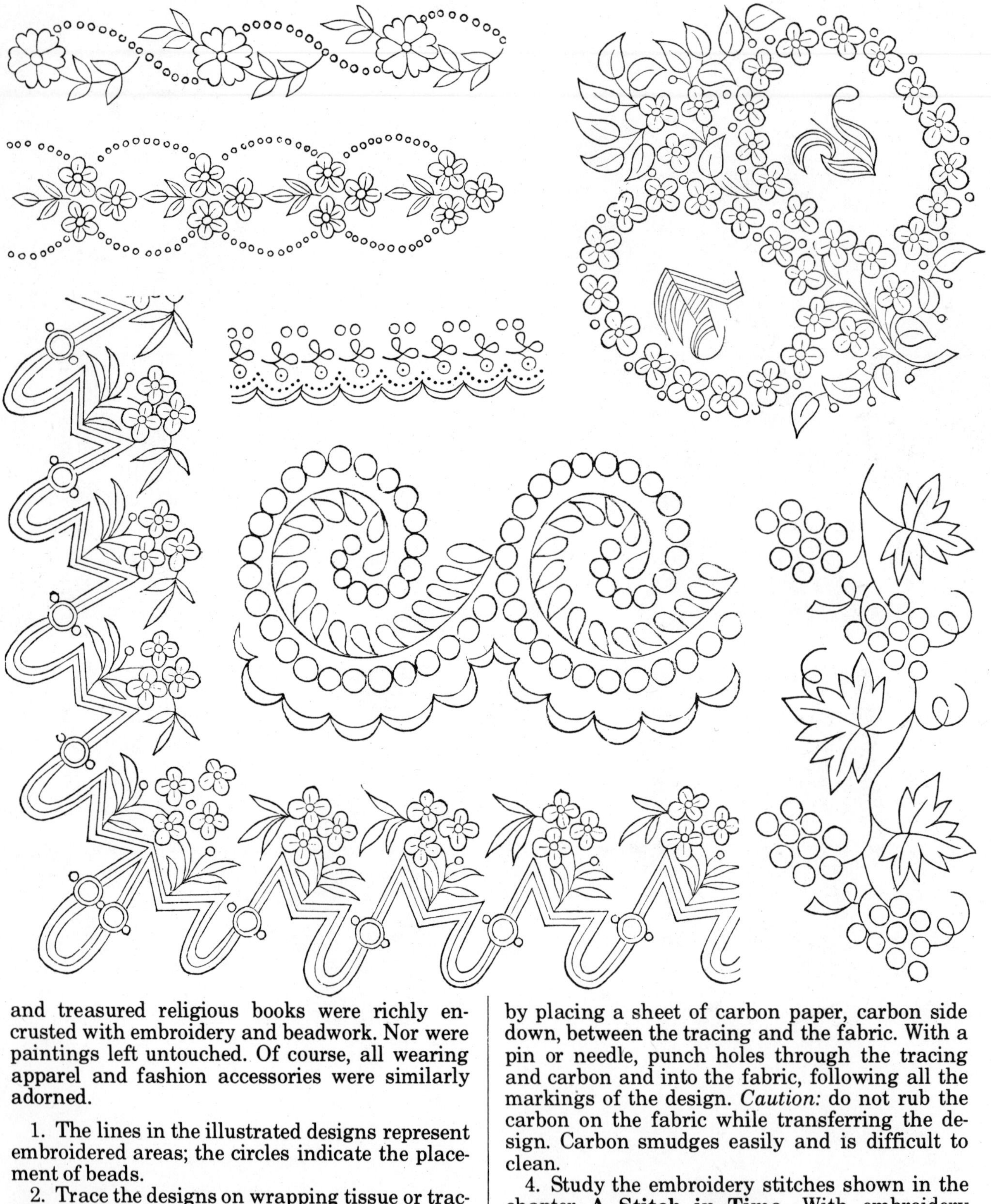

and treasured religious books were richly encrusted with embroidery and beadwork. Nor were paintings left untouched. Of course, all wearing apparel and fashion accessories were similarly adorned.

1. The lines in the illustrated designs represent embroidered areas; the circles indicate the placement of beads.
2. Trace the designs on wrapping tissue or tracing paper. To make a continuous pattern for a border or trim, use a long strip of paper, and trace the motif repeatedly.
3. Pin the tracing to the designated area. (You can also transfer your motifs directly to the fabric by placing a sheet of carbon paper, carbon side down, between the tracing and the fabric. With a pin or needle, punch holes through the tracing and carbon and into the fabric, following all the markings of the design. *Caution:* do not rub the carbon on the fabric while transferring the design. Carbon smudges easily and is difficult to clean.
4. Study the embroidery stitches shown in the chapter **A Stitch in Time.** With embroidery thread, embroider along the lines of the tracing or the dotted carbon-transfer.
5. Add beads where the designs call for them.
6. Pull away the tracing paper and it's done.

MONOGRAMS

Around the turn of the century it was considered quite stylish to monogram handkerchiefs and articles of clothing—a sense of personal pride sewn into one's wardrobe.

1. Monogram designs are simple enough to require no tracing. Use the monograms given in the chapter **A Stitch in Time,** which are clearer and less elaborate than these old fashioned ones. The line details shown here do give definition to the letters and the embroidered flower designs are quite nice; however, consider both optional. (If you choose to work the delicate flower designs, use a running or outline stitch, and dot the flower with a French knot.)

2. What would be very nice and is much the simpler, is to sew pearls or beads of graduated size along both sides of the widest part of each letter, as in the letter L.

3. When using three letters in a monogram, make the center letter larger than the other two.

BOW NECKLACE

(Shown in color on cover)

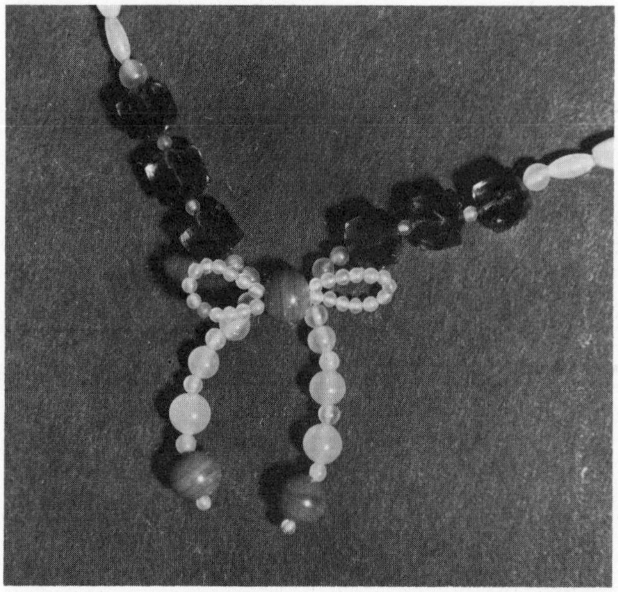

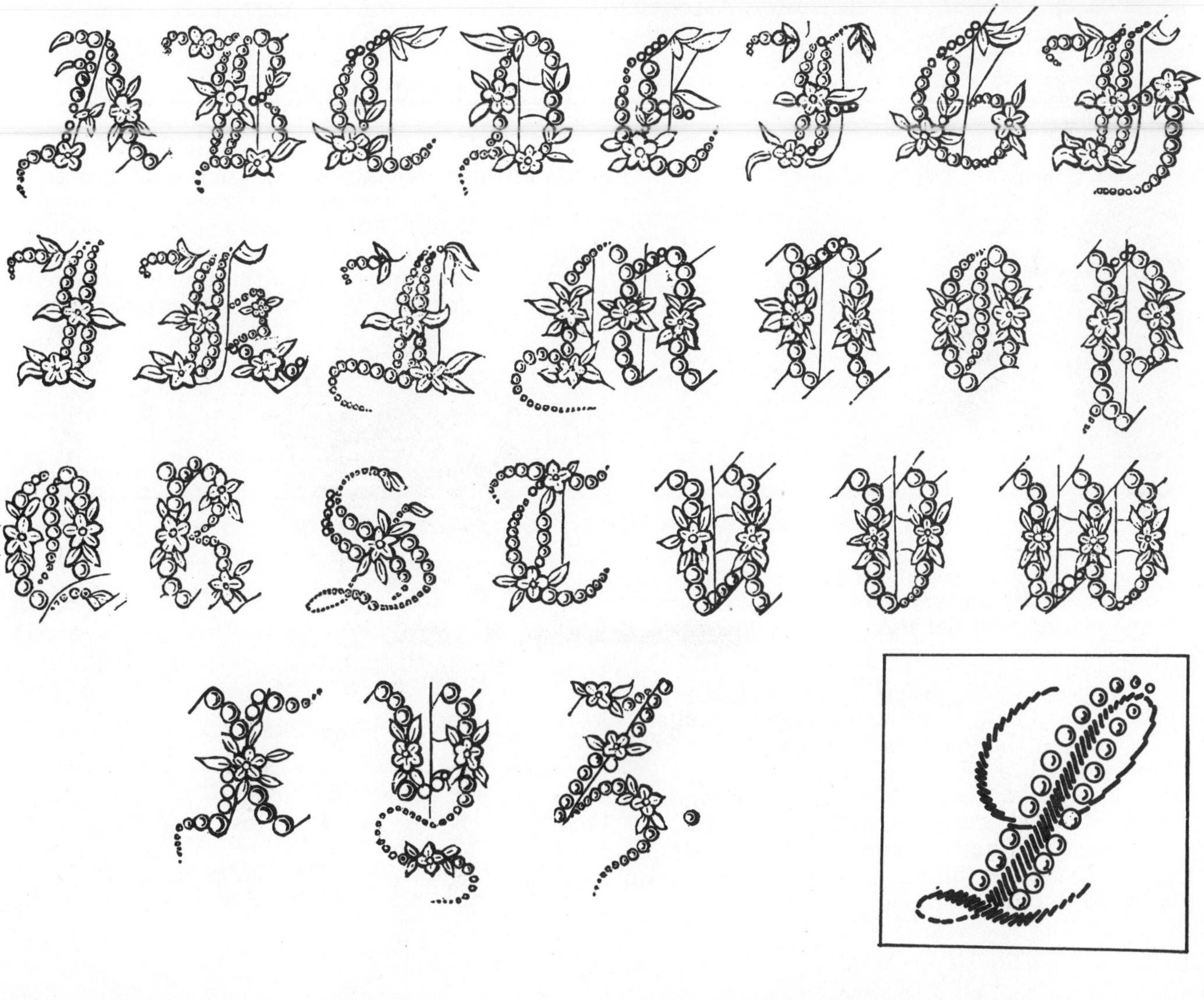

Some of the more beautiful necklaces worn in the late nineteenth century were made by European jewelers from a combination of beads and crystal, and other semiprecious stones.

1. This necklace consists of two beaded lengths of nylon or plastic yarn that meet in the middle.
2. Start at the top of each strand with a hook and eye or a bead clasp.
3. Using two needles, thread both strands of yarn with beads in an identical arrangement.
4. When you have reached the desired length, pass both needles through a large bead, as shown in the left-hand illustration.
5. String small seed beads on both loose ends, and pass the needles back through the center bead again to form loops (right-hand illustration).
6. Continue to bead the ends to a comfortable length. Secure the ends after the last beads. *Note:* Some plastic and nylon yarns will melt with the light of a match, forming its own knot. This is a sturdy way to finish off beaded ends.

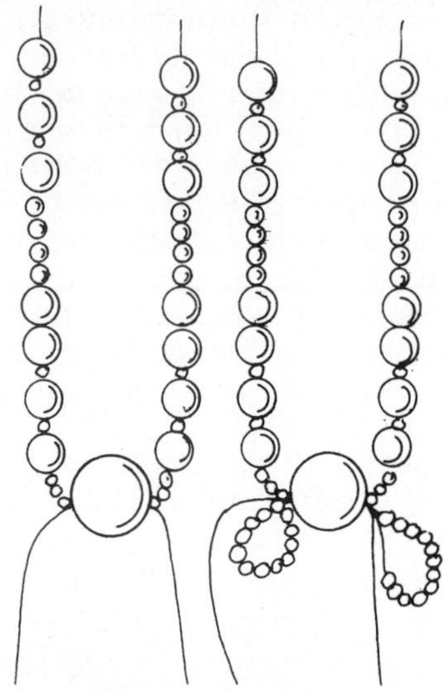

BEAD PENDANTS

This pendant consists of an embroidered patch from which delicate strings of beads are suspended. Today one can buy ready-made appliqués in all sizes and shapes, so you can coordinate a variety of beads with different appliqués. You can also experiment with different stringed-bead designs (two possibilities are shown here).

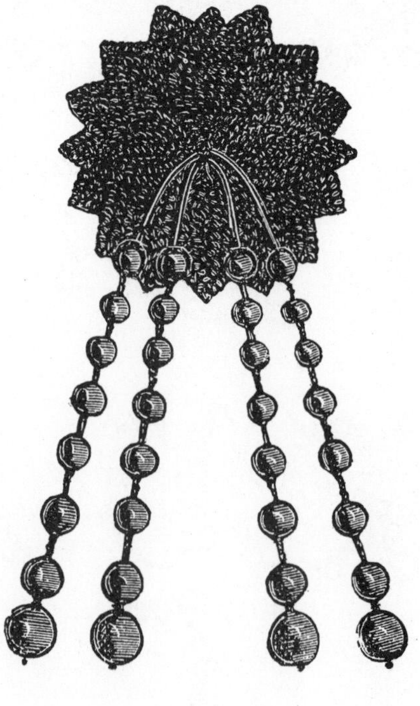

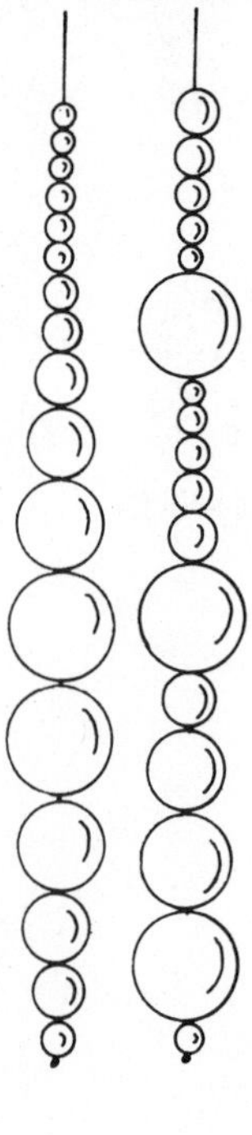

Attach the bead pendants on gowns, shawls, pillow corners or on the base of a lampshade.

1. The base of the pendant is an embroidered-patch appliqué. (Sewing centers and trimming shops carry these.) You can also use single motifs cut from some of the fancy trims that are sold by the yard.
2. Knot one end of a length of yarn. Trim the knot and dip it into melted wax from a small birthday candle.
3. Thread your beads, knotting the yarn between each bead.
4. Sew four or more lengths of beads into the center of the patch. Secure the thread in back.

BEAD AND EMBROIDERY BAG

Pocketbooks were once less cumbersome than they are today; it seems women had less to carry. In the Edwardian era, petite bags were the rage—bags just large enough to hold a pair of opera glasses and maybe some powder to touch up the nose. The charm of these little reticules, as they were called, lay in the beautiful beadwork stitched all around.

1. The outside of this bag is made from two 6 x 10-inch pieces of velvet. The lining is made from two pieces of acetate, same size.
2. Trace the embroidery design on wrapping tissue or tracing paper. Reverse the flower-cluster motif at the base of the design and add it at the left side of the central flower.
3. Pin the tracing to the nap-side of one velvet shape.
4. Embroider along the dotted lines with a running or an outline stitch, through the tracing.
5. Add beads where circles are indicated on the design.
6. Pull away the tracing when the design is completed.
7. Sew the two pieces of velvet together, right sides facing, with ½-inch seams. Leave the top open.
8. Sew the lining pieces together, wrong sides facing, with ½-inch seams. Leave the top open.
9. Cut a length of wire coat-hanger the length of the bag.

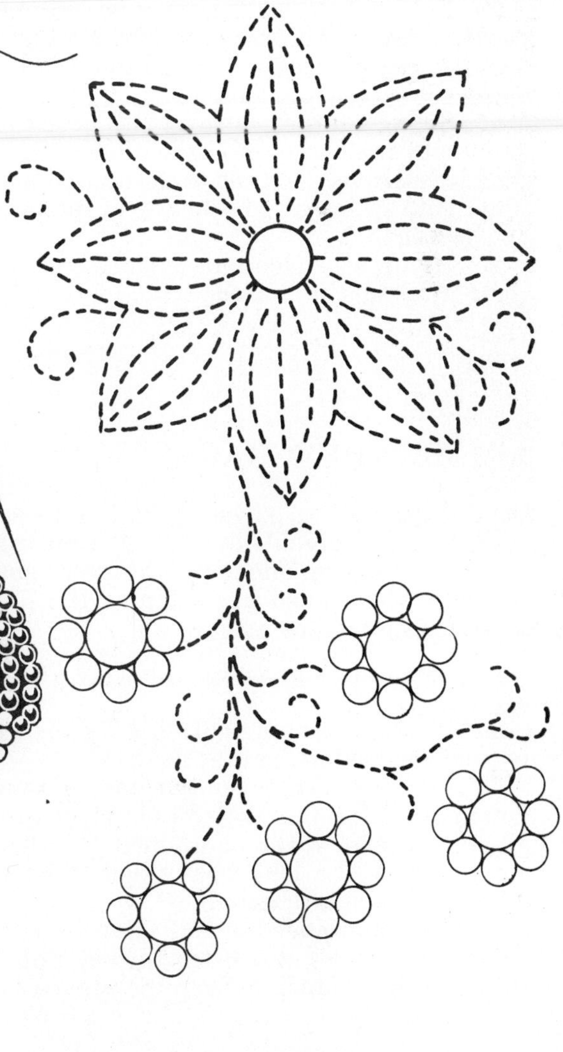

10. Sew the wire into the bottom seam allowance.
11. Turn the lining right side out and slip it over the velvet bag. Sew the top edges of the bag to the top edges of the lining.
12. Turn the bag inside out through the unsewn top edge of the lining.
13. Blind-stitch the bottom lining together, tucking both edges into the bag ½ inch.
14. The handle is made of beads threaded on thin wire or, better still, on nylon cord.
15. Thread both ends of a long piece of wire or cord with needles.
16, Thread nine beads on the wire and center them. Form a loop by passing one needle through the last bead.
17. Thread four beads on one needle and five on the other needle. Pass the needle on the four-bead strand through the last bead on the five-bead strand (Fig. 1).
18. Continue this thread-and-loop process until your handle reaches the desired length. Tie both ends securely.
19. Sew the handle to the top corners of the bag.
20. Each side tassel is formed by stringing and securing loops of beads, as in Fig. 2. Allow a long end of thread to extend beyond the first loop and tie all the succeeding loops to it.
21. String a large bead over the loose thread at the top of the clump of beaded loops. Sew a finished tassel over each end of the beaded handle.
22. Add satin bows to the top of the purse and the handle.
23. If you wish, loop an extra fringe of beads along the bag's bottom edge.

ALL-BEADED BAG

Beaded bags are so expensive to buy these days, it seems inconceivable that at one time a stylish woman might own one to go with every gown. To this day, the beaded bag remains the finishing touch to fine evening attire.

1. The patterns given for the body and handle are actual size.
2. Cut two oval shapes of satin for the bag and two more of acetate for the lining.
3. The bead design on the bag is shown by dotted lines. The thin dotted lines represent small glass seed beads; the short heavy dotted lines, small pearls; the long heavy dotted lines, long pearls (this last is optional).
4. First embroider the leaf shapes at the top. Follow with the bottom design, beginning with the outer line (¼ inch in from the edge) and working inward. Then do the free-form squiggly design in the center.
5. Place the two outer sides together with the beaded faces turned inward, and hand-stitch the bag together ¼ inch in from the edge. Stop at the points marked on the drawing with an X. Sew the lining-pieces together in the same way, right sides facing.
6. Turn the bag inside out, but leave the lining as it is, with the outside of the fabric facing in.
7. Place the lining inside the bag.
8. Pin a 6-inch zipper along the top edge of the bag by slipping one side of the zipper between the front lining and the bag front. Turn both edges ¼ inch under so they are flush with the teeth of the zipper. Do the same with the back side of the bag.
9. Hand-sew the zipper in place.
10. Cut the handle and its lining to the width shown and to the length desired. Both ends should come to a point.
11. Bead the handle following the design given.
12. To line the handle, turn both the handle and lining edges under ⅛ inch and blind-stitch the two fabrics together.
13. Sew the handle to the sides of the bag.
14. Camouflage the side seam by sewing additional beads along the length of the bag.

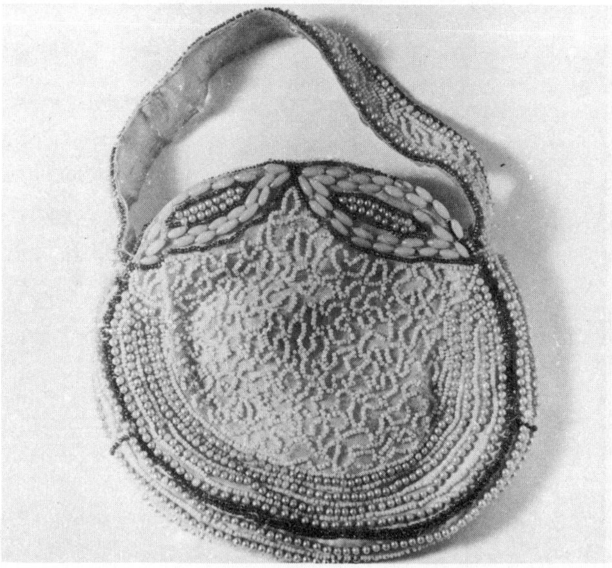

BEAD AND NEEDLEPOINT BAGS

Beads and needlepoint are a lovely combination. In Victorian times, they were used to ornament footstools, chair seats, and evening bags. Three different bag designs are offered here.

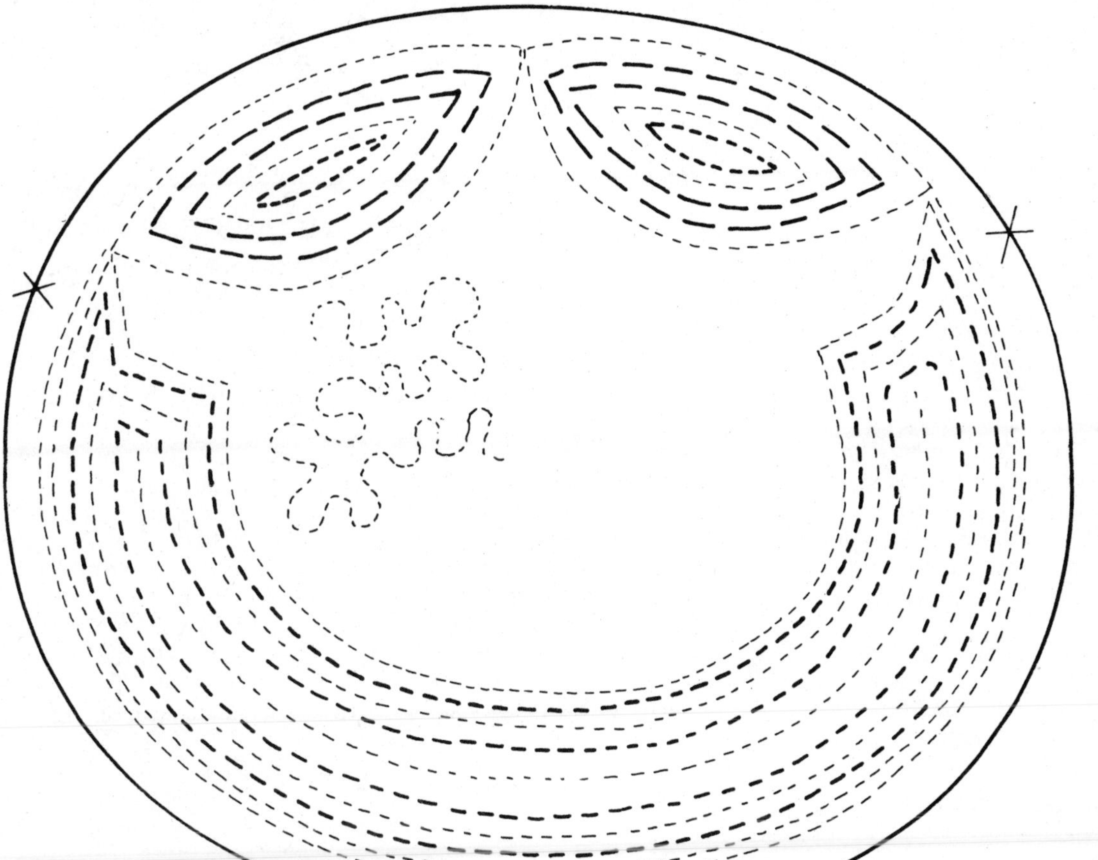

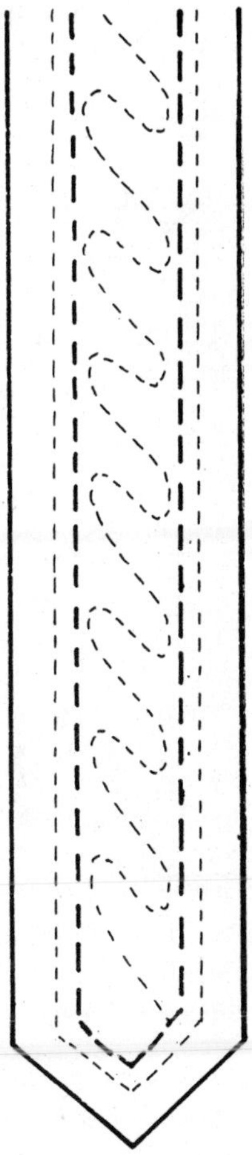

FLAP BAG

1. The size of the bag is up to you. Both sides are made of needlepoint canvas. The back piece should be about 1 ¾ the length of the front piece, but the same width.
2. If you are using large beads, they should be placed before you stitch the needlepoint. Sew a simple outline of beads onto the canvas, following the canvas weave. The bead design can be repeated on the back of the bag or just used on the flap.
3. If you are using seed beads or other tiny beads, they should be worked later, on top of the completed needlepoint.
4. Needlepoint the front and back of the bag following the Basic Needlepoint Instruction in the chapter **A Stitch in Time.** Work the needlepoint up to two spaces from each edge, but only up to *2 inches* from the top edge of the front piece.
5. Attach the front of the bag to the back by whip-stitching the sides together with yarn.
6. Turn the outside edges of the flap under and sew down with yarn or embroidery thread. Finish off the raw edges by sewing on bias tape or a narrow ribbon.

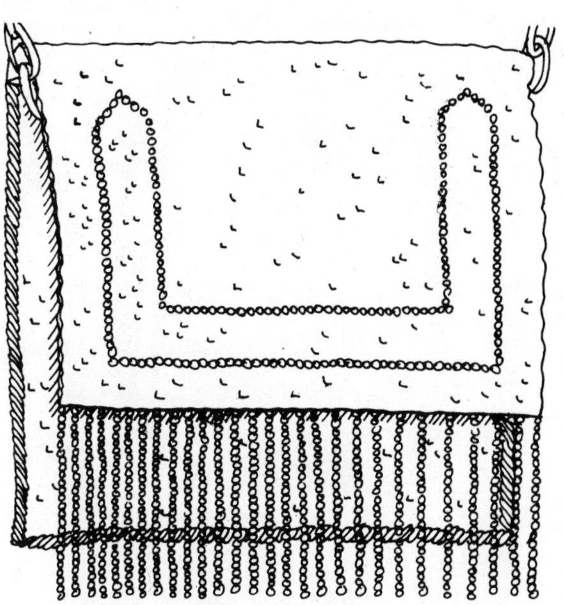

7. String seed beads in even lengths on nylon or plastic thread, and sew them in a row to the bottom edge of the flap. Space the fringe as desired.
8. Attach a length of chain to both sides of the bag for a handle. You can also use a braided-yarn or rope handle.
9. Line the bag if desired.

TOTE BAG

1. The front and back of this bag are the same size.
2. Work needlepoint up to two spaces from the bottom and side edges and up to 2 *inches* from the top edges.
3. Stitch on beads as described above. You might experiment with a more elaborate design than the one used in the preceding project.
4. Whip-stitch the completed pieces together with yarn along the bottom and sides.
5. Turn the 2-inch top edges and sew down with yarn.
6. Sew on a sturdy ribbon handle.
7. Fringe the bottom edge with beaded loops sewn in a row.
8. Line the bag if desired.

EYEGLASS OR CHECKBOOK CASE

1. The front and back of the case are cut to the same size. The size depends on its intended use.
2. Needlepoint up to two spaces from the side and bottom edges and up to one inch from the top.
3. Construct as the Tote Bag.

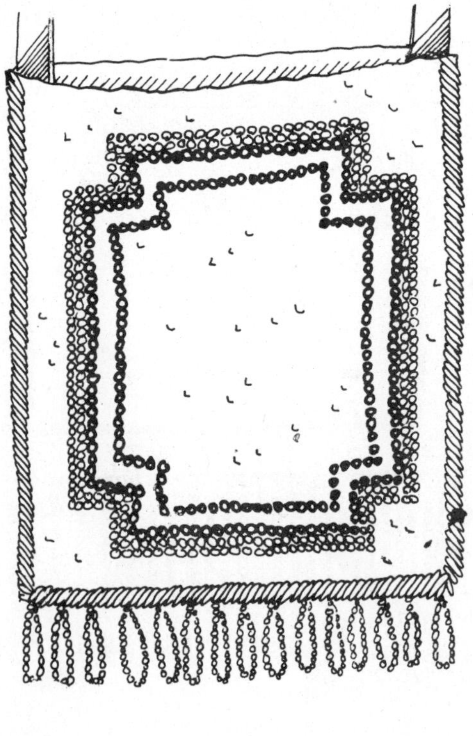

BEADED LACE

Beaded lace is the most elegant trim for a gown, makes any pillow a jewel, and is stunning as a choker.

1. The base of the lace is formed by two lengths of ribbon or eyelet lace.
2. Begin by passing a threaded needle through the inner edge of one ribbon.
3. String the thread with seed beads to fill the desired space between the two ribbons.
4. Sew the end of the bead strand to the inner edge of the second length of ribbon.
5. Continue to add equal lengths of beads between the two ribbons, or between appropriate points on the eyelet lace.
6. To thread a velvet ribbon through the beads, bring the first and third beaded lengths up over the second one. Pass the ribbon through the three crossed strands, beneath the middle strand (see illustration).
7. Continue to thread the ribbon through every three strands of beads in the same fashion.

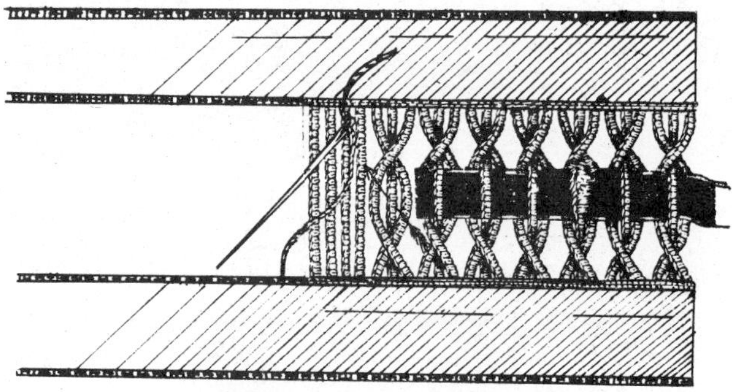

INTERLOCKING NECKLACES

These necklaces of interlocking bead strands look like macramé. Though popular in Victorian times, this mode of beading originated in some of the earliest civilizations. Certain African tribes still do highly intricate work with interwoven beads, and American Indian beadwork is renown. In tribal societies, the beads are usually set in symbolic folklore motifs.

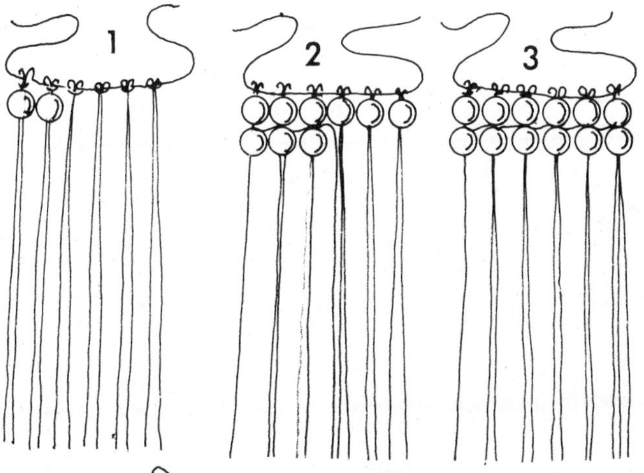

1. Fold in half equal lengths of wire, plastic or cotton thread and knot them at regular intervals along the base cord which will go around the neck. The more threads you use, the wider the necklace. The base cord can be chain, yarn or a decorative metallic cord.

2. String one bead, starting at the left, on each pair of hanging threads (Fig. 1). If you are using cotton thread, dip the ends of individual strands in melted wax from a small birthday candle to add body.

3. Begin the second row of beads by threading the first bead on a single strand. The second strand is threaded through the next bead along with one strand issuing from the second bead on the top row. The remaining strand from the second bead is then threaded through the third bead, along with one strand from the third bead in the top row. Continue until you reach the last bead, which will be threaded on three strands (Figs. 2 and 3). The next row follows the same weaving pattern starting on the right.

4. At certain points in the necklace you might keep some strands free and string them in lengths, instead of interlocking them with adjacent strands.

5. The ties of the necklace on the left are made by large beads strung on the base thread. A hook is added at one end.

6. The ties of the necklace on the right are made by continuing the necklace pattern on separate threads tied on *above* the base cord. The beads are strung straight (the strands do not interlock), and are divided and tied in two equal clusters. The base thread at the bottom of the necklace is strung at each end with seed beads and finished with a larger bead before securing. Loops of seed beads have been added between them.

BEAD WEAVING

With the aid of a simple loom, you can do quite sophisticated bead work, the applications for which go far beyond the three suggestions given here.

1. A bead-weaving loom is very inexpensive and can be purchased at most craft, hobby and art centers. If you care to, you can make your own loom from a shoe box, by cutting slits, ¼ inch deep and 1/16 inch apart, at both short sides of the box.

2. String the store-bought loom according to the enclosed instructions. Use nylon or plastic thread, or beading wire. To string the box loom, tie together threads cut 6 inches longer than the box. The number of threads used will determine the width of your weaving. Pass each thread through a slit at one end of the box (knot remains on the outside), and then down through the corresponding slit at the opposite end. Pull taut and tie with all the other loose threads into a single knot.

3. To begin weaving, thread a length of your wire or nylon with enough beads to fit one between each long base thread on the loom.

4. Pass this beaded length beneath the long threads and adjust so there is one bead in every space (Fig. 1).

5. Then bring the needle over the last long base thread and back through all the beads. This locks them in place (Fig. 2).

6. Each row of beads is placed under the long threads and then secured by passing the needle

over and back through the beads.

7. When you come to the end of a length of thread, sew it to the last long thread in that row before snipping it off. Start a new thread of beads as you did the initial thread.

8. To remove the weaving from the loom, cut two threads at a time from the end knot and tie them together. Snip off the excess thread.

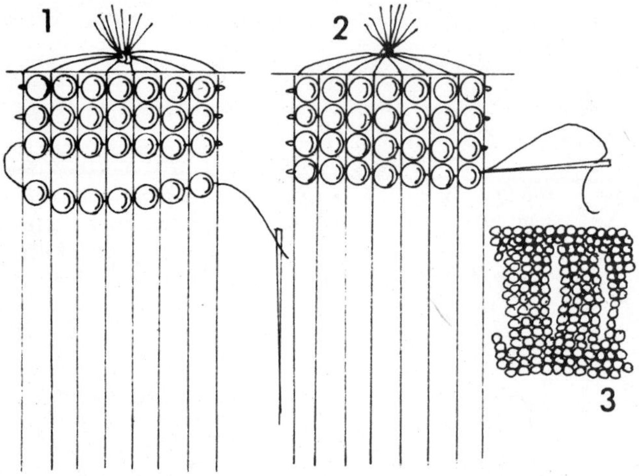

BELTS

(Shown in color on cover)

1. String a store-bought loom with extra-long lengths of thread and weave with beads as described above. Belts cannot be worked on the shoe-box loom.

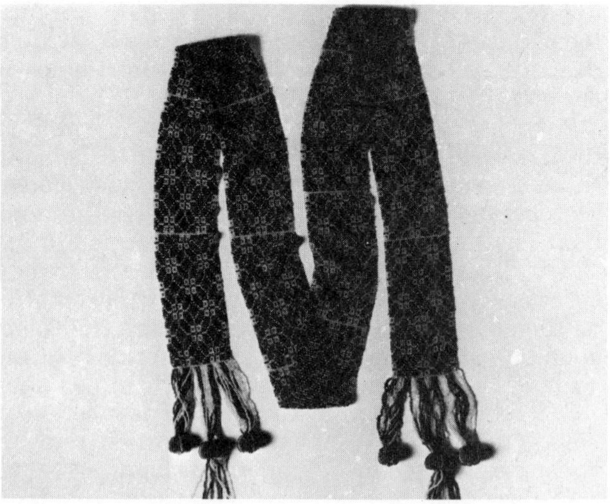

BAGS

1. The two sides of a bag are worked separately and then sewn together. The size of the bag is up to you.

2. Weave a solid pattern of beads across the loom to a depth of ½ inch.

3. For the next ½ inch, slits are left between vertical rows of beads to accommodate a pull-cord. To make the slits, start at one edge of the loom and weave beads across to cover ½ inch. Weave back and forth across this ½-inch section to a depth of ½ inch. Continue to weave slits in this manner across the width of the bag (Fig. 3).

4. When the slit portion is completed, go back to weaving straight across the loom to make the body of the bag.

5. Taper off the bag at the bottom by narrowing each row of beads as you approach the base of the loom.

6. When both sides of the bag have been completed, whip-stitch them together along the side and bottom edges.

7. Add a fringe to the bottom edge.

8. The pull-cord can be either a beaded ribbon that you have made or a decorative cord. Weave the pull-cord in and out of the top slits and sew the ends together.

PICTURES

1. Cut out a color picture from a magazine to use as a guide for your weaving.

2. Place the picture on top of the threaded loom and clip in place.

3. String the first line of beads by laying the thread over the top of the picture and stringing the colored beads to match the drawing.

4. Flip the drawing over and weave the first line of beads.

5. Replace the drawing above the warp and bead the second line following the picture. Continue working down from the top in this way.

BEAD MAT.

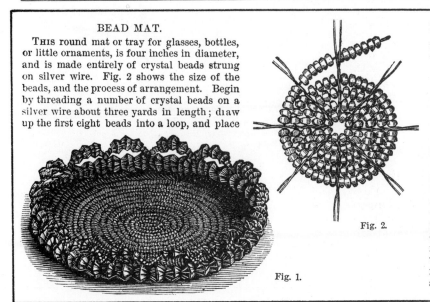

THIS round mat or tray for glasses, bottles, or little ornaments, is four inches in diameter, and is made entirely of crystal beads strung on silver wire. Fig. 2 shows the size of the beads, and the process of arrangement. Begin by threading a number of crystal beads on a silver wire about three yards in length; draw up the first eight beads into a loop, and place eight wires, five inches long, in between the beads, doubling them over the loop, and twisting the two ends together close to it. Then wind the long wire threaded with beads round the loop, passing it between the open ends of the double wire, and leaving two beads between them, twist the ends together again, and repeat this process, leaving a greater number of beads between the wires in each successive row, till the mat has reached the required size; the ends of the wires should be tightly twisted together, and fastened down underneath the mat. Now proceed with the raised rim. Make a ring of large cut crystal beads round the mat, observing that the number of beads must be divisible by three. Take another wire and fasten it between two of these large beads, thread three small crystal beads, three large cut beads, three small beads, pass the wire round the wire of the edge, missing three of the beads of the last row; repeat from all round, cut off the wire and fasten in the end, and turn the scallops upwards to form a rim.

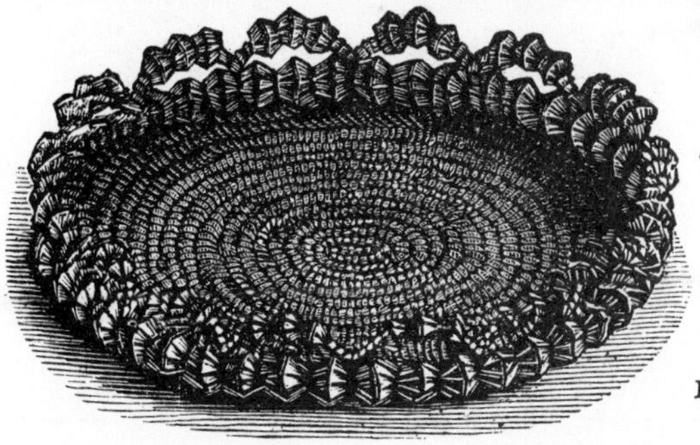

Fig. 1.

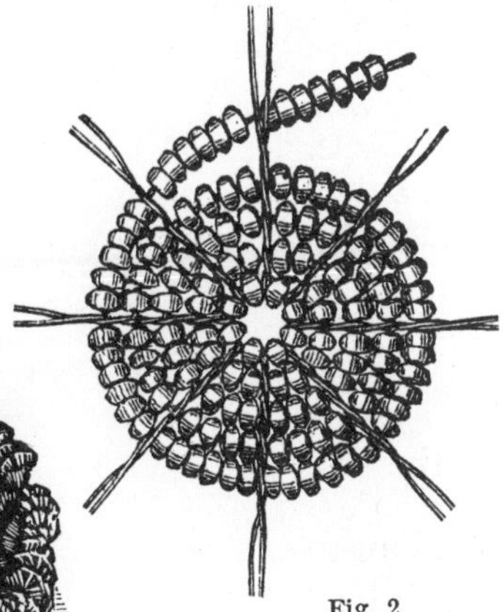

Fig. 2.

HOT PLATE

This turn-of-the-century hot plate was designed as a woven mat, but it is simple enough to work in beads. Glass or wooden beads will withstand the heat of serving dishes straight from the oven.

1. Cut out a simple square or rectangle from a piece of felt. The design shown is a rectangle with corners cut off.
2. Use glass or wooden beads (large or small) for the hot plate.
3. Sew beads onto the felt in rows, starting ½ inch down from the top edge and ½ inch in from the side edge.

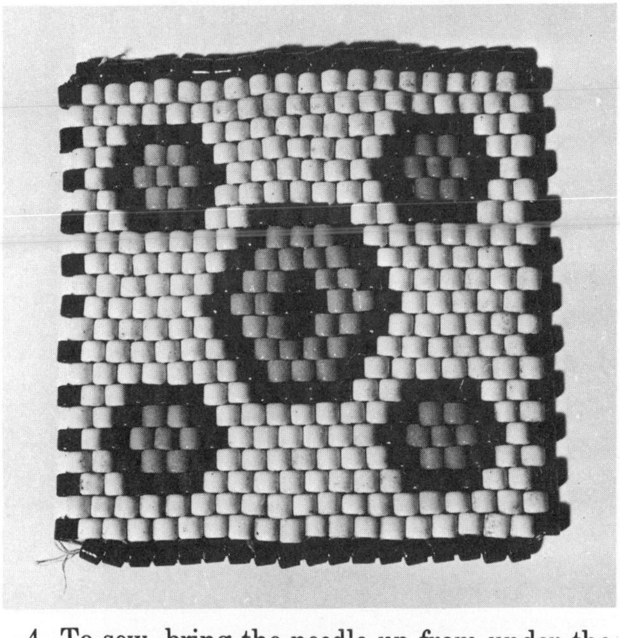

4. To sew, bring the needle up from under the felt, string two or three beads and sew them to the fabric. Continue straight across the felt. When sewing the second row of beads, the stitches should fall between the stitches of the first row.
5. The beading can be solid or patterned. Carry the beading up to ½ inch from the bottom edge.
6. Cut out a piece of heavy cardboard exactly the size of the beaded area.
7. Place the beaded felt over the cardboard and turn the ½-inch edges under. Use a bond cement to glue the edges down.
8. When the edges are secure, cut a second piece of felt slightly smaller than the mat but identical in shape.
9. Glue the felt over the bottom of the mat.
10. Sew a looped fringe around the edges.

FRINGED LAMPSHADE

A popular lampshade in the early 1900s was made of a canvaslike material and fringed with strings or loops of clear glass beads. The beads catch the light and reflect it in a shimmering circle beneath the shade. Fringe a shade for one of those old-fashioned wall-hung fixtures.

1. For a hanging fringe, string seed beads on pre-measured lengths of thread. Sew the strands close together at regular intervals along the bottom edge of the shade.
2. For a looped fringe, sew a fairly long length of thread to the base of the lampshade. String enough beads to form a graceful loop and stitch the loop to the shade. Continue to string, loop, and sew all the way around. Add a second row of longer loops attached midway between the points where the first loops start and end. Finish with a single row of loops around the top edge of the shade.

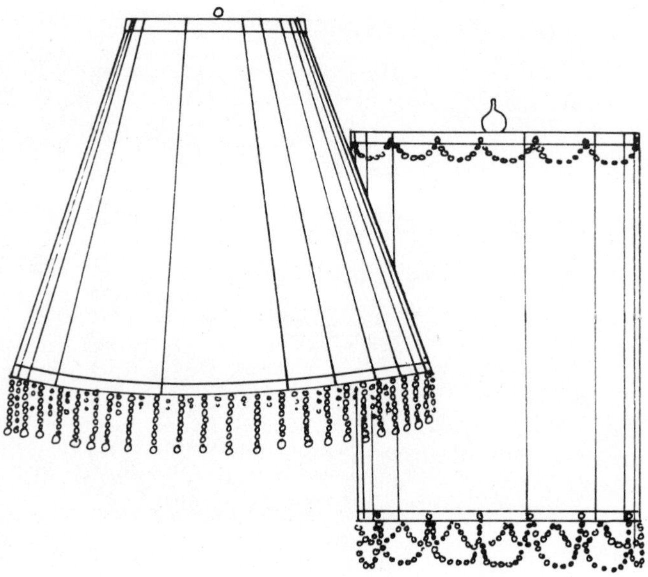

BUTTERFLY PINCUSHION

This old Victorian butterfly design lends itself beautifully to that sewing must, the pincushion. To be truly Victorian in spirit, your adaptation should be lavishly decorated with beads and sequins. If you are already rich in pincushions, you can enlarge the butterfly and make yourself a throw pillow instead.

1. Draw the single butterfly wing on a grid that's been enlarged so that one square equals ½ inch. (See page 13 for how to enlarge patterns

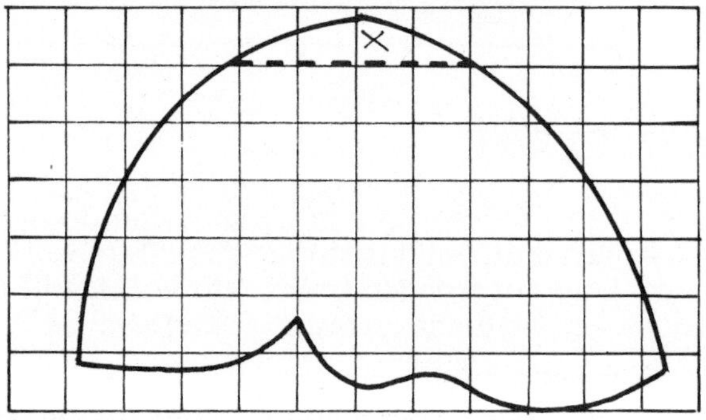

placedon grids.) Once you have your pattern, cut four wing-shapes from satin, two with the wings facing left and two facing right.
2. Embroider a design similar to the one shown in the old illustration on the right and left wings (optional).
3. Place the two right wing shapes together with the right sides of the fabric facing it. Sew around the wing beginning and ending at the dotted line. Sew the two left wing shapes together in the same way.
4. Turn the wings right side out and stuff firmly with cotton.
5. Sew closed along the dotted line.
6. Sew the two wings together by overlapping the section marked X.
7. The body of the butterfly can be made from a few lengths of yarn looped and clumped together. Tie the loops at ½-inch intervals with gold thread.
8. Sew on the body between the wings.
9. Fringe the edges of the wings with short strands of seed beads ending with single pearls.
10. Attach two pipe cleaners for the antennae.

FLOWERPOT COVER

If you study old home décor magazines, you will

find that the word "ornate" appears with surprising frequency. Though today's taste tends toward straight lines and a minimum of ornamentation, this "ornate" Victorian beaded flowerpot is certainly pleasing to the eye.

1. The body of the flowerpot cover is made from plain white drinking straws (plastic or paper).
2. Pierce a straw near the bottom with a threaded needle. Knot the end of the thread.
3. Thread a bead on the needle and then another straw. Continue sewing beads and straws to a length that will just fit around the base of your pot. Form the straws in a circle and sew together at the base. Place the pot in the cover.
4. Midway up the straws, start to sew a second row of beads. This row will require more beads between each straw to fan out the straws so they'll accommodate the girth of the pot.
5. Sew a third row of beads between the straws slightly down from the top. You'll need still more beads to fill the wider gaps between straws.
6. String a length of thread with enough seed beads to form a loop between sets of beads in the top row. Attach and add more beads to make a second loop. Continue all the way around.
7. Attach more loops to the strand by stringing lengths of seed beads with a large bead at the base of each strand, and suspending each length at intervals from the wider loops.
8. Glue large beads to the top of each straw. To glue beads to the bottom of the straw, remove the pot from the cover and turn the cover upside down.

BEADED EGG

Here's an egg that any chicken would be proud of. Make a basket of them.

1. Take an egg at room temperature and gently twist a straight pin into both ends. Enlarge the hole on the blunt end of the egg to ⅛ inch. Blow through the pinhole on the tapered end. The egg will push through the larger hole. Wash the egg shell.

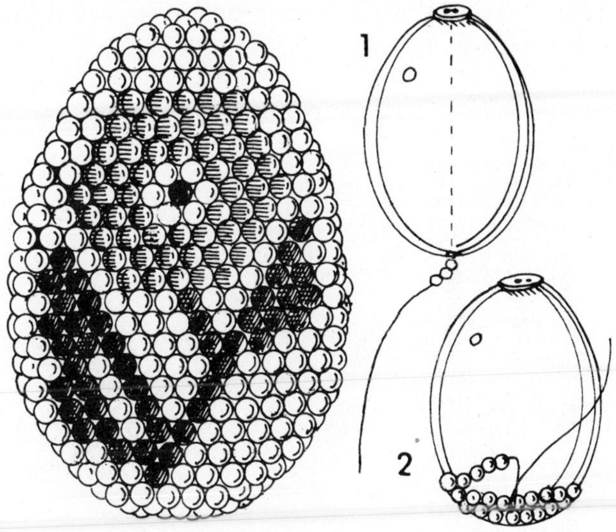

2. String a small button on one end of a length of beading wire and secure in place.
3. Push the wire through the small pinhole and out the larger hole (Fig. 1).
4. String three seed beads on the wire and loop them in a circle at the base of the egg.
5. Add more beads to the wire to form a ring around the first circle of beads. Wire the two rings together.
6. Keep forming new circles of beads and wiring them to the preceding one. Follow the shape of the egg as you bead.
7. The ring widens as you work up the wall of the egg. About every tenth bead, wire the ring you are working on to the previous ring (Fig. 2).
8. Continue to the top of the egg. Snip off the button before you complete the egg.

GRAPE CLUSTER

On a sunlit table, these beaded grapes look like a bowl of amethysts—shimmering and tempting. At the turn of the century, artificial fruits were either made of glass beads or wax.

1. The base of each grape is cotton. Wad up some cotton into a compact ball and wrap it in every direction with thread.

2. Bead the grapes following steps 2–8 for the Beaded Egg (the beads are strung in rings and wired together, Fig. 1).

3. Make grapes in several sizes. Add a length of unbeaded wire to each completed grape.

4. Tie the grapes together in a tight cluster, starting at the top with the largest grapes and ending with the smaller ones. Twist all the wire ends together to form a stem.

5. To make the leaves, bend a straight section of wire for the stem and center vein. Add three beaded petal shapes to the main stem, two on the bottom, and a third encasing the upper part of the stem (Fig. 2). Wire in the remaining veins.

6. Add two of these beaded leaves to the cluster's stem.

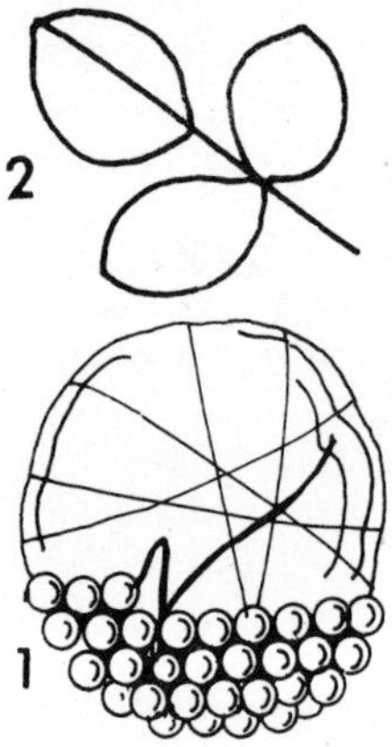

PETAL FLOWERS

(Shown in color on page 165)

Where today we have plastic and paper flowers, once they were of porcelain and bead. A bouquet of beaded blossoms will add unwilting grace to a hallway or to any other room in your home.

ROUND PETAL

1. Thread three beads so they are centered on a length of wire. Twist the beaded part of the wire into a tight circle (Fig. 1).

2. Twist the end of a second length of wire around the first (base) wire just beneath the beads.

3. Add beads for half a second ring and attach to the beaded core by twisting the wire into the beaded inner circle. (Fig. 2). Then add beads to complete this circle.

4. Continue to bead and wire on concentric rings to form a circular petal (Fig. 3). Always bead half a ring and twist it to the center of the proceeding ring before completing the new ring of beads. For pansies, use blue and purple beads on

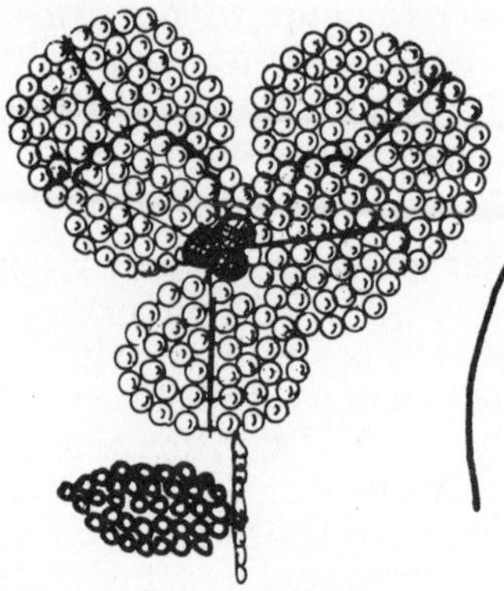

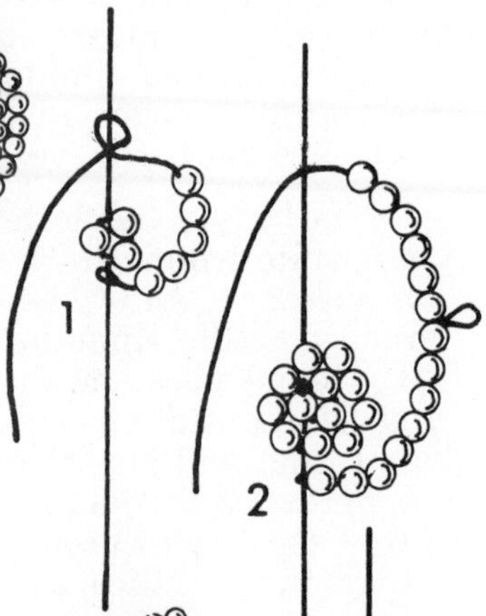

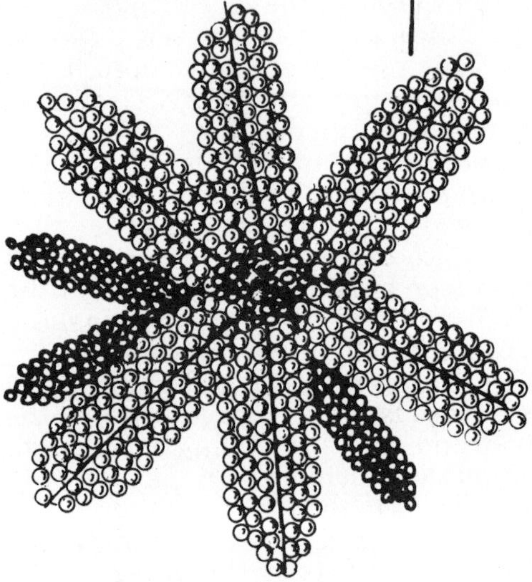

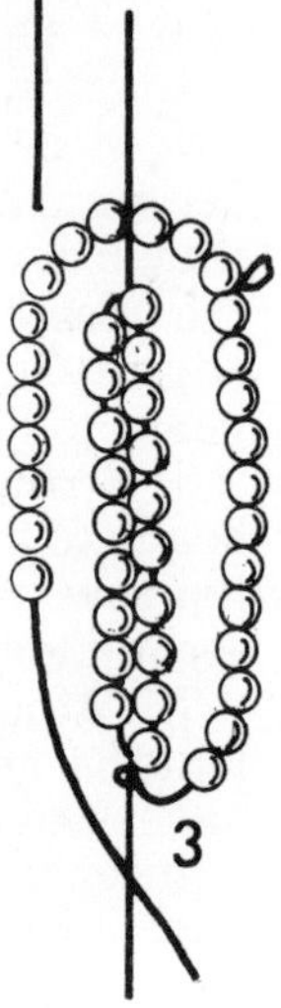

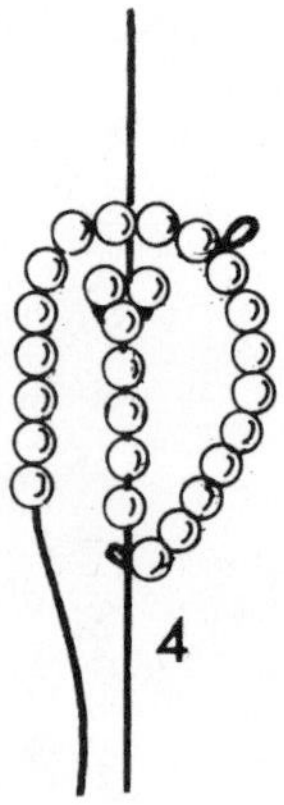

the upper half of the circle and yellow beads on the lower half.

5. Make three smaller circles for the central cluster and two larger ones for the outer petals.

6. The core of the pansy is made by attaching three large beads to one end of a length of wire. Wire on the petals below the beaded core by twisting together the exposed wires at the base of each.

7. Cover the wire with florist's tape.

8. The leaf, tucked into the florist's tape stem, is a Pointed Petal.

POINTED PETAL

1. Thread a strand of beads on a long piece of wire (the number depends on the intended size of the petal) and fold the wire double to form a tight loop of beads. Twist the short end of the wire securely around the longer end. Add a second length of wire to the top of the loop to form the upper base wire (Fig. 4).
2. Bead and twist the remaining concentric rows of the petal as described in Round Petal, steps 3 and 4.
3. Attach the completed petals to a beaded core (see step 6) in a circular pattern, as shown, or make a chrysanthemum by layering the petals and bending them upward.

TEARDROP PETAL

1. The center of this petal is a length of beads *topped with a tight three-bead circle.* Add a second wire to form the base above the beaded portion. Continue to string beads in concentric rings.

BEAD TREE

The art of beading enjoyed a renaissance during the frugal Depression years, when women salvaged the fringe and jewels from the dresses they had loved and worn in the 1920s. It was then that this intricate tree became a popular item.

1. Each branch begins with a loop of beaded wire at the top. String a few more beads straight on the wire beneath the loop.
2. Add enough beads to form a second loop. Twist this loop securely and follow it with a single bead. Add beads to form a third loop and twist in place on the opposite side of the branch stem.
3. String more connecting beads, followed by two more loops.
4. Make the tree's top branch from one large center loop and two side loops. As the branches move down on the trunk, make them longer by adding extra loops to each base wire.
5. Attach all the branches to a length of coat hanger that has been cut to the desired height of the tree. The last branches should fall about 1½ inches above the bottom of this wire.
6. When all the branches are in place, camouflage the center wire by beading a long length of flexible wire and twisting it down around the trunk. Cover all loose ends of wire from the branches in the same manner.

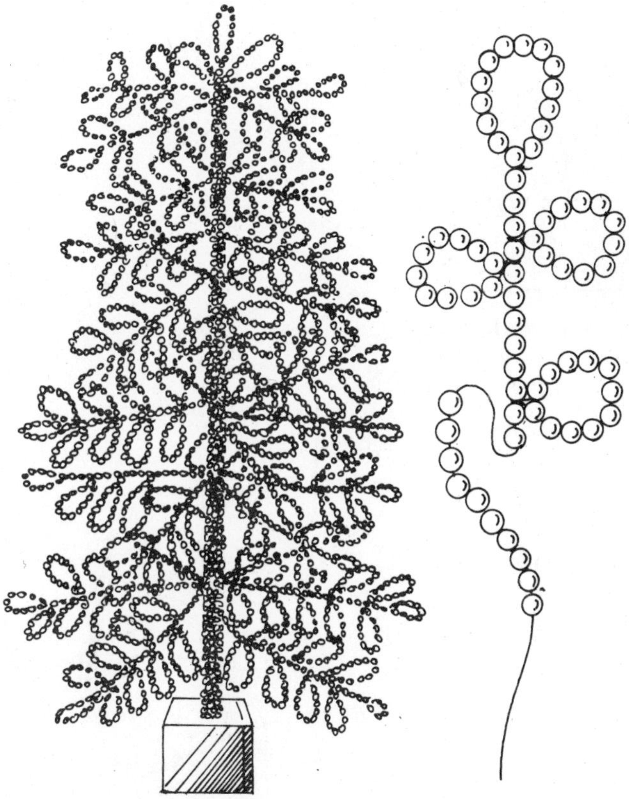

7. Insert the tree into a block of foam or a frozen-juice can that has been half-filled with plaster of Paris.

BEAD AND EMBROIDERY PICTURE

This lovely scene would look spectacular on a pillow or on a wall hanging hung in some special place.

1. Draw the heavy solid lines of the simple landscape on a grid and enlarge it so that one square equals one inch. (See page 13 for how to enlarge patterns placed on grids.) Use tracing paper.
2. Pin the tracing to the fabric you have selected and embroider the fabric through the tracing paper along the heavy lines. Use the embroidery stitches given in the chapter **A Stitch in Time.**
3. The round circles indicate beads. The dotted lines emanating from the sun should also be beaded. The X points on the hills suggest the placement of beaded flowers. Use your imagination to create pretty flower shapes.
4. When you have completed the needlework, pull away the tracing.

ALL-BEADED PICTURE

An all-beaded picture is the sign of a true beadwork devotee.

1. The owl in the illustration is actual size. Place a lightweight fabric over the drawing and trace. (You can also trace designs from magazines.)
2. Stretch the fabric on an embroidery hoop.
3. String beads on a threaded needle and sew the picture beginning at the top. Tack every third bead to the fabric. Always sew the beads in straight rows, making sure that they fall between (not directly under) the beads in the previous row. (Seed beads work best for beaded pictures.)
4. Use different colored beads for different areas.
5. Stretch your finished piece on cardboard, gluing edges under, and frame.

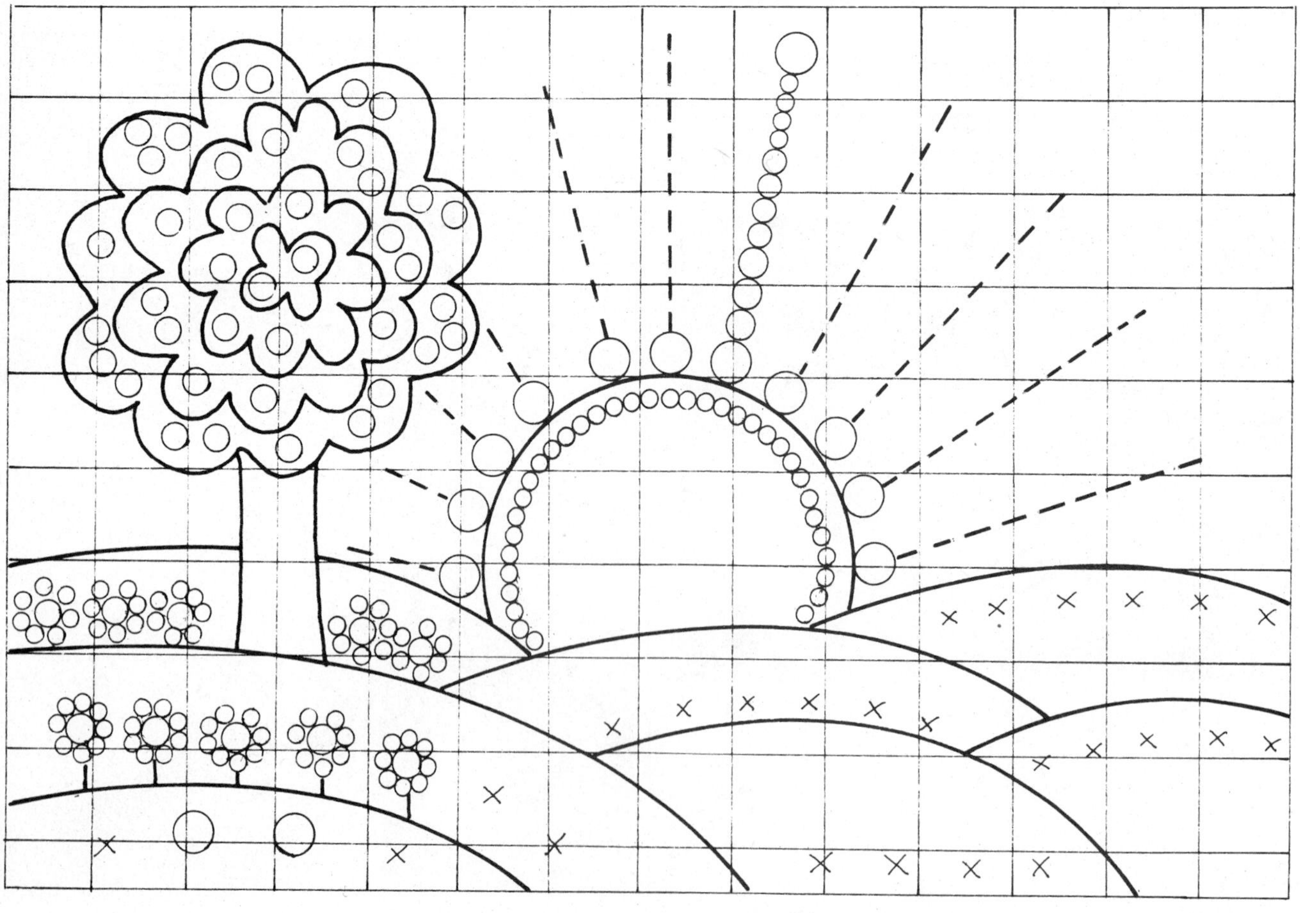

It's Only a Paper Moon

It's Only a Paper Moon

We are so indebted to the invention of paper—for the annals of history that might never have been recorded, for the pleasure of the letters we write and receive, for all the things we transport in paper, from groceries to garbage. The publishing industry alone uses more than half of the paper manufactured in the world today.

It is said that a Chinese sage, while watching wasps build their nests, conceived of paper as we now know it. If you take a look at a hornets' nest, you'll see that it does look like a paper house. The female hornets with their strong jaws shave off tiny particles of wood from trees. They chew them into a pulp which they spread out in thin layers. As they dry, they turn into a tough springy paper.

The early Egyptians, some 3,000 years before the Christian era, made a writing material from the papyrus plant that grew along the banks of the Nile. (Our word "paper" comes from papyrus.) Thin slices of the plant's stem were laid side by side over slices running in another direction. The layers were moistened with water, pressed down, and the rough places smoothed with a piece of ivory or a shell. The natural gum contained in the fresh stems glued the slices together into a tough ivory sheet. Left to age, it became brown and brittle like the papyrus you see in museums. Papyrus became so indispensable that a failure of the papyrus crop during the reign of Tiberius threatened to upset the ordinary business of life in the Roman Empire.

Over the centuries, parchment and vellum came to be used, the former made from the skin of sheep and goats, the latter from thin calf or lamb gut. The development of wood pulp paper, as used today, accompanied advances in printing, and by 1800 there were sophisticated paper-making machines.

It wasn't until paper became readily available that it was used as a crafts material. One interesting exception was China, where as long ago as the second century A.D., work was done with papier-maché.

Most of our paper-craft techniques come to us by way of Europe. Perhaps so few of them originate here because of the scarcity of paper in colonial times. Regardless, every kind of paper is available here now—rainbows of colors, textures, weights, sheens—and there is almost nothing that cannot be made with it.

SIMPLE PAPER CLASSICS

Below are three simple paper creations that rank among the oldest and best loved.

PAPER-DOLL CHAIN

(Shown in color, page 68)

1. Fold a long strip of paper back and forth, accordion style. The width of the paper and the number of folds determine the number and height of the dolls in the chain.
2. Draw a simple doll shape on the top fold. The hands should extend to the folded sides (Fig. 1).
3. Cut around the figure. Do not cut apart the hands on the folds, however.
4. Open the doll chain. Form a ring by gluing together the hands of the last dolls at each end.

PAPER BEADS

1. Cut out triangles of colored construction

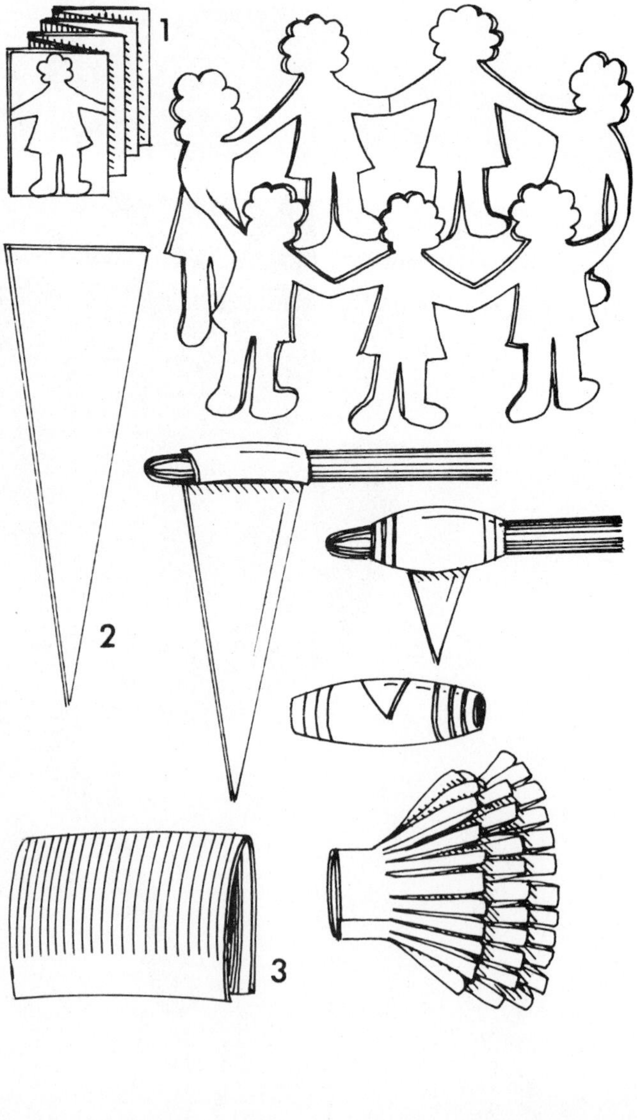

paper or colorful prints from magazines.

2. Brush one side of a triangle with white glue.

3. Roll the triangle, glued side in, around the handle of an artist's paintbrush or a drinking straw. Begin with the wide end and roll toward the point (Fig. 2).

4. Paint the paper bead with a light coating of glue.

5. Slip the bead off the handle and dry on wax paper. String when dry.

POULTRY RUFFLES

1. Fold a 4 x 4-inch piece of lightweight paper in half, without creasing the fold.

2. Cut slits in the folded edge, 1/8 inch apart and 1 inch deep (Fig. 3).

3. Wrap two or three ruffles around a cooked bird and pin under the legs.

PAPER LACE

Victorian ladies were the first to adapt intricate lace designs to paper. Bakers took to this parlor pastime, making doilies for their cakes, and by the turn of the century, greeting cards were heavily paper-laced.

1. Work with sheets of colored tissue or other lightweight paper.

2. For squares and rectangles: fold paper in either shape three or four times, as size permits. Cut out shapes along the folded sides, going no deeper than the center of the paper.

3. For Valentine hearts: cut out a heart shape, and fold it down the center. Fold in half again lengthwise so that the heart looks like a pie wedge. Cut out shapes on the folded side (not the side of the outer edges). Don't cut into the rounded sides.

4. For snowflakes: cut out a circle from a sheet of paper and fold in half three times. Cut out shapes along the top rounded edge.

5. Carefully open lace cuttings.

PAPERCUTS

Sentimental papercuts like these were popular in the eighteenth and early nineteenth centuries.

1. To make a pattern for either scene, enlarge

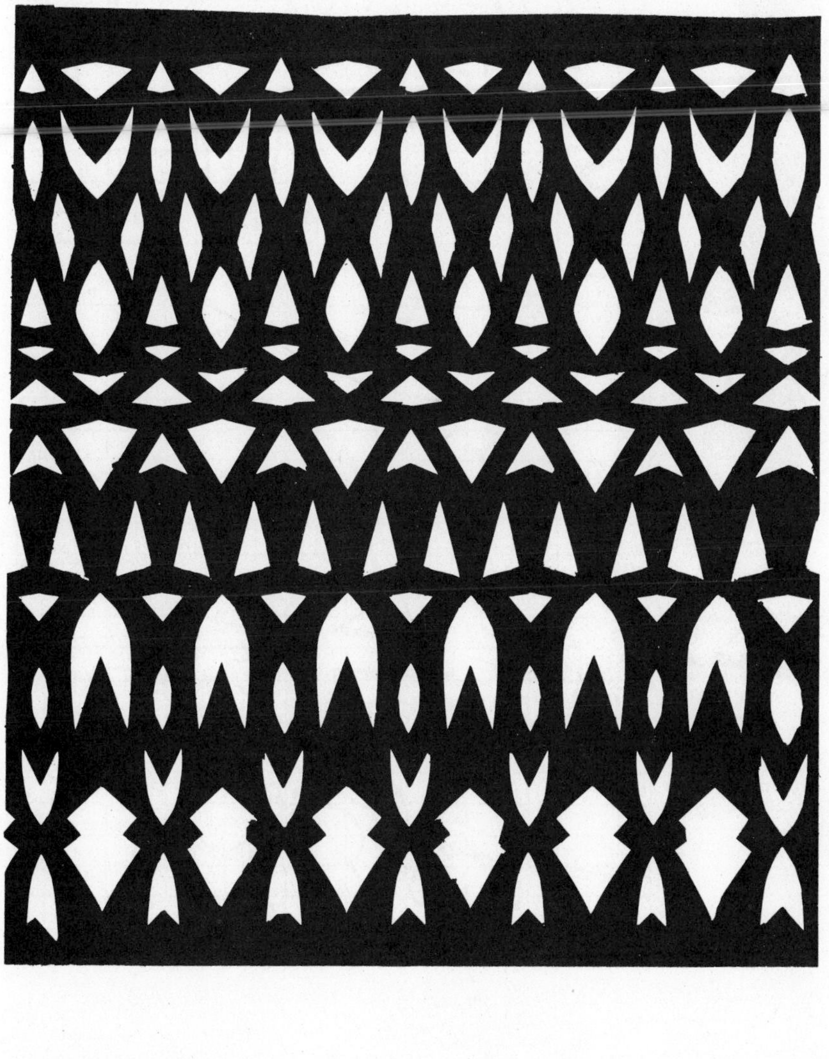

the grid on a piece of tracing paper so that one square equals one inch. Then draw the scene on the enlarged grid. (See page 13 for detailed directions on how to enlarge patterns from a grid.)

2. Rub the side of a sharpened pencil over the underside of the tracing.

3. Tape the tracing on colored paper, drawing facing up, and follow along the lines of the design with a sharp pencil. This will transfer the outline of the drawing to the paper.

4. Cut out the designs carefully with a pair of pointed scissors or a single-edge razor blade.

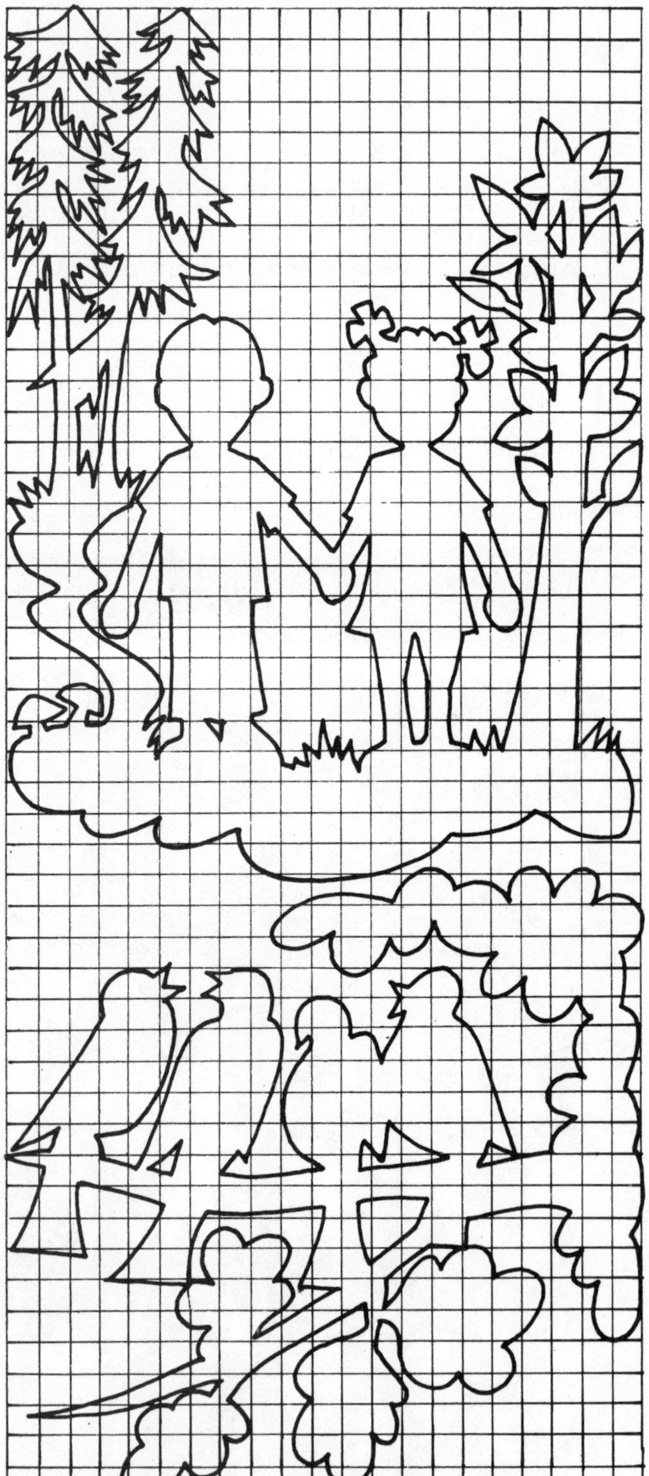

5. Apply paste or glue to the underside of the cutout with a paint brush and carefully place it on white or colored paper. (Rubber cement can also be used, although it is a less durable adhesive. Remember to rub away any excess with your fingers.)

6. Cut the background paper to fit the frame you intend to use.

Note: You can transform magazine photos into papercuts by tracing the major shapes and either filling them in with a black marker or using them as patterns.

PORTRAIT SILHOUETTES

Before the invention of the photograph, the silhouette was the leading form of protraiture.

1. If you can sketch, make your own portraits. Draw an egg shape for an adult head, or a somewhat more circular one for a child's. The eyes come halfway down the head. An exaggerated hairline with a few curls or stray wisps should be included. Add a collar line.

2. To make more accurate silhouettes, take black-and-white close-up side views of the members of your family. Shoot as close as your camera will allow.

3. Select the shots to be used and blow up your negatives to 5 x 7-inch prints.

4. To make your patterns, trace the portraits carefully on tracing paper.

5. Rub the side of a sharpened pencil on the underside of the tracing, covering the entire portrait area. In effect, you are making it into a piece of carbon paper.

6. Place the tracing, line drawing facing up, on a piece of black paper. Tape in place.

7. Draw over the traced line, pressing down firmly on the pencil. The outline will appear on the black paper.

8. Cut out the portrait carefully and paste it to white or colored paper or a piece of fabric.

9. An oval frame is best suited to silhouettes.

GRILLWORK

Another popular Victorian paper craft, this one inspired by the delicate grillwork that has been a part of European architecture since metal was first twisted and shaped.

1. To make a pattern for the daisy, enlarge the grid on a sheet of tracing paper so that one square equals ½ inch. Then draw the design on the enlarged grid. (See page 13 for detailed directions on how to enlarge a pattern from a grid.)

2. Rub the side of a sharpened pencil over the underside of the tracing.

3. Tape the tracing on a piece of black or col-

ored paper, drawing facing up, and follow along the lines of the design with a sharp pencil. This will transfer the outline of the drawing to the paper.

4. Cut out the design with a single-edge razor blade.

5. Paste or glue a sheet of colored paper to the underside of the design.

6. Use the razor blade again to cut out sections of the under color from the sun, flowers and leaves in the design.

7. Paste a third sheet of paper in a different color to the underside of the second layer.

8. Trim the outer border of the design to fit the frame you intend to use.

THREE-DIMENSIONAL COLLAGES

This effective technique, employed in colonial times, enhances the illusion of depth and extends a picture's plane out toward the viewer.

1. Cut a piece of cardboard to fit the frame you intend to use.

2. Paint the cardboard or cover it with fabric (either a solid color or a print.)

3. From another piece of cardboard, cut a simple vase shape and smaller shapes with which to highlight it. Paint each separately and then glue the highlights to one side of the vase (see illustration).

4. Glue the vase to the backing, near the bottom of the field.

5. Cut simple flower and leaf shapes from cardboard. Chrysanthemums have four layers of petals of graduated sizes. Daffodils have pointed leaves with a large circle in the center, topped with several smaller circles. Daisies consist of two concentric layers of scalloped petals topped with a circle. Lilies of the valley and leaves are also made from double layers of similar shapes.

6. Paint all the pieces individually before gluing them together into a three-dimensional arrangement.

7. Glue the assembled flowers and leaves in a spreading bouquet above the vase. Green-painted stems should link the flowers together.

8. If you painted the entire collage, backdrop and all, you can protect it with a coat of liquid plastic or a découpage finish.

PAPER "LEADED" BOX

Early American metal forgers created quite marvelous things—both utilitarian and decorative. This little "leaded" box resembles the ornate handwork that adorned sconces and lanterns in

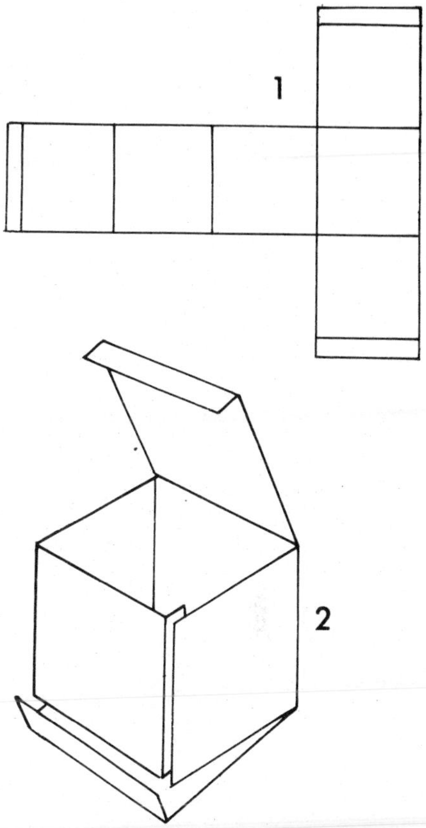

those days before machines.

1. The design shown is actual size. Trace it four times in a row on lightweight paper, forming a continuous pattern.
2. Retrace the design directly above and below the last square on the right of your pattern.
3. Add ½-inch extensions to the left, top and bottom squares (see Fig. 1).
4. Carefully cut out the motif on all six squares with a single-edge razor blade.
5. Paste a piece of colored tissue or cellophane to the underside of each motif.
6. Fold the first four squares of the pattern to form a cube. Fold the extending tab into the cube and glue (Fig. 2).
7. Fold the top and bottom squares over the cube and tuck in the tabs to form a box.
8. Glue the tabs for added security.
9. Place the box before an artificial light source or hang in a window where sunlight can pass through it.

QUILLWORK

Quillwork is a delicate lacy art that was first practiced by Italian nuns in the seventeenth and eighteenth centuries. They called it quillwork because a bird's quill (minus the features) was the tool originally used for rolling the narrow strips of paper and vellum into spirals. The craft spread to France, then to England. Though it was not unknown in colonial America, it would be lost but for a few dedicated artisans who have kept it alive.

1. The basic round coil in Fig. 1 is made by wrapping long strips of white or colored paper (about ⅛ to ½ inch wide) around a hatpin. The wider and longer the strips, the larger the coil. Wrap tightly. Unwrap the coil and rewind by hand into a looser circle. Add a dab of glue with a toothpick to keep the coil intact. Coils can be loosely or tightly wound according to your needs. The following coils follow the same procedure.
2. Teardrop coil (Fig. 2) is made by pinching one end of the constructed coil into a point.
3. A heart-shaped coil (Fig. 3) is made by pinching one end of the constructed coil into a point, and making a depression in the opposite end with your thumb.
4. A leaf-shaped coil (Fig. 4) is made by pinching both ends of the constructed coil into points.
5. A butterfly coil (Fig. 5) is made by wrapping both ends of a paper strip inward, leaving the connecting portion uncoiled. Fold this strip in half so that the glued coils now turn outward. A

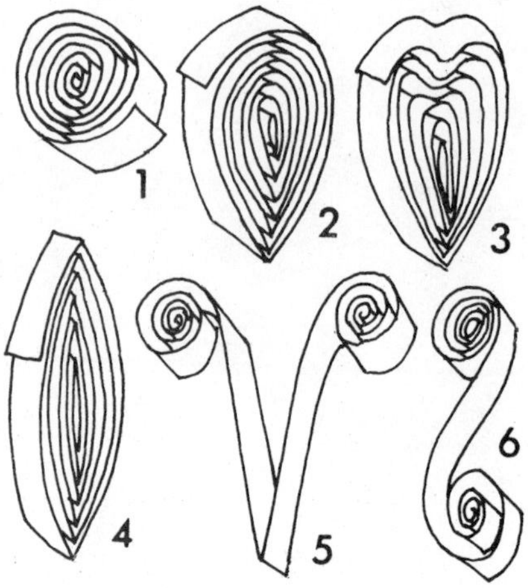

reversed butterfly is made with the glued coils facing inward.

6. The "S" coil (Fig. 6) is a strip of paper with the coils on either end going in opposite directions.

7. Quilled flowers have round-coil centers flanked by teardrops, hearts or leaves. The stems are made from very loosely-coiled strips of paper.

8. Arrange the elements of your design on a sheet of colored or white paper. Add small dabs of glue with a toothpick to the under edges of each coil. Press to the backing and allow to dry thoroughly.

PAPER BASKETS

(Shown in color, page 165)

A sewing catchall, a basket for flowers, a candy container, a tree trim, a make-up caddy—baskets hold everything.

WOVEN BASKET

1. The size of the basket is determined by the size of the center square (Fig. 1). The larger the square, the more slits you can cut in each side, and therefore the deeper the weave.

2. Draw the center square on heavy colored paper. Then draw four more squares adjacent to the four sides of the original square (Fig. 1).

3. In the four surrounding squares, cut slits ½ inch apart, running toward the center square. The slits should begin and end ½ inch in from the edges of each square.
4. Cut long strips of paper ½ inch wide in a contrasting color.
5. Fold the four slit squares upward to form a box.
6. Weave the long strips in and out through the slits. When turning a corner, alternate the weave so that if the strip went under the last slit, it goes over the first slit on the next side. The ends of the strips should fall inside the box. Trim each end and glue it to another strip.
7. The second row of strips is woven in the opposite direction. Continue to alternate the rows of strips until the basket is completed.
8. Glue on a paper handle.

PLEATED BASKET

1. Accordion-pleat a sheet of paper by folding it in and out in ½-to one-inch intervals (Fig. 2). The length of the paper will determine the fullness of the basket.
2. Glue the ends of the paper together to form a cylinder.
3. Sew the base of the cylinder with colored embroidery thread, passing through the center of each fold about ½ inch above the bottom edge (Fig. 3).
4. Pull the thread in to make the sides of the basket slant as much as you wish, and tie securely.
5. Sew the top of the pleats in place.
6. Cut a cardboard circle one inch larger than the base opening and rest it inside the basket.
7. Add a paper handle.

BASKET FOR SWEETS.

THIS little basket is made of paper and thin card-board. For the bottom take a circle of card-board, two and a half inches in diameter; and for the side, a strip seven inches long, and one and a half inch wide. Join the strip around, and gum it to the bottom. Next take a strip of tinted note-paper, seven inches long, and two wide; fold it in half, lengthwise, and cut it in strips to within the eighth of an inch at the edge. Open it, and gum it at the two edges to the foundation, letting the cut part stand out, as seen in engraving. The edges are bordered with gilt, or other ornamental paper; the handle is of a narrow strip of card-board, also covered with ornamental paper.

1

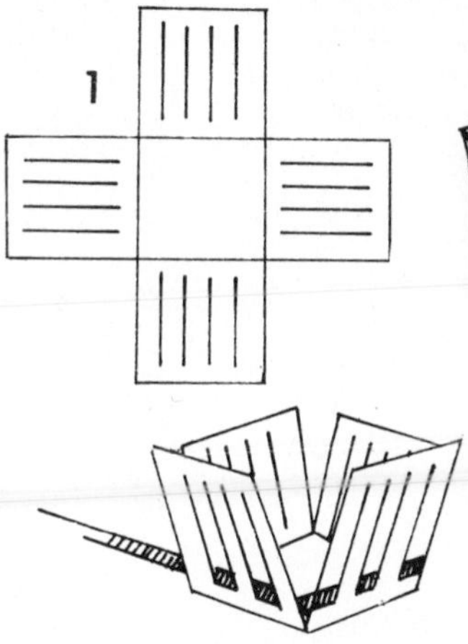

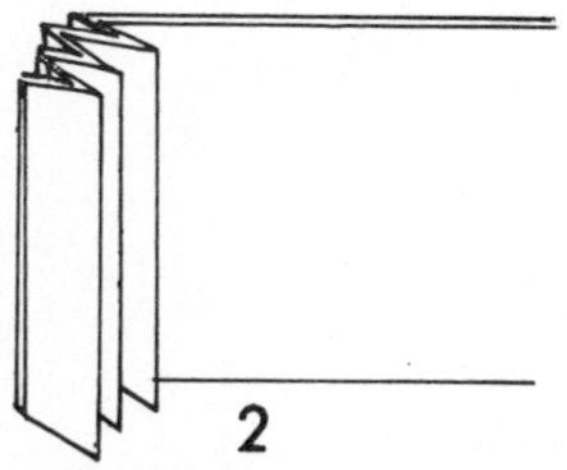

2

3

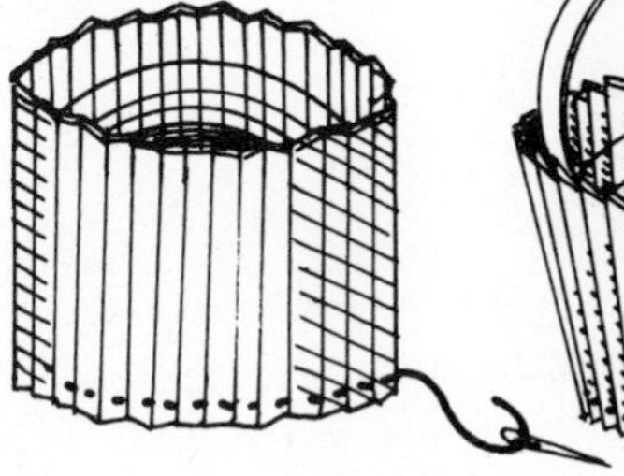

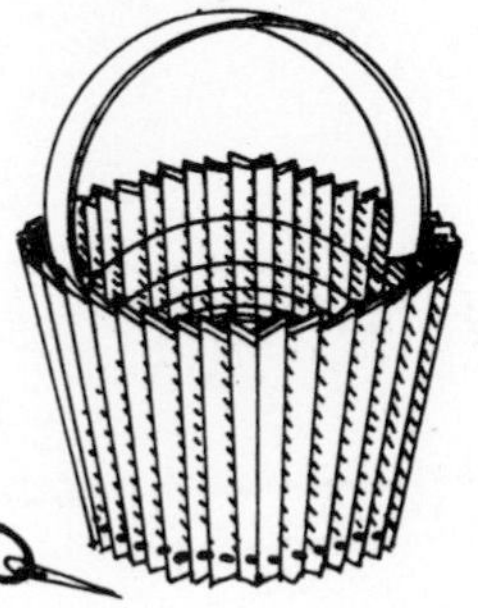

PAPER FLOWERS

(Shown in color on cover)

Before plastic was invented, paper bouquets were the rule when flowers were not in season. These flowers have a wire stem made from coat hangers or thin wire covered with green crepe paper.

DAISY

1. For each daisy, take a 4-inch-wide strip of white crepe paper and cut one edge into pointed petals (Fig. 1).
2. The center of the daisy is a 1½-inch-wide strip of yellow crepe paper rolled into a tight bud (Fig. 2).
3. Twist florist's wire around the base of the yellow center, and twist the white petals around both (Fig. 3). Bend the petals outward to open the flower.
4. Cover the base of the petals and the stem wire with florist's tape, winding downward.

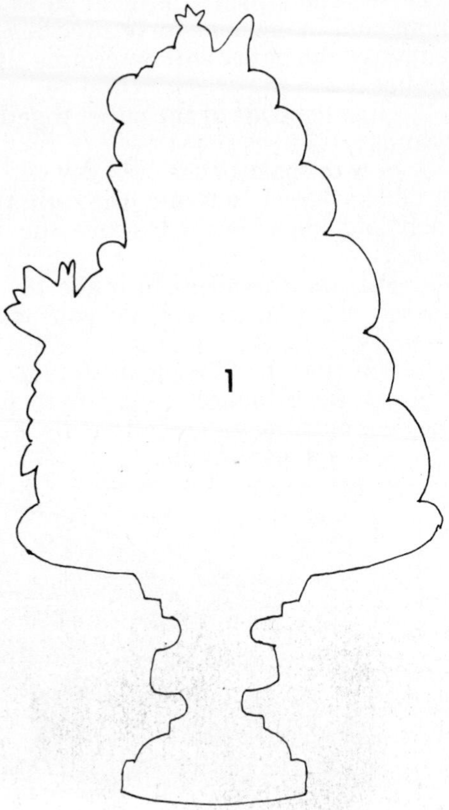

FACING PAGE
1. Topiary Tree, page 76

CENTER SPREAD
1. Topsy-Eva Doll, page 91
2. Shoe-Box-Woven Doll, page 94
3. Soap Dolls, page 96
4. "Yo-Yo" Doll, page 84
5. Braided-Limb Animals, page 95
6. Puppet Theater Puppet, page 115

E
C
L
Z

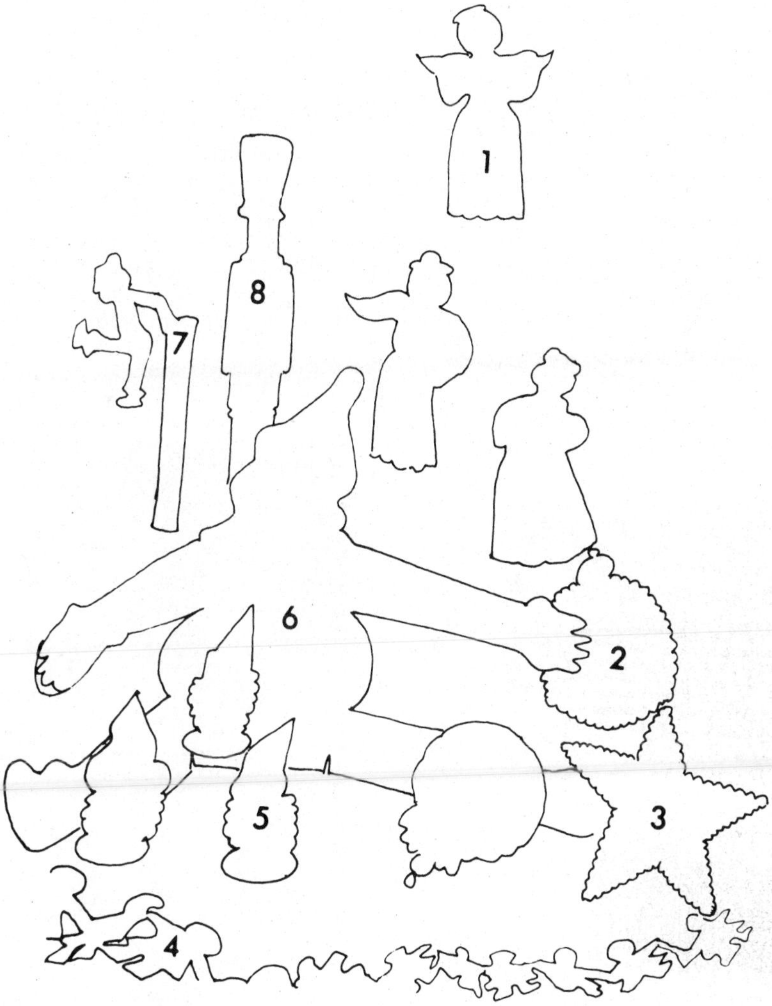

FACING PAGE
1. Cornhusk Angel, page 82
2. Jeweled Balls, page 129
3. Beaded Star, page 130
4. Paper Dolls, page 56
5. Pine Cone Elves, page 136
6. Hinged Clown, page 112
7. Tumbling Acrobat, page 109
8. Spool Soldier, page 103

1
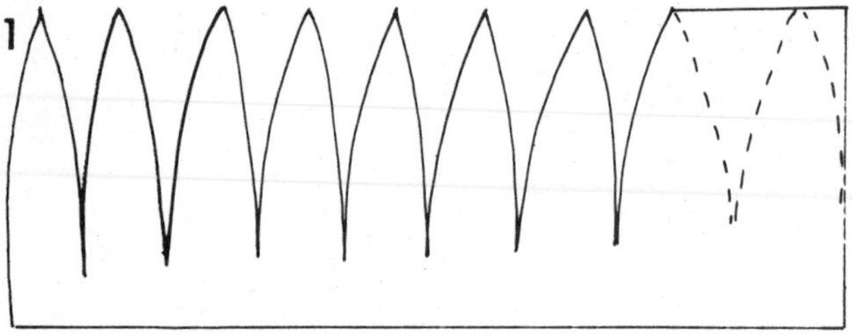

2
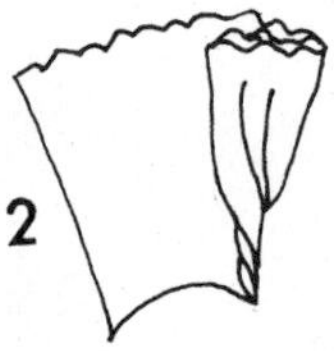

3
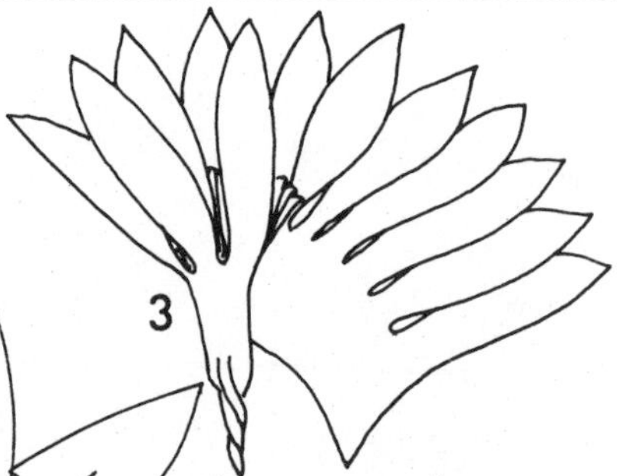

4
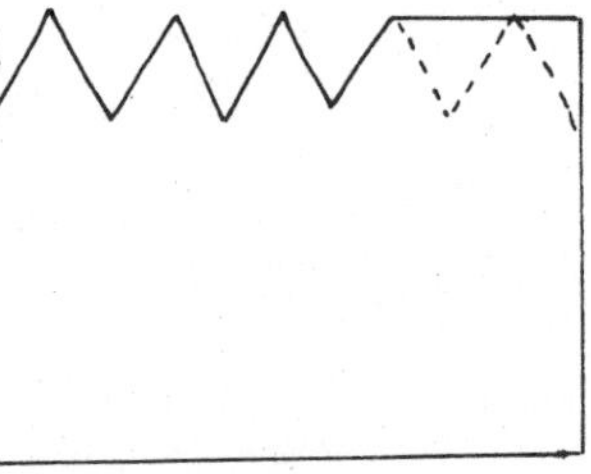

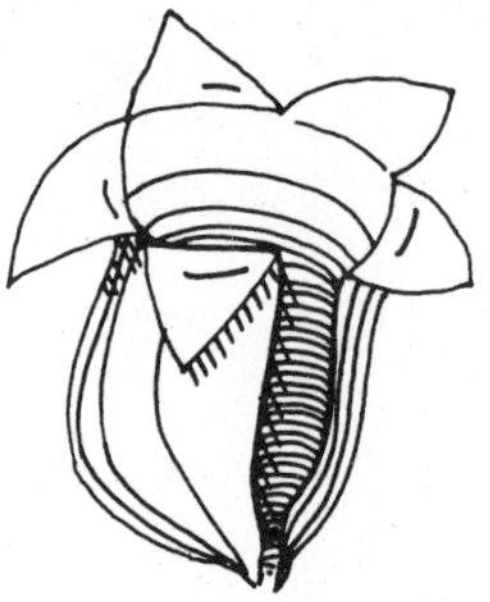

MINIATURE FIELD DAISIES

1. These flowers are exactly like the daisy just described but scaled down to half the size. Use white crepe paper for field daisies or purple for thistles.

2. Twist several buds into one wire stem and cover with florist's tape.

CANTERBURY BELLS

1. Cut five small wedges along the top edge of a 2-inch wide strip of red or yellow crepe paper (Fig. 4).
2. Roll the paper to form a circle. Overlap the first and fifth petal slightly.
3. Twist the bottom of the roll tightly between your fingers.
4. Place one finger inside the flower and push out the base so it bulges slightly.
5. Attach one or two cotton swab tips to one end of a length of wire. Wrap the wire with florist's tape, tucking in bells here and there to form a spray.

PORCELAINIZING

Enhance your paper flowers with this glossy finish.

1. Make flowers following the instructions given in the preceding project. (You can use lightweight colored paper as well as crepe paper.)
2. Brush the flowers with a plastic-base finish, découpage finish or white glue.
3. Allow the first coat of finish to dry completely before you apply a second one. The more coats you add, the more convincing the porcelain look.

PAPER ROSE.

Materials.—Pale yellow, white, or red, and light green tissue-paper; thick gum, fine wire, paint-brush, pincers, hyacinth hook, the thickest wooden rounding pin, green leaves, and green wax calix; light green wool.

Fig. 1.

Fig. 2.

Fig. 4.

Fig. 3.

Fig. 5.

Fig. 6.

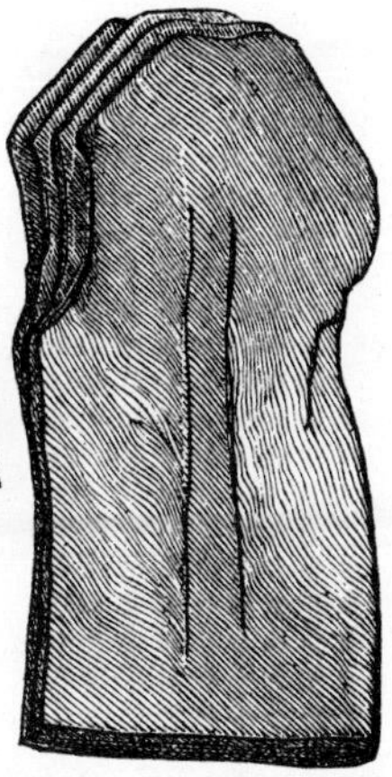

Fig. 7.

Fig. 8.

Fig. 9.

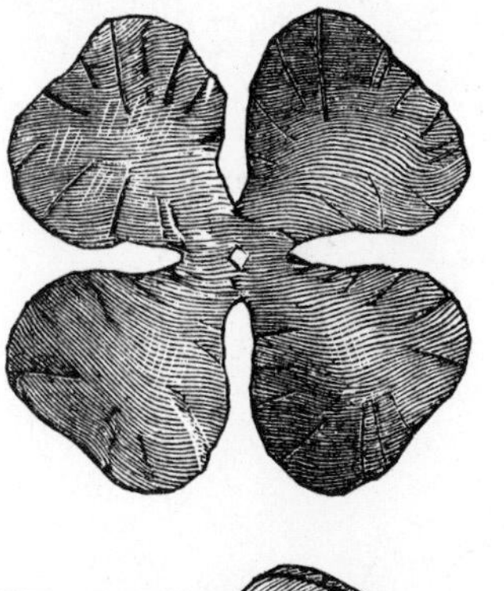

Fig. 10.

OUR model is a light yellow rose, with a reddish pencilling; any pink will do as well.

The coloring is painted with carmine. The several leaf parts are folded four or eight times double, and then cut. The stamen calix, represented in Fig. 2, consists of a few light green loops of wool fastened to a wire. These are carefully combed out and surrounded with stamens of gold thread, touched at the points with fine white sand. Six double leaves, curled with what is called a hyacinth hook, are then pressed together at the under end, as shown in Fig. 3, and bound round the calix. They are one inch and a quarter long and half an inch wide, with a little piece cut out of the middle in a tapering form to within a quarter of an inch of the bottom of the paper. Then make three hollow pads, each formed from one inch and a half square by inclosing and pressing the corners together carefully (see Fig. 4). The our leaves, which are all cut in one piece, are for the smaller size, two inches long and one inch broad, quite straight at the bottom, folded together at the top, and slightly rounded, so as to give a little curve exactly in the middle. The larger ones are one inch and a quarter broad, two inches and a half long, shaped at the top as described for the smaller one. Four of both sides (see Fig. 5) are pressed between the thumb and fore-finger of both hands, then opened out again, and, lying fourfold upon each other upon the palm of the hand, are crimped with the hyacinth hook, according to Fig. 6. The scalloped edges are then drawn lightly over the scissors in order to give the part that turns over the delicate form natural to the rose-leaf. Then the separate parts of the petal must be quite unfolded and separated from each other, and the four petals in one piece must be pressed together at the under end; then the so-far prepared petal part is again laid in the palm of the hand, and pressed up with the hook several times, so as to form the shapes represented in Figs. 7 and 8. First the four smaller, then the four larger petal parts; the latter, reversed, are bound round the hollow pad; then follow three circles of the petals cut four in one piece, with a little opening in the middle for pushing on. These are cut in the exact form shown in Fig. 9.

Each leaf is two inches and a quarter at the widest part, and is the same length from the highest point to the hole shown in the middle to draw the wire of the stamen calix shown in Fig. 2. The largest round of the wooden pin will be needed for rounding the large petals. As soon as a separate circle of the so-far finished rose is closely pushed on, the edges of the petals are very carefully gummed over each other at the side edges. Twelve leaves taken from this pattern are placed in reversed lines, and again carefully gummed over each other at the under points and side edges.

Suitable branches of moss are firmly gummed at regular distances under the roses. The stalks are covered with light green tissue paper, and a calix of green wax completes the rose. The mode of placing on the wadding and yellow tissue paper bud is shown in Fig. 10.

PAPER FLOWERS.—DOUBLE PINK.

THE materials are cherry-colored (carmine) paper and pale green paper, also blue-green paper, all three without gloss; watered-silk paper in pink or light lilac, and green; thin flower-wire, etc.

Fig. 1.

Fig. 2.

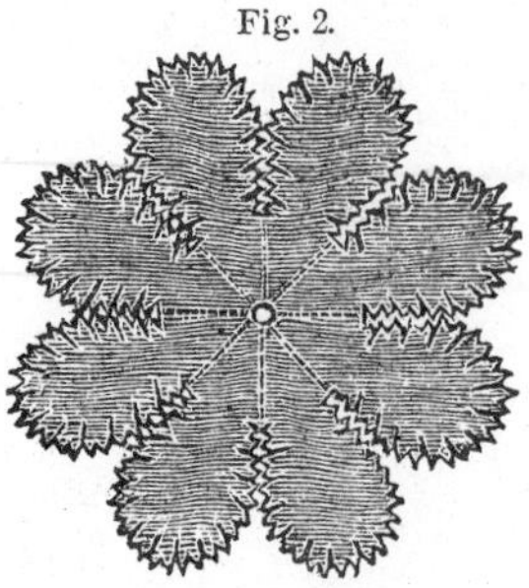

Fig. 5.

Fig. 3.

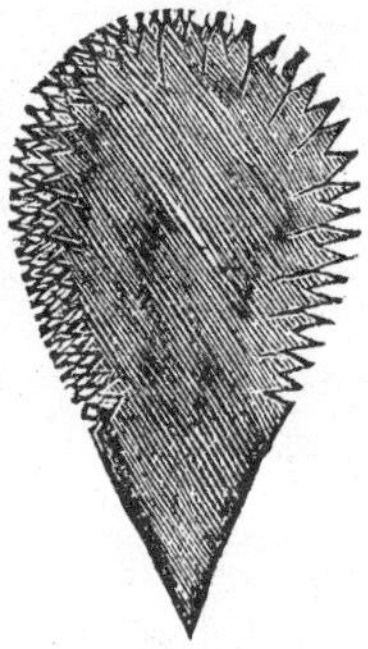

Fig. 4.

Fig. 1.—Should thin paper be taken for this pink, four petal circles of the same size are required for each; but if the thick so-called carmine paper is used, of which the model flower is made, then three are sufficient. Fig. 2 gives one petal in a small size spread out. Fig. 3 shows the same in the full size folded together eight times. The edges of this folded-together flower part, to be next cut out in points, are to have small slits between every two points; after being opened, the pointed edges are drawn over a knitting-needle or scissors, in order to curve them, and this throughout and only on one side; a narrow stripe of white paper in the same way is then slit up one and a quarter inch deep in a fringe-like way, and twisted around a piece of wire, gives the bunch of stamens (shown in Fig. 4); more natural, however, is a small piece from the feather part of a goose-quill. The petal circles are slipped on singly, and tied on the wire stalk, letting the thus-far finished flower slip between the thumb and first finger of the half-closed left hand, so that the petals may come closer together. The calyx of the pink, the edges of which must be pasted over each other, are cut out of the pale green, dull paper, after Fig. 5, filled with a little cotton-wool, and the flower stalk then slipped through. The lower edge of the calyx disappears when caught together by twisting over the flower stalk with green paper. The long, pointed leaves of pale green paper are next broken (folded together, pressed with the finger, and again opened) along the middle, then drawn over the scissors the whole width, and, only at the lower end, finished with a fine wire stalk twisted over with green. Then the green closed pink buds can be formed of cotton-wool, and covered with a mixture of green wax and gum Arabic; but these are so cheap at flower-shops that it is quite unnecessary to make them. Open buds are of one petal circle, and one calyx of only three points.

PAPER FLOWERS.

FULL-BLOWN MALLOWS ARRANGED AS A BOUQUET FOR A VASE.

Materials.—Colored and white tissue paper, several shades of water color paints, fine yellow sand, flower wire, thick dissolved gum, pincers.

FIG. 1 represents a branch of mallow in reduced size, with graduated buds and flowers. About twelve such branches are required for a vase. Fig. 2 gives a flower in full size. For a shaded flower, white tissue paper, covered with carmine, or any other color suitable to the flower, may be used. For the colored flowers, tissue paper of the proper color must be selected.

Circles of paper of two sizes may be cut out for each flower. The flowers look more natural not cut too much of a size; these must be folded together from the middle to form a triangle, and then, having folded the flower part so that the paper is threefold, cut so that scallops are formed. Then take the under part of the triangle with the left hand between a piece of thin old linen, lay it with its contents upon a corner of a table, hold it firmly, and push with a twisting movement, pressing the ball of the right hand with great force over it several times, which gives the necessary folds for the circle of petals. Afterwards the triangle of white tissue paper must be painted and dipped in clean water, and then laid upon the edge of a plate that the color may gradually run; and,

Fig. 2.

Fig. 3.

Fig. 4.

Fig. 5.

Fig. 1.

take the leaves made with the feathers from which the fringe has not been shaved off; the leaves, buds, and small blossoms are made of petals are placed in regular order; sometimes, also, two of the smallest are first pushed on the wire stalk, and pressed on to it, which must have a pistil of wadding and colored sand (see Fig. 3).

The smaller the corolla the fewer the number of petal circles; the smallest have no pistils. The bud represented in Fig. 4 is composed of wadding wetted with gum, and painted green; the point is squeezed with the pincers crosswise, according to Fig. 5. All the stalks have light green tissue paper twisted round them.

The green leaves may be purchased at very little expense.

DÉCOUPAGE BOX

(Shown in color on cover)

Découpage as practiced today is a revival of an art which flourished in eighteenth-century Europe. The French word (from *couper,* to cut) made

its way into the English language in the early 1900s. It describes a method of laminating paper cutouts onto hard surfaces. It is only in the past ten years that découpage has become a popular art form in this country.

1. Surfaces appropriate for simple découpage range from scraps of wood for wall plaques to jewelry boxes, furniture, kitchen cabinets or old china plates.
2. The picture to be used can be clipped from a magazine, a book, a greeting card or wallpaper. You can also use the printed designs made especially for découpage and sold at crafts counters.
3. Carefully cut out the design or figure you have chosen.
4. Sand the edges of the cutout on the underside with extra-fine sandpaper, working out from the edges in order not to bend them.
5. If you are using scrap lumber, cut it down to the appropriate size and sand the edges.
6. Stain or paint the wood.
7. Pour liquid white glue into a small paper cup and brush the glue on the underside of the cutout.
8. Place the glued print on the selected surface.
9. Place a sheet of paper over the glued print and press down, beginning in the center of the print and working out to the edges. This pushes out excess glue and smoothes out air bubbles.
10. Wipe off any excess glue with a damp sponge.
11. Allow the print to dry.
12. The print is to be set like a bug in amber beneath several layers of transparent finish. Buy special découpage finish, or use liquid plastic or liquid white glue. Do not use an oil-base finish such as shellac or varnish. Brush on the first coat of finish and allow to dry.
13. When dry, buff with steel wool or extra-fine sandpaper and follow with a second coat of your finish. Let dry.
14. Continue to buff and apply coats of finish until the print has sunk beneath a thick veneer.
15. Your last finish can be a high gloss or a more subdued low-luster finish achieved by a final buffing with fine steel wool.
16. To antique the final finish, rub in an oil-base walnut stain or a layer of artist's oil paint.
17. The raised design on the box in the illustration was made by squeezing white glue directly from the bottle in decorative designs once the print was in place. The glue was allowed to dry thoroughly before the coats of finish were applied.

TOOLED PAPER DÉCOUPAGE

A form of découpage that did gain popularity in this country was embossing. Look at turn-of-the-century post cards, book covers and greeting cards and you'll notice how certain areas are raised, how they have a three dimensional effect.

1. Without trimming the edges of the print you have chosen, place it face down on a triple layer of scrap felt. Prints on heavyweight paper work best.
2. Gauge where major areas of the design fall, and sketch these areas in pencil on the back side of the print.
3. Use the handle of a spoon or another instrument with a blunt but fairly pointed tip to tool or emboss between the penciled lines. Keep working an area until you have made a slight depression in the paper. Be gentle, too much tooling will crack the print.
4. Glue the tooled print to the surface you have chosen to decorate. Don't press down on the embossed portions or you'll flatten them.
5. Finish with several coats of découpage sealer, liquid plastic or liquid white glue.

REPOUSSÉ DÉCOUPAGE

This technique involves stuffing the découpage item with papier-mâché.

1. Repoussé is most effectively applied to a

rounded object, such as a metal coffee pot, a vase or an old-fashioned milk can. If you use a flat surface as your base, eliminate step 3 below (do not moisten the first print).

2. You will need two identical sets of prints. The ones sold expressly for découpage are best for this project.

3. Cut out the first print and lay it face up on a damp sponge.

4. When moist, brush white glue on the back of the print and mold it to the rounded surface of the object you have chosen to decorate.

5. Decide what parts of the print you wish to have raised. Choose larger areas in the design —an apple, for instance, rather than its leaves. Cut out these areas from the second print.

6. Make a papier-mâché mixture with chopped-up facial tissue, white glue and a teaspoon of glycerine. The glycerine keeps the dried pulp from cracking. Mix the ingredients together with a spoon to obtain a smooth consistency similar to moist mashed potatoes. The tissue can be reduced to a fluff in your electric blender for easier mixing.

7. The mold for the raised pieces is made in a block of hard craft foam. With the handle of a spoon, make depressions in the foam slightly smaller than the cut-out pieces. Each indentation should be smooth and rounded, with no sharp angles. Sand the indented places if necessary.

8. Place the cut-out shapes face up on a damp sponge until they are moist.

9. Carefully fit the prints into the mold, face down, pressing them evenly into the recesses.

10. Fill the molded prints with your papier-mâché mixture. Even off the papier-mâché with a knife.

11. Unmold the cutouts and brush white glue on the leveled area.

12. Place them over their identical counterparts on the découpage surface.

13. Press down the edges with the end of an artist's paintbrush or any other narrow instrument.

14. Indentations can be made in the raised areas with the end of the brush—for instance, on a highlight.

15. Allow the repoussé découpage to dry for ten days before you proceed to coat the piece with an appropriate finish. (See procedures described under Découpage Box.)

ILLUMINATED DÉCOUPAGE

Many new craft techniques evolve when two craft materials are used together. Illuminated découpage combines cut-out prints with paper foil. The effect of illumination is achieved by cutting away highlighted areas of a design so that the foil layer behind shows through.

1. With a single-edge razor blade, cut out small areas in your print that you wish to illuminate: veins in leaves, for example, or glints of light on fruit. You might also consider making a narrow illuminated border around your design.

2. If the item you plan to decorate has a curved surface, moisten the underside of the print on a damp sponge.

3. Cut out pieces of foil slightly larger than the cut-out portions of the print. Use white glue to paste the foil, shiny side down, to the back of the print. If you are bordering the print as well, glue the entire design to a sheet of foil and trim so that the foil is ⅛ inch larger all around.

4. Brush the back of the illuminated print with white glue.

5. Place the print on the item you are decorating and roll from the center of the print out to the edges, pressing down with a small glass or the handle of an artist's paintbrush.

6. Wipe away any excess glue with a damp sponge.

7. When dry, proceed to give the item a finishing coat following the directions for Découpage Box.

POTICHOMANIE DÉCOUPAGE

Potichomanie découpage is a technique that originated in Victorian England at a time when Chinese vases were in vogue. For those with expensive tastes but little cash, remarkably convincing substitutes for the genuine article were produced by placing découpage designs inside clear glass vases and giving the interior of these vessels a bright porcelain-like finish. The new craft acquired a hybrid name that literally means "pot-crazy," from the French words *potiche,* or Oriental vase, and *manie,* or craze.

1. Choose a glass item with a wide mouth, such as a large brandy snifter.

2. Choose a print that will fit comfortably inside the glass and cut it out.
3. Moisten the print with a damp sponge.
4. Brush liquid white glue on the *face* of the print.
5. Place the print inside the glass. Press on the print and mold it into the curve of the glass, working outward from the center of the design. Be sure to remove all air bubbles, as they are easy to see through the glass.
6. Allow the print to dry thoroughly. The white glue will dry clear and become invisible.
7. When dry, paint the inner surface of the glass and slightly over the edges of the print.

ILLUMINATED POTICHOMANIE DÉCOUPAGE

If you have mastered all the preceding découpage projects, this last technique will be somewhat like a final exam.

1. Place the print inside the glass following the process outlined for Potichomanie Découpage. Before you begin, however, cut out areas of the design that you wish to highlight in the manner described for Illuminated Découpage.
2. When the print inside the glass container is dry, brush the entire inner surface including the print with white glue.
3. Press pieces of aluminum foil (about 2 inches square) onto the glued inner surface. Do not allow any rough edges to protrude. Overlap the foil pieces until you have covered the entire inside of the glass, print included.
4. Press all air bubbles out from under the foil.
5. The top of the glass can be trimmed with a decorative ribbon, after excess foil has been trimmed flush with the rim of the glass.

PULP PAPIER-MÂCHÉ

The first papier-mâché plant operated in this country was run by one John Keating as early as 1771. By the mid-nineteenth century, there were small factories everywhere. Papier-mâché was the plastic of the nineteenth century. Though it is nothing more than mashed paper pulp mixed with a binder of glue or gum arabic, it is endlessly versatile.

1. Papier-mâché pulp is made with finely shredded newsprint or facial tissue, wheat or wallpaper paste and water. The ingredients are mixed together to the consistency of moist mashed potatoes. The facial tissue or newspaper can be reduced to a fluff first in an electric blender. (You can make extra mixture and store it in a plastic bag for future use.) Dry papier-mâché is sold by the bag, if you prefer not to make your own. In that case, all you do is add water.
2. Pulp paper-mâché is shaped by spreading the wet mixture over a mold. Molds can be made of clay or aluminum foil, or improvised with such household items as mixing bowls or gelatin molds. Grease the outside of your mold generously. Spread the pulp over the mold in a layer ¼ to ½ inch thick. Press the pulp firmly into any recesses. Allow to dry thoroughly before unmolding.
3. Papier-mâché can also be shaped by hand, without a mold, but when the sculpture is thick it takes longer to dry and may turn moldy in the process.
4. Sand the finished item with fine sandpaper and give it a base coat of white paint. Follow with a layer of base paint, applying color detail for decoration. Water-base paints can also be used. A high-gloss or mat-finish varnish or a coat of liquid plastic finishes off the piece.

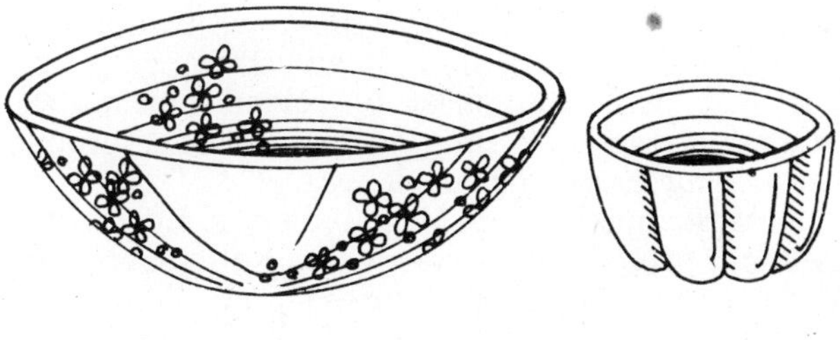

STRIP PAPIER-MÂCHÉ

A more recent addition to the papier-mâché craft repertoire is the strip method. Instead of molding objects, you paste strips of paper over molds. The molds remain part of the final project.

1. Tear newspaper in strips, small strips for small items, larger ones for large items. Make a mixture of wheat or wallpaper paste and water that has the consistency of heavy whipped cream.
2. Select a household item such as an old jar, a bottle or a tin tray to serve as a permanent mold for the strip papier-mâché. Dip the strips of paper into the wet mixture. Layer the strips, overlapping slightly, so that they cover the entire item. Repeat this process with two more layers of paper. Press the strips down, removing any excess paste.
3. Let the item dry thoroughly, smooth with fine sandpaper, and apply a base coat of white paint before giving the piece a final painting.

BALLOON MOLDS

Blow up round balloons and knot the ends tightly. Cover with moistened paper strips, let dry, and finish the surface according to the above

directions. You can paint and decorate the balloons in countless ways, a few of which are suggested here.

1. Make giant fruits or vegetables to hang in your kitchen or play area. Strawberries, peas in a pod (the pod is a sheet of folded newspaper, stapled at the ends and painted green) or onions are among many you can design.
2. Make masks from large balloons, by carefully slicing the dried, strip-covered balloon in half. Cut out the eyes. Glue on a nose made from paper or a ping-pong ball. Paint on a funny expression, add fringed paper hair, and tie ribbons to both sides of the mask.
3. Christmas balls are made with small round balloons. Paint and decorate them with beads, sequins, glitter and bits of ribbon.
4. Make party favors by slicing small papier-mâché balls in half. Remove the balloon and sand the inside of the ball. Fill with candy or small toys for children and then tape the ball closed. Decorate as you wish.

FOAM BALL MOLDS

Hard foam balls are covered with strips and finished following the directions given above. The foam can be easily carved with a knife to look like fruit, dolls' heads, eggs for Easter, beads or practically anything else you can imagine. Here is a single example of what you can do.

1. To make a topiary tree, (shown in color on page 65), carve balls of different sizes into apples, peaches, pears, strawberries, lemons and plums. A pomegranate has a wedge cut into it, and ½-inch balls, cut in half, are glued into the wedge with white glue. Oranges, grapefruit and small watermelons remain circular. Bananas are cut from block foam. Grapes are ½-inch balls strung together on wire before the papier-mâché strips are added.
2. The base of the tree is made by gluing together a pair of foam bases. Similar plastic bases or flowerpots can substitute for foam if not readily available. The base is glued to a block of

foam at the bottom and then topped with a 12-inch foam circle. The rim of the circle is spotted with ½-inch foam balls, split in half. Glue the base together with white glue.

3. Roll a narrow paper (oaktag) cone about 12 inches high. Staple or tape them together. Then trim the bottom edge. Tape or glue the cone to the center base so that it stands straight and secure.

4. The base and the fruit are covered with papier-mâché strips, and painted and varnished separately, before the tree is assembled. Stick wooden match-stick stems to the fruit. Glue green paper leaves to the apples, peaches and pears, and a star-shaped cap to the top of each strawberry.

5. Use five-minute epoxy to start the fruit tower. Glue larger-sized fruit around the bottom of the cone or the rim of the base. Add another ring of smaller fruit. Bananas point upward toward the peak. Grapes are arranged in clusters falling down from the top. Dot the mound at random with small fruits such as strawberries or cranberries.

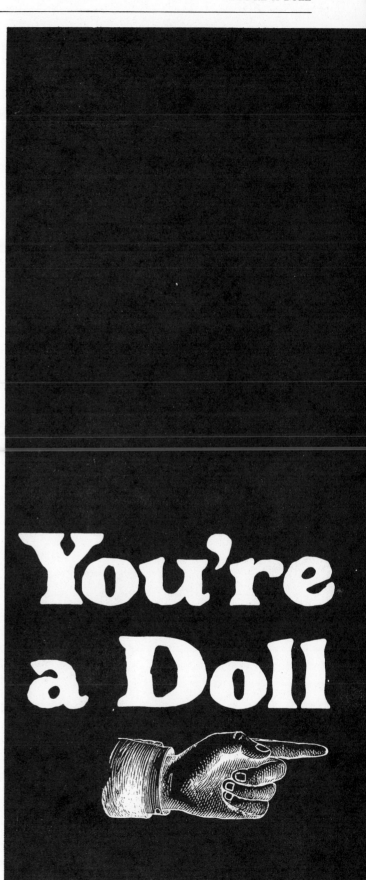

You're a Doll

You're a Doll

Open any kind of toy chest, and you will discover, somewhere amidst the clutter and confusion of this compact, miniature kingdom, the happy face of a doll. Everyone has had the experience of befriending a doll. To a child a doll is the closest thing to a friendly person, a member of the family or a best friend. It fills the owner's quiet moments with imaginary play and stands sentry, protecting little boys and girls from a fiery mouthed dragon or mysterious ghost that might interrupt a good night's sleep.

Dolls know no sexual boundaries although when the word is mentioned little girls usually come to mind. What about stuffed animals? Toy soldiers? Try to remember the years of love you shared with your favorite doll and how oneday it no longer occupied your world. Tenderly it was put to rest. Look into your collection of memorabilia and you just may find a lace-clad doll your grandmother called her very own.

Fantasy is as old as the days. Dolls more than

3,000 years old have been found in the tombs of ancient Egypt. They have flat wood bodies, carved and painted, and for hair, clay beads strung on thread. The dolls of ancient Greece and Rome were slightly more sophisticated, with well shaped heads and jointed arms and legs that could be moved by pulling a string. In America's pioneer days, a child usually had one doll, the one her mother made for her, and it was there from birth. It might be one of a variety of dolls, depending on the availability of construction materials. Some of the styles were brought to America from Europe while others were native to this country.

The cornhusk dolls were first made by the Indians for their children and eventually they were adopted by the settlers. The hoop snake dolls have a story that explains its peculiar design. As the folklore goes, the old-timers of the mountainous regions believed that a hoop snake, in order to make speed coming down a mountain, took its tail in its mouth and rolled down in hoop fashion. Rag dolls, yarn dolls, paper dolls, as well as ceramic-head dolls were the prototypes of true-to-life dolls children play with today.

Dolls have played interesting parts in America's past. Besides providing enjoyment for young children, they were cunningly employed during times of military engagement. As ships carrying dolls were accorded neutrality between nations at war, precious medicines and drugs were smuggled through to Confederate soldiers inside dolls' heads. Dolls were used as models for little girls' domestic training, in preparation for their future role as mother.

No matter how real or how imaginative a doll may be, it is, nevertheless, an object of love and affection, a love far different than any other imaginable. Owning a doll helps children adjust to their world. It gives them the necessary confidence to communicate with other children and share their world with them. Just as the world is comprised of different races of people, so too, the doll kingdom has many faces and figures. Children can learn to love any doll you make for them. On the following pages you and your children will be surprised to see the many interesting shapes and smiles dolls can have. All are guaranteed to generate interest and encourage collections. Create for your children a history of dolls that stretches from the pioneer days to more contemporary types.

CLOTHESPIN DOLLS

In this age of electric dryers, your children may never have seen a clothespin. Drive along any back road or country lane during the warm weather to convince them that they're still very much in use. The clothespin doll came out of the American backwoods. To make these dolls you will need the good old-fashioned variety.

1. The body of the doll is a flat or rounded wooden clothespin.
2. Use enamel paint or nail polish to paint cheeks, eyes, and lips on the round top of the pin. Glue on yarn for hair and paint on shoes.
3. Wrap a pipe cleaner under the face. Glue felt hands to the ends of the pipe cleaner.
4. Make a dress from a gathered piece of scrap fabric.
5. Make a bonnet from a circle of gathered fabric.

YARN DOLL

The yarn doll was born from an overflowing knitting basket. It is one of the simplest and most colorful dolls you can make.

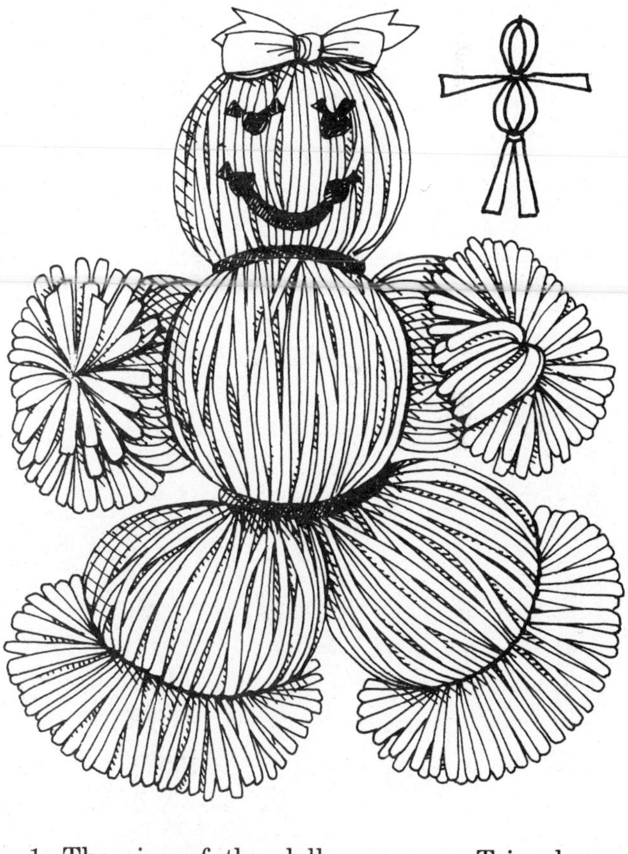

1. The size of the doll can vary. Trim long strands of yarn to the same length and tie them together in the center.
2. Fold in half, keeping the tied center on top. About an inch or so below the top knot (depending on the size of the doll you are making), tie a single strand around the yarn to form a head.
3. Divide the hanging yarn in half, and divide one of the two bunches in half again. The quarter sections will be the arms and the half section is the body.

4. Tie the quarter sections together, a few inches below the head. Trim off the excess yarn one inch below the knot.
5. Tie the remaining yarn to form the body.
6. Divide the hanging yarn in half to form the legs.
7. Tie the legs a few inches down from the waist and trim as you did with the arms.
8. Use contrasting yarn to tie on knots for facial features. Tie a bow on the top of the head.

CORNHUSK ANGELS

(Shown in color, page 68)

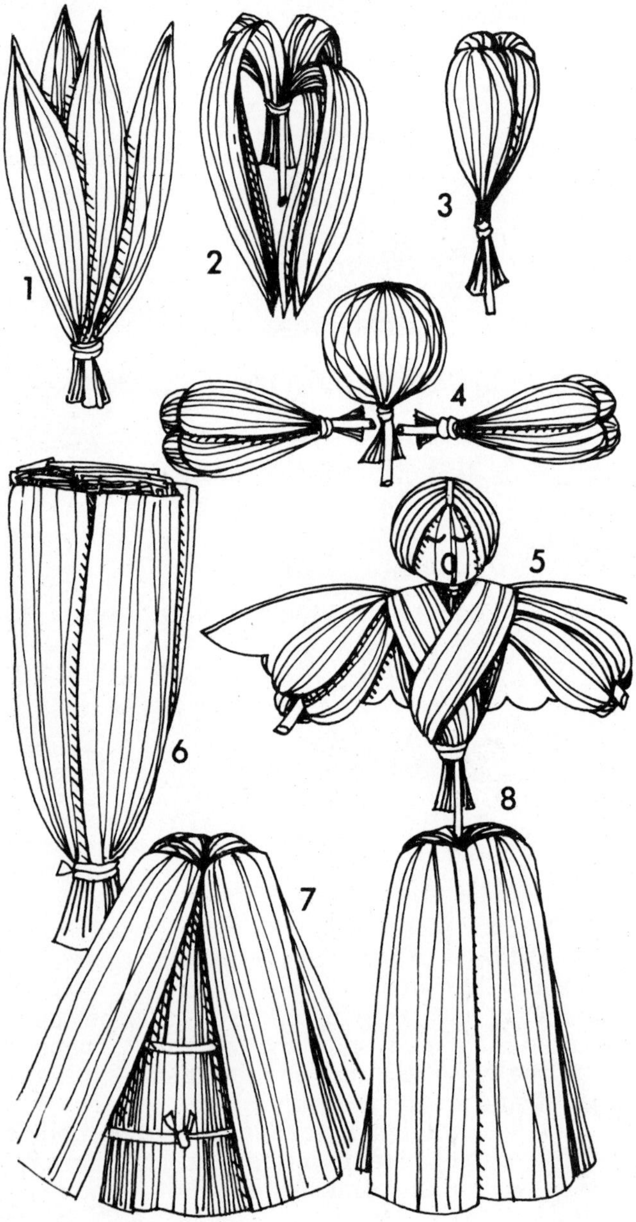

The cornhusk doll comes to us from the American Indians. One of the prettiest of all cornhusk dolls is the angel.

1. During the corn season, carefully remove the husks from corn. Pile the husks in loose, flat stacks and tie them together. Allow the husks to dry in an arid place, such as a closet or an attic.
2. Cut four strips of husk about ½ inch wide and gather the end tightly with thin beading wire (Fig. 1).
3. Bend the husks back over the gathered part and fold down to form a puff (Fig. 2).
4. Gather the ends with wire (Fig. 3). Make two more puffs in the same way.
5. Cover a large bead with husk. To cover, take a piece of husk slightly larger than the bead, brush it with white glue, and fold it around the bead. Gather the ends of the husk with wire, close to the bead. Trim the excess husk. This is the doll's head.
6. Wire on two puffs, for arms, just under the bead head (Fig. 4).
7. Push the twisted wire of the head and arms into the top of the remaining puff.
8. Make the bodice of a dress by winding a strip of husk around the neck and crisscrossing it over the body front (Fig. 5). Wire securely.
9. Push match-stick hands into each arm-puff and glue or pin on wings made of foil or paper.
10. The skirt is made from a generous wad of husks wired together at the base. Arrange the husks around each other, forming a cylinder. The four innermost husks should be large perfect strips (Fig. 6).
11. Fold all the husks down over the gather.
12. Lift up the top husks and wire the inner

ones securely (Fig. 7). Then glue the top husks to the skirt, covering the wiring underneath.

13. Fit the gathered wire ends of the upper body into the center gather of the skirt (Fig. 8).

14. Thee hair is gathered straw, raffia or embroidery thread glued to the center of the head. Form a braid or ponytail.

15. Paint on a simple face.

APPLE-FACE DOLLS

In pioneer days, after the New England apple harvest, and after all the ciders, pies, butters, and preserves were made, leftover apples were peeled, dried and made into apple-face dolls.

1. McIntosh, Jonathan, Winesap or Delicious apples are recommended. Choose a well-formed apple with no scars.
2. Peel the apple carefully and remove the stem.
3. Divide the face into imaginary thirds. Cut out hollow eye sockets, a slight slit for the mouth and a rather broad nose. Carve away a pronounced chin. Shrinkage will reduce the size of the features so it is important that they be well-defined initially (see Fig. 1).
4. To keep the face from turning too dark during the drying process, either brush the apple with lemon juice and sprinkle with salt, or dip the apple in a mixture of 50 percent water and 50 percent vinegar or lemon juice.
5. To disinfect the core of the apple, bore a small hold through the top and fill it with powdered sulphur.
6. Fold a length of florist's wire or a thin coat hanger in half. Insert the two ends of the wire through the top of the apple face, extending down through the bottom. Twist the ends together and use the loop at the top to suspend the apples.
7. Hang the apples in a cool but dry place. Apples can also be left in a warm dry place, but there is a chance that they might rot.
8. Apples will dry differently, some with fewer wrinkles or different shades of coloring than others.
9. Check the apples in two weeks. Make adjustments to the face at this time by pinching and molding the features.
10. Dry the apples for an additional two weeks. After this second drying period, check the face for excess wrinkles. To smooth out wrinkles or add fullness to parts of the face, make an opening in the back of the head and plump up areas you wish to fill out with cotton.
11. If you have sprinkled the face with salt, wash it off at this time. Dry thoroughly and return the apple to its drying place for two more weeks. The heads should be ready to be attached to bodies after this final drying.

1

2

12. Using tempera or water-color paints, color the features. Place clove or bead eyes in the still-soft eye sockets. You can lacquer the apple at this point. Glue on wool or fur for hair or beards. The apples should still be soft and will dry further.
13. Create a body shape with heavy coat-hanger wire by twisting four pieces of wire to form arms and legs (Fig. 2). The arm wires are cut shorter than the leg wires. Loop the ends of the wire to form feet and hands. Twist the wire extending beneath the apple onto the body wire.
14. Pad the body with cotton and wrap the limbs with cut strips of old nylon hose. Sew or glue the ends of the wrapping to the body.
15. Cut simple hand and feet shapes from felt. Sew and stuff them and attach them to the limbs.
16. Create costumes. Use calico prints and lace for the women's dresses and denim from old dungarees for pants for the men. Check pattern catalogs for dolls' clothes patterns.

"YO-YO" DOLL

(Shown in color, page 67)

The "Yo-Yo" doll was a classic patchwork doll common in the days when cloth was quite dear. It is made from yo-yos which are actually gathered into small circular puffs.

1. Cut dozens of 4-inch circles from scrap fabric to make yo-yos for the doll's arms and legs.
2. Sew a running stitch ¼ inch in from the outer edge of each circle (Fig. 1). Pull the thread taut, gathering the entire edge into a center core. Secure the thread with a triple stitch and clip the edges straight (Fig. 2). The yo-yos for the body section can be larger.
3. The head of the doll is a 4-inch foam ball. Cover the ball with a section of nylon stocking. Gather the nylon and tie with string.
4. Knot two lengths of string or lightweight yarn and thread each one on a wide-eyed needle. String a bead or a button on each.
5. Thread the gathered yo-yos on each length to form the legs. How long you make the legs is up to you.
6. Tie the two lengths of string together, attaching the legs (see the skeleton stick figure).
7. Take both lengths of string and thread on one needle.
8. Thread larger yo-yos to the strings to form the body.
9. Tie the body strings to the nylon gather of the head. Secure and clip off the excess thread.
10. Knot two shorter lengths of thread for the arms. On each length, first thread a bead, then follow with yo-yos.
11. Tie both arms to the gather at the neck.
12. Tie a bow under the head.
14. Add a felt cone for a hat and felt or embroidered facial features.

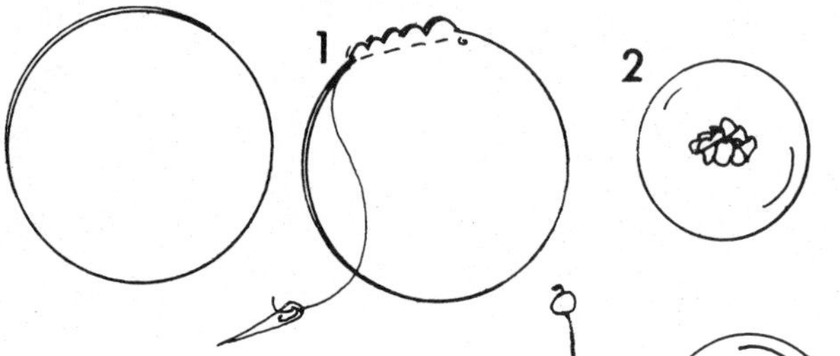

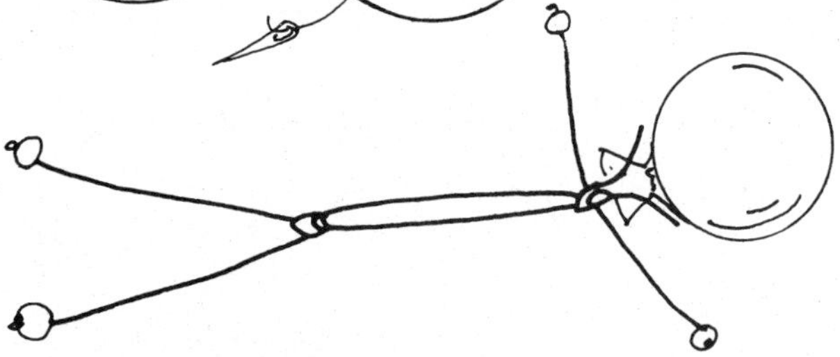

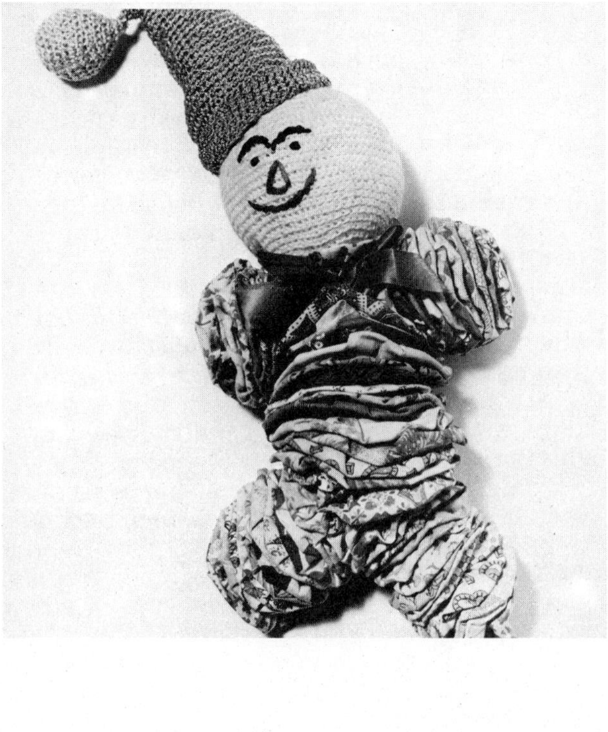

SOCK DOLL

This cozy doll is made from a sock, and it has that soft, comfortable old-shoe charm.

1. Choose a large sock (preferably a man's). The best sock dolls are made from heavy cotton or wool. An argyle sock will create a fine calico doll.
2. Cut the sock following the diagram pictured: Section 1 will be the body; Section 2 the legs; Section 3 the arms.
3. Fill the body (1) with cotton stuffing and handsew the open end closed.
4. Tie the upper third of the body with a length of yarn to form the head.
5. To make the arms and legs, sew closed the length and one width of each of the four smaller sections (2 and 3 in the diagram). Round off the edges to make hands and feet. If the sock has a right side and a wrong side, sew the limbs with the right sides facing.
6. Turn the limbs right-side out and stuff with cotton. Sew the open ends closed.
7. Sew the limbs in their proper places on the body.
8. The face can be designed with buttons or felt features, or with a mixture of both. Sew on the buttons and glue on the felt.
9. Sew yarn hair along the center of the head. The hair can be styled in bangs, center-parted and long, or tied in pigtails.
10. Clothes can be made of scrap material and should be simple in design. To plot out a dress, lay the doll on a folded piece of fabric and draw an outline using the outstretched doll as a guide. Add a zipper or buttons for opening and closing the dress. Sew elastic around the arm openings.
11. Make a pinafore by sewing a ¼-inch hem

all the way around a square piece of white fabric. Gather one side with a broad running stitch. Cut and hem a smaller square of white fabric to fit above the gathered side of the larger square. Sew it over the gathers. Add a long length of white ribbon, between the two joined squares, for a sash. Add a second small looped ribbon to the top of the pinafore for straps.

You can also use old doll clothes or check the back section of your pattern catalog for doll clothes.

HARLEQUIN ON A STICK

Everybody loves a clown and this sprightly little harlequin is a charmer.

1. The head is a 4-inch foam ball or a 4-inch stuffed felt circle. For a felt head, sew two circles together, ¼ inch in from the edge, leaving ½ inch unsewn. Stuff firmly with cotton and sew closed.

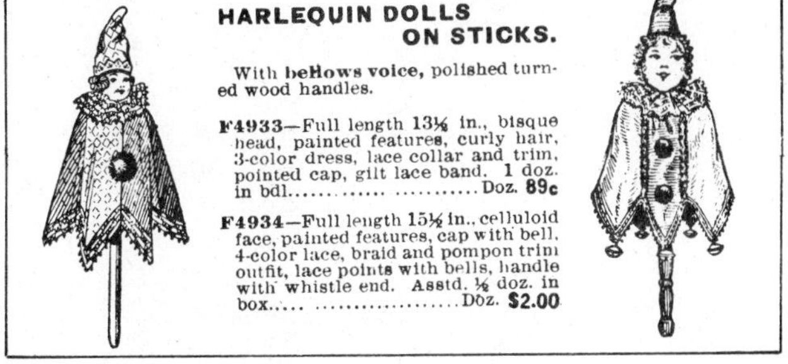
HARLEQUIN DOLLS ON STICKS.

With **bellows voice,** polished turned wood handles.

F4933—Full length 13½ in., bisque head, painted features, curly hair, 3-color dress, lace collar and trim, pointed cap, gilt lace band. 1 doz. in bdl.......................Doz. **89c**

F4934—Full length 15½ in., celluloid face, painted features, cap with bell, 4-color lace, braid and pompon trim outfit, lace points with bells, handle with whistle end. Asstd. ½ doz. in box.........................Doz. **$2.00**

2. The face is a combination of embroidery and glued-on felt appliqués. Glue tufts of yarn hair to the foam ball with white glue. Yarn hair can be sewn into the seams of the felt head before stuffing, or stitched onto the head after it has been assembled.

3. The stick is a dowel 12 inches long and ¼ inch wide. Shave one end to a slight point.

4. Insert the pointed end of the dowel into the foam ball or the fabric head.

5. Glue the base of the ball to the stick with white glue.

6. Place a ½ x 2-inch piece of cardboard with rounded corners under the dowel, pierce a hole in the center, and glue the cardboard to the stick ½ inch below the head.

7. To make patterns for the harlequin's robe and hat, enlarge the grid on a sheet of paper so that one square equals one inch. Draw shapes 1, 2 and 3 on the enlarged grid. (See page 13 for detailed directions on how to enlarge patterns from a grid.) Using the pattern, cut four Fig. 1 panels and 2 Fig. 2 panels. A satiny fabric is ideal. Use contrasting colors for the wide and narrow panels.

8. To construct the robe, sew a panel 1 on either side of a panel 2, with right sides facing. Repeat with the remaining panels and sew the constructed front and back together. Turn the robe right-side out.

9. Sew a ball fringe along the bottom of the robe and large felt buttons along the front panel.

10. Sew a running stitch along the top edge of the robe.

11. Slip the robe over the head and pull the thread tightly under the neck. Secure the thread.

12. To make the ruff, gather a length of fabric that has been hemmed on both long edges. Fit it around the head and sew together in back, securing it to the robe at the same time.

13. Cut two hat patterns (Fig. 3) in felt.

14. Sew the hat together, ⅛ inch in from the edge. Sew a strip of gathered fabric or lace around the bottom of the hat and add a bell at the tip.

BONNET BABY

This early American patchwork motif is the inspiration for a doll that features a frilly bonnet—an item of apparel which little girls and their mothers were seldom without.

1. To make a pattern for the doll, enlarge the grid on a sheet of paper so that onesquare equals one inch. Draw figures 1, 2, 3 and 4 on the enlarged grid. (See page 13 for detailed directions on how to enlarge patterns from a grid.) Using your pattern, cut out two body shapes (Fig. 1), two shoes (Fig. 2), four arms (Fig. 3), two baskets (Fig.

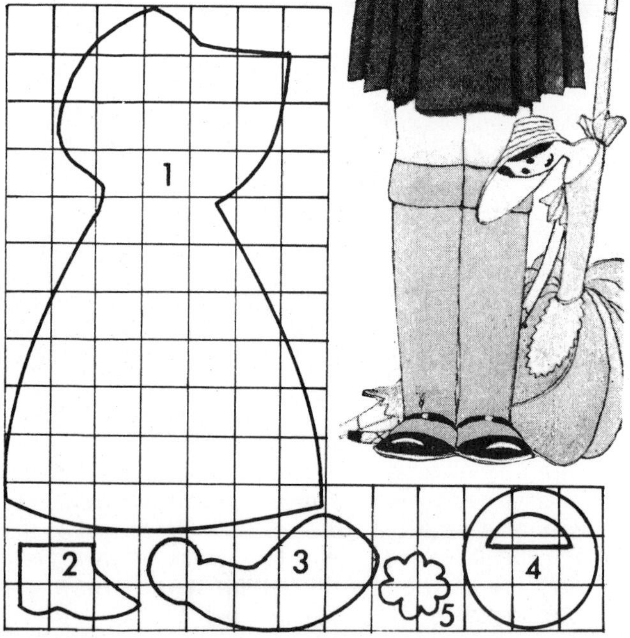

4) and several flowers (Fig. 5)—all from felt.

2. Sew the shoes together, stuffing them lightly.

3. Sew pre-gathered lace along the rim of the bonnet on both body shapes.

4. Sew the two body shapes together, ¼ inch in from the edge. Tuck the shoes into the bottom hem as you sew. Leave 2 inches of the skirt unsewn on one side.

5. Stuff the doll and close the open seam.

6. Cut four skin-tone hands, using the hand on the arm as a pattern, and sew them on at the base of the arm shapes. *Note:* two arm shapes should be cut facing left and two facing right.

7. Sew two of each arm shape together, with the right sides of the felt facing out, stuffing the arms lightly.

8. Add large snaps on the underside of each arm and at the appropriate places on the body. Snap the arms in place.

9. Sew the two basket shapes together around the outer edge. Fill the basket with flowers.

10. Add a snap to the handle of the basket and snaps to the flowers and the hands. This way the baby can carry the basket and the individual flowers in either hand.

SALLY SLEEPER

Dolls do all sorts of things these days—eat, blink, cry, wet their diapers. Perhaps the precursor of such mechanical invention was Sally Sleeper, a simple sweet doll, wide-eyed on one side and asleep on the other.

1. To make a pattern for Sally, enlarge the grid on a sheet of paper so that one square equals one inch, and draw figures 1, 2, 3 and 4 on the enlarged grid. (See page 13 for detailed directions on how to enlarge a pattern from a grid.) Using your patterns, cut out two body shapes (Fig. 1), one nightie front (Fig. 2), two raincoat fronts (Fig. 3, up to the dotted line), two hat shapes (Fig. 4) and four shoe shapes (Fig. 5). Use felt.

2. Each body shape has a different face worked with embroidery thread and felt, one face wide-awake and the other sound asleep. Baste-stitch yarn hair to the inside of one head shape.

3. Place the two body shapes together, right sides facing *out,* and sew together ¼ inch in from the edge. Leave 2 inches unsewn on one leg.

4. Stuff the doll and sew the open seam closed.

5. To assemble the dual outfit, place the two coat patterns next to each other, overlapping slightly (for a raincoat, use oilcloth), and sew them to the nightie, stitching along the shoulder and along the sides. The right sides of both fabrics should face *out.*

6. Add a felt collar, pocket and button to the coat; stitch pre-gathered lace to the nightie. The coat is closed with snaps.

7. Sew the hat around the upper curve, using the same two fabrics you used to make the outfit. Add lace to the nightcap half and glue a felt flower to the rain-hat half.

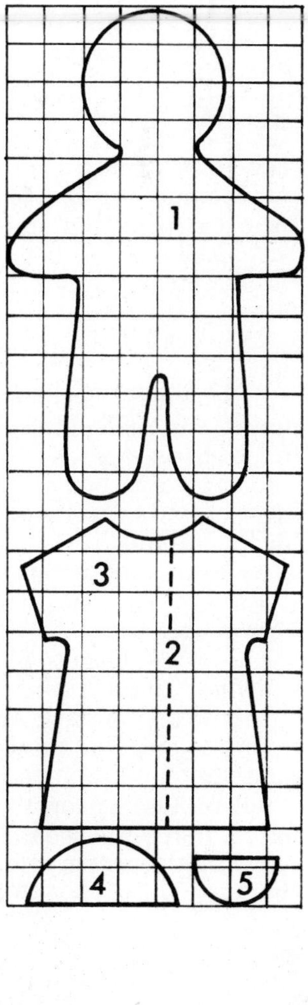

8. Use coordinating colors for the shoes, and sew them together along the curved part. Add a ball from a strand of ball fringe to the slippers; glue a felt buckle to the shoes.

Note: This doll can also be made of cotton. Sew two body shapes together, with the right sides of the fabric facing *in,* about ¼ inch in from the edge. Leave two inches on the leg unsewn. Turn right-side out, stuff firmly, and then hand sew the open seam closed.

KEE WEE AND BROWNIE

Two favorite turn-of-the-century characters—Brownie, from the comic strip bearing his name, and Kee Wee, the famous sailor.

1. To make Kee Wee and Brownie patterns, enlarge the grid on a sheet of paper so that one square equals one inch. Draw figures 1 through 7 on the enlarged grid. (See page 13 for detailed directions on how to enlarge patterns from a grid.) Kee Wee's body shape is Fig. 1; his arm is Fig. 2; and his leg is Fig. 3. Brownie's body shape is Fig. 4; his arm is Fig. 5; his leg is Fig. 6; and his hat is Fig. 7. Using your patterns, cut two of each body and hat shape and four of each leg and arm shape from felt.
2. Kee Wee's legs are white and his arms are blue. Cut and pin black shoes and pink hands to fit over the feet and hands on the base pieces.
Note: two legs face left and two face right.
3. Kee Wee's body is white and his jacket, blue. Cut two jacket fronts (marked X in Fig. 1). The jacket back combines two front shapes into one, and is cut along the dotted line in the pattern at the neck. Also cut a black belt, three red stripes to be placed on the chest between the two jacket fronts, and a blue hatband and ribbon. Pin in place.
4. Sew all these appliqués to Kee Wee's costume.
5. Brownie's legs are gold and his arms are brown. Cut and pin green shoes and gold hands to the base shapes, as you did with Kee Wee.
6. Brownie's body is also gold. Cut two brown jacket fronts (marked X in Fig. 4). The jacket back combines two jacket fronts, extending the sides until they meet. Add green buttons in the front. Finally, cut two green hat shapes with brown stripes.
7. Sew all these appliqués in place, and stitch Brownie's hat to his head.
8. Sew two of each arm and leg together with the right sides of the fabric facing out, making the seam about ¼ inch in from the edge. Leave a small portion unsewn each time; stuff the limb lightly and sew closed.
9. Pin the arms and legs between two body shapes.

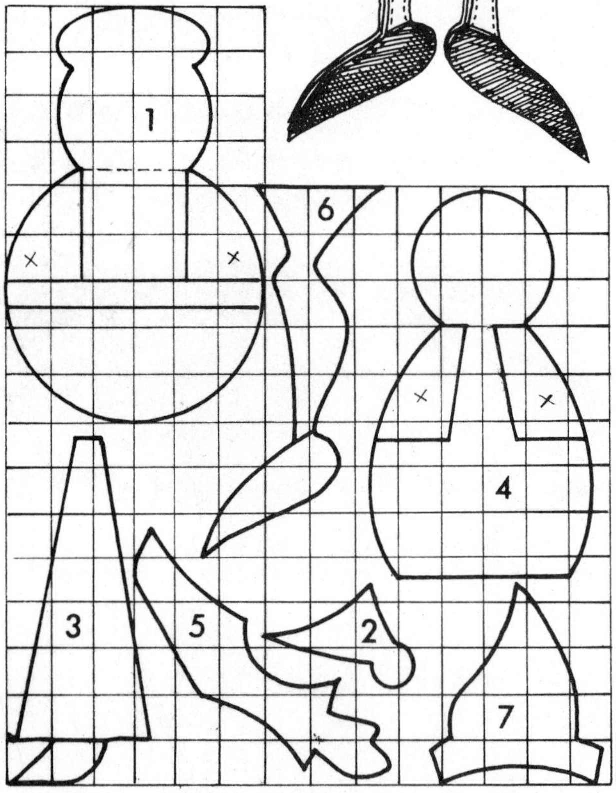

10. Sew the body shapes together, ⅛ inch in from the edges. Leave one inch unsewn on the side of each.
11. Stuff each body and then sew the open seams closed.

ACTION ACROBATS

(Shown in color, page 68)

Hand-operated toys were very popular around the turn of the century. One such toy involved two athletes connected by a pin and set in a shadow box. When you turned the metal pin, the athletes performed all sorts of acrobatic tricks. The same principle applies here, only this version is much simpler.

1. To make patterns for the acrobats, enlarge the grid on a sheet of paper so that one square equals one inch. Draw figures 1 through 5 on the enlarged grid. (See page 13 for detailed directions on how to enlarge patterns from a grid.) Use your patterns to cut, for *each* acrobat, two body shapes (Fig. 1), four legs (Fig. 2), four arms (Fig. 3), two hair shapes (Fig. 4) and one moustache (Fig. 5). Make the acrobats in felt.

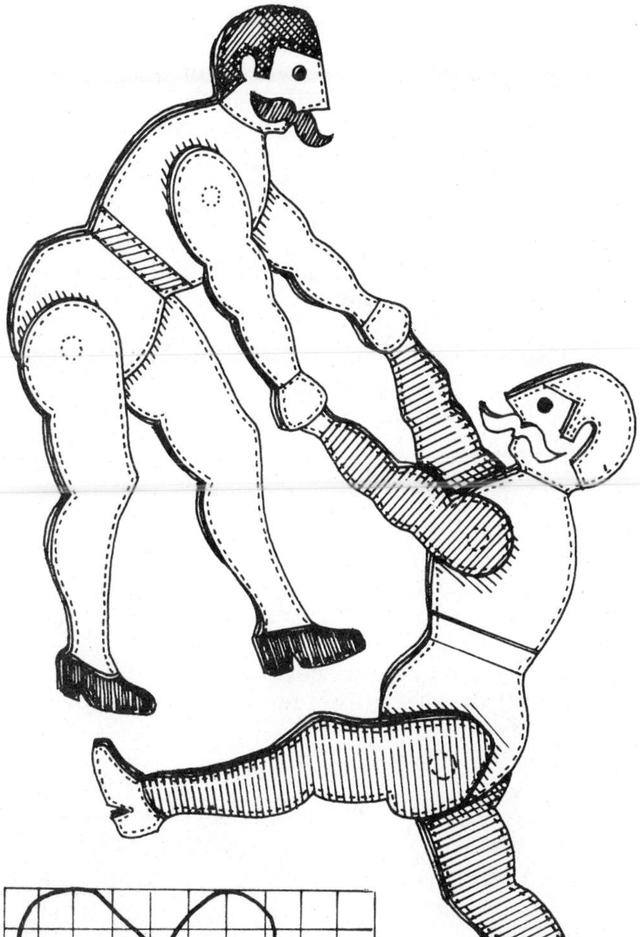

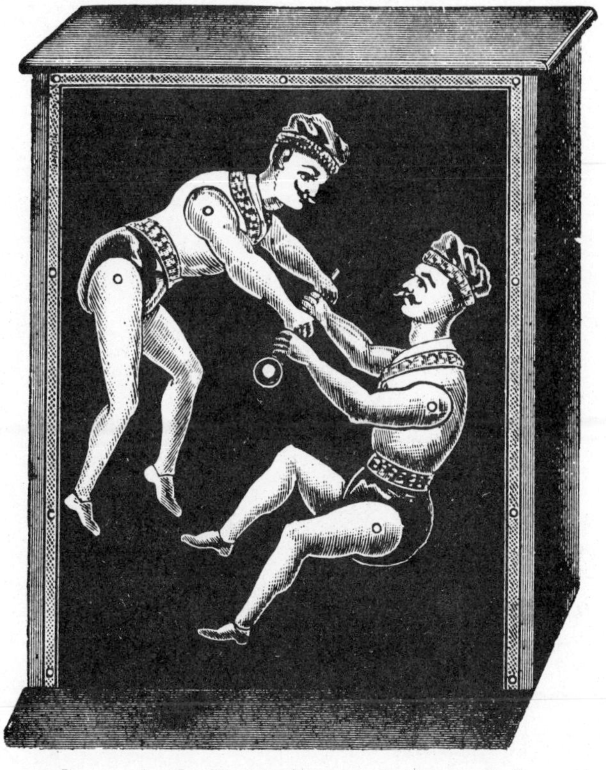

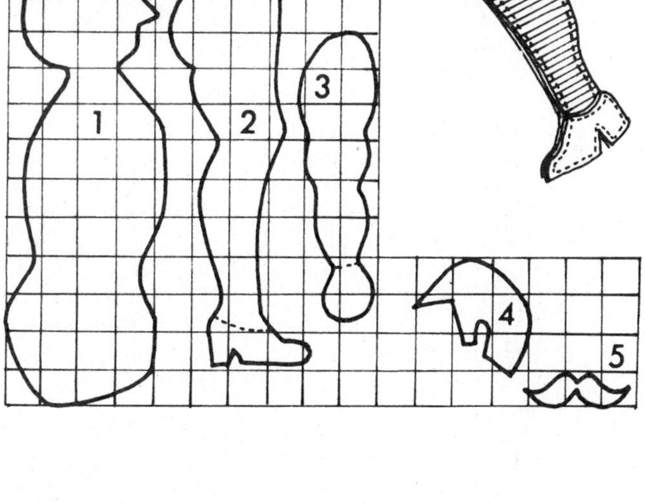

2. Cut shoe and hand shapes in contrasting colors, using the shoes and hands of the base shapes as patterns. Pin them to the legs and arms. *Note:* two of each limb face left and two face right. Also add belts around the waists and hair on both sides of the heads. The moustaches and a button eye appear on only one side of each head.
3. Sew all the appliqués in place.
4. Place a light layer of cotton or polyester between each pair of arms, legs and body shapes, with the right sides of the felt patterns facing out.
5. Sew the bodies and limbs together ¼ inch in from the edges.
6. Attach the arms and legs to the bodies with large snaps.
7. Join the two acrobats at the hands, again with large snaps.
8. Twist the arms and legs on the snaps to put the acrobats into action.

RAG-DOLL SISTERS

More dolls made from recycled garments. It is said that all good things, like these rag dolls, come in pairs.

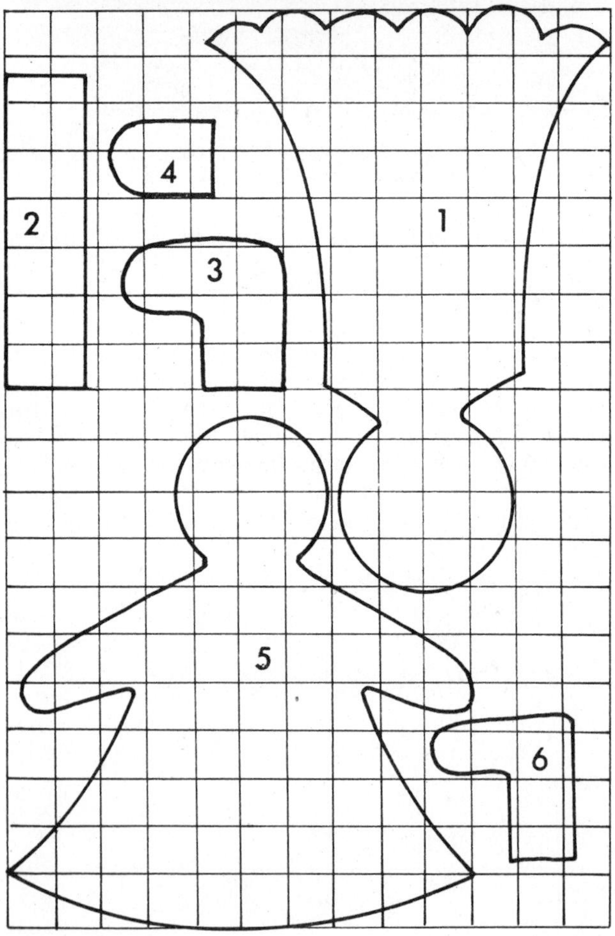

1. To make patterns for the dolls, enlarge the grid on a sheet of paper so that one square equals ½ inch. Draw figures 1 through 6 on the enlarged grid. (See page 13 for detailed directions on how to enlarge patterns from a grid.) Use your patterns to cut out two Big Sister body shapes (Fig. 1), four legs (Fig. 2), two shoes (Fig. 3) and two hands (Fig. 4). Then cut two Little Sister body shapes (Fig. 5), and two shoes for her (Fig. 6). The bodies should be made of felt and the trimmings of scrap fabric.

2. To construct the legs of Big Sister, sew two legs together along the sides with ⅛-inch seams. Sew with right sides facing. Sew the other two together. Turn the legs right-side out, stuff them and hand-sew the open ends closed. Sew the feet to the legs, and cover the seams between each leg and foot with a scrap-fabric cuff. Add lace panties around the top of each leg.

3. Big Sister's arms consist of scrap-fabric sleeves that have been gathered and sewn to the sides of the doll. Hem the sleeves at the wrist and sew on the hands just inside the cuffs.

4. Sew the two halves of Big Sister's body together on the right side of the fabric with embroidery stitches. Sew in the legs at the bottom of the skirt and the arms at the sides. Stuff the body before closing all the seams. Add lace to the bottom edge of the skirt.

5. Use embroidery thread to sew Little Sister's body shapes together with an overhand outside stitch. Tuck an edging of pre-gathered lace just inside the skirt hem, to suggest panties. Stuff the body before completing the outside stitches.

6. Sew Little Sister's shoes to the inside hem of the panties.

7. Little Sister's dress is a length of lace wrapped around the neck and attached to an apron made of scrap fabric. Tie a sash around the waist.

8. Add yarn hair to both dolls, and indicate their features with embroidery or felt appliqués.

KEWPIE DOLL

At old-time amusement parks, an amorous gentleman would do his best—shooting bottles or tossing quoits—to win his lady friend a Kewpie doll. The original doll had tiny wings, fashioned after Cupid, the god of love.

1. To make the patterns for the Kewpie doll, enlarge the grid on a sheet of paper so that one square equals ½ inch. Draw figures 1, 2 and 3 on the enlarged grid. (See page 13 for detailed directions on how to enlarge patterns from a grid.) Use your patterns to cut two body shapes (Fig. 1), four arms (Fig. 2) and four legs (Fig. 3). Make the doll out of cotton or a cotton blend.

2. On one side of the head embroider features or draw on a face with indelible felt-tip markers.

3. Pin two arms and two legs to each body shape with the right sides of the fabric facing.

4. Sew the limbs to the body shapes about ⅛ inch in from the edge.

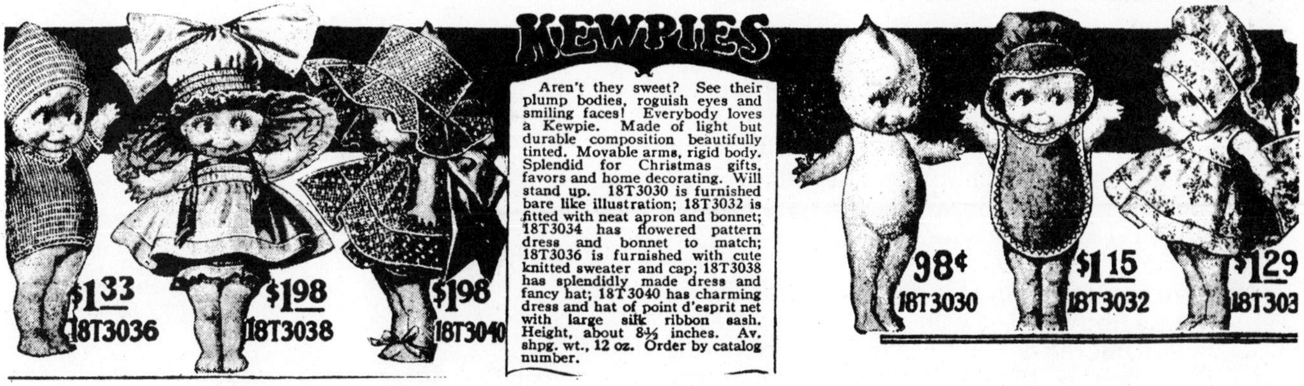

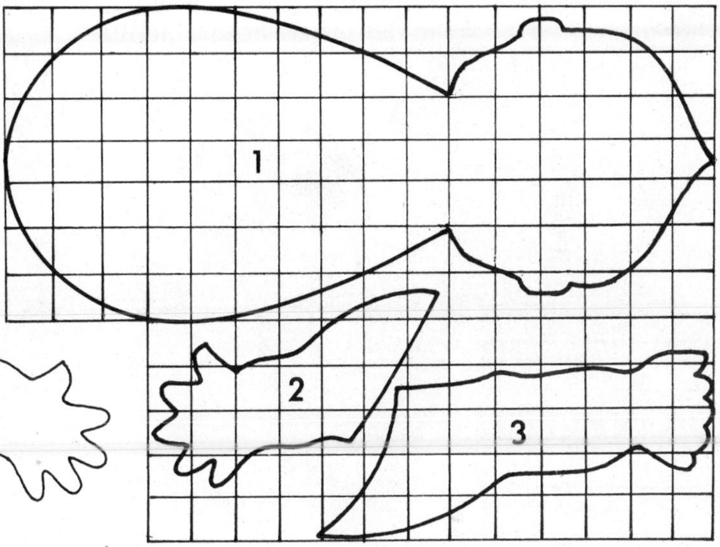

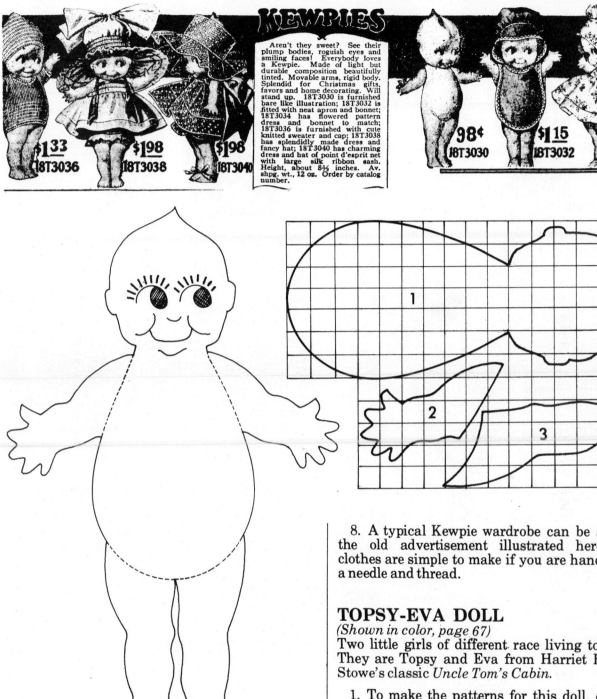

5. Pin the two completed body shapes together, right sides facing, and sew them ¼ inch in from the edge. Leave 2 inches on the tummy side unsewn. Slit the seams slightly wherever they are curved—at the hands, the neck, the armpits, etc.

6. Turn the doll right-side out and stuff it firmly with cotton or polyester.

7. Hand sew the open seam closed.

8. A typical Kewpie wardrobe can be seen in the old advertisement illustrated here. The clothes are simple to make if you are handy with a needle and thread.

TOPSY-EVA DOLL

(Shown in color, page 67)

Two little girls of different race living together. They are Topsy and Eva from Harriet Beecher Stowe's classic *Uncle Tom's Cabin.*

1. To make the patterns for this doll, enlarge the grid on a sheet of paper so that one square equals one inch. Draw figures 1 and 2 on the enlarged grid. (See page 13 for detailed directions on how to enlarge patterns from a grid.) Figure 1 is the body shape. Figure 2 is the blouse. Also draw on the enlarged grid the upper part of Fig. 2 (from the heavy line up) to make back pieces for the blouse. To begin, cut four Fig. 1 shapes, two in brown and two in pink, from a cotton or cotton-blend material.

2. Pair each pink body with a brown one and sew the two pieces of fabric together at the waist-

line. Consider one pair the front of the doll and the other the back.

3. Sew the pairs together as you would sew together the front and back of any doll. (This doll just has a head in place of feet.) Sew with right sides facing about ¼ inch in from the edge. Make sure that the pink and brown sections are properly matched. Leave 3 inches of seam unsewn on the top of one head.

4. Turn the doll right-side out, stuff with cotton or polyester and hand-sew the open seam closed.

5. Following the dotted lines in Fig. 1, machine or hand-stitch to separate the arms from the chest and head.

6. For each doll, add a snap to the front of one hand and the back of the other, at the points marked *O* on the pattern.

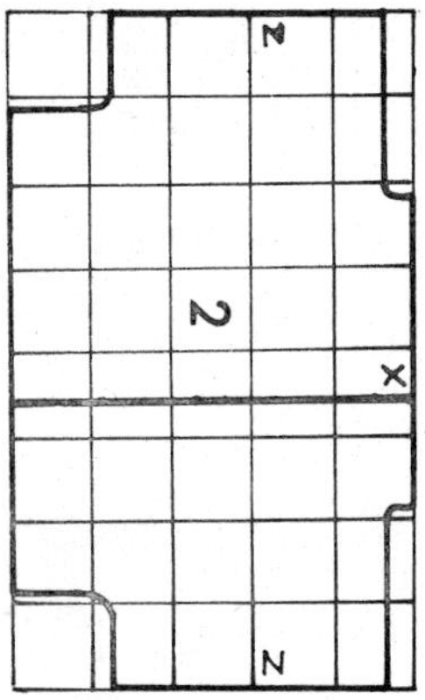

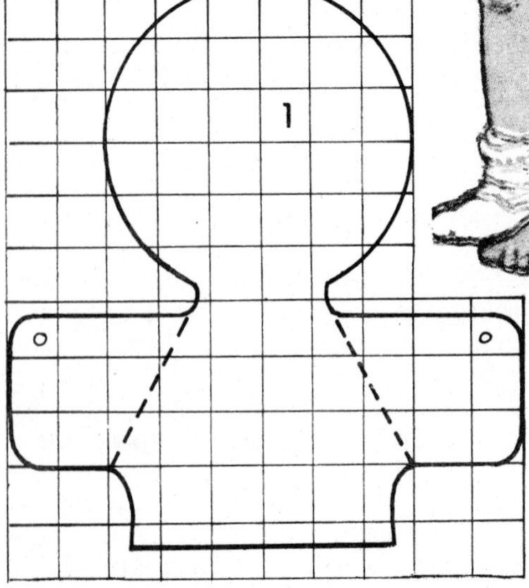

7. Sew on brown ball-fringe hair for Topsy; make Eva's hair flower appliqué. Start the hair on the outside edge of each face and spiral it towards the center of the head's back side.

8. Use felt pieces to design the dolls' faces. Topsy's round blue pupils and Eva's black ones should be glued to slightly larger white circles. Make a nose of the same color as each doll and pink lips for both. Glue these features to the two doll faces.

9. Cut two blouse fronts, using the whole of pattern 2. Cut four blouse backs following the *upper* part of the pattern, above the heavy line. Each doll should have one front and two backs in contrasting colors.

10. Sew the two contrasting blouse-fronts together at the waistline (*X* marks the neck) with ¼-inch seams. Pin the four backs to the constructed front, with the right sides of the fabric facing. Sew the front to the back with ¼-inch seams. Leave neck portions *(X)* and the arm openings *(Z)* unsewn. Turn the blouse right-side out.

11. Sew a bib to one blouse-front and a collar to the other. Run small snaps down the back sides of the blouse for closing.

12. Fit the blouse on the doll and snap shut.

13. The skirt can either be A-line, gathered or circular. Plot the skirt to fit comfortably around the waist. It should be wide enough to fit over the arms and long enough to fall below the head of the doll underneath. The skirt is made in two layers, each side coordinated with the color of one blouse.

14. Fold a long, broad strand of ribbon over the gathered waistline of the skirt and sew it in place.

15. Tie the skirt to the waist of the doll, matching the colors of each blouse and skirt.

16. The hands of the doll under the skirt should be snapped together. Reverse the doll with a flip of the skirt, unsnapping the clasped hands and snapping the other pair as you make the change.

Note: The skirt can also be sewn between the two waists of the blouse.

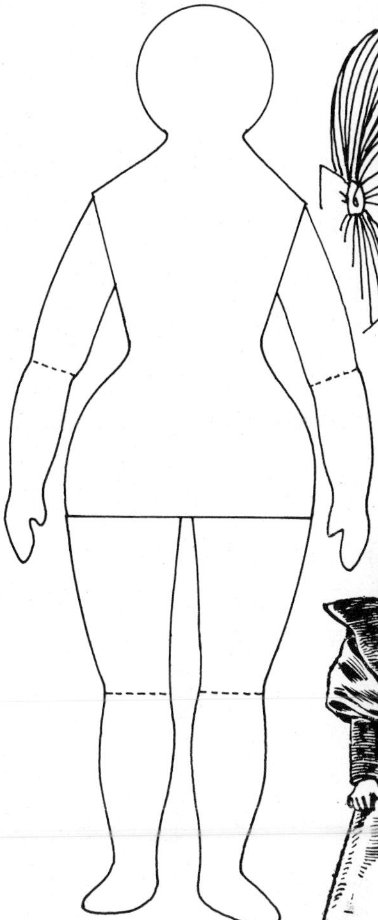

VICTORIAN JOINTED DOLLS

The Victorian doll's claim to fame was its flexible joints. Also its porcelain head. (In time, composition, a substance that resembles papier-mâché, came to replace porcelain.) You can make your own mock porcelain head from an eggshell or—a less fragile proposition—make it from cloth. Instructions are given for both.

FABRIC-HEAD DOLL

1. To make a pattern for the doll, enlarge the grid on a sheet of paper so that one square equals ½ inch. Draw figures 1, 2 and 3 on the enlarged grid. (See page 13 for detailed directions on how to enlarge patterns from a grid.) Use your patterns to cut out two body shapes (Fig. 1), four legs (Fig. 2) and four arms (Fig. 3) from a cotton or cotton-blend material.

2. Sew two of each limb together, right sides facing, ¼ inch in from the edge. Leave the straight edge at the top of each limb unsewn. Cut small slits in the seams around sharp curves.

3. Turn each limb right-side out and stuff it firmly up to the knee or elbow.

4. Stitch across the joints of each limb, as indicated by the dotted lines on the doll.

5. Stuff the remainder of each limb and stitch across the open seam at the top by hand, ¼ inch down from edges and without turning edges into the limb.

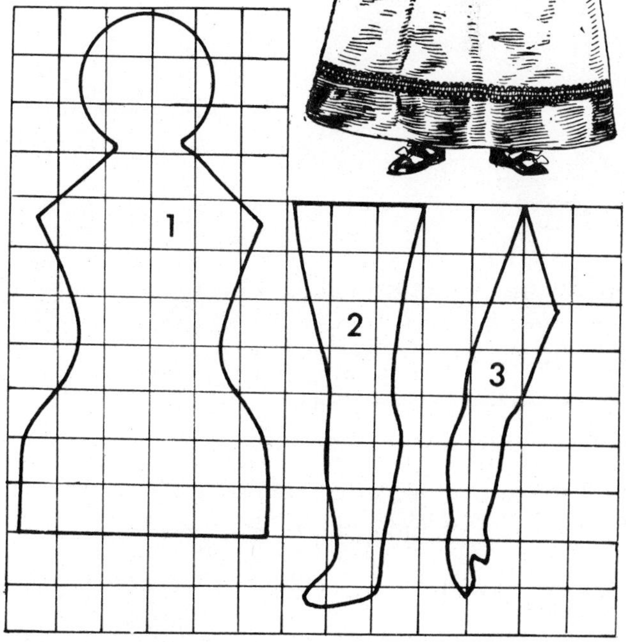

6. Sew the legs and arms to one of the body

shapes, 1/8 inch in from the joined edges, right sides facing.

7. Place the second body shape over the first one with right sides facing. The arms and legs should be tucked in between the body shapes.

8. Sew the two body shapes together, 1/4 inch in from the edge. Leave 2 inches of seam unsewn along one side. Slit the seams slightly around the curves of the body and head, and turn the doll right-side out.

9. Stuff the doll firmly.

10. Hand-sew the open seam closed.

11. Embroider the face as shown in the illustration and sew on yarn hair arranged along a center point.

"CHINA" HEAD DOLL

1. The body for the "China"-head doll is the same as the one used for the fabric-head doll. Cut the body shapes straight across at the neck, omitting the head, and sew directly from one shoulder to the other.

2. The base of the "China" head is an emptied eggshell. To remove the contents, twist a pin

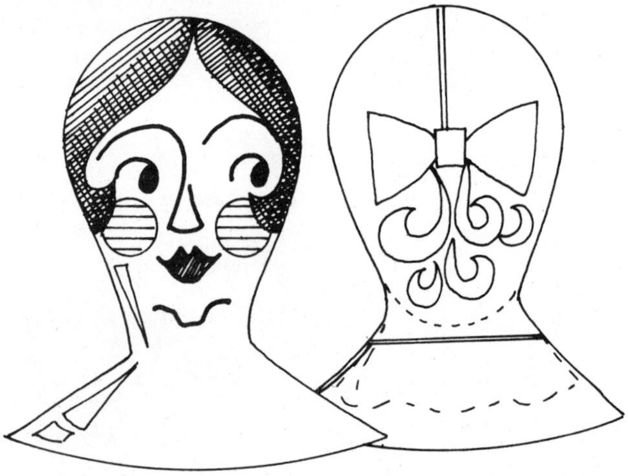

gently into both the blunt and the tapered ends of the egg until you break through the shell. Enlarge the hole at the tapered end to 1/4 inch. Blow through the pinhole forcing the egg out through the blunt end. Wash the shell.

3. Cover and shell with old nylon hose, gathering the fabric at the tapered end.

4. Stuff the gathered nylon with a little cotton to make the neck. Shape the neck by wrapping it in cellophane tape. Fit the head to the body and attach by sewing the nylon snugly over the shoulders.

5. Make two paper bibs to camouflage the juncture of the nylon and the fabric on the back and front of the body. The bibs should be cut straight across the base of the neck and down along the shoulder seams, but curved at the bottom.

6. Glue the bibs to the front and back of the doll. Trim off any excess nylon that falls beneath the bottom curve.

7. Cut strips of newspaper one inch long and 1/2 inch wide.

8. Use wheat paste and water to make a papier-mâché mixture with the consistency of loose mashed potatoes.

9. Dip the paper strips into the paste mixture and lay them on the egg, around the neck, and over the bibs. Cover the head with four or more layers of paper. Wipe off any excess paste. To protect the rest of the doll from paste, wrap it in cellophane or foil before you start to apply the papier-mâché.

10. Allow the paper to dry thoroughly.

11. When dry, smoothe all the papered areas with very fine sandpaper.

12. Paint the head with an undercoating of water-base white paint and then a skin tone. Paint on facial features and hair. The back view of the head shows the egg (indicated by the dotted line) in relation to the bib.

13. Varnish the head with a high-gloss finish.

SHOE-BOX-WOVEN DOLL

(Shown in color, page 67)

The shoe box is best used for almost anything but storing shoes. In the 1920s, they were made into simple looms to make woven dolls.

1. Using a sharp single-edge razor blade, cut vertical slits in the rim along both widths of a shoe box. The slits should be 1/8 inch apart and 1/4 inch deep. Each one should correspond to a slit directly across the box.

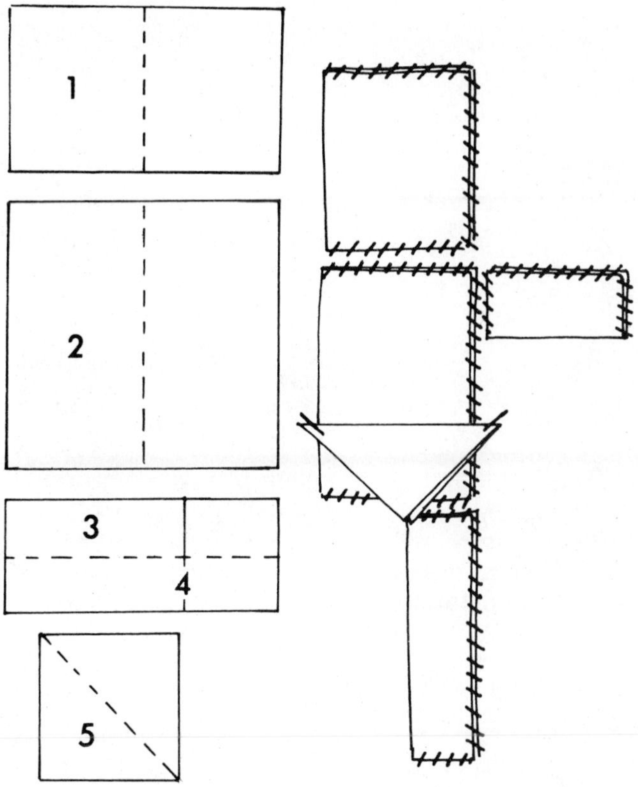

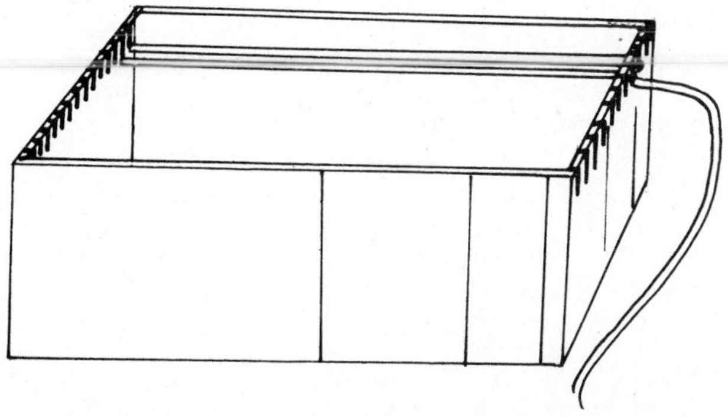

2. String 4-ply yarn back and forth across the box, starting at one corner and continuing until all the slits have been filled. This is your base yarn.

3. To weave, knot the end of a strand of yarn to the outside base yarn, close to one side of the box. The cross yarn is woven in and out of the base yarn. When you reach the last base yarn in a row, turn the yarn under and then weave back through the base yarn, in and out. To make your task easier, roll the cross yarn into a tight ball. Continue to weave to the specified length. When you have finished, tie the loose ends of cross yarn to the outer base yarn and snip off any excess.

4. The doll's body is put together as follows. The head (Fig. 1) is the width of the box and 4 inches long. The body (Fig. 2) is the width of the box and 6 inches long. The arms (Fig. 3) are woven across only 4 inches of base yarn, and should each be 2½ inches long. Make two. The legs (Fig. 4) are the width of the box and 2½ inches long. Make two.

5. The top of each woven piece (next to the box end) and the sides do not require finishing. To finish the bottom edge (the end of each weaving) cut two strands of base yarn at a time and knot them together, clipping off excess ends. Continue to cut and knot across the entire side.

6. Slip the weaving off the box loom.

7. Fold the legs, arms, body and head pieces in half (along the dotted lines) and sew them each together with yarn, along three sides.

8. Stuff each piece firmly and stitch up the last seam.

9. Sew the body pieces together.

10. Embroider on a simple face with embroidery thread, and sew on yarn hair.

11. The doll's diaper (pattern 5) is a woven 4-inch square, folded on the diagonal. Make two, and sew one triangle to the front of the doll and one to the back.

12. To make the doll a dress, gather a wide piece of weaving along one edge and tie it around the doll's neck. For booties, weave two small pieces just a little wider than each leg, sew them together on three sides and slip them over the doll's feet.

BRAIDED-LIMB ANIMALS

(Shown in color, page 66)

These little animals with their floppy braided limbs were popular among farm children. The same basic pattern is used for all animals; only the length of the legs, the shape of the ears and the expression on the face differentiate between species.

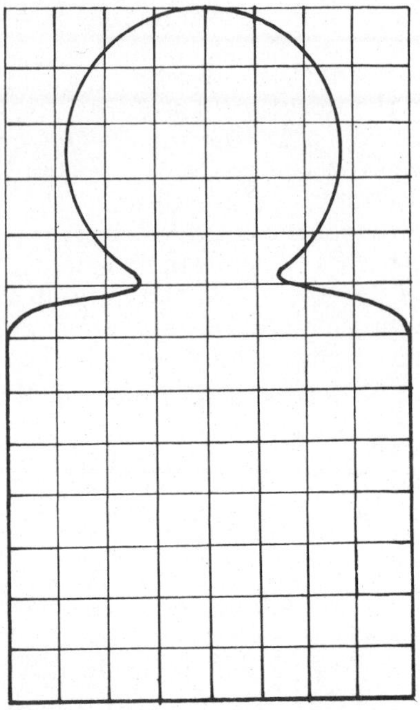

1. Make a pattern for the body of the animal by enlarging the grid on a sheet of paper so that one square equals ½ inch. (See page 13 for detailed directions on how to enlarge patterns from a grid.) Use your pattern to cut two body shapes from felt.

2. Each ear is constructed of two matching felt circles with a pink inside ear stitched to one. Sew the two circles together, slightly stuffed, ¼ inch in from the edge.

3. Cut simple facial features from felt and sew them to the face of one of the body shapes. Pin the ears to its underside.

4. To make the limbs, cut strands of rug yarn 11 inches long—18 strands for each limb. Machine-stitch each bunch together, several times over, about ½ inch below the bundle top. Braid each of the four limbs and tie the ends securely with yarn bows. Sew the limbs to the underside of one body shape at appropriate points.

5. Pin the two body shapes together and sew them ¼ inch in from the edge. Leave 3 inches of the hem unsewn.

7. Stuff the body with cotton and sew the open seam closed.

SOAP DOLLS

(Shown in color, page 66)

These sweet little things are not to be washed with. If you can find soap on a cord, use that.

1. Choose round or oval soap with a smooth side.

2. Draw on faces with felt tip markers.

3. Glue on bows, scrap-yarn hair, a bow tie or any other detail that will complete a happy face.

WIRE AND THREAD MINIATURES

(Shown in color on the cover)

Often tiny things can be larger than life. Ask any child; he'll know.

1. Make a simple stick-figure body shape with beading wire.

2. The head can either be a large bead or a small roll of crepe paper. Attach one or the other to the wire body.

3. Wrap the entire wire body with embroidery thread. Secure the ends with a dab of glue.

4. Paint on a simple face and add paper or fabric clothing.

Playthings that Never Grow Old

Playthings that Never Grow Old

Toys have kept little hands occupied since the beginning of time. Toy manufacturing is today one of the most profitable industries in this country. When all other markets are down the toy industry seems to constantly flourish. It seems a plaything is somewhat of a basic need for children, and children there will always be. Toys keep them busy, a relief to parents. They provide recreation, stretch the imagination and educate young minds. In pre-school years, the learning

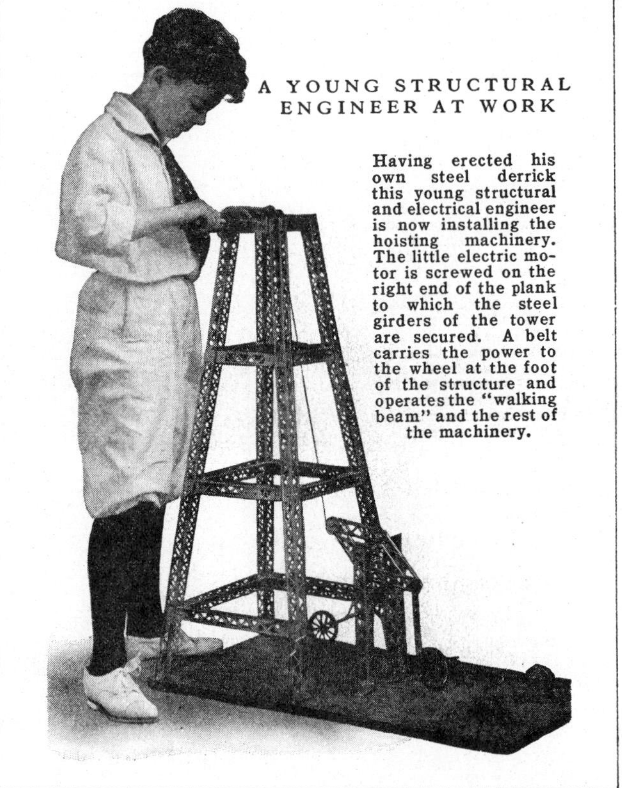

A YOUNG STRUCTURAL ENGINEER AT WORK

Having erected his own steel derrick this young structural and electrical engineer is now installing the hoisting machinery. The little electric motor is screwed on the right end of the plank to which the steel girders of the tower are secured. A belt carries the power to the wheel at the foot of the structure and operates the "walking beam" and the rest of the machinery.

curriculum revolves around games and toys that provide learning experiences without drudgery.

Only until recently the vast majority of toys were homemade. At the rudimentary level, children created playthings out of sticks and rocks and other objects from nature and any discards from the home. The existence of a toy-making industry as we know it today is a comparatively recent phenomenon, originating in Germany in the sixteenth century. Before that time, what commercial toy making there was existed as a sideline of various artisans, who would work on special order from wealthy parents.

By the late sixteenth century, the products of the Toymakers Guild of Nuremburg were being distributed across Germany. Individual toys were

still handmade products of skilled craftsmen, and the only families who could afford them were landowners and other gentry. It wasn't until the Industrial Revolution in the early nineteenth century, which brought manufactured goods down in price while increasing the living standards of large numbers of people, that the toy industry as we know it today came into being.

In the United States, most early toy production was of large, wooden outdoor toys, such as sleds, wooden horses and other cumbersome playthings. In the 1860s, indoor toys began to be distributed, but these were mostly European imports. Aiding the growth of the burgeoning toy industry in the latter half of the nineteenth century were the great mail-order houses. Items such as sleds, velocipedes, wagons and hobby horses were introduced into catalogs to tempt the younger set. Each year more and more toys surfaced and would be displayed for this ever growing profitable market. The wholesale suppliers who served the general stores of the frontiers and the small merchants of the rural Midwest found playthings a fast moving, high-profit product area.

Manufactured toys didn't reach the hands of all people. Farmers and mountain people continued to design and make their own toys, folk toys. Though primitive in appearance, they sometimes utilized principles of physics that might stagger our mechanized imaginations. The flipperdinger is one such folk toy. (Air passing through a blowpipe causes a ball at the end, resting on an open hole, to rise through a wire hoop several inches above the hole. You could say it was a stepping stone to basketball.) Hundreds of folk toys have come out of the mountain areas. Today they're being copied by toy manufacturers.

Children nowadays have the most intricate

and elaborate toys imaginable. Unfortunately, they lack the charm and integrity of some of the old-fashioned toys. They are not as open-ended; they leave less to the child's imagination. Make a few of these oldies with and for your children—they will be enjoyed.

STRING FAVORITES

Two toys that have remained popular for generations are the Yo-Yo and the spinning top—both simple devices to which string adds the dimensions of motion and speed. Other classic playthings made with string include the parachute, the buzz saw and the walkie-talkie. All three have been in the hands of American children since the beginning of the century, and even today no toy collection would be complete without them.

PARACHUTE

1. Cut four equal lengths of lightweight cord. Tie one length to each corner of a handkerchief.
2. Tie the strings together in a knot 3 inches from the ends.
3. Tie all four ends to a single eye screw that has been inserted into the head of a wooden clothespin.
4. Roll the clothespin up inside the handkerchief and throw the parachute into the air.

BUZZ SAW

1. Cut out a cardboard circle and punch two small holes in the center, about 1/8 inch apart.
2. Thread sturdy cord through the holes and knot at both ends.
3. Tie a small piece of dowel to each end of the cord.
4. Center the circle on the cord. Hold both dowels and spin the cardboard circle so that the cords become tightly entwined. Then pull the dowels apart with a jerk and let the cardboard circle spin.

WALKIE-TALKIE

1. Remove one lid completely from two small cans.
2. Sand or file the raw edges, if any.
3. Punch a hole in the center of each remaining lid.
4. Take a long strand of cord and insert one end into each can. Knot the ends tightly.
5. Each player takes a can, goes into a different room, pulls the can tightly on the cord, and talks into and listens through his can.

PAPER FAVORITES

Though the Japanese have perfected origami, there are a number of folded paper projects that

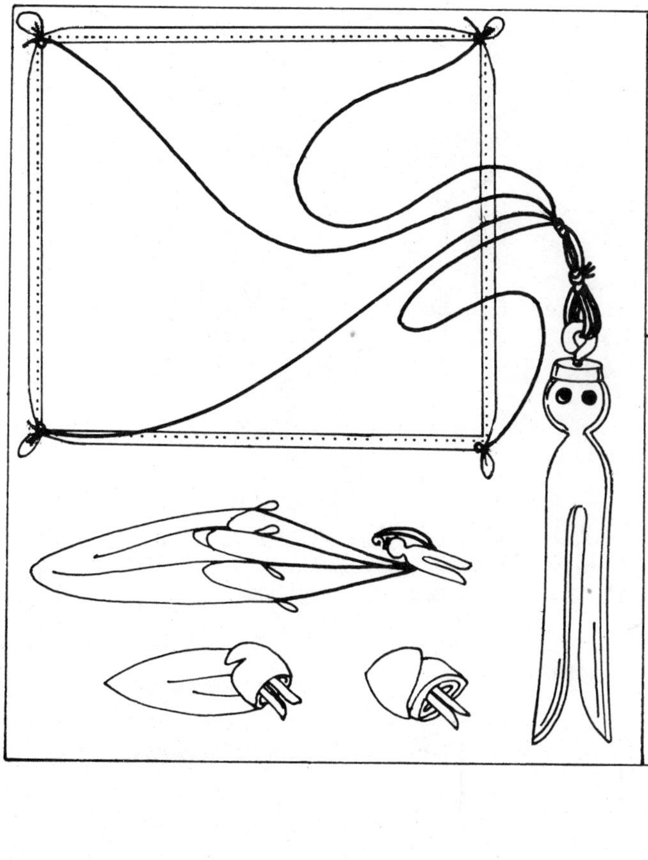

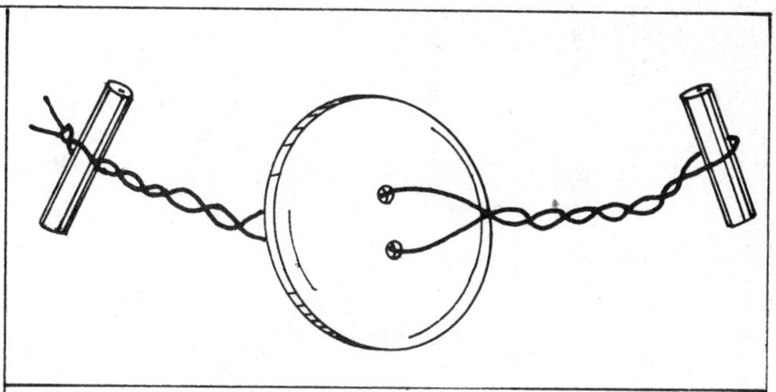

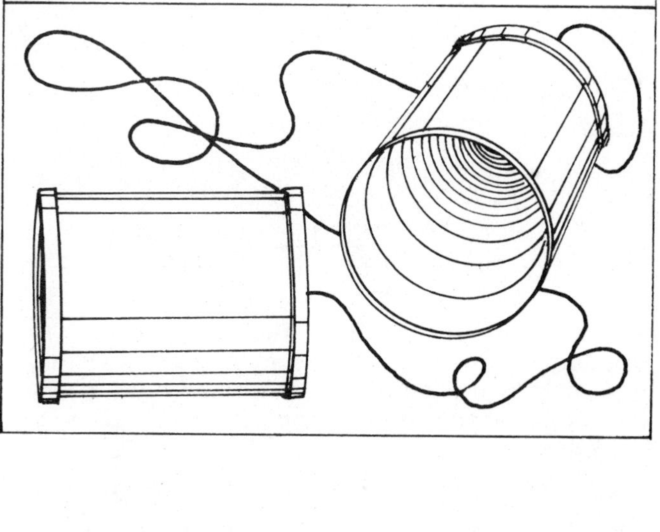

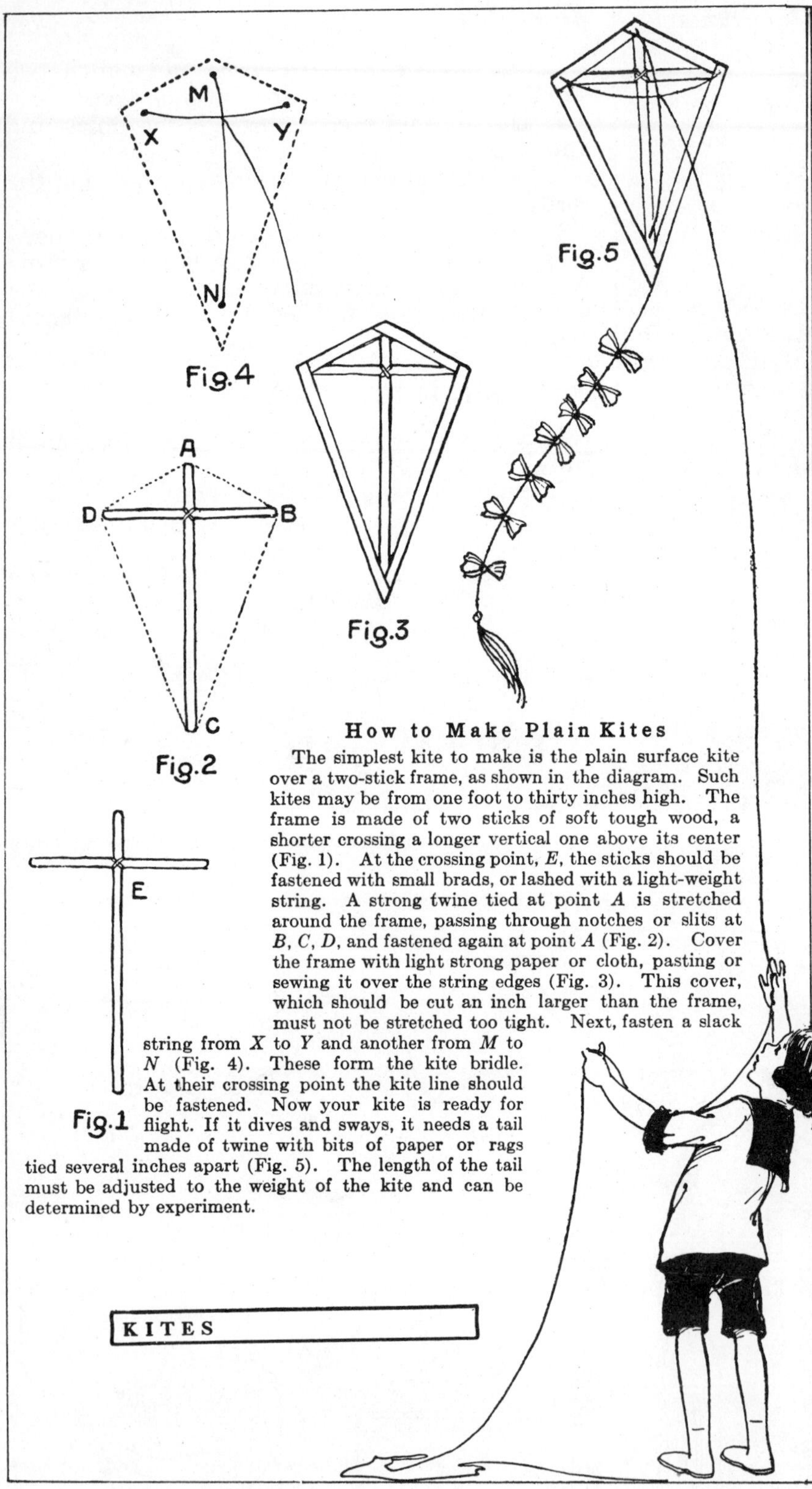

How to Make Plain Kites

The simplest kite to make is the plain surface kite over a two-stick frame, as shown in the diagram. Such kites may be from one foot to thirty inches high. The frame is made of two sticks of soft tough wood, a shorter crossing a longer vertical one above its center (Fig. 1). At the crossing point, *E*, the sticks should be fastened with small brads, or lashed with a light-weight string. A strong twine tied at point *A* is stretched around the frame, passing through notches or slits at *B*, *C*, *D*, and fastened again at point *A* (Fig. 2). Cover the frame with light strong paper or cloth, pasting or sewing it over the string edges (Fig. 3). This cover, which should be cut an inch larger than the frame, must not be stretched too tight. Next, fasten a slack string from *X* to *Y* and another from *M* to *N* (Fig. 4). These form the kite bridle. At their crossing point the kite line should be fastened. Now your kite is ready for flight. If it dives and sways, it needs a tail made of twine with bits of paper or rags tied several inches apart (Fig. 5). The length of the tail must be adjusted to the weight of the kite and can be determined by experiment.

KITES

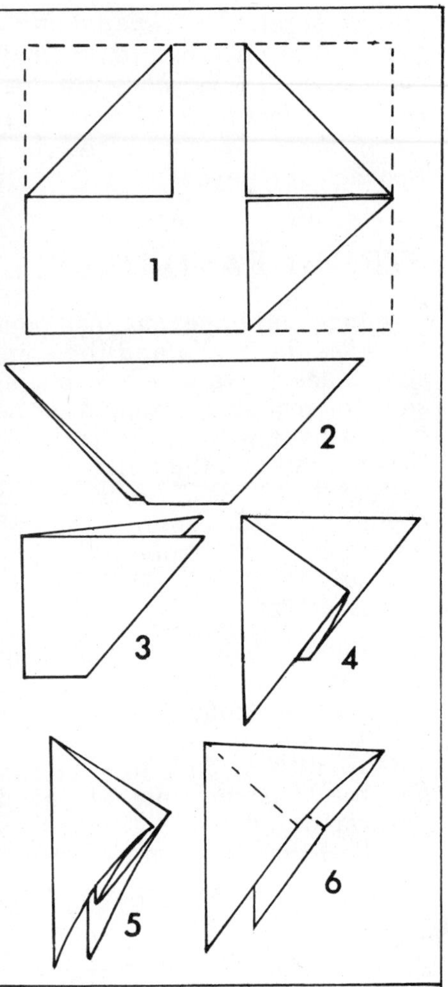

are singularly American—like the popgun and the paper top. The origin of the kite is uncertain, but there is no doubt that on a windy day every boy or girl wishes they had one.

POPGUN

1. Take a double sheet of tabloid-size newspaper and fold the top and bottom corners toward

the center so that they meet in a horizontal line (Fig. 1).

2. Fold the paper in half along the center horizontal so that the top and bottom meet, with the corners tucked inside (Fig. 2).

3. Fold the paper in half again along the center vertical, so that the top corners meet (Fig. 3).

4. Fold the front corner point down on the diagonal, so that the top side now lies flush with the left side of the paper (Fig. 4).

5. Turn the paper over and repeat with the remaining corner point (Fig. 5).

6. To make the gun pop, hold the two bottom points between your fingers and snap your wrist. The inside fold will pop out. To close, push the fold back to its original position (Fig. 6).

PAPER TOP

1. Cut out a paper or cardboard circle.
2. Draw a swirling pattern on the circle pointing clockwise (see illustration).
3. Force a short sharpened pencil through the center of the circle.
4. Lay the top on a sheet of paper and spin by twirling the pencil.

SPOOL FAVORITES

There seems to be a shortage of almost everything these days. The good old days are looking better than ever. Wood products have become rather scarce. Maybe you've noticed that the spools sewing thread comes on are no longer wooden but cardboard or plastic. There was a time when children couldn't wait until a spool came empty so they could appropriate it for a racer or a spool knitter. You can still find some wooden spools at the sewing counters, but you better hurry because the supply won't last.

SPOOL RACER

1. Hammer two small nails with heads three-fourths of the way into one end of a wooden spool. The nails should be opposite each other, next to the hole.
2. Wrap a 4-inch rubber band around both nails and pull it through the spool.
3. Thread the rubber band through a bead with a large eye.
4. Slip a 3-inch piece of dowel through the loop of the rubber band that extends beneath bead, and twist the band tightly. Place the spool on the floor, let go of the dowel, and watch it go.

SPOOL KNITTER

1. A large wooden spool is ideal for this project. Enlarge the hole in the spool with a drill and sand the opening until smooth.
2. Hammer five wood staples into the top of the spool at equal intervals, slanting them outward slightly so that the yarn loops will not slip off.
3. The "knitting" is done around the top of the spool. When completed, the knit tubing passes through the spool and out the hole at the bottom.
4. To use the knitter, first run the loose end of a ball of yarn down through the spool until several inches emerge from the bottom. Begin at the top and run the yarn counterclockwise around every other staple, to form a starlike shape (Fig. 1). When the star is complete and you are back at the first staple, start "knitting" the stitches. "Knitting" consists of passing the original strand up and over the new strand, from outside the staple to the inside (Figs. 2 and 3). Use a crochet hook. Carry the yarn to the second staple, wrap it, and again pass the original strand up and over the new strand from outside the staple to the inside. Keep working around the spool, but every few stitches give a little pull on the knitted yarn rope that is emerging from the bottom of the spool (Fig. 4).

SPOOL SOLDIERS

(Shown in color, page 68)

1. Stack wooden spools of various sizes to make the soldier's head, body and legs. Secure in place with white glue.
2. Top the spools with a wooden cabinet doorknob.
3. The arms are made with ice cream sticks. The hands on the soldier in the center were cut off the ends of the sticks and glued back on at an angle.
4. Paint the spools to look like a soldier's uniform using enamel paints. Check hobby counters for small, inexpensive bottles of paint.

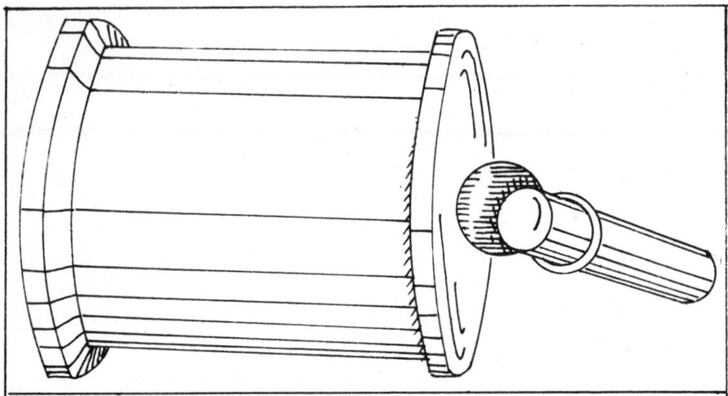

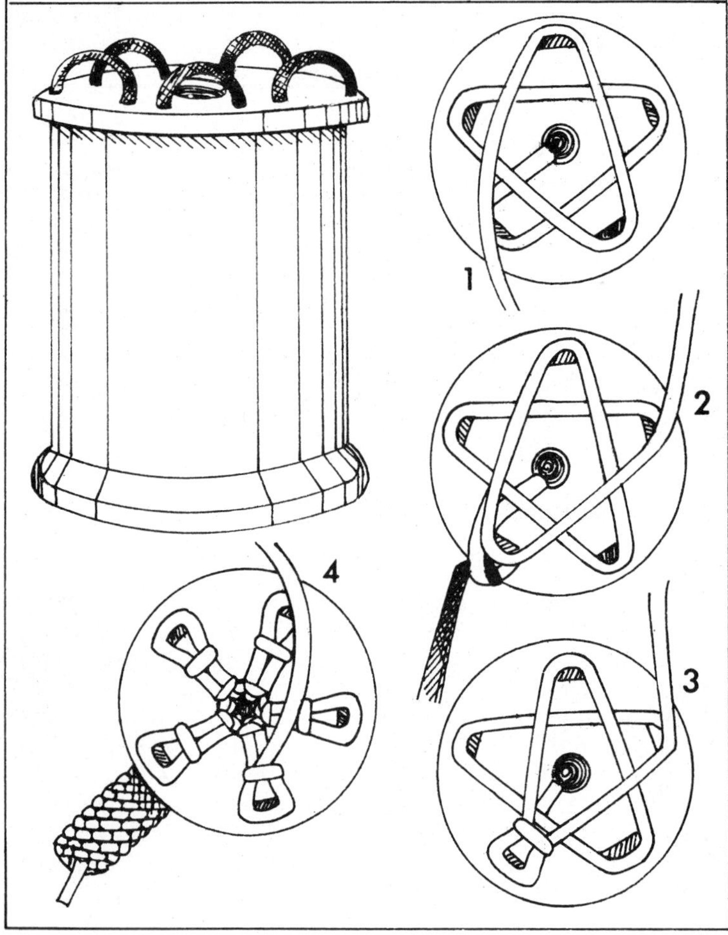

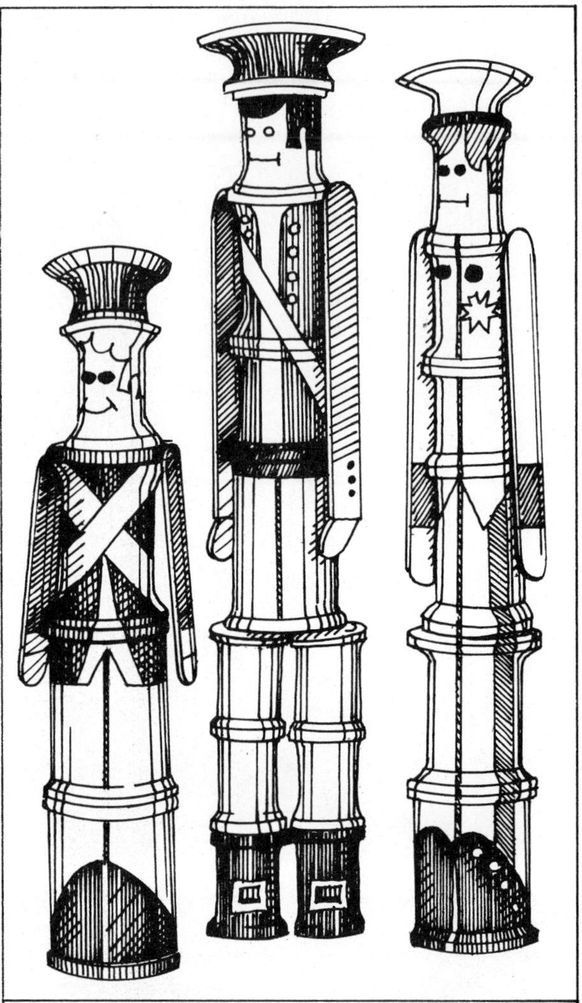

ROLY-POLY CLOWN

Gone are the days when the circus paraded through local towns announcing "the greatest show on earth is coming." The clowns, marching up front, were every child's favorite. And if we don't see so many walking down the streets anymore, it certainly doesn't mean we like them less.

1. Cut a one-inch circle in an old 3-inch rubber ball.
2. Squeeze a generous amount of bonded cement to the inside bottom of the ball. Wedge a stone into the ball, resting on the cement. Keep the ball's opening facing straight up so that the stone will dry centered on the bottom of the ball.
3. Wrap an 8-ounce drinking cup in red construction paper. Paste the paper at the back and trim away any excess from the top and bottom. Make the clown's face with a pink paper strip, his collar with a white scalloped strip and his belt with a black strip. Draw on facial features and a button with felt-tip markers. Add a curled feather at the top.
4. Glue the cup over the hole on the ball with bonded cement.

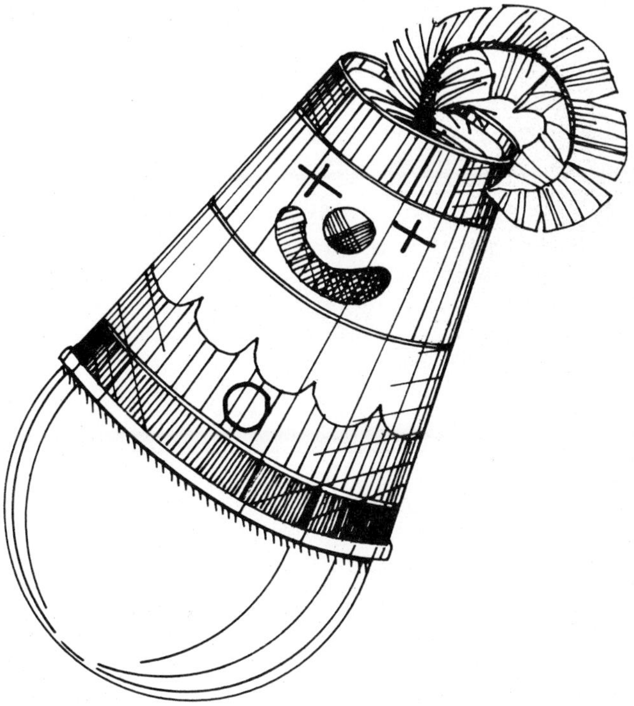

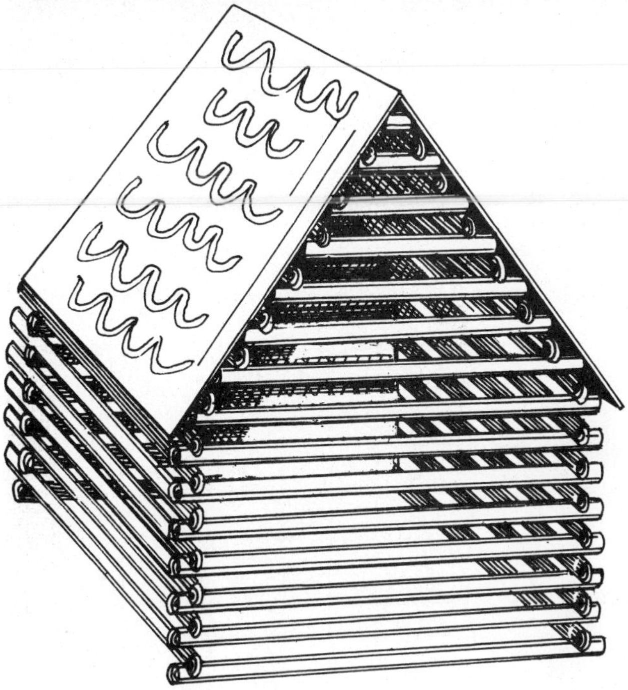

STRAW LOG CABIN

We use straw logs here to build that earliest of American homes—the pioneer log cabin. The log cabin makes a suitable house for westward-wandering dolls.

1. Lay four drinking straws on the table so they form a square. The straws in the vertical position should be on top of those that lay horizontally and should cross them about ½ inch in from the edge. Use a bonded cement in a squeeze-top tube to hold the straws in place. Allow the glue to dry thoroughly before proceeding.
2. Raise the four walls of the cabin to a height of 5 inches, layering horizontally- and vertically-placed straws in the same manner. Glue each vertical pair to the horizontal pair beneath.
3. Start to narrow the front and back walls into peaks by snipping off a ¼ inch from one set of horizontal straws. Place the shortened straws on top of the last set of vertical straws. The next set of vertical straws are forced to move in a little to maintain the ½-inch overlap.
4. Cut each set of horizontal straws ¼ inch shorter than the preceding and glue the straws down, set by set, until the sides, front and back of the cabin meet.
5. Cut out windows and a door. Glue supporting straws to the inside of the openings.
6. Add a folded paper roof with shingles drawn to the cabin's pitch.

JUMPING JENNY

Everybody knows this toy. You pull a string at the top and puppet kicks its legs and arms about. This toy was originally French and originally called *pantins*. There have been jumping Humpty-Dumptys and jumping Jacks—ours is Jenny.

1. To make a pattern for Jenny, enlarge the grid on a sheet of paper so that one square equals ½ inch. Then draw the four shapes on the enlarged grid. (See page 13 for detailed directions on

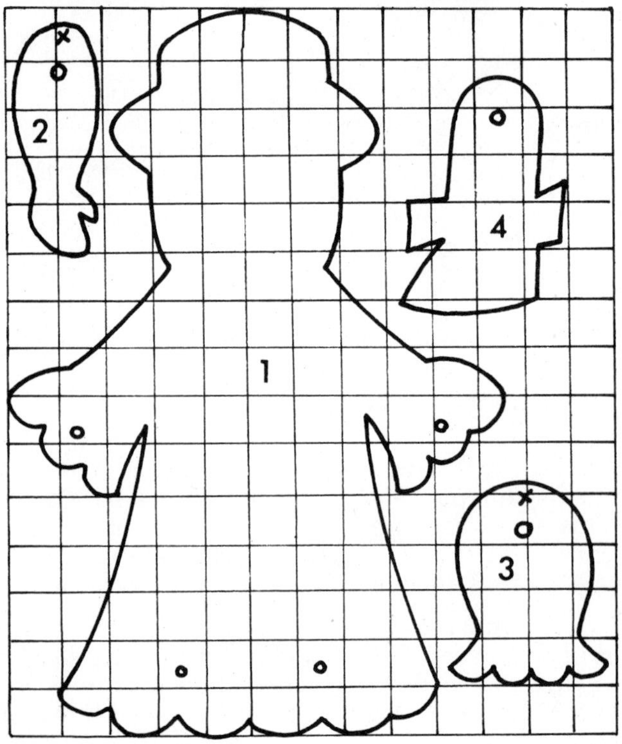

how to enlarge patterns from a grid.) Use the patterns to cut out one body shape (Fig. 1), two arms (Fig. 2), two pantalets (Fig. 3) and two legs (Fig. 4) from pieces of cardboard.

2. Before assembling, paint all of the shapes or color them with felt-tip markers.

3. Punch holes with a hole puncher in the places on the body and limbs marked 0 on the patterns. A second smaller set of holes should be punched with a nail on the arms and pantalets, as indicated with an X.

4. Attach the arms to the body with metal paper-fasteners. Attach the legs to the pantalets and the pantalets to the skirt. You can also use string to attach the limbs to the body, passing it through a button or bead, then through the limb and body, and finally through a second button on the back side. Secure the thread with knots. The limbs must swing freely.

5. To prepare the figure for jumping, thread and knot cord through both small holes (the points marked X) on the tops of the arms. Do the same with the tops of the pantalets. Take a third cord and knot it to the center of the arm cord and then the center of the leg cord, letting the end hang down below the doll's shoes. Thread a bead on the end of this cord and secure.

6. To make Jenny jump, hold her head and pull the hanging cord.

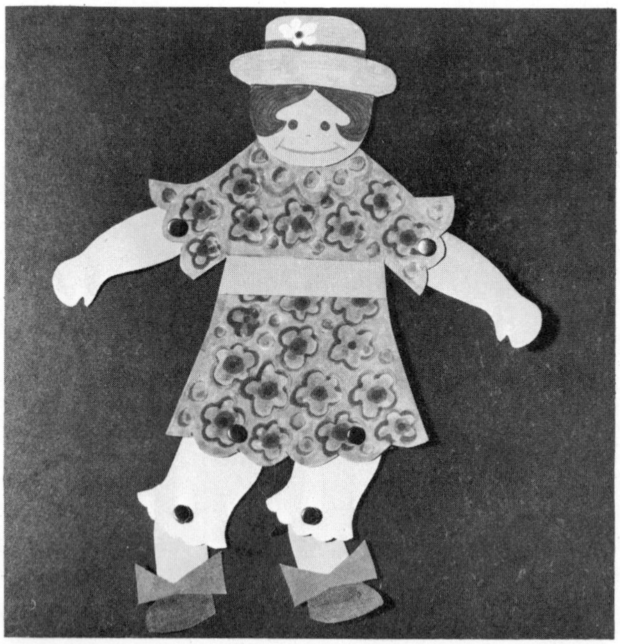

BEAN-BAG CUP AND SAUCER GAME

Bean-bags are most fun when there is a game attached to them—like Hot Potato or the following game we've dreamed up. This one's terrific practice for aspiring pitchers.

Child's Decorated China Tea Set.
Given for only 20 trial subscribers at 10 cents each; or, for only 10 trial subscriptions and 50 cents extra in cash.
The handsomest toy set we have ever given, consists of 23 pieces handsomely decorated in gold, Tea Pot, Sugar Bowl, Cream Pitcher, 6 Plates and 6 Cups and Saucers. Plates are 2¾ inches in diameter, other pieces in proportion. Size of set can be judged accordingly. The shape is new and unique, made in Germany for us and imported expressly for the LADIES' HOME JOURNAL little ones. By having them made in large quantities we can afford to sell them at a low price, only $1.00, carefully packed in a strong wooden box and can be sent to any address with safety.
Should be sent by express, which will be but a trifle to any point east of Rocky Mountains, can be sent by mail to distant points for 50 cents extra.

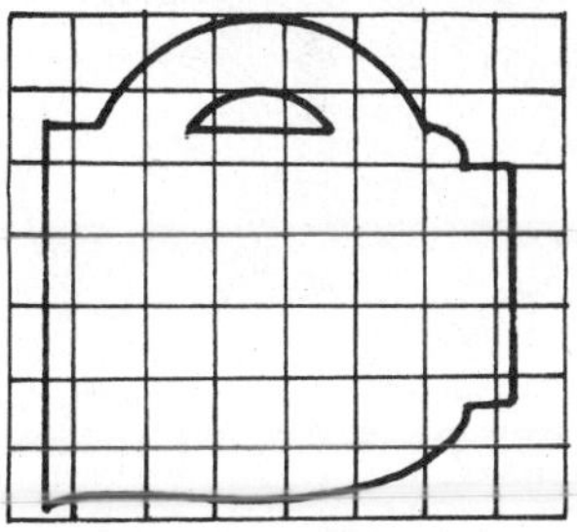

1. To make a pattern for the cup, enlarge the grid on a sheet of paper so that one square equals one inch. Then draw the cup shape on the enlarged grid. (See page 13 for detailed directions on how to enlarge patterns from a grid.) Use the pattern to cut out two cup shapes out of felt for each bean-bag.
2. Sew a palm tree design on both sides of each cup.
3. Sew the cup shapes together, ½ inch in from the edge. Leave one inch unsewn on the top edge.
4. Fill the cup half full with dried split peas or lentils.
5. Sew the open seam closed.
6. Make the plate from a 12-inch circle of heavyweight paper or cardboard. Draw the palm tree in the center with felt-tip markers.
7. Place the plate on the floor and try to throw the bean bag on to it.

TOY TRAIN

The invention of the locomotive changed the lives of Americans in a way nothing may ever affect us again. After that historic first train trip, every male child decided he would grow up to be a railroad engineer. Toy trains proved to be a pretty good substitute until the kids were old enough for the real thing.

1. To make a pattern for the train, enlarge the grid on a sheet of paper so that one square equals one inch. Then draw the four shapes on the enlarged grid. (See page 13 for detailed directions on how to enlarge patterns from a grid.) Use your patterns to cut two felt locomotives (Fig. 1), two cabooses (Fig. 2) and as many pairs of passenger-car shapes (Fig. 3) as you want. Also cut out assorted simple window shapes, smokestacks, and so on. The wheels (Fig. 4) are 2½-inch circles.
2. Sew the windows and any other accessories you have made to both sides of each car.
3. Place a thin layer of cotton or polyester between the two sides of each car.
4. Sew each car together ¼ inch in from the edge.
5. Make the wheels by sewing two circles together with a thin layer of stuffing in between.
6. Add a large snap to the back of each wheel and to the corresponding points on the cars. Snap on the wheels. (You can add wheels to the other side of the train, as you prefer.)
7. Join the cars together with snaps.

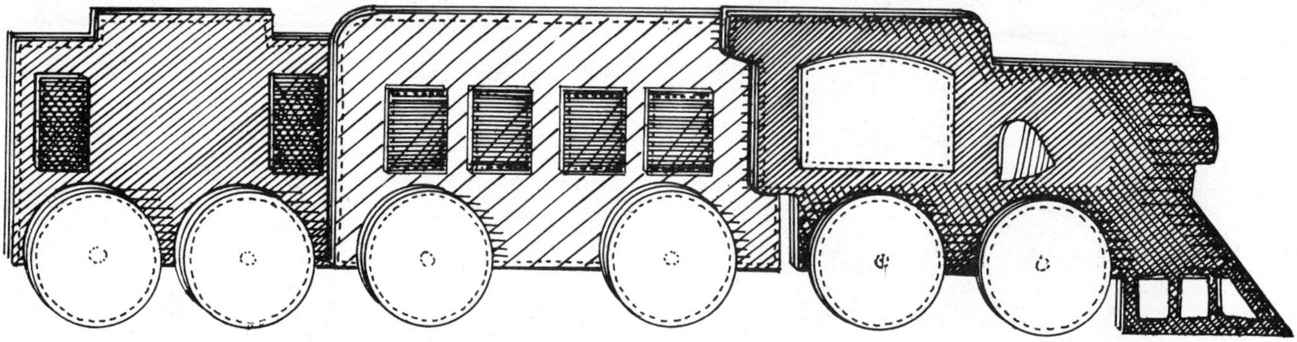

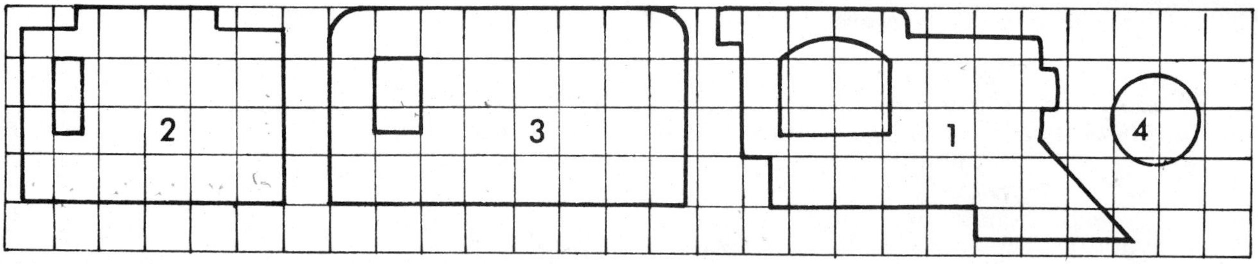

ZIP-UP DELIVERY WAGON

Around the turn of the century almost all deliveries—ice, bread, wood, coal, milk—were made by horse-drawn wagons. Lucky children had miniature metal versions to play with. Ours, which is quite as nice, is made from fabric.

1. To make patterns for the wagon and its accessories, enlarge the grid on a sheet of paper so that one square equals one inch. Draw the seven shapes onto the enlarged grid. (See page 13 for detailed directions on how to enlarge patterns from a grid.) Cut out two wagon shapes (the *entire* Fig. 1 outline), six wheels (Fig. 2), one of each medallion (Figs. 3 and 4), one wagon opening (Fig. 5) and two bottles of milk (Fig. 6). Make the delivery wagon in felt.
2. Sew the medallions and the wagon opening to the front wagon shape. Add three small rectangles under the medallion and the letters M-I-L-K inside the medallion. Draw the letters on felt before cutting or cut them out free-hand.
3. Sew a 7-inch zipper to the straight back edge of both wagon shapes.
4. Sew the wagon shapes together along all the other sides, ¼ inch in from the edges of the felt.
5. Sew free-cut triangles to three of the wheels.
6. Sew each pair of wheel shapes together with a thin layer of cotton stuffing in between.
7. Add a snap to the back of each wheel, and sew snaps to the tabs that protrude below the wagon body.
8. The third wheel should be snapped onto the front of the other side of the wagon.
9. Zip open the wagon and pop in bottles.
10. Follow the same procedure to make delivery wagons for ice (Fig. 7 is your ice block) and for pies (Fig. 8).

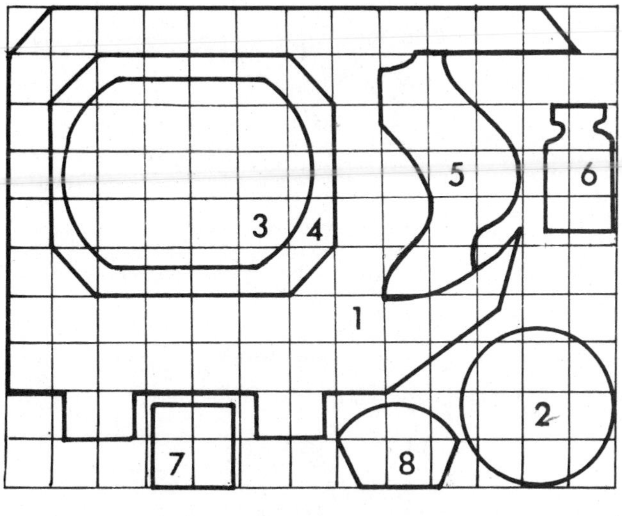

TUMBLING ACROBAT

(Shown in color, page 68)

The tumbling acrobat is one of those hand-operated toys that never fails to amuse. Unlike toys meant to sit on shelves and look pretty, this one goes through all the acrobatic tricks athletes do on horizontal bars. This sort of hand-driven toy was very popular before electricity powered the toy industry.

1. The two upright bars are pieces of ¾-inch screen molding cut 10½ inches long.
2. Drill two small holes in each bar, ¼ inch and ¾ inch below the top, or pierce the bars with hammer and a finishing nail.
3. The connecting bar is a piece of pine 2½ inches long. Round the ends of this bar slightly with sandpaper.
4. Place the connecting bar 4¾ inches down from the top of the two upright ones and hammer it in place.
5. The little acrobat illustrated is actual size. Trace one body shape (Fig. 1), two legs (Fig. 2) and two arms (Fig. 3) on cardboard and cut them out.
6. Punch holes through the limbs and the body with a nail. Attach each pair of limbs to the body with a single piece of thin wire (see illustration). Thread the ends of the wire through small beads and knot them securely. The limbs should swing freely.
7. Punch two holes through each hand, one above the other.
8. Attach the acrobat's hands to the upright bars with a length of cord. First pass the cord through the two holes on one bar. Then twist the cord once, so that the upper strand passes through the lower holes in the acrobat's hands and vice versa. Twist the cord once more so that the lower cord again becomes the upper one, and thread the two strands through the holes in the second bar (see illustration). Tie the ends of the cord together.
9. Press the bottom of both upright bars simultaneously, and watch the acrobat swing on his trapeze.

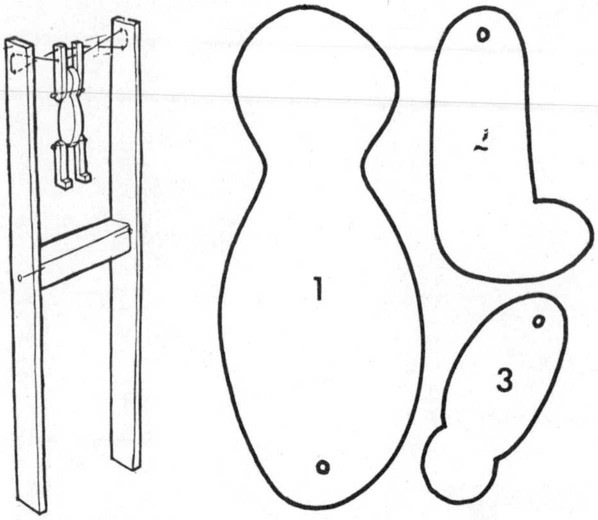

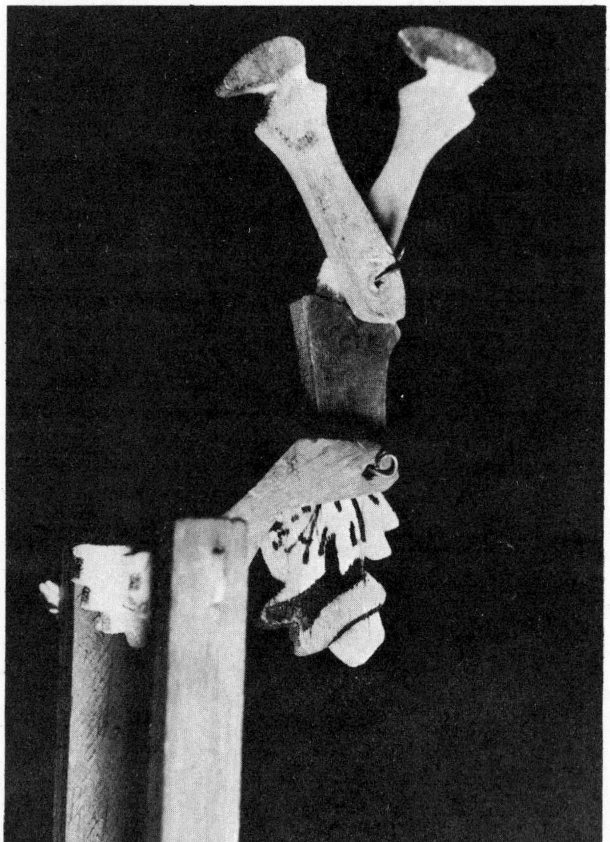

PLAY STOVE

Some toys that were made commercially in the early 1900s resembled the actual item in every detail—even the construction materials might be the same. Witness the toy stove that was sold sev-

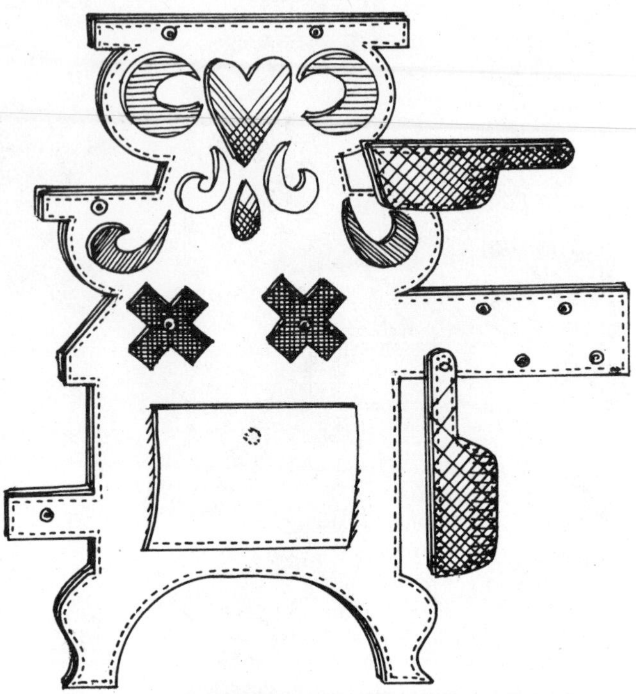

H 9039 "Pet" Toy Range, a handsome little model like illustration; polished and nickel-plated, with full set of utensils; large enough for the first stove and exceptional value; will please any little tot. Size, 10$\frac{1}{4}$x5$\frac{1}{2}$x5 in. Shipping weight, 4 lb. Each......**45c.**

enty years ago: it appears to be the real thing in miniature. There is no way you can duplicate the original with today's materials, but this felt replica is a pretty fair imitation of the real thing.

1. To make patterns for the stove and its pots, enlarge the grid on a sheet of paper so that one square equals one inch. Draw the two shapes on the enlarged grid. (See page 13 for detailed directions on how to enlarge patterns from a grid.) Cut out two stove shapes (Fig. 1) and ten pots (Fig. 2). Make both the stove and accessories from felt. (You might make the pots in two sizes.)
2. Cut out decorative grillwork and two criss-cross burners and sew to the stove. Cut a door and sew it along its bottom edge to the lower part of the stove. Close the door with a snap.
3. Sew the two stove shapes together with a layer of cotton or polyester between them. Sew ¼ inch in from the edges.
4. Sew each pair of pot shapes together with a light layer of padding between. Make five pots.
5. Sew large snaps on the handles and bottoms of each pot, on the burners of the stove and on the shelves. The dots on the grid indicate placement.
6. Snap the pots on the burners for cooking, and on the shelves for storage.

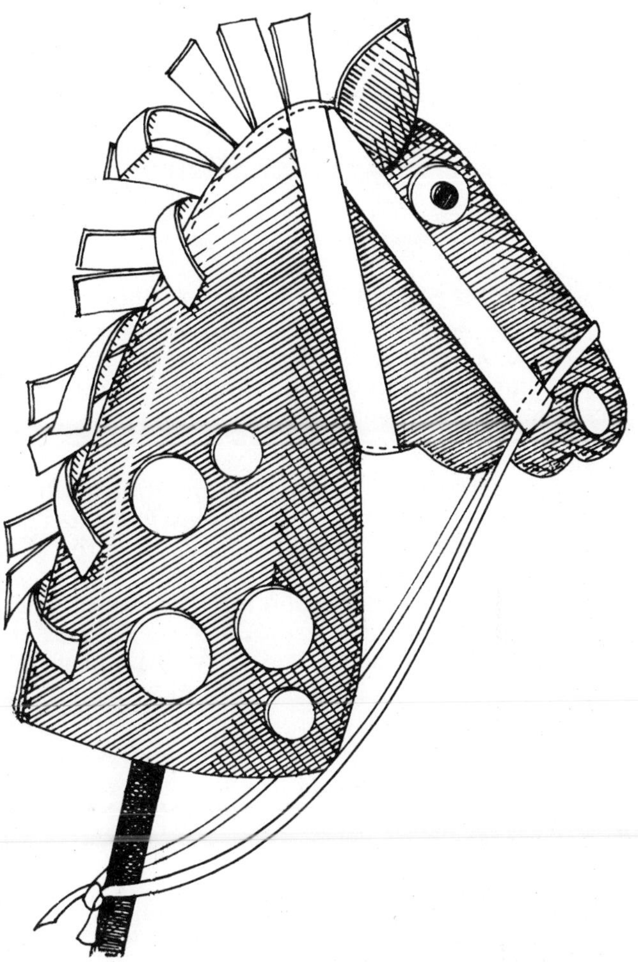

PONY-ON-A-STICK

Cowboys and Indians still dominate the childhood play scene, and what "pardner" wouldn't like to own his own horse? The wooden pony was a favorite toy among farm children in the West—practice for the day when they would hop onto their first mount and ride the open range.

1. To make a pattern for the pony, enlarge the grid on a sheet of paper so that one square equals two inches. Draw the four shapes on the enlarged grid. (See page 13 for detailed directions on how to enlarge patterns from a grid.) Using felt, cut out two head shapes (Fig. 1), two ears (Fig. 2) and two eyes (Fig. 3). Cut mane strips 5 inches long and one inch wide.
2. Sew the mane strips in place, just inside the back edge of one head shape. Sew a felt ear, eye and nose onto each side of the head, and dot with felt polka dots.
3. Sew the two head shapes together, ¼ inch in from the edge. The bottom edge stays unsewn. Stitch two lengths of ribbon to each side as you sew, one from the top of the head to the neck and one from the top of the head to the nose. Leave the ribbon to the nose hanging free for the moment.
4. Stuff the head firmly with cotton or polyester.
5. Fit a broom into the neck. You may have to

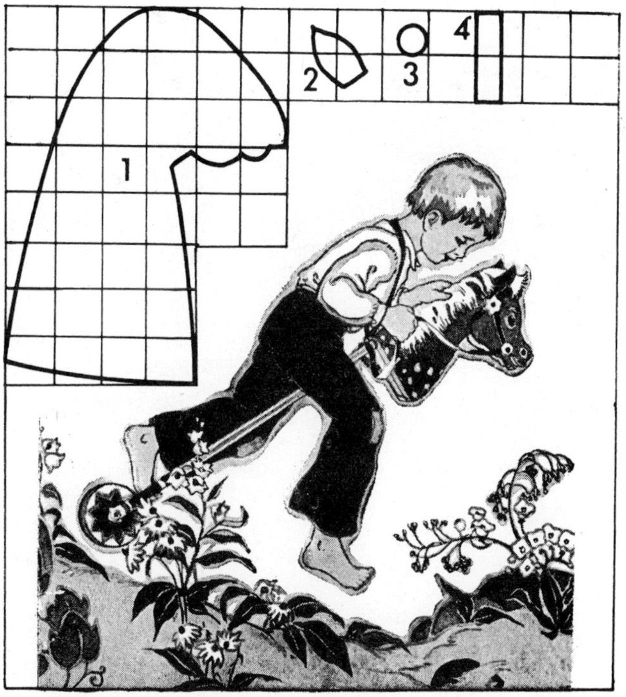

trim the bristles to fit.

6. Continue to stuff the head and neck around the broom.

7. Sew the bottom edge of the pony's head closed.

8. Sew the loose-hanging nose-ribbons over a long cord, and tie the cord around the broomstick to make reins.

SKATEBOARD

A pair of old roller skates, a 4-foot section of 2 x 4 lumber and an orange crate and you can be the terror of 143rd Street. Scooters and wagons have been around for a long time.

1. Cut scrap lumber into a shape that is blunt on one end and tapered on the other. The cuts can be straight rather than rounded, provided the corners are not too sharp.

2. Remove the clamps and the back brace from an old roller skate and screw the skate to the bottom of the board in the center. Additional skate wheels or individual wheels (bought at hardware stores) can be used for the four corners of the board.

HINGED CLOWN

(Shown in color, page 68)

This toy clown comes from a design that was found in an old trunk at a flea market. Because of its hinged construction, it can sit up without the aid of props and stretch out its hands to greet passersby.

1. To make a pattern for the clown, enlarge the grid on a piece of paper so that one square equals one inch. Draw the three shapes on the enlarged grid. (See page 13 for detailed directions on how to enlarge patterns from a grid.) Cut out the patterns and trace them on plywood. You'll need one body shape (Fig. 1), two arms (Fig. 2) and two legs (Fig. 3). Cut them out with a jigsaw and sand the edges.

2. Attach the limbs to the clown with small brass hinges.

3. Paint the clown with paints in colors similar to the original.

Note: The clown can also be made of heavy cardboard. In this case, make the hinges from fabric or paper and glue them to the body with white glue.

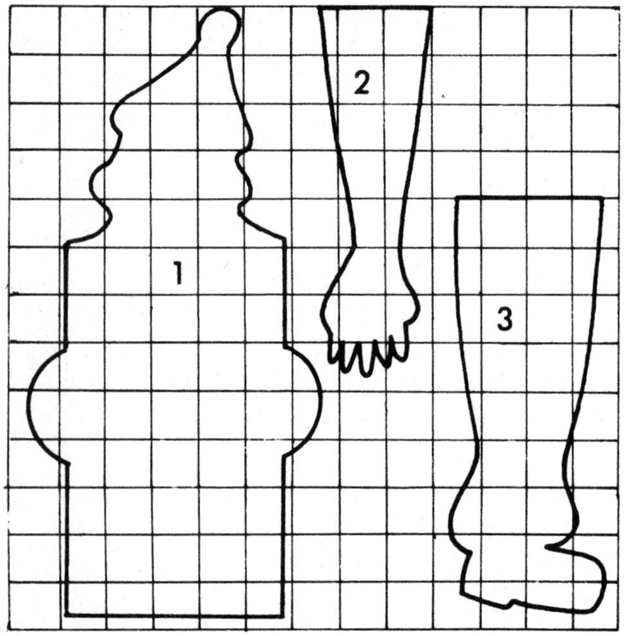

CLATTER BLOCKS

Clatter blocks may be the best toy to come out of the early years of the twentieth century. How does the first block tumble down past the middle ones to become the last block? The secret lies in the way the blocks are taped together. If you want to learn more, read on.

1. Cut seven 2½ x 3½-inch rectangular plywood slabs, or use wide lattice. Sand the raw edges.
2. The blocks are attached to one another with twill tape. Staple the ends of two 28¼-inch lengths of tape to the top edge of the first block, 1½ inches apart. Weave the tape in and out of the seven blocks and then staple the ends to the bottom edge of the last block.
3. Weave a third length of tape 21¼ inches long in and out of the blocks in the reverse direction. Staple the ends to the inside edges of the top (first) and the bottom (last) blocks (see illustration).
4. To make the clatter blocks work, hold the second block and allow the top block to tumble down to the bottom block.

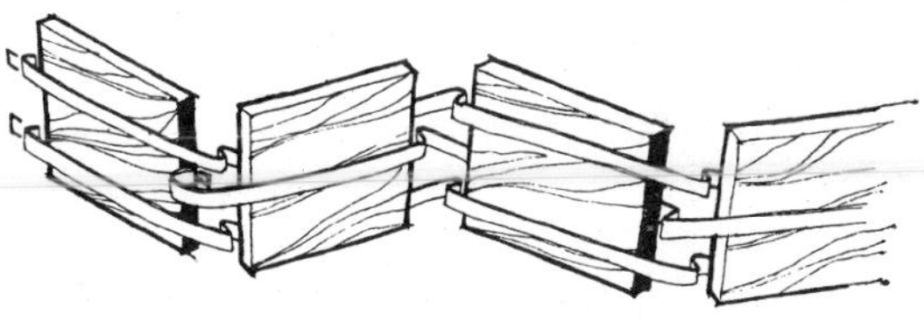

SAILBOAT

Sailboats have a fascination for children (also for parents). They float! And then there's the magic of water and wind. This version is perfect for a bathtub lake.

1. The base of the boat is made from scrap lumber. It should be cut straight across one end and tapered to a point at the other.
2. The cabin is a smaller rectangle of scrap wood glued to the boat's base with bonded cement.
3. Drill a hole in the cabin to accommodate a thin dowel. If you do not have a drill, pound a hole into the wood with a hammer and a large nail. The hole should be close to the front of the cabin.
4. Glue the dowel into the hole.
5. Make the sail by cutting a triangle from oilcloth. Hem the cloth along the vertical edge.
6. Slip the dowel into the hem and glue the sail in place one inch above the cabin.

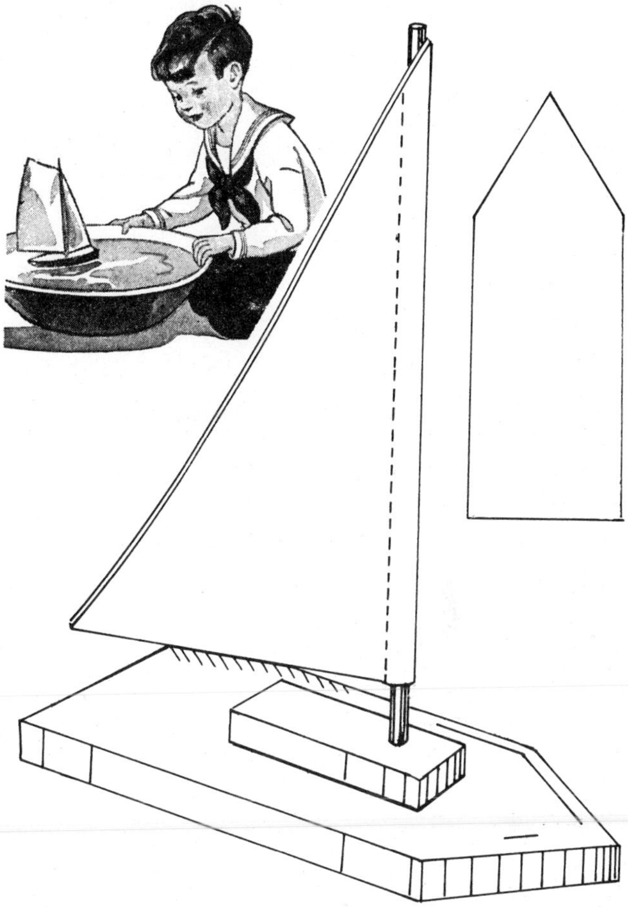

SOFT BLOCKS

Toddlers like picking up blocks, throwing them, stacking them. These blocks, with the letters of the alphabet and coordinated pictures, are an early reading tool. This is also a very safe toy, as it is made of felt.

1. Make the block patterns (Fig. 1) on a sheet of paper. Measure four 4-inch squares side by side. The first and last squares have ½ inch added to the length. The top and bottom squares have ¼ inch added to all sides. The dotted lines show the additions. Use felt for the squares and appliqués.
2. Sew the two ends of the row of squares together, ¼ inch in from the edge (Fig. 2).
3. Sew the bottom square into the connected squares, making the seam ¼ inch from the edge on all sides (Fig. 3).
4. Turn the block over and sew two sides of the top square and half of the third side to the block.
5. Stuff the block firmly and sew the open seam closed.

Each block will have three letters and three

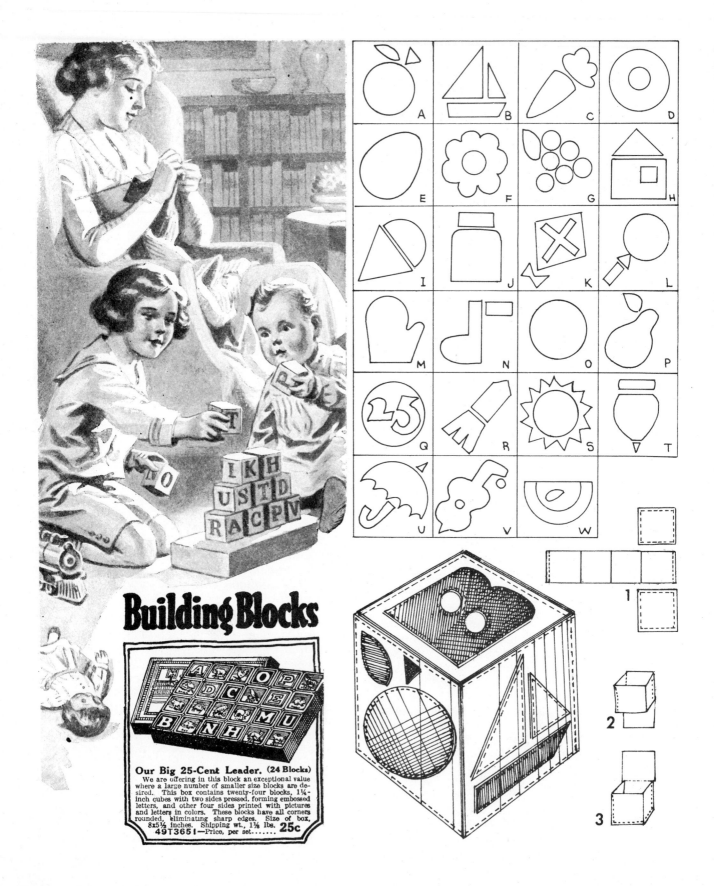

Building Blocks
Our Big 25-Cent Leader. (24 Blocks)
We are offering in this block an exceptional value where a large number of smaller size blocks are desired. This box contains twenty-four blocks, 1¼-inch cubes with two sides pressed, forming embossed letters, and other four sides printed with pictures and letters in colors. These blocks have all corners rounded, eliminating sharp edges. Size of box, 8x5½ inches. Shipping wt., 1⅛ lbs.
49T3651—Price, per set....... 25c

A
B
C
D
E
F
G
H
I
J
K
L
M
N
O
P
Q
R
S
T
U
V
W

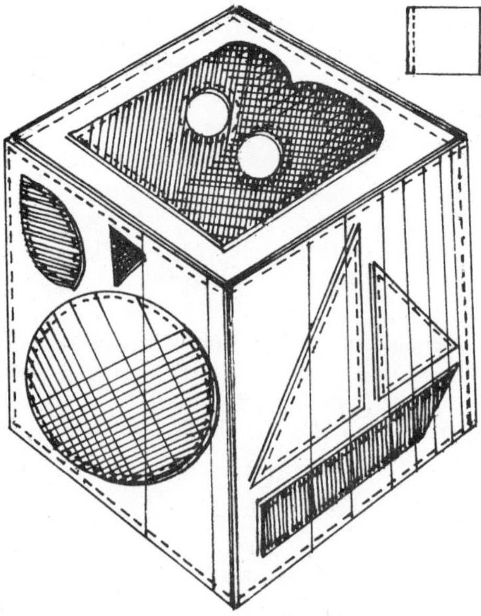

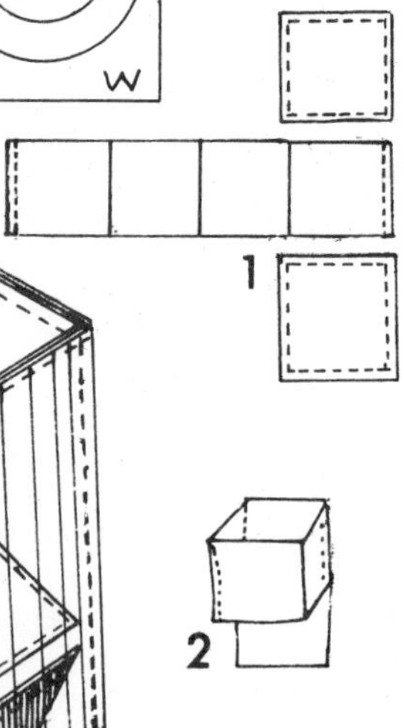
1
2
3

appliquéd symbols that correspond to the letters. On the last block, put X and Y together on one side. Z stands alone on the remaining side. *Note:* Sew all the appliqués before you assemble the blocks. They are as follows: A, apple; B, boat; C, carrot; D, doughnuts; E, egg; F, flower; G, grapes; H, house; I, ice cream; J, jar; K, kite; L, lollipop; M, mitten; N, note; O, orange; P, pear; Q, quarter; R, rocket; S, sun; T, top; U, umbrella; V, violin; W, watermelon. There are no appliqués for X, Y and Z.

DOLLHOUSE

For children who dream of running their own households a dollhouse is the perfect toy.

1. The house can be made either of plywood or of corrugated cardboard and assembled with 5-minute epoxy glue or another strong glue or cement. A cardboard house can be pasted together. You can use paper hinges for extra support on cardboard and angle irons on wood.
2. To plot the back of the house, start by drawing a 20-inch square. Measure 7 inches up from the center of the top of the square and mark this point.

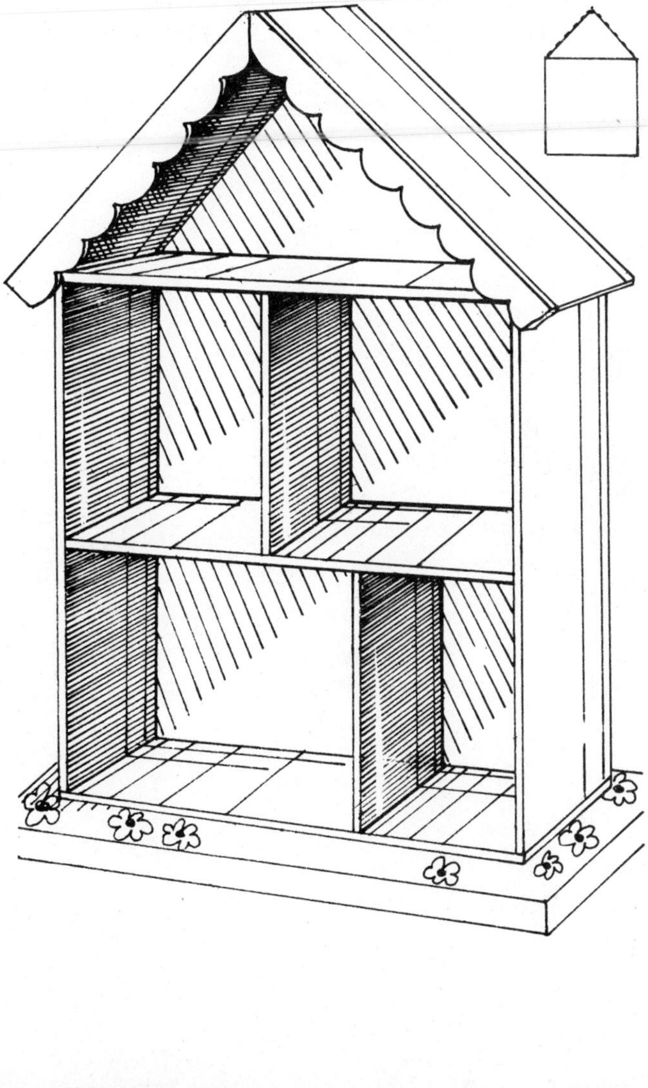

3. Connect this point with the top corners of the square and cut out the final shape.
4. Cut out all the other parts you'll need. All the sides of the house—the walls, floors and roof—are made from either 4-inch wide lattice or plywood or cardboard. Make the sides 20 inches long. Make the bottom of the house 20½ inches. Both sides of the roof are 13 inches long.
5. Glue the sides to the back of the house. Then add the bottom. Follow with the two sides of the roof.
6. Add all interior walls and floors as desired.
7. Add decorative molding along the roof.
8. Paint the house in whatever color you choose.
9. The house should be glued or nailed to a broad wooden base that has been painted green and dotted with painted flowers.

PUPPET THEATER AND PUPPETS

Interestingly enough, puppet theaters—as a children's plaything—are fairly new. Previously, the world of drama was exclusively the province of professionals. Children might see a puppet show when the puppet troupe came to town, but there were no theater-related toys until the beginning of this century. As it happens, the puppet theater may be one of the best teaching toys one could give a child.

1. The puppet theater can be made either of plywood or of corrugated cardboard and assembled with 5-minute epoxy glue or another strong glue or cement. A cardboard puppet theater can be pasted together. You can use paper hinges for extra support on cardboard and angle irons on wood.
2. To plot the triangular peak (at the top of the theater), start by drawing a rectangle 20 inches long and 3 inches high. Mark a point centered on the rectangle and measure 7 inches up. Connect this point with the top corners of the rectangle. Cut out the final peak shape.
3. The footlight board at the bottom of the theater is 20 x 3 inches. Cut this piece out of whatever material you're using.
4. Cut out all the other parts you'll need: the two side pieces are 20 x 4 inches. Use 4-inch wide lattice or cardboard or plywood. Both sides of the roof are 13 inches x 4 inches. The bottom floor of the stage is 20½ x 4 inches.
5. To assemble the stage, attach the sides to the footlight board and then the peak to the sides.

6. Add the bottom of the theater and two sides of the roof. Nail or glue the assembled theater to a wide bottom board.

7. The curtains are made from scrap fabric 14 inches long and 12 inches wide. You'll need two curtains. Hem the sides and bottom ½ inch. The top hem is sewn last. Make it one inch wide.

8. Thread heavy cord through the top hem of each curtain.

9. Pull the cord taut, and staple or nail the ends to each side of the peak on the inside of the theater.

10. Paint the theater with gay designs or decorate with decals.

STICK PUPPETS

1. Insert a dowel into a foam ball, a Ping-Pong ball or any other round item (even blown-out eggshells). Hold the head in place with glue.

2. Decorate the head with paint, bits of felt or yarn, or with a face cut out of a magazine.

3. Make the puppet's garment from a piece of gathered scrap fabric and secure it under the head with cord or glue.

HOLIDAY TIMES

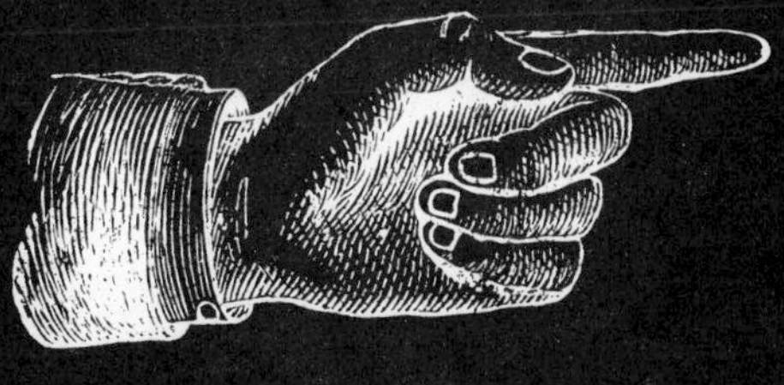

HOLIDAY TIMES

Th: Nast.

Sunday has been a sort of holiday for centuries—the day when the family sat around the dinner table and talked. The day on which all the aches and pains of the working week received their share of relief. In early America, people often went visiting on Sunday. Society was less mobile, and people had more time for each other, both on Sunday and on those special holidays that were times of joyful celebration.

Today Sunday may be a day of non-productivity for most of us, but the phrase "a day of rest" retains little of its original meaning. Few people now work a full six-day week, and fewer still perform chores that are absolutely essential for maintaining life. And we have become so transient a people, it takes a special occasion to bring most families together. Not all holidays have this effect, but there are three each year that do; first comes Valentine's Day, then Easter, and finally Christmas.

In America, we have exchanged love tokens on Valentine's Day since the arrival of the first settlers. Fond messages and love poetry would be sent on handmade cards, and such missives still occupy the postman every February. The heart-shaped box of candy soon became a standard gift, as a doubly appropriate symbol of the day: the heart for love, and the contents to promise sweets for the sweet. Today, of course, we give each other many other Valentine's presents as well.

Easter is probably the most sacred of all holidays for members of the Christian faith. One of the oldest Easter customs is exchanging the colored eggs that symbolize rebirth and Christ's resurrection. Children love this holiday, knowing that if they are good, the Easter rabbit will reward them with baskets of sweet things to eat. Although Easter is a short holiday, it is still a time when relatives can renew their acquaintance with each other and keep abreast of one another's news.

Christmas is surely the season most widely responsible for bringing people together. Like Easter, it has been celebrated in one form or another for almost two thousand years. During America's early days, the entire family took part in the preparation of the Christmas feast. If extra help was needed for any holiday project, the neighbors would be called in. People chopped down their own fir trees to put in the parlor or kitchen, and every decoration for the house and delicacy for the table was handmade. When everything was ready, the family would kneel down to worship and then sit down to dine.

Today most Christmas preparations are made

for us, and modern conveniences have reduced our labor to a minimum. All we really have to do is buy whatever we decide we need. Yet the family reunion, and the spirit of love that fills the air, are Christmas qualities that still remain in the happiest homes. We can increase the pleasure of Christmas—or Valentine's Day or Easter—by going back to some of the old ways, and undertaking craft projects that involve the whole family. Families can make the world a better place to live in, and special holidays help keep strong family ties alive.

SATIN SWEETHEART PILLOW

Satin pillows were part of the American parlor for many decades. Which of us cannot remember some aunt whose sofa boasted such a pillow with a view of Niagara Falls indelibly stamped on the front? This heart-shaped valentine pillow is a sentimental reminder of yesterday's forgotten sweethearts.

1. The size of the pillow is optional. Small hearts can be used as sachets or pincushions. Whatever the size, the fabric should be red bridal satin.
2. Fold a large sheet of paper in half. Draw half a heart on the fold. Cut out the half-heart shape and open the paper.
3. Now fold your fabric double, pin on the heart pattern, and cut out two shapes, one for each side of the pillow.
4. Using an embroidery hoop, stitch a simple message in the center of one fabric piece. Use the simplest running stitch, worked tightly. If you do not have a hand for embroidery, sew on flower patch appliques (sold at your local notions store or sewing counter).

5. Sew pre-gathered eyelet lace in the shape of a small heart around the embroidered message.
6. Place the two satin hearts together, right sides facing in. Sew them together ½ inch in from the edge, leaving a 3-inch section unsewn.
7. Slit the seams slightly at ½ inch intervals, taking care not to cut the stitching.
8. Turn the pillow right-side out and stuff with cotton, chip foam, or polyester.
9. Hand-sew the open seam closed.
10. Select beads in two sizes for the fringe. You may purchase these at sewing counters, or break up old necklaces. Buy a package of red embroidery thread. Separate the strands of embroidery thread into thicknesses appropriate for the size of the holes in the beads.
11. Thread a single length onto a needle. Knot the long end tightly, trimming off any thread that extends beyond the knot.
12. Thread a large bead followed by smaller beads. Sew the beaded lengths securely along the outer seam of the pillow, at regular intervals.

LACY VALENTINES

An old-fashioned valentine is the perfect setting for an intimate message to someone extra special.

1. Buy paper doilies. (They come in all sizes.

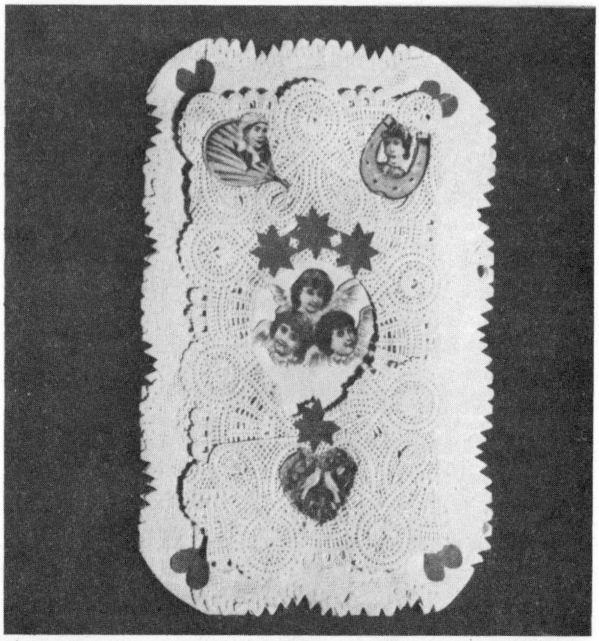

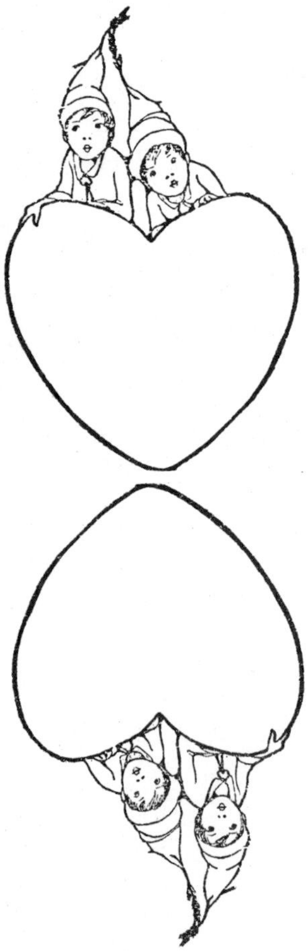

Larger ones can be cut down to the size and shape you wish.)

2. Cut out a piece of colored paper in the shape of a square or circle slightly larger than the doily. Tack on the doily by dabbing small spots of glue on the larger areas of the doily's underside.

3. Cut flowers from old greeting cards or flower seed catalogs.

4. Paste a flower (or flowers) to the center of the doily.

5. Cut small hearts from colored paper and paste them on the doily to compliment the central flower.

6. Write your message on the face or back of the card.

7. Make an envelope by folding a piece of paper over the valentine. Seal with the small paste-on hearts that can be bought at stationery counters.

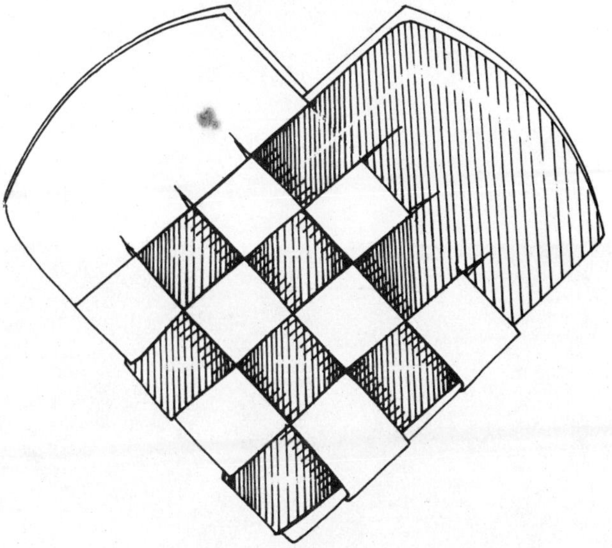

WOVEN HEART ENVELOPES

Originally made of leather for use as pen wipers, these woven heart cases were an attractive item on many early desks. With the advent of the modern pen, new uses for them had to be found. Since the heart is a classic symbol of love, why not transform this former leatherwork pattern into a fine envelope for your favorite valentine's card?

1. Cut two base shapes in contrasting colors. The base shape is a strip of colored paper folded in half. Trim the open ends in a curve (see diagram). The length of the paper should be 1½ times the width—2 inches x 3 inches, or 4 inches x 6 inches. The size is optional.

2. Cut an even number of slits into the folded edge, to a depth that is slightly longer than the width of the paper. Cut as many slits as you wish.

3. To weave the first row, slip slit 1 into slit A, slit A into slit 2, slit 3 into slit A, and slit A into slit 4.

4. To weave the second row, slip slit B into slit 1, slit 2 into slit B, slit B into slit 3, and slit 4 into slit B.

5. Row C follows the same weaving as row A, and row D follows row B.

6. Adjust the strips until they fit neatly.

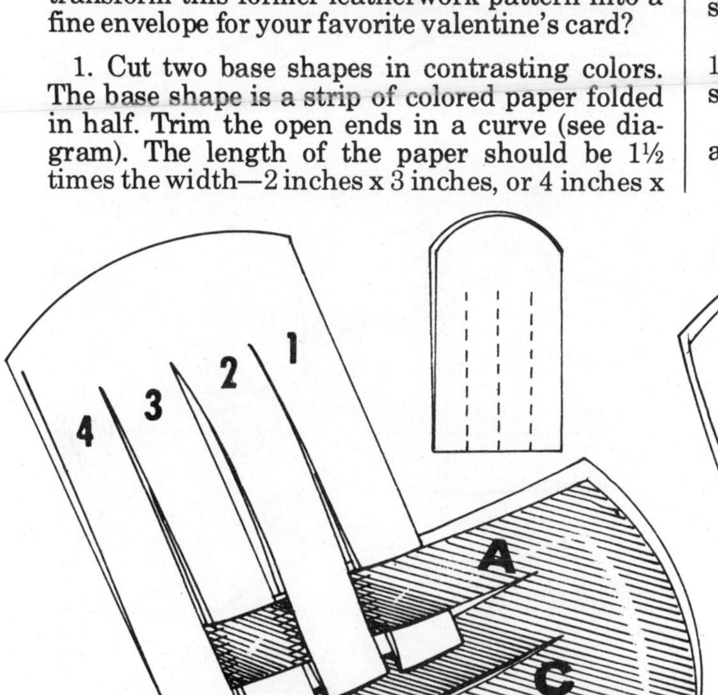

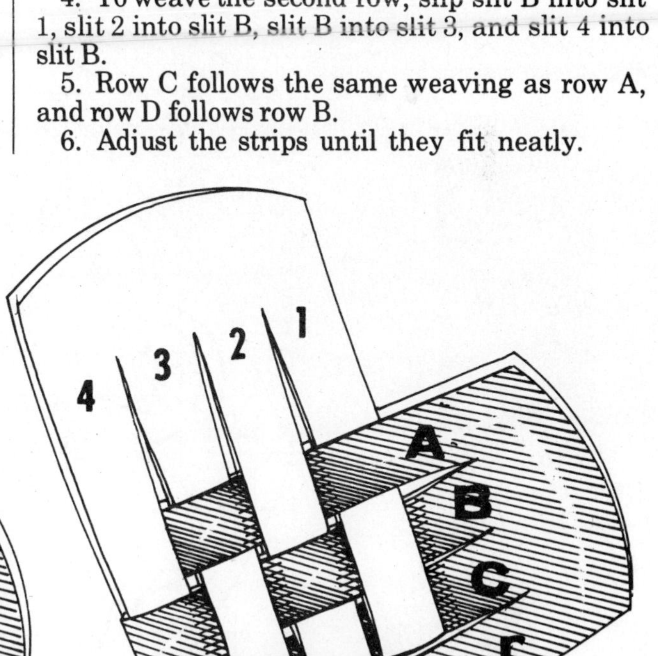

LOVE

To my Valentine

Love's Greeting
Some of the other girls expect Valentines.

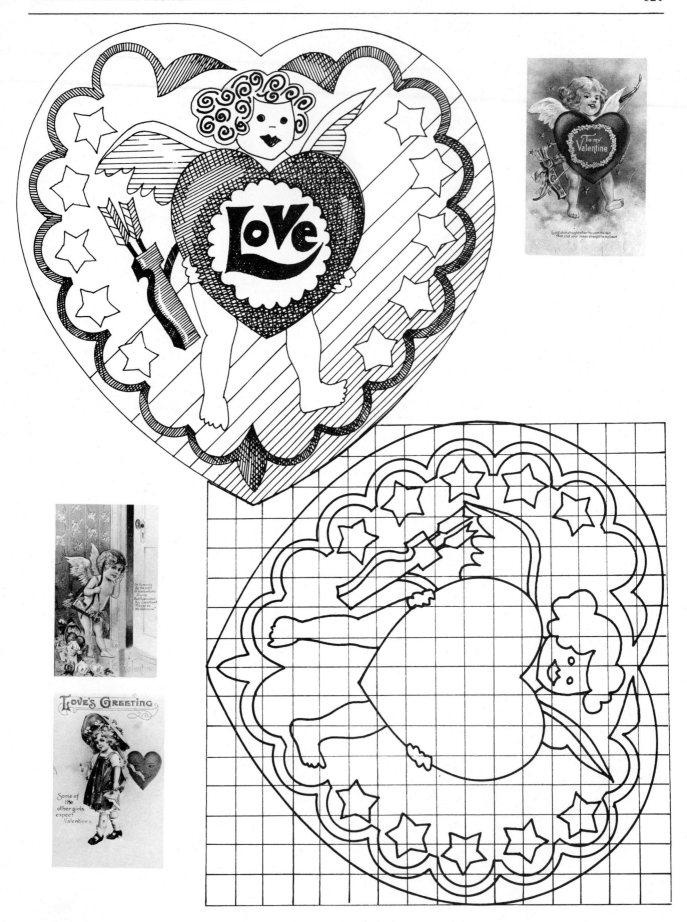

NEEDLEPOINT CUPID

This design was inspired by a valentine post card sent at the turn of the century. (Then it only cost a penny to mail.) Try the cupid in needlepoint.

1. Buy a piece of needlepoint canvas that will accommodate a 16-inch pillow.
2. Enlarge the grid and the design on your backing with an indelible fine-tip felt marker so that one square equals one inch. (See page 13 for detailed directions on how to enlarge a pattern from a grid.)
3. For colors, you may wish to follow the original card: a pink (or light brown) cupid, yellow hair, beige and white wings, red heart, gold center flower, red "LOVE," light blue background, gold stars, and dark blue scalloping. Cupid's arrows and case are in browns and oranges.
4. See the needlepoint section in the chapter **Spin a Yarn,** for further information.

HEART-SHAPED SCENT SACHET.

THESE pretty little sachets should be made by every lady, to be scattered through her drawers, so as to impart a general fragrance to the various articles of her wardrobe. The trouble is very slight, and the material no more than any trifling remnant of silk of the size shown in our illustration, and three-quarters of a yard of ribbon to form the bow. The little group of flowers which we have given is to be embroidered on the sides as slightly as possible; the two parts are to be laid face to face and stitched together, with accuracy, to their shape, leaving an opening at the top; after this they are to be turned and filled with fine cotton wool, impregnated with any perfume most agreeable to taste; after which the aperture is to be closed, and the rosette of ribbon laid upon the place. Ladies who are not inclined to undertake the embroidery may take any piece of fancy silk, or even such as are quite plain, and nake them up in the same way, without this decoration. These little sachets make pretty presents, and it has been with reference to this that the "Forget-me-not" has been selected for its embellishment.

SHADOW BOX EGGS

Remember as a child how intriguing those candy egg landscapes were?

1. To prepare an egg for the following crafts, see, Beaded Egg in **Baubles, Bangles and Beads.** If you plan to make a front-window egg, pierce an additional hole in the face of the egg.
2. For windows on the end of an egg, carefully enlarge the hole by chipping away bits of shell. For a front window, start to chip away the pinpoint hole made previously.
3. When you have formed the desired opening, gently sand the edges with extra-fine sandpaper.
4. Dye the eggs in egg dye or food coloring.
5. Gently blot dry.

HANGING EGG

1. Glue gold cord around the front window edge of the eggshell. Add a tassle.
2. Cut out a small oval Easter design from a greeting card. Glue it to the inside of the egg.
3. To hang, knot a length of thread on a small needle, insert the needle into the egg, and push it out through the smaller pinhole at the top of the egg.

LACY EGG

1. Glue pre-gathered lace around the opening of an egg.
2. Cut out a bunny, chicken or other Easter symbol from a greeting card. Leave extra paper on the bottom of each cutout.

3. Fold under the extra paper on each cutout and glue it to the inner floor of the eggshell.
4. Add Easter grass around the cutout.

CONFECTIONERY EGG

1. Decorate the outer shell with designs inscribed in icing. To make the icing, combine 3 egg whites (at room temperature), one pound confectioner's sugar, and ½ teaspoon cream of tartar in a clean bowl. Beat at high speed for 7 to 10 minutes. Warning: any touch of grease will break down the icing. The mixture will harden quickly, so work fast and keep the bowl covered with a damp cloth.

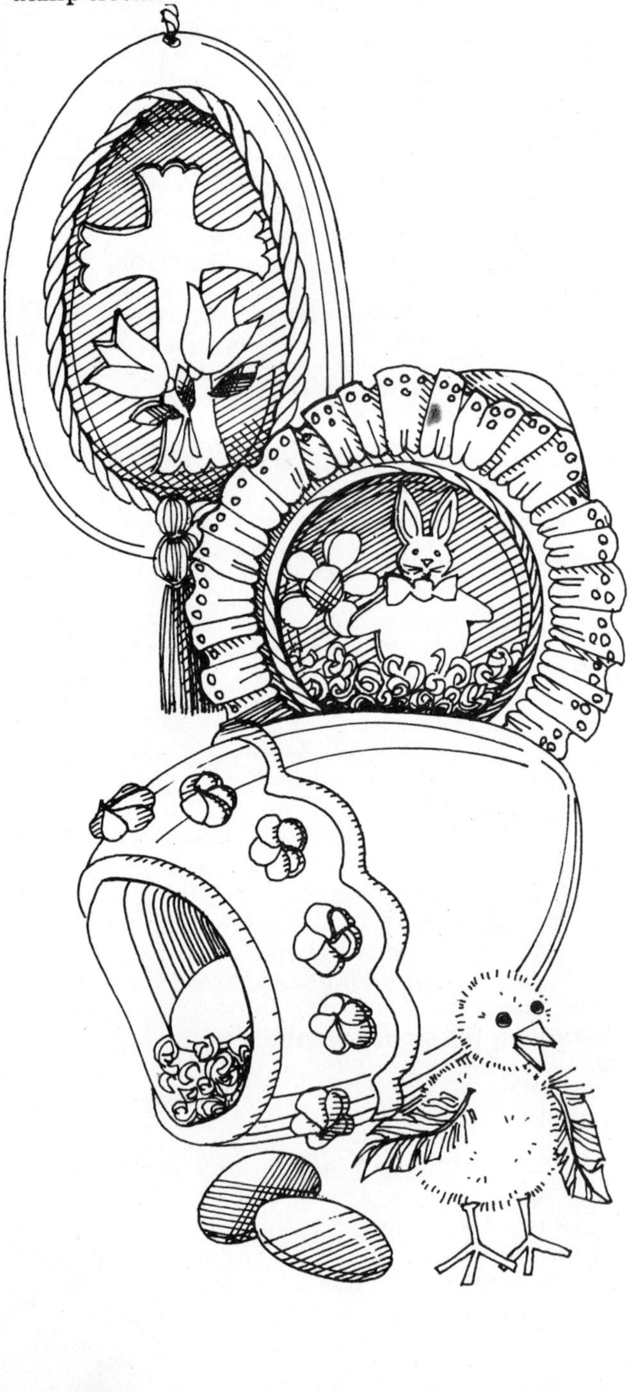

2. Fill an icing bag, with a decorative tip in place, and draw icing designs onto egg. Allow to harden.
3. Fill the egg with jelly beans and Easter grass.

BUNNY GO-CART

In the 1930s the bunny go-cart came close to replacing the Easter basket as a receptacle for all those good Easter sweets kids like to eat.

1. The exact-size pattern illustrated here shows one side of the bunny cart and the base. The second side of the cart is identical to the first.
2. Draw the pattern on a large sheet of tracing or lightweight paper. To make the second side, turn your tracing over and retrace only the bunny. Both bunny shapes should face the same direction.
3. Cut out your pattern along the heavy solid lines. The dotted lines are for folding. Trace the cart on heavy yellow paper (the oaktag type sold at art centers or stationery stores is good).
4. Cut out the slots on the sides of the bunny.
5. To assemble the bunny cart, fold both sides of the bunny and the sides of the base upward to form a box. Fit the tabs into the slots on the bunny's sides.
6. Punch holes in the tabs on the bunny's feet.
7. Cut four wheels from heavy cardboard (corrugated cardboard will work well). Cover the wheels with colored construction paper.
8. Punch a hole in the center of each wheel.
9. Push a drinking straw through the bottom tabs on each side of the cart.
10. Slip a wheel on both ends of each straw.
11. Glue a paper bow and a cheek, eye and inner ear of construction paper onto the bunny's head.

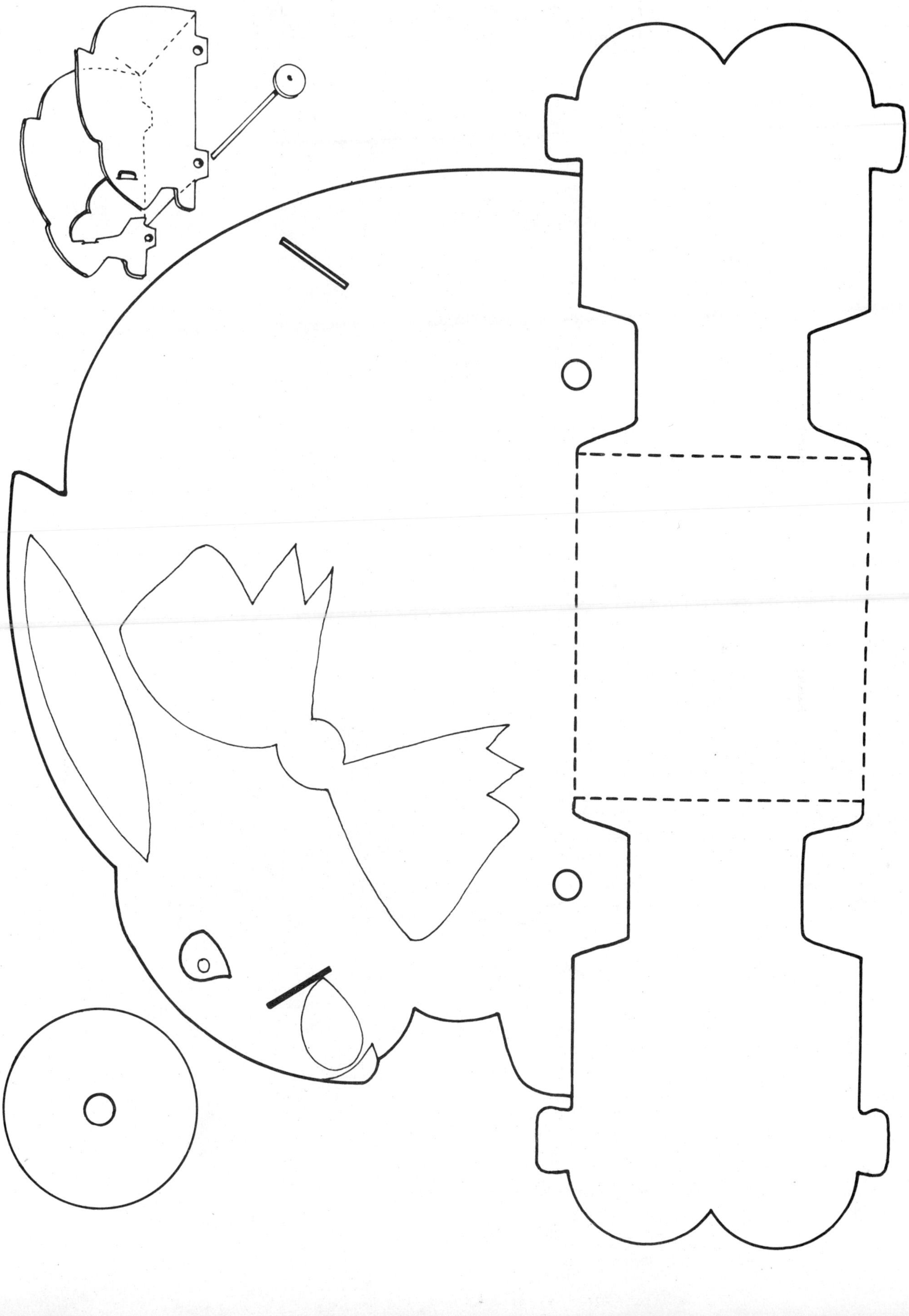

CHRISTMAS BEGINS WITH THE TREE

In the old days, stringing popcorn, looping garlands, and weaving wreaths used to keep whole families busy for weeks. Unfortunately, much of this Christmas magic is gone, and the commercial clamor of the season often drowns out quieter strains of joy. A blend of old and new in your tree decorations will help keep alive the best of the Christmas tradition.

CARD TRIMS

Back when printed matter was a scarce commodity, greeting cards were cut into ornaments and hung from the Christmas tree. It was a lovely idea and those sentimentalists who have saved Christmas cards from year to year should try it.

1. Cut a cardboard circle for a base.
2. Take an old Christmas card and cut out a scene (preferably one with an old-fashioned theme) to fit the cardboard.
3. Trim outer edge with decorative cords or ribbon and embellish with a fabric flower and/or tassel.

CONSTRUCTED BALLS

Another nice thing to do with old Christmas cards. This simple constructed ball makes a spectacular tree ornament. Its heyday was the forties.

1. Use a five and dime compass to draw 2-inch circles on last year's Christmas cards. Cut out 20 circles.
2. Form a triangle out of each circle by folding the outer edges toward the center in three even sections (see Fig. 1).
3. The center base of the ball is made of ten circles with their folded sides stapled together into a long band. To form this band, adjacent triangles at the center of each circle must face in opposite

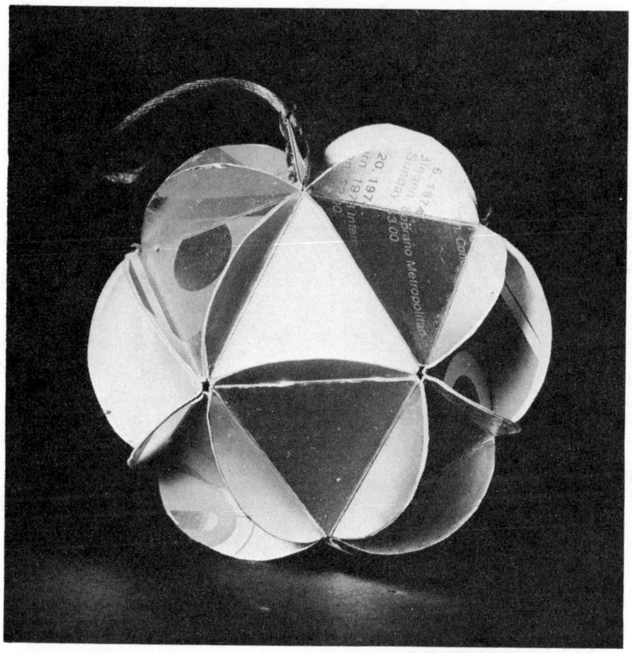

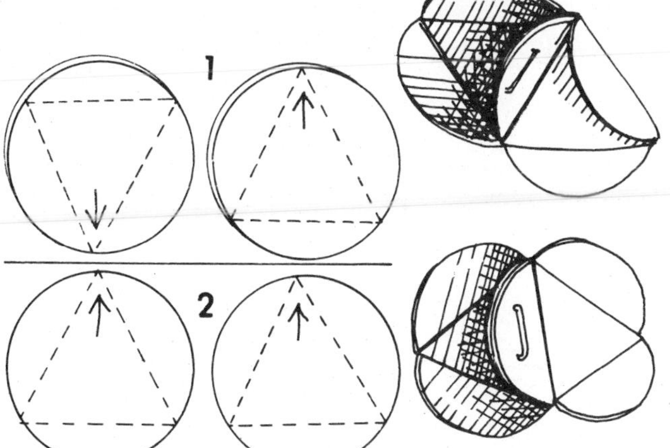

directions (as indicated by the arrows in Fig. 1).

4. Form this band into a circle and staple securely.

5. This center band will be flanked top and bottom with a cap of circles. To form each cap, staple 5 circles together, this time with the triangles facing in the same direction (see arrows in Fig. 2).

6. Staple each cap to the center band of circles.

JEWELED BALLS

(Shown in color, page 68)

This ornament is European in origin but has graced American Christmas trees since the turn of the century. It remains among the most popular tree ornaments being made in homes today.

1. The base of each ornament is a 4-inch foam

ball. (These can be purchased wherever Christmas decorations are sold.) Wind two lengths of satin ribbon around the ball so that they intersect each other and mark off four equal sections of foam. Pin the ribbons to the ball at the points where they cross and where the ends meet.

2. Next, you stud the surface of the ball with beads. The number needed will vary according to the size of bead you select. Any size will do, so long as a straight pin will fit through the bead's eye easily and without slipping. You might choose to thread each pin with a single large bead, layered with a sequin, or with a medium-sized bead followed by a tiny seed bead, or with any other combination that strikes your fancy.

3. Push the pinned beads into the foam ball along the edges of the ribbon. Then fill in the spaces between the ribbons, until all the foam is covered.

4. Cap the top and bottom of the ball with a hatpin pushed through a fancy button or a bit of old jewelry.

5. Hang the ball by tying a loop of beading wire or a thin cord around the uppermost pin.

CONES AND CHAINS

(Shown in color, page 165)

This simple construction of colored paper is a favorite Christmas project with children of all ages, in all parts of the country.

1. To form each cone, roll colored construction paper into a cone shape and tape or staple securely.

2. Trim the top edge, and scallop or wedge. Punch holes for a lacy effect.

3. Make a handle from a strip of paper and decorate in similar fashion. Staple to the inside of the cone. Add bows or felt-marker designs.

4. To form the chains, cut 1 x 5-inch strips of colored construction paper and punch decorative holes along their length. Paste or glue the first strip into a circle. Insert the next strip into the first circle and glue so that it too forms a circle. Continue this process until you have a long chain.

5. The chain can be draped about the tree and the cones filled with candy and hung from branches.

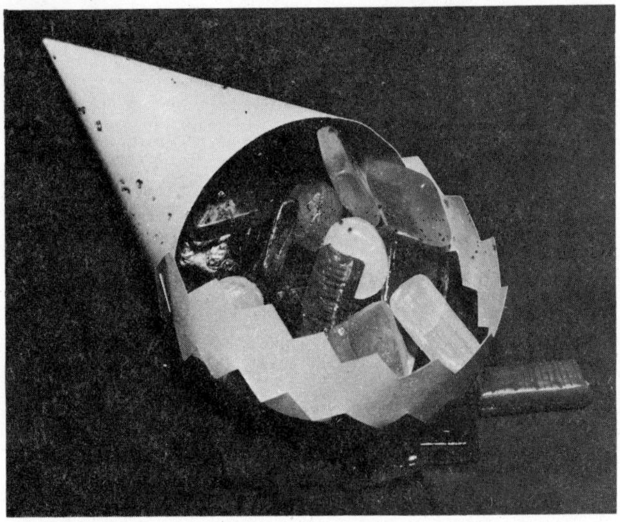

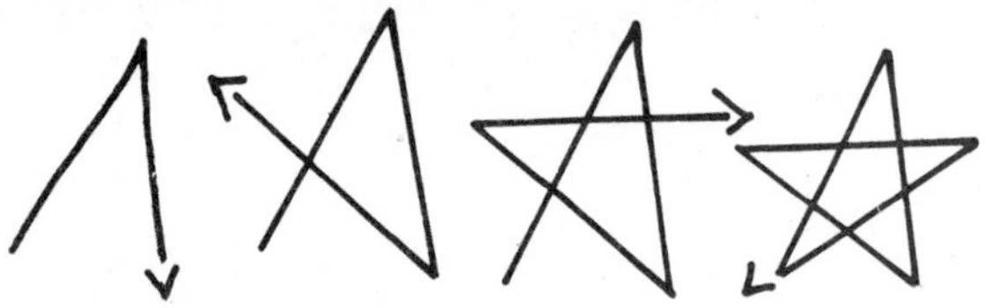

BEADED STAR

(Shown in color, page 68)

Today, plastic ornaments have replaced the more fragile and delicate ones, and people forget the things that once were. Beads brighten any tree—catch light, are all warmth and shimmer. Stars are particularly nice and here is an easy way to make them.

1. String small iridescent beads on a piece of thin florist's wire, 21 inches long.
2. Make slight bends in the wire at 4-inch intervals.
3. Curve the bent wire so that the 4-inch sections form a star shape, as indicated in the diagram. Twist the loose ends together.
4. Make a second star in the same way.
5. Attach the two stars with two wired beads connecting each point.
6. Wire larger beads into the point areas.

POMANDER BALLS

Certain smells pervade the air during the Christmas season: pine and bayberry, and perhaps the aroma of sugar cookies baking, or the fainter scent of citrus and brandy escaping from a fruit-cake tin. Years ago a common fragrance was the delicate perfume of the pomander ball. This ornament is a cook's delight, for fruit and

spices are the prime ingredients. You will need cloves, ground cinnamon, and a thick-skinned lime, lemon, or orange. Begin early; the ball takes several weeks to ripen to perfection.

1. Wash a lime, lemon, or orange and dry thoroughly.
2. Using a skewer to start holes, insert whole cloves in the skin of the fruit, covering the entire surface.
3. Put a heaping teaspoon of cinnamon in a small bag along with one of the fruits. Shake the bag to coat the fruit well.
4. Wrap each fruit loosely or place it with others on a foil covered tray.
5. Store in a dry place until the fruit shrinks and hardens. This should take three to four weeks.
6. Tie the pomander ball with colored ribbon and hang.

CITRUS TREE

This decoration can be eaten when it comes time to put the Christmas ornaments away.

1. The base of the tree is a large grapefruit.
2. Use toothpicks to attach oranges and pomander balls to the grapefruit.
3. Begin to form a tower by adding circles of oranges and pomander balls in decreasing numbers. Hold the tree together with toothpicks.
4. Lavish the top pomander ball with a fruit bow.
5. The tree will hold for three weeks. After Christmas, make a giant fruit salad.

CALICO TREE

There is no happier fabric than calico. Its simple pioneer charm is captured in the layered skirts of this patchwork Christmas tree.

1. Roll oaktag (sold at stationery stores) into a cone. The width and height of the cone is optional. Staple or tape the cone securely.
2. Trim the base of the cone so that it stands straight and firm.
3. Cut the first strip of fabric with pinking shears, to avoid hemming. If you do not own pinking shears, machine hem the length of cloth on one side. Gather the opposite side until it just fits around the base of the cone.
4. Pin the layer so the pinked or hemmed edge falls at the base of the cone. Trim any excess fabric after pinning.
5. Make the next layer in the same way and pin it to the cone so that it overlaps the first layer slightly.

6. Repeat the layering process until you reach the peak of the cone.
7. Top with a starburst of gathered fabric.

SANTA'S WORKSHOP BANNER

This Santa's workshop banner comes to you directly from a 1920's mail-order house special Christmas catalog. Kids will love it.

1. The banner base and the background for Santa are both constructed of felt. Buy ½ yard for each. The smaller appliqués can be cut from felt sold by the piece.
2. To make patterns for the appliqués, enlarge the grid on drawing or typing paper so that one square equals one inch. Then draw the appliqués on the enlarged grid. (See page 13 for detailed directions on how to enlarge patterns from a grid.)
3. Cut out the patterns, pin to the felt, and cut the fabric.
4. The color and pattern identifications are as follows: 1. Background: beige; 2. Santa's face: pink or brown (cut along the dotted line); 3. Santa's beard: white; 4. Mouth: red; 5. Mustache: white; 6. & 7. Nose and cheek: pink; 8. Eyes: black; 9. Eyebrows; white; 10. Sleeve: red; 11. Sleeve details: brown; 12. Cuff: white; 13. Hand: pink or brown; 14. Boat: green; 15. Sails: white; 16. Flag: green; 17. Cabin with window: yellow; 18. & 19. Boat and roof: red; 20. Dress: light blue; 21. & 22. Bow and cuffs: orange; 23. Hands: pink or brown; 24. Hat: orange; 25. Face: pink or brown; 26. Hair: yellow; 27. & 28. Lollipop and candy cane: red and white.
5. The base fabric is white felt about 13 inches wide and 32 inches long, or larger if you prefer. Cut the bottom edge into a point.
6. Pin all the cut appliqués to the base fabric following the illustration.
7. Glue on the appliqués with white glue. Those who are more ambitious may wish to sew them on instead.
8. Stitch a length of folded felt to the top corners of the banner, to form loops.
9. Sew a ball fringe along the pointed bottom edge.
10. To hang, slip a one-inch dowel, cut a little longer than the banner's width, through the top loops. Suspend by looping a ribbon around the dowel.

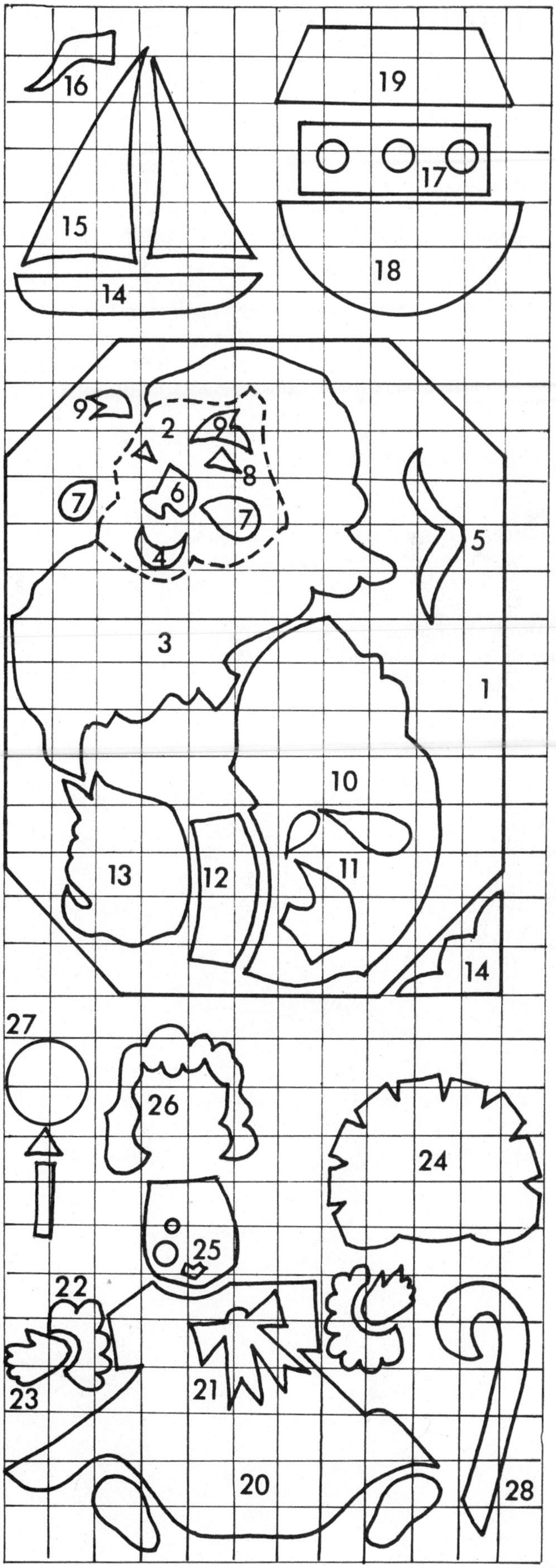
16
19
17
15
18
14
9
2
9
8
7
6
7
4
5
3
1
10
13
12
11
14
27
26
24
25
22
23
21
20
28

CORNHUSK WREATH

These wreaths were popular in pioneer days, and there will always be something very American about them. At holiday time, drive along rural back roads and you may see a few around.

1. During the corn season, remove the husk (the leafy casing) from several ears of corn. Stack the leaves in loose bundles and tie them just tight enough to hold in place.
2. Keep the stacks in a dry spot in the house, such as a closet or attic. Store until you are ready to make the wreath.
3. Cut sheets of husk into strips one-inch wide.
4. Loop five or six of these strips in bow-like fashion and tie them together at the center with heavy beading wire or lightweight florist's wire. Make dozens of clusters.
5. The base of the wreath is a 12-inch foam circle, which can be purchased at five-and-dime stores during the Christmas season.
6. Push the wires through the wreath.
7. Tie each pair of wires together on the back side of the wreath. Trim up to one inch of wire. Push the remaining inch back into the foam.
8. For a color accent spray-paint some of the clusters red before attaching.
9. Add a thick red satin or velvet bow.

TREE BLANKET

Back in the days when candles burned on Christmas trees, the tree blanket was used to protect floors from melting wax.

1. The blanket is best made in felt, and will last generations. Felt comes in 70-inch widths, so two yards will suffice to give you a generous blanket. Other sturdy fabrics can also be used.
2. If the fabric has a crease, steam press it out before plotting the circle.
3. To plot the circle, first locate and mark with a pin the center of the felt. Use a yardstick to measure out equal distances (34 or 35 inches) in all directions from the center. Mark your own measurements with straight pins. The more measurements taken, the more accurate the circle.
4. Cut out the circle.
5. Cut a straight slit from the edge of the circle to the center mark.
6. Cut out a circle at least 4 inches wide in the center.
7. Felt does not require hemming. For all other fabrics, hem all raw edges ¼ inch.
8. The ornamental appliqués should also be made of felt. The design is quite simple. Each figure consists of a large circle topped with a smaller one. An even smaller circle is then placed below

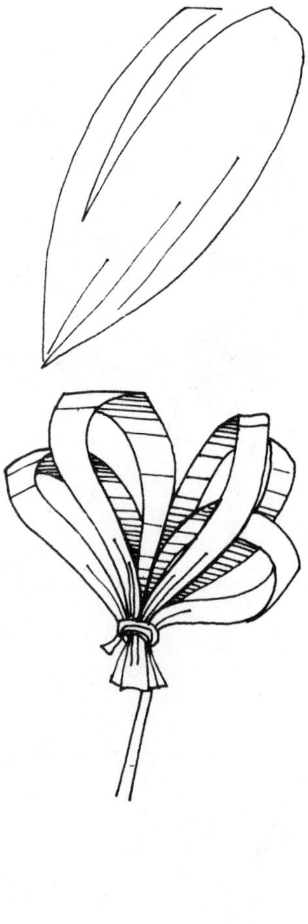

the main circle, followed by a triangle. Above the large circle is another triangle, with its top peak snipped off. Finish with a very small circle at the uppermost point.

9. Chains of small circles go all the way around the blanket, linking one figure to the next.

10. Pin all felt appliqués in place.

11. Glue on the appliqués with white glue or machine-stitch down.

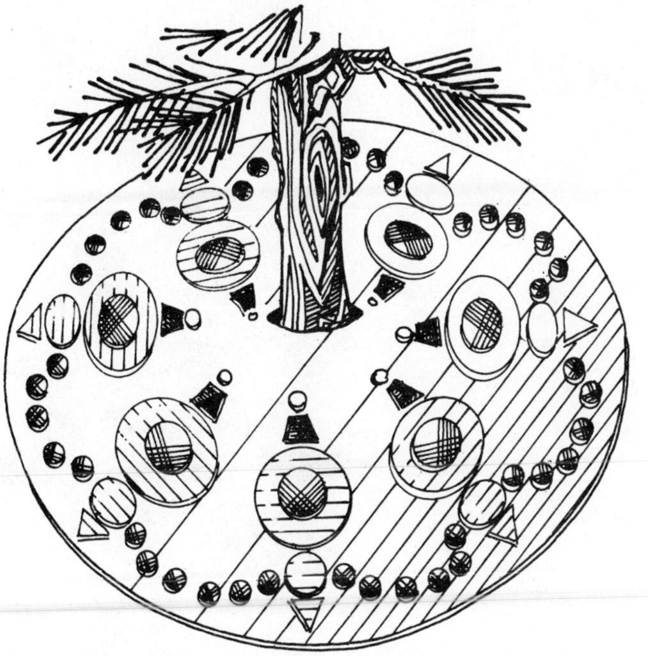

THE TIMELESS GINGERBREAD HOUSE

This truly admirable concoction is not edible. (It will last forever.)

1. The patterns for the house should be mapped out on cardboard.
2. Draw a 9 x 6½-inch rectangle on a large piece of cardboard.
3. Center a 6-inch measurement on the bottom of the 9-inch side (see Fig. 1), and connect the top corners of the rectangle to the 6-inch measurements, as shown.
4. Center a point 5½ inches up from the top of the rectangle and mark it.
5. Connect this point to the top corners of the rectangle (Fig. 2). You now have the pattern for the front and back of the house.
6. The sides of the house form a rectangle 6¾ inches high and 7 inches wide. The roof is 7¼ inches high and 7 inches wide.
7. Cut out the patterns from cardboard.
8. To make your clay, mix together 2 cups cornstarch, 4 cups baking soda, and 2½ cups cold water.
9. Cook these ingredients in a saucepan over medium heat for 4 minutes, stirring constantly. The mixture should resemble mashed potatoes.
10. Remove from heat and cover with a damp cloth until cool.
11. Knead the clay as you would bread dough.
12. Roll out the clay to a thickness of ¼ inch.
13. Use the cardboard patterns to cut two pieces of dough in each shape.
14. Cut out simple shutters, windows, a cookie, two candy canes, and a door.
15. Add design details by rolling out the dough in thin strips. Trim the windows with crosses or panes, and make an inner door and stripes for the candy canes. The shingles on the roof are also made of rolled dough. Gently press all these details into the sheets of dough that form the house.
16. When dry (about twenty-four hours later), glue the sides together with bond cement or epoxy. When bonded, glue on the roof.
17. The candy cane circles are candy wafers with swirls of red drawn on with an indelible felt-tip marker. (The wrapped peppermint candy circles available at this time of year will not last.)
18. Paint the house with poster paints.
19. For a look of gingerbread without painting, tint the dough with brown food coloring, dye, or cocoa before rolling it out.

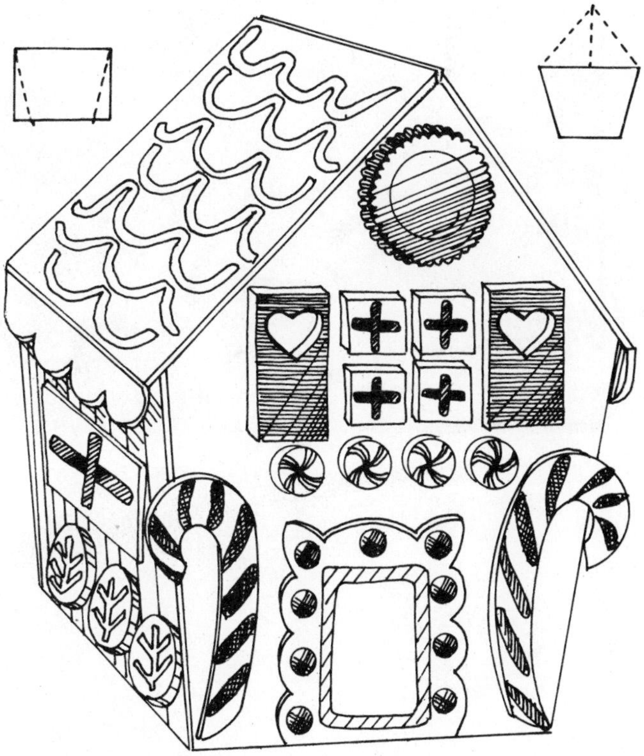

PINE CONE ELVES

(Shown in color, page 68)

The versatile, wonderful pine cone transformed into kindly creatures to live in your gingerbread house.

1. Collect small pine cones. Paint the tips with white paint. Sprinkle on salt or glitter for a snow-like shimmer.
2. Glue two beads to the center of a white circle of heavy cardboard.
3. Glue the tip of the pine cone to the beads. (Cut off part of the cone's tip if necessary.) This is the elf's body.
4. The head can be made from either a one-inch foam ball, a large bead, or an acorn.
5. For arms, wrap a colored pipe cleaner around the head so that it extends evenly on both sides.
6. Add a felt or fur beard and a paper or felt cone cane. If the head is a bead or acorn, paint on facial features. If you used a foam ball, make a face from pins with colored heads.
7. Glue paper cymbals, a pipe cleaner horn, or a rolled paper lantern to the elf's hands.

[redacted]

The Patchwork Story

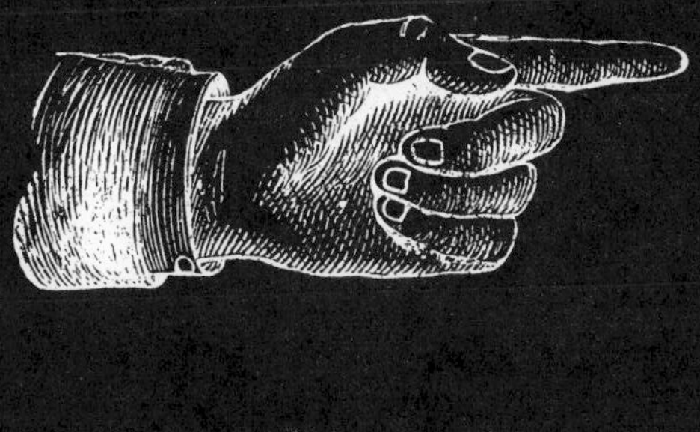

The Patchwork Story

Patchwork quilts are as seductive as kaleidoscopes—the wondrous colors and symmetrical designs, the magical things that happen when bits and pieces of fabric are tossed together.

This art was born of necessity. The first settlers in this country found life a good deal harder than they'd anticipated. The winters were cold, the deprivations many, their supplies short. As the quilts they had brought with them from the Old World began to wear out, there was no way of replacing them. No new material could be obtained. Women were obliged to patch them, and their clothing, as best they could. When an entirely new blanket was needed, pioneer women would piece together scraps into a solid fabric and stuff two lengths of it with straw or twigs or another stuffing to provide insulation and warmth. This was the first patchwork quilt.

As life became less harried for the settlers, you could see the difference in their quilts. Patches were more neatly cut and less randomly positioned. Geometric patterns began to emerge. Patchwork became one of the few artistic outlets available to these hardworking women. If you catch a quilt show at a local museum or have an heirloom quilt that's been passed on to you from another generation, you can see yourself the time and love that was devoted to them. Symbolic designs reflecting the occurrences and concerns of everyday life—log cabins and sunbursts, lilies and wild geese—became quilt motifs with the birth, settlement, expansion and struggle of the new nation woven into every swatch, snip and stitch.

THE TWO BASIC SQUARES

This chapter is a simple guide to the basics. The intention is to give you the hang of it—the elements that once understood enable you to create not just your own quilts, but your own designs. Read the first half of the chapter through before beginning.

The idea is to attach multi-square patchwork blocks to one another to form a fabric. The multi-square blocks can be pieced together from full squares or diagonal squares (squares made from two triangles). In this chapter, squares and diagonal squares measure 3 inches square. Fabric is cut to 3½ inches square to allow for ¼-inch seams on all sides.

The full square and half of the diagonal square are shown here actual size. The dotted line is your cutting line and the solid line is the size of the sewn square. Note that the diagonal square is

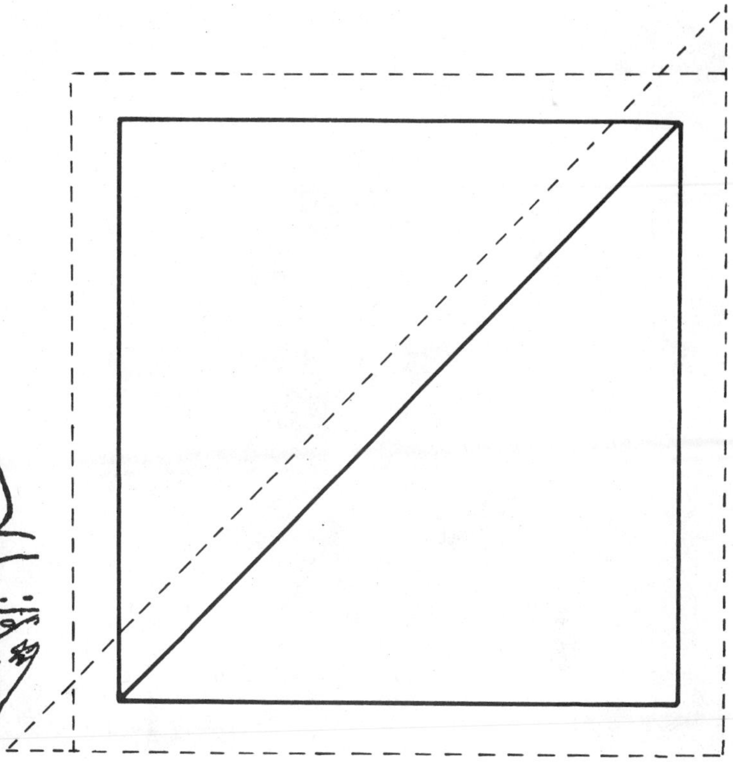

made from two triangles that are pieced together, right sides facing. Stitching the two triangles together along the diagonal with a ¼-inch seam will give you a 3½-inch square—3 inches when hemmed.

When assembling your squares into a patchwork block there are two important rules which you must follow to the letter. First, always cut your fabric exactly to the fraction of an inch specified. Second, take pains to make all seams exactly ¼-inch wide. Precise cutting and sewing will assure that all your finished squares match each other perfectly.

To make patterns for the above squares, carefully trace the full square and the half of the diagonal square along the dotted line. (The patterns are superimposed here so naturally you must draw each one separately.) Glue the tracings on cardboard and cut out the shapes. With a soft pencil trace the cardboard pattern you are using directly onto the wrong side of your fabric. To save time, you may pin several layers of fabric together and cut the patches simultaneously. In this case, however, you must be doubly sure to cut the pattern with meticulous care.

In choosing fabric for patchwork, it is a good idea to use odds and ends salvaged from your sewing projects, as well as worn or outdated clothing. The only rule of thumb is to select fabrics that are similar both in weight and in washing instructions. (Don't mix heavy wool with lightweight cotton, or washable fabrics with materials that should be dry-cleaned.) You *can* mix either solids with prints or different prints with each other. The diagonal square works best when the contrast between the two triangles is clearly marked.

Although a motif can be designed with as few as four assembled squares, we have chosen to start with the nine-square motif. The larger the assembled motif, the more design possibilities you have. The nine-square motif comprises three squares placed in a horizontal direction and three on the vertical. If you add one more square going across and another going down you will be working the sixteen-square motif. (To determine the total number of squares needed for a motif, simply multiply the number of horizontal squares by the number of vertical ones.) The most versatile arrangement uses thirty-six squares—six across and six down. This motif will be discussed at length later in the chapter.

HOW TO DESIGN AND ASSEMBLE A MOTIF

The following designs represent no more than the tip of the iceberg; there are literally thousands of motifs among which you can choose.

1. Invest in a small pad of colored construction paper at your local five-and-ten to use in making your design.
2. Cut out 3-inch paper squares in different colors.
3. Cut about one-third of the squares in half along the diagonal.
4. Tape contrasting triangles together to form complete squares.
5. On a table, begin to arrange full squares and diagonal squares in a specific pattern.
6. First try designing a nine-square motif, building with three squares across and three down.
7. Once you have mastered the nine-square motif, move on to a larger motif.
8. When you have arrived at the design you wish to use, tape the squares together to form a permanent pattern which you can refer to as you work.
9. Cut the required number of full and diagonal squares from cloth, following the method described in the preceding section. Stitch triangles together to form diagonal squares before you begin to assemble each motif. Remember to make all your seams exactly ¼-inch wide.
10. Press open the seams on every diagonal half-square.
11. Sew the squares in the top row together, right sides facing. Then sew together the squares in the remaining rows, working down from the top. Reassemble the motif on the table.
12. Pin the top row and second row from the top together. If the corners do not match, make the necessary adjustments at this time. When the two rows are lined up exactly, corner to corner, sew them together.
13. Follow with the remaining row or rows.
14. Press all seams open and flat.

THE NINE-SQUARE MOTIF

The nine-square motif has three squares across and three down. Designs formed with this motif are simple and bold. The total size of each completed motif will measure 9½ inches on a side.

Pattern 1. Place diagonal squares made of two contrasting fabrics on each corner. The same fabric always faces in. Complete the motif with five full squares as shown in Fig. 1.

Pattern 2. This one's harder to explain than do. Note (Fig. 2) that only one full square is used.

Pattern 3. In this motif, six identical diagonal squares—three in the top row, two in the middle row, and one in the bottom row—face in the same direction. The diagonal squares in the middle and third row are of the same fabric but arranged differently. A full square in a contrasting fabric occupies the lower left-hand corner.

Pattern 4. The center square of this motif and the four corner squares are full. The four remaining squares are diagonals arranged with two facing upwards and two facing down.

If you study these nine-square motifs carefully, you will be able to figure out the construction of the more complex motifs that follow.

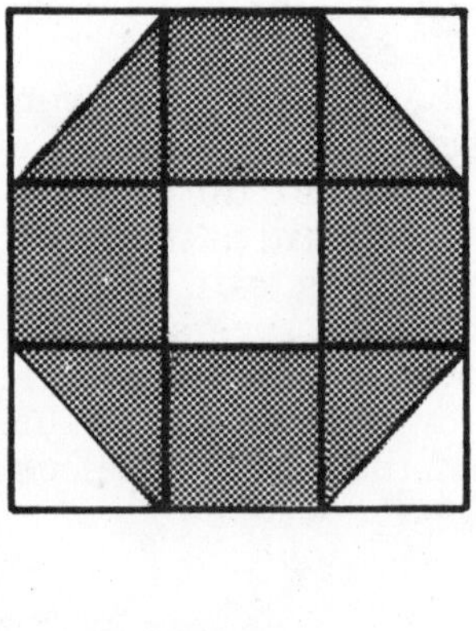
1

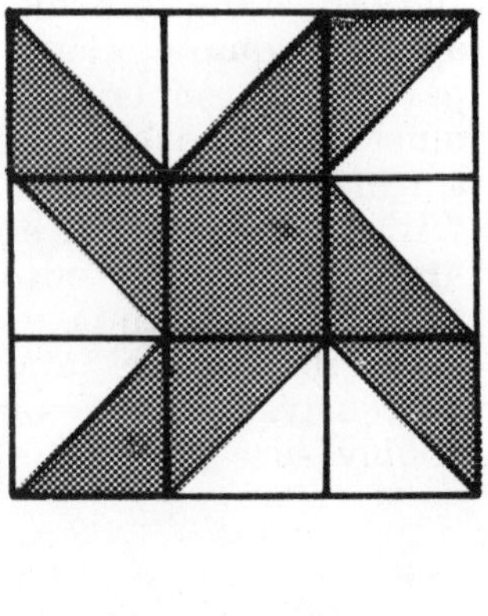
2

3
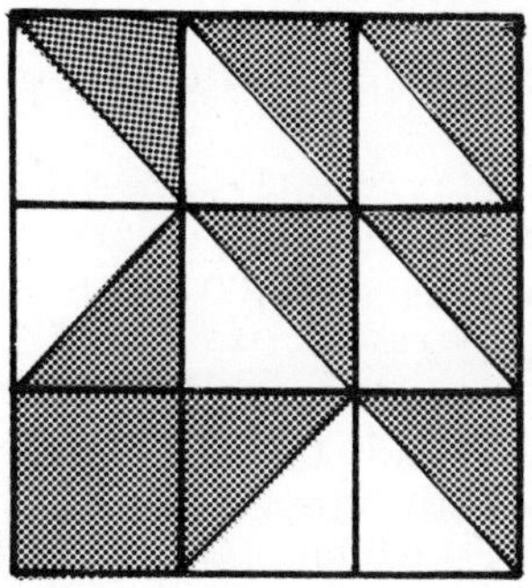
4
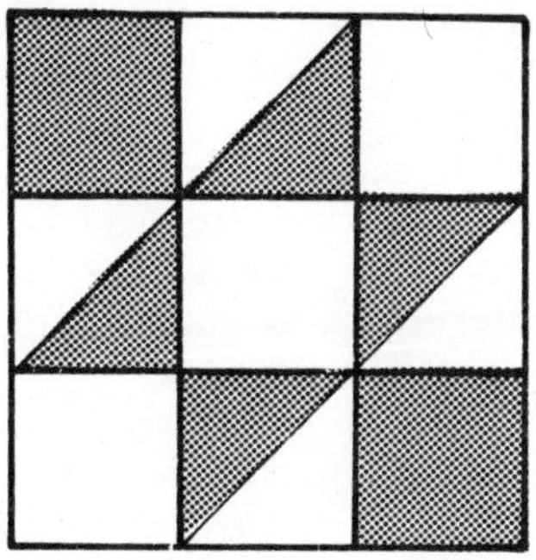

THE SIXTEEN-SQUARE MOTIF

The sixteen-square motif has four squares across and four squares down. The total size of each completed motif will be 12½ inches on a side. All the designs shown here are symmetrical, except the second one. If you divide any of these motifs visually into four equal sections or quadrants, each section containing four squares, you will be able to see the plan of each pattern more clearly.

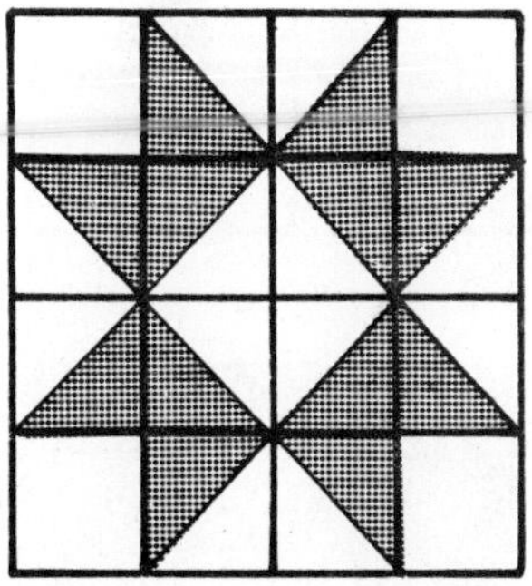
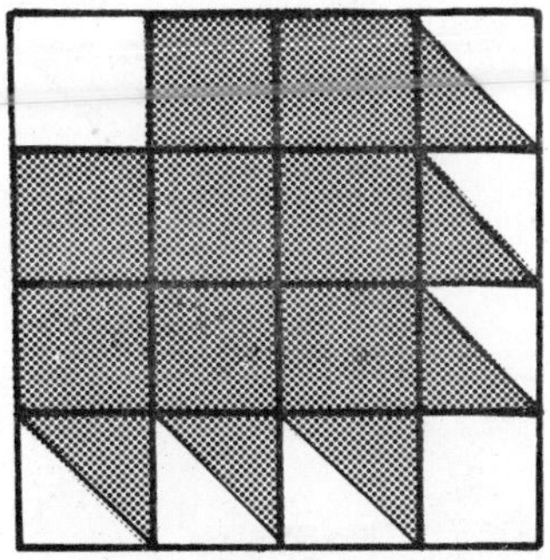
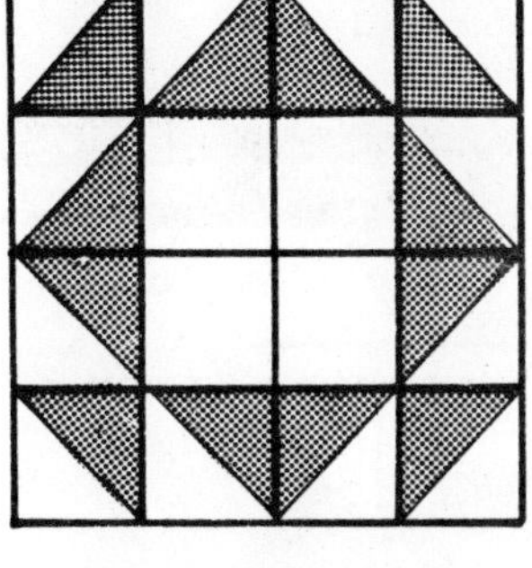
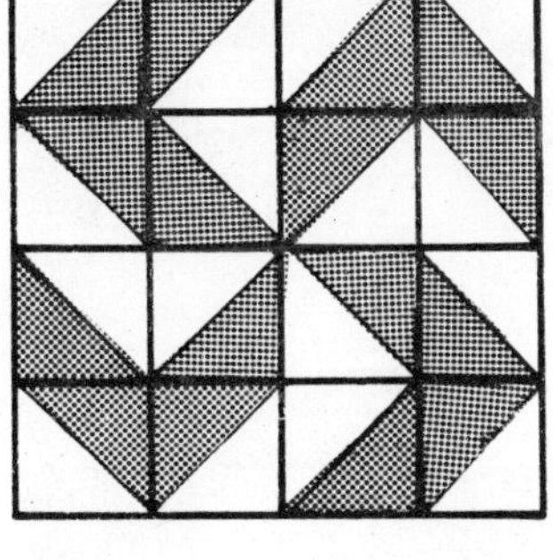

THE TWENTY-FIVE-SQUARE MOTIF

The twenty-five-square motif has five squares across and five squares down. The total size of each completed motif will be 15½ inches on a side.

As the number of squares increases in a motif, the designs can become more intricate. Many motifs can be built around a single center square, using various symmetrical arrangements of full and diagonal squares. Note, however, that the second motif from the left in the top row uses no diagonal squares. In the first and last patterns in the bottom row the role of the central square in the design is less evident at first glance.

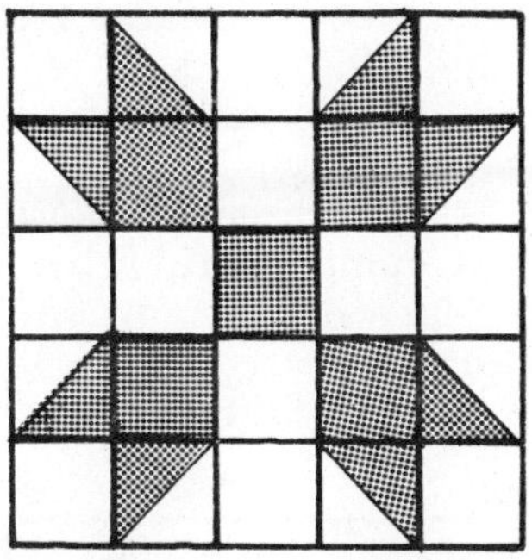
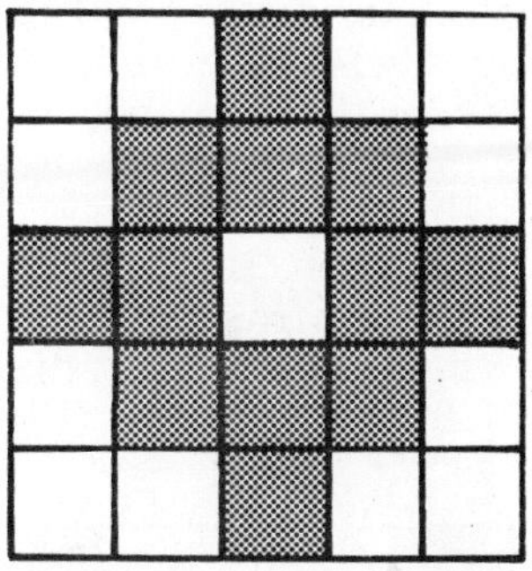
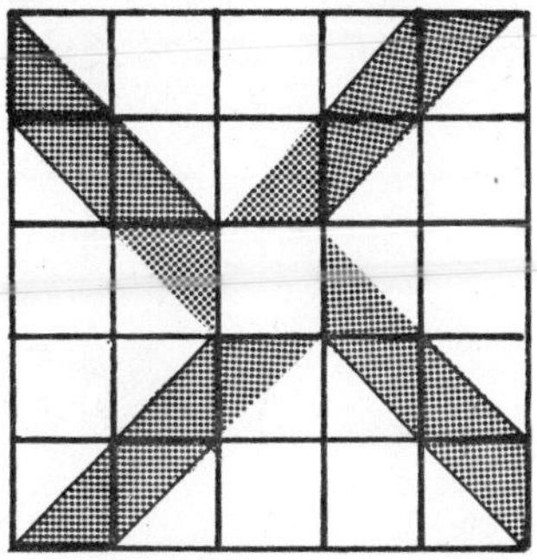
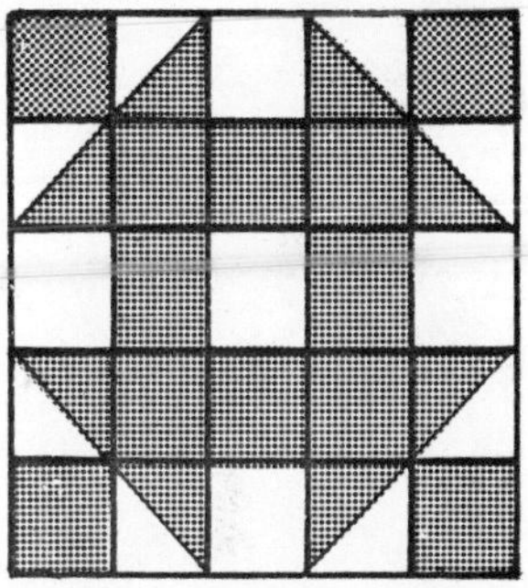
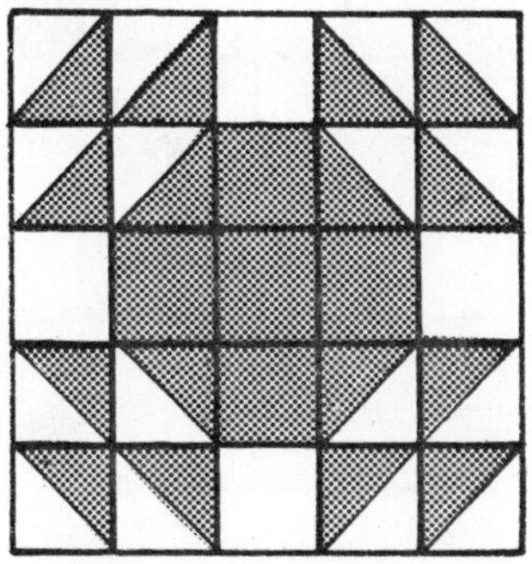
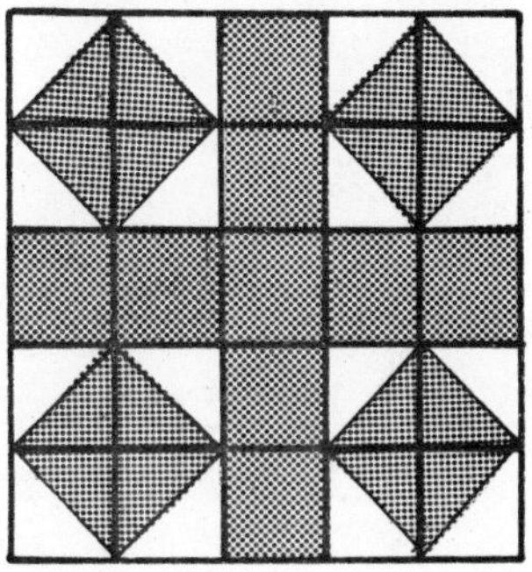
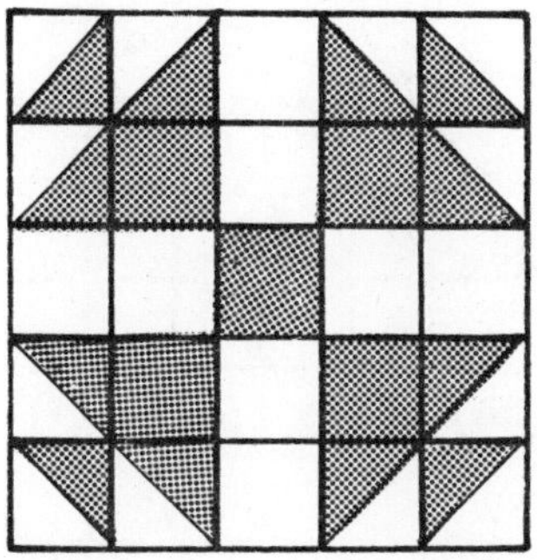
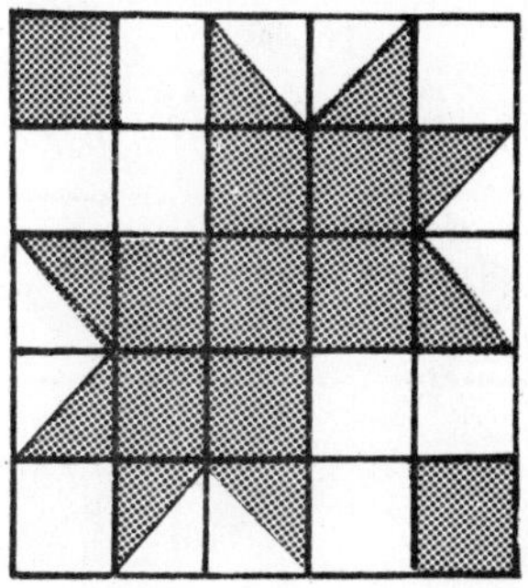

THE THIRTY-SIX-SQUARE MOTIF

The thirty-six-square motif is the one most frequently used. It has six squares across and six squares down measuring 18½ inches on a side.

Now that you have acquired an understanding of how patchwork motifs are planned, we can use the thirty-six-square type to show you how to alter the total look of a design by shifting the position of a few component squares.

In the first row (Fig. 1), four bold designs are created with full squares and diagonal squares. These designs are worked in two contrasting fabrics.

In row two (Fig. 2), the designs directly above have been changed simply by using a third fabric in a contrasting color in place of some of the original full and/or diagonal squares.

In the third row (Fig. 3), a third fabric is used again to vary the basic designs in the top row. This time diagonal squares are substituted for full squares.

The eight variations on a star (Fig. 4) offer still more dramatic proof that changes in color or minor rearrangements of the basic squares in a design can make the appearance of a motif totally different.

Although the full square and the diagonal square should provide you with enough designs to last a lifetime, there are three other basic patchwork squares—the half square, the three-quarter square and the diagonal three-quarter square—that will enlarge your repertoire immensely. These squares can be worked into a motif using only the full square, or they can be added to designs which incorporate both the full and diagonal square. To create designs which include one of the following units, make 3-inch squares of construction paper and add them to

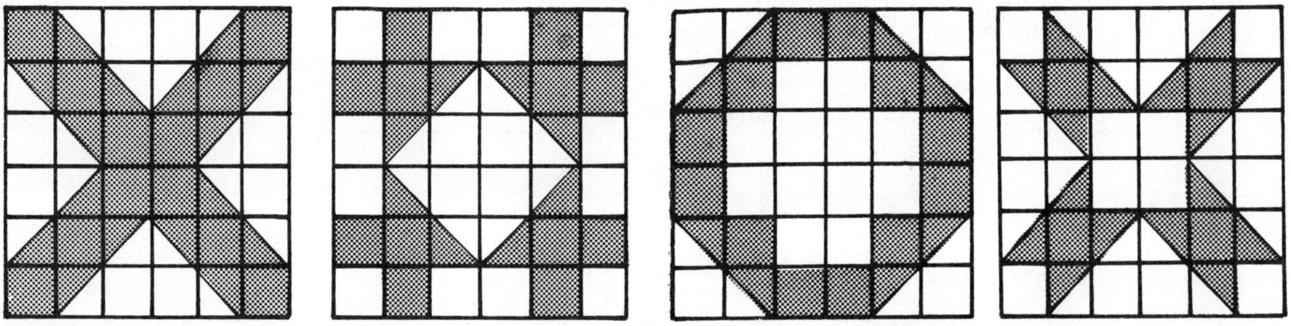

1

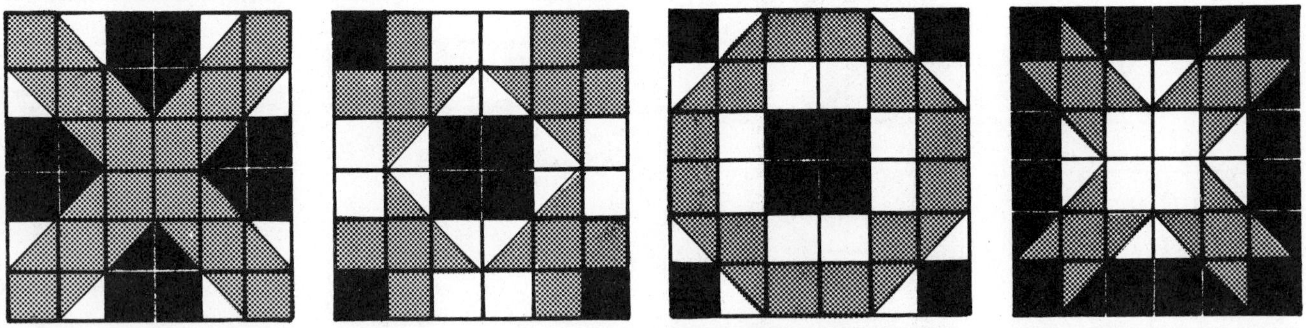

2

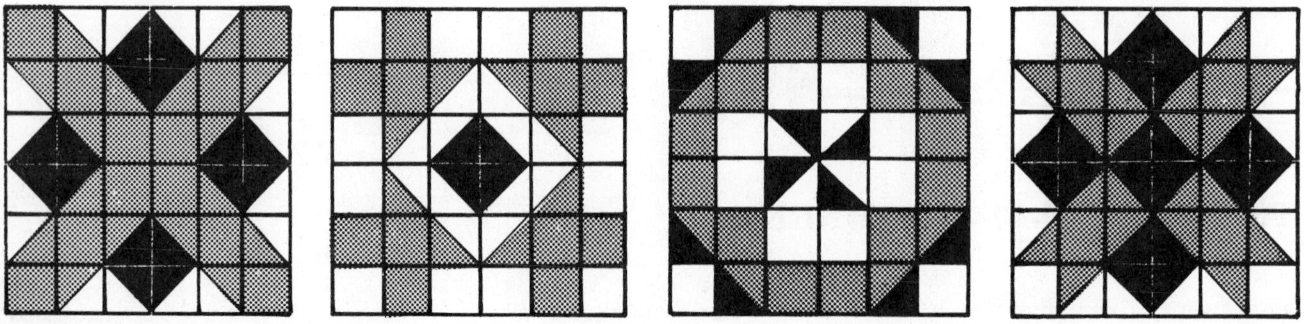

3

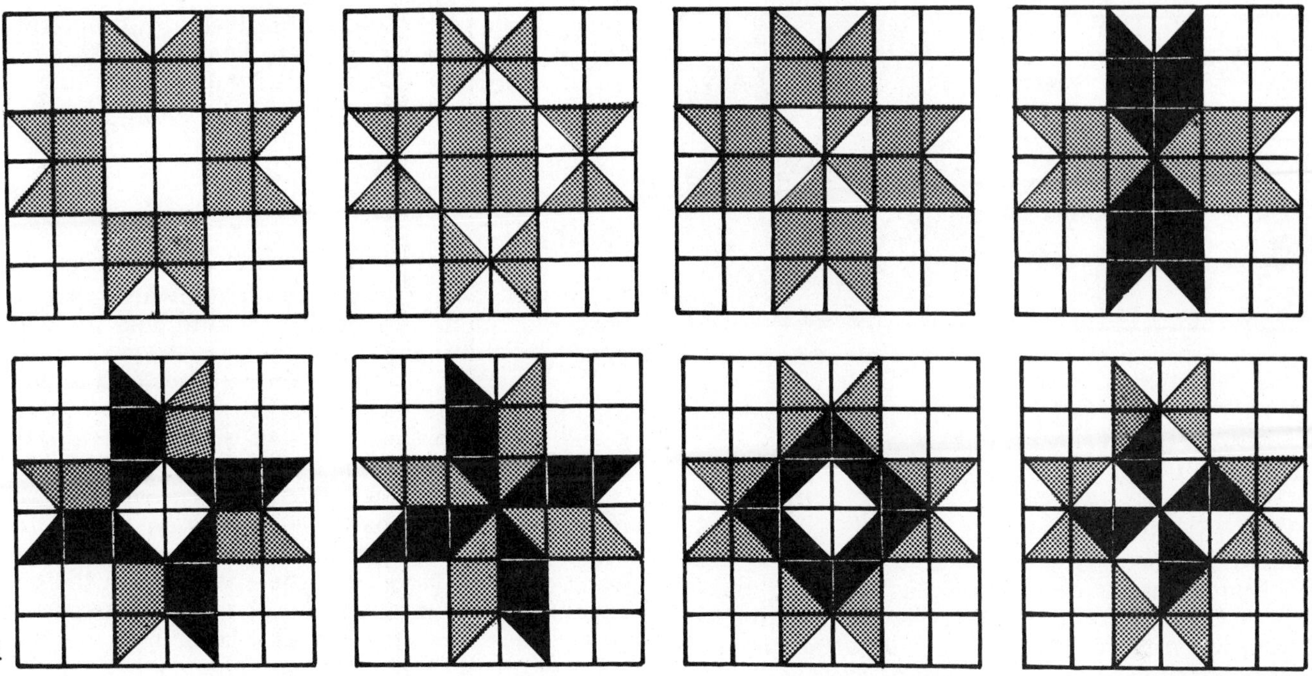

4

cutouts representing the two basic squares when you plan your motifs.

THE HALF SQUARE

This square is composed of two rectangles sewn together to form the complete square (see illustration). Each rectangle should be cut 3½ inches long and 2 inches wide. Pin two rectangles of contrasting fabric together, right sides facing, and sew with a ¼-inch seam. Press the seam open. When hemmed, the completed square should be 3 inches on a side. The three motifs shown here use the rectangular half square in conjunction with full squares.

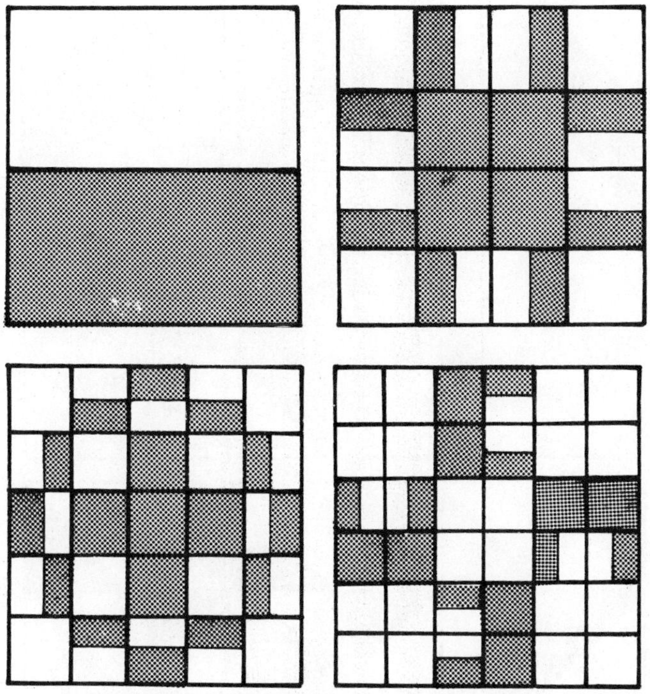

THE THREE-QUARTER SQUARE

This square is composed of a rectangle topped by two smaller squares that together make up the length of the rectangle. The rectangle is 3½ inches long and 2 inches wide. Each smaller square measures 2 inches on a side. The rectangle and one square should be made of matching fabric. First sew the two small squares together; then stitch the joined squares to the rectangle, following the instructions given above for the half square. Press the seams open. The three motifs illustrated here use the three-quarter square and the full square together.

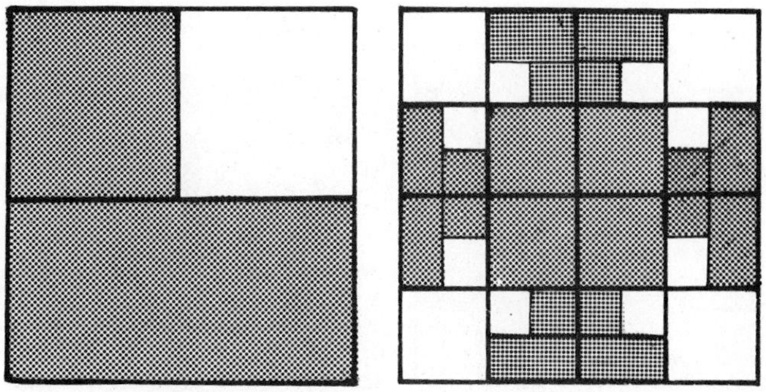

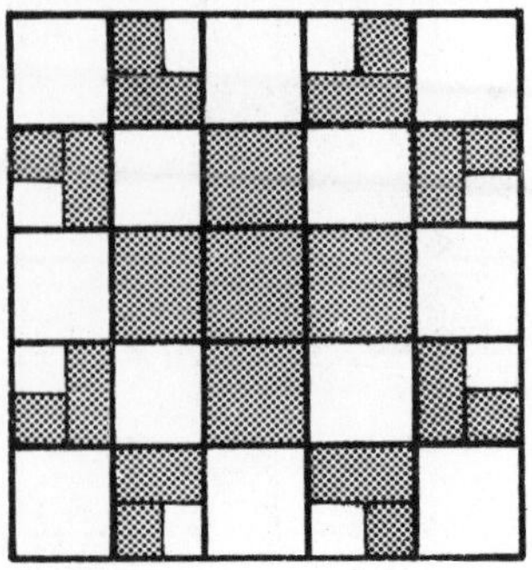

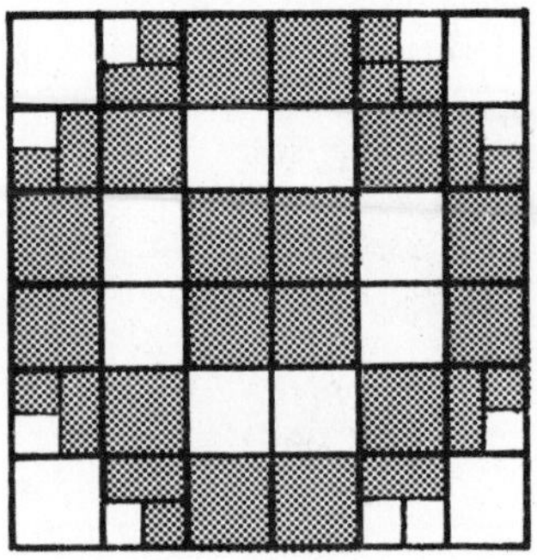

THE DIAGONAL THREE-QUARTER SQUARE

This square is composed of half a diagonal square topped with two smaller triangles. The bottom triangle can be traced from the book, using the pattern on page 141 Glue it to cardboard for a working pattern. To make a pattern for the smaller triangle, trace this shape a second time. The smaller triangle is half the size of the larger with an additional ¼ inch added for seam allowance. Cut the tracing out and fold in half exactly. Trace this half triangle onto a piece of paper but extend the line of the fold ¼ inch for seam allowance. This is your final shape. Glue it to a piece of cardboard and trim.

The larger triangle and one of the smaller triangles should be cut from matching fabric. Sew the two smaller triangles together along the sides. Stitch them to the larger triangle along the diagonal as you would two halves of a diagonal square. Press the seams open. The three motifs in the illustration combine full squares with diagonal three-quarter squares.

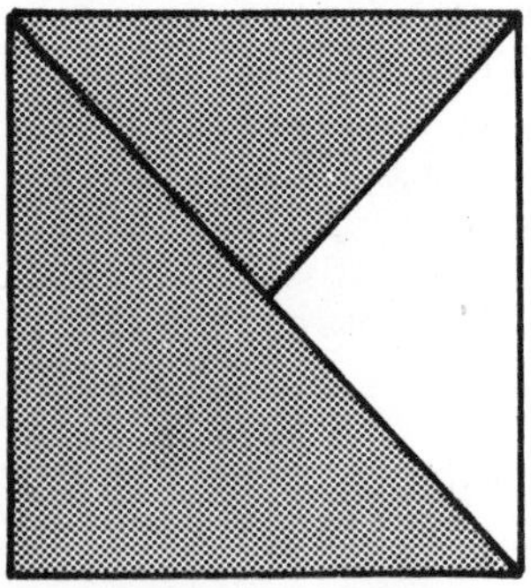

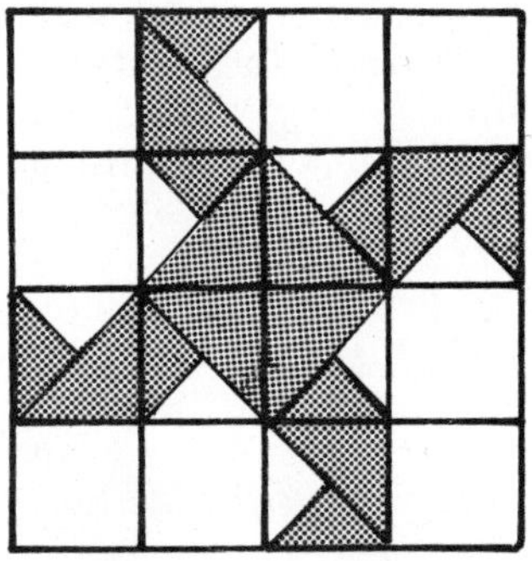

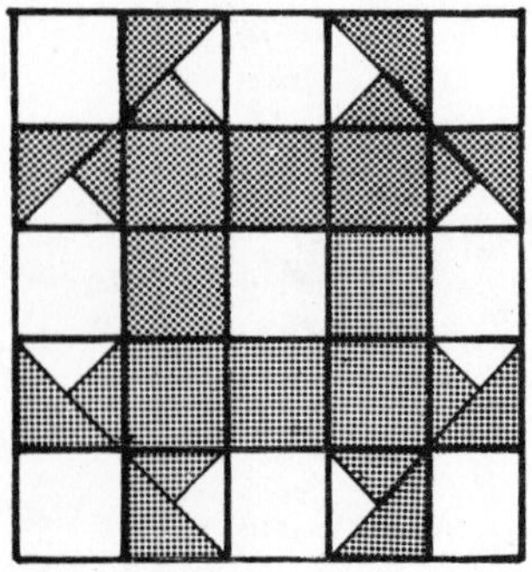

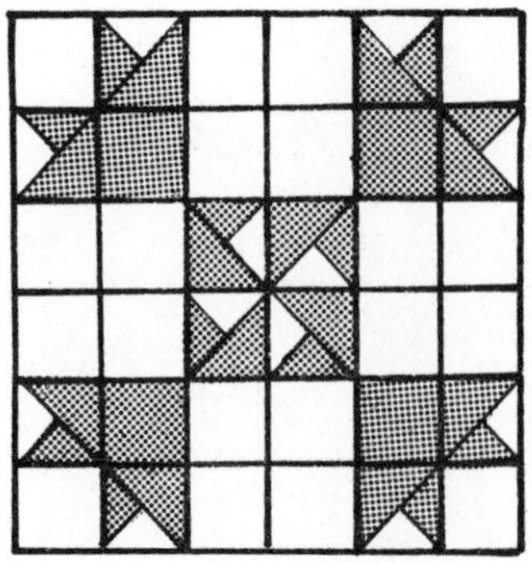

BORDERS

There is no written law that a patchwork must be bordered, but an edging of this kind does make a lovely finishing touch.

These borders comprise full squares and diagonal squares. The examples shown here are composed of one or two rows of squares, and are therefore either 3 or 6 inches wide.

For bolder borders, you can enlarge the pattern for your full squares to 6½ inches on a side. In this case, cut the diagonal squares from a pattern exactly double the size of the one given at the beginning of the chapter. Borders can be used on three sides of a patchwork (excluding the top edge) or on all four sides.

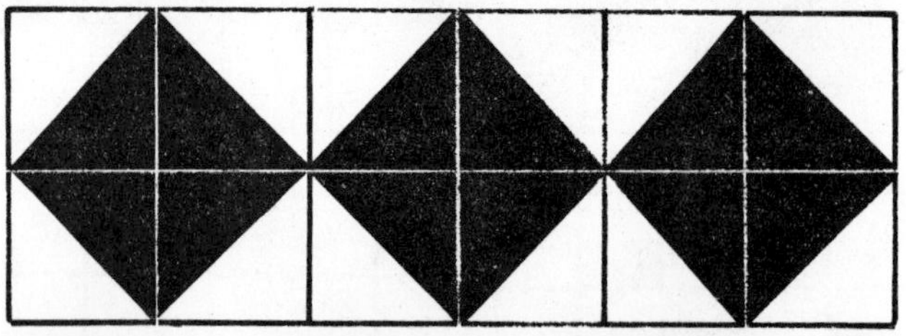

COMBINING THE FIVE BASIC SQUARES

Once you have mastered the five basic squares, you can begin to paint pictures in fabric. The two motifs illustrated here are shown in completed form (left) and broken down square by square (right). To make designs of your own, work with squares of colored construction paper, as discussed earlier in this chapter.

Pineapple and Apples on a Stand (Fig. 1), has red apples, a yellow pineapple, green leaves and a blue stand. The fabrics can be either solids or prints that fall into the color scheme.

Wild Rose (Fig. 2), is a red and pink flower with green leaves at the bottom. Again, you may use solids, prints or both, provided the colors are right.

DETERMINING THE SIZE OF A PATCHWORK BEDSPREAD

Either measure the size of the existing spread on

1

2

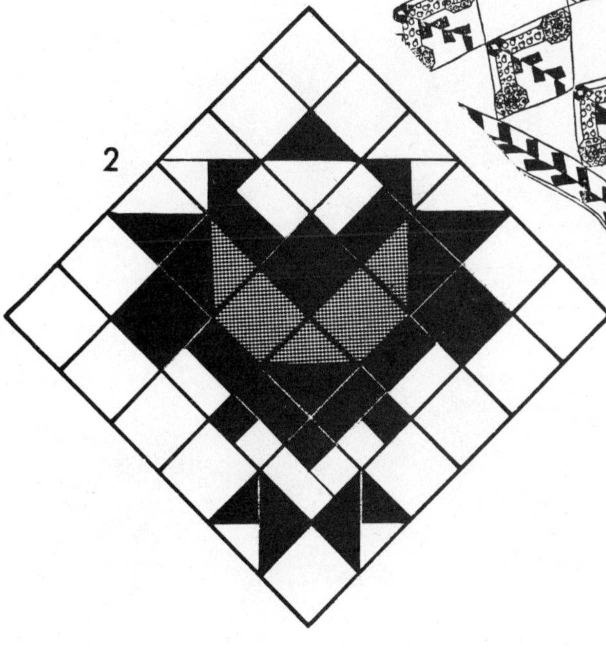

the bed you wish to cover, or take new measurements. A spread should fall to within about 3 inches of the floor. Remember to allow extra inches at the head of the bed for tucking under the pillow. Determine the number of inches that will be taken up by the border, and substract this figure from the total area of the spread. Then divide the remainder by the number of square inches covered by a single motif to ascertain how many motifs you will need. Obviously, the larger the motif, the fewer you will have to make.

HOW TO CONSTRUCT A PATCHWORK SPREAD

1. Complete all the individual motifs before you begin to assemble the bedspread.
2. Pin together as many motifs as you need to make up a single width of spread.
3. Sew these motifs together with ¼-inch seams.
4. Pin and sew a second row together.
5. Pin the two completed rows together.
6. If the corners of the motifs in the two rows don't meet, make adjustments at this time.
7. Sew the rows together.
8. Continue row by row, as just described, until you have completed the spread.
9. Sew together enough border squares to equal the width of the spread.
10. Pin the border to the width of the spread, making any necessary adjustments so the squares will line up neatly with the adjacent motifs. Sew the border in place.
11. Now make borders for the sides of the spread.
12. Pin, adjust and sew as above.

Note: The spread can double as a tablecloth.

HOW TO QUILT A PATCHWORK SPREAD

1. A sheet is the ideal backing for your patchwork spread. A double-bed sheet will fit a twin-bed patchwork; a queen-or king-size sheet will fit a double-bed patchwork. For larger quilts, sew two twin sheets together. Choose a solid, striped or flower-printed sheet.
2. Lay the sheet on the floor with the right side facing down.
3. Spread the quilt stuffing of your choice (see page 14) over the sheet in an even layer.
4. Lay the patchwork over the stuffing with the right side facing *up*.
5. Baste the three layers together, starting from a central point and fanning out first to the four corners and then to the four sides. Finish basting along the edges of the patchwork.
6. Begin quilting with the center motif. With short running stitches, sew the three layers together along the outer seams of the motif.
7. Continue quilting around each motif, working out from the center in a spiral direction.
8. Finish quilting the spread along the border.
9. Trim off the excess sheet so that it is even with the edges of the patchwork.
10. Fold about ¼ inch of both patchwork and sheet in toward the lining and blind-stitch the two layers together.

SIMPLETON PATCHWORK

(Shown in color, page 166)

A handmade patchwork quilt is a glorious accomplishment but a long-range project. For people lacking the time or ambition, this quilt is for you.

1. This quilt is made from solid squares of fabric instead of pieced motifs. As before, you may choose fabrics in solid colors, prints or both.
2. Squares of any size may be used, so long as they are all cut to exactly the same dimensions.
3. Pin and sew together the number of squares needed to make up a single width of spread.
4. Pin and sew a second row together.
5. Pin the two completed rows together. If the squares in the two rows do not line up properly, adjust them at this time. Sew the rows together.
6. Continue adding rows in this manner until the spread reaches the desired size.
7. Border the patchwork with a ruffle of whatever width you like. To make the ruffle, stitch long strips of fabric together, figuring on twice the length of a given side of the quilt for each flounce.
8. Hem one edge of the strip by machine and

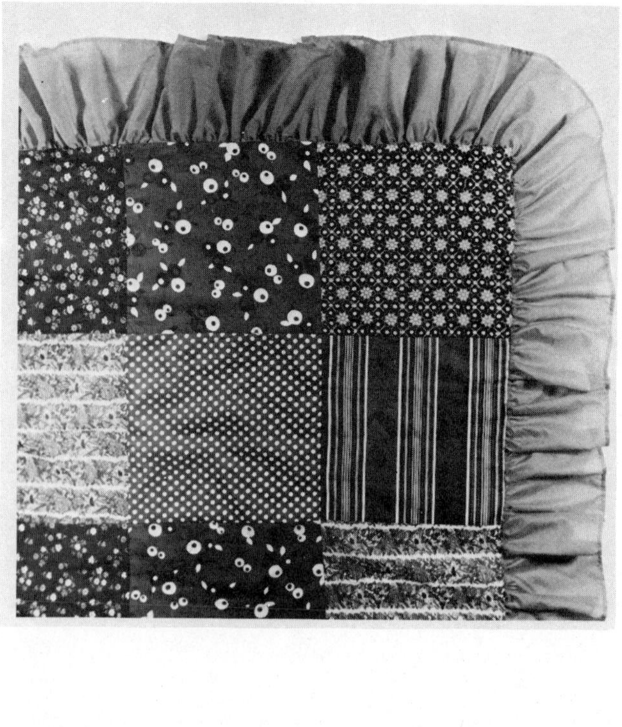

gather the other edge.

9. Pin the ruffle to the quilt, right sides facing, and tighten or ease out the gathers where needed to make it fall smoothly.

10. Sew the ruffle to the patchwork.

11. If you wish to line and quilt this patchwork, follow the instructions for the preceding project.

CRAZY QUILTS

The crazy quilt is the finale in the patchwork story. This quilt has no set pattern. Instead it employs scraps of all sizes pieced together randomly.

1. Cut out 16½-inch squares of inexpensive muslin. Your crazy-quilt patterns will be stitched onto this interlining.

2. Baste scraps of fabric onto each square until none of the muslin is left showing.

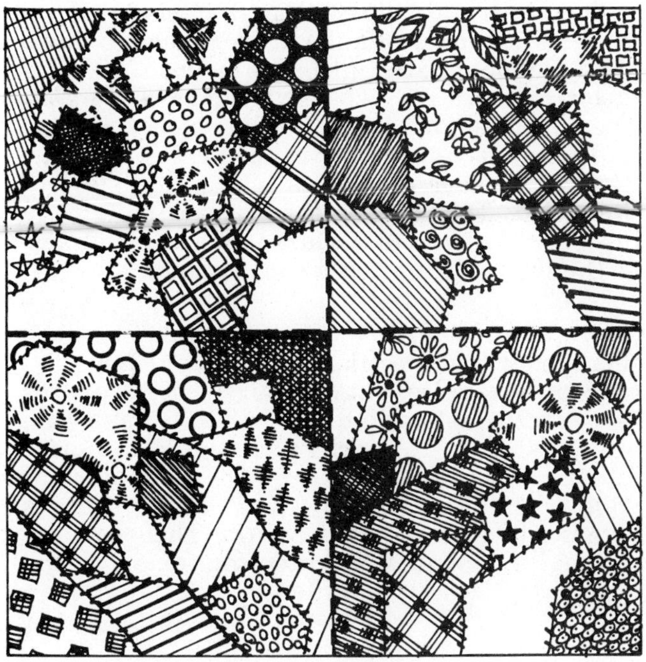

3. With a needle and embroidery thread, embroider over the raw edges of the patchwork pieces. Or use a decorative machine stitch instead.

4. Sew the crazy-quilt squares together, following the instructions given for the Simpleton Patchwork.

5. Quilt the crazy squares as described earlier in this chapter.

6. To separate the crazy-quilt motifs, you can sew ribbon over the seams by hand or by machine.

SQUARE PATCHWORK PILLOWS

(Shown in color, page 167)

These pillows are made from simple squares and rectangular patches grouped in harmonious designs.

1. Each pillow is based on a 16½-inch square. Be sure to sew all squares or rectangles together with ¼-inch seams. Hems too should always be ¼-inch wide.

2. The back of the pillow can be either a solid piece of fabric or a repeat of the patchwork pattern on the front.

3. Place the two faces of the pillow with the right sides of the fabrics facing, and sew them together ¼ inch from the edge. Leave 4 inches unsewn.

4. Turn the cover inside out.

5. For pillows with a ruffle at the edge, make a long, gathered strip of fabric and hem it along one edge. (The whole ruffle should be about twice as long as the circumference of the pillow.) Sew the ruffle to one face of the patchwork cover, right sides facing, with a ¼-inch seam. Then pin the two pillow sides together, right sides facing, with the ruffle tucked in between and stitch up the cover as directed above. Turn the cover right-side out.

6. Stuff the pillow with cotton, chipped foam or polyester.

7. Sew the open seam closed by hand.

The flag pillow (Fig. 1) is made from six rectangles. Cut one 4½ x 16½ inches, one 4½ x 12½ inches, and four 3½ x 12½ inches. The larger rectangles should be cut from the same printed or lacy fabric, and the smaller ones from two contrasting solid-color fabrics. Sew the four smaller rectangles together with ¼-inch seams. Sew the 4½ x 12½-inch rectangle perpendicular to the first four. Then sew the largest rectangle parallel to the first four to complete the flag design.

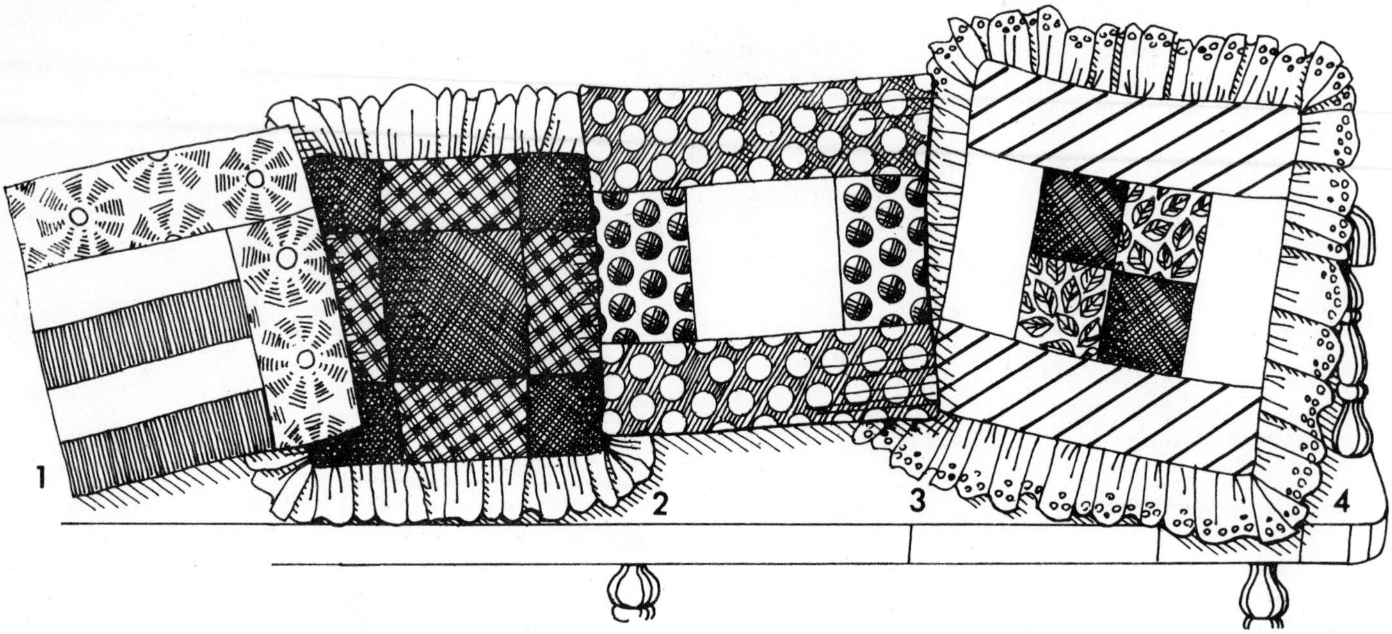

The cross pillow (Fig. 2) consists of a large center square surrounded by smaller squares and rectangles. Cut one 8½ -inch square, four 4½-inch squares and four 8½ x 4½-inch rectangles. The squares and the rectangles should be made of contrasting fabrics—a solid for the squares and a check for the rectangles, for instance. Sew a rectangle to opposite sides of the large center square to form the middle row, then sew a smaller square to each side of the remaining two rectangles for the other two rows. Sew the first row to the middle row and the third row to the middle row. Add a ruffle around the edges.

The Railroad Pillow (Fig. 3) is made with a large center square flanked by rectangles of two sizes. Cut out one 8½-inch square, two 4½ x 16½-inch rectangles and two 4½ x 8½-inch rectangles. The square should be in a solid color, the large and small rectangles in two contrasting prints. Sew the smaller rectangles to opposite sides of the square. Then sew on the larger rectangles to the top and bottom of the large square (rectangles on the side), as shown in the illustration.

The Window Pillow (Fig. 4) is made from four small central squares, flanked above and below by pairs of rectangles. Cut out four 4½-inch squares in two contrasting fabrics (one solid and one print), two 4½ x 16½-inch rectangles of the same fabric, and two 4½ x 8½-inch rectangles of another fabric. Sew the four small squares together to form a larger square. Then sew the rectangles around the center square as in the Railroad Pillow. Add a ruffle.

PINWHEEL PILLOWS

(Shown in color, page 166)

The pinwheel pillow is based on a circle 16 inches in diameter. Pie-wedge shapes, 8 inches long, are sewn together to form the completed circle.

1. Draw your 16-inch circle on a large sheet of paper using a compass set to an 8-inch radius or an 8-inch string tied to a pencil. (Hold the base end of the string firmly at the center point, pull

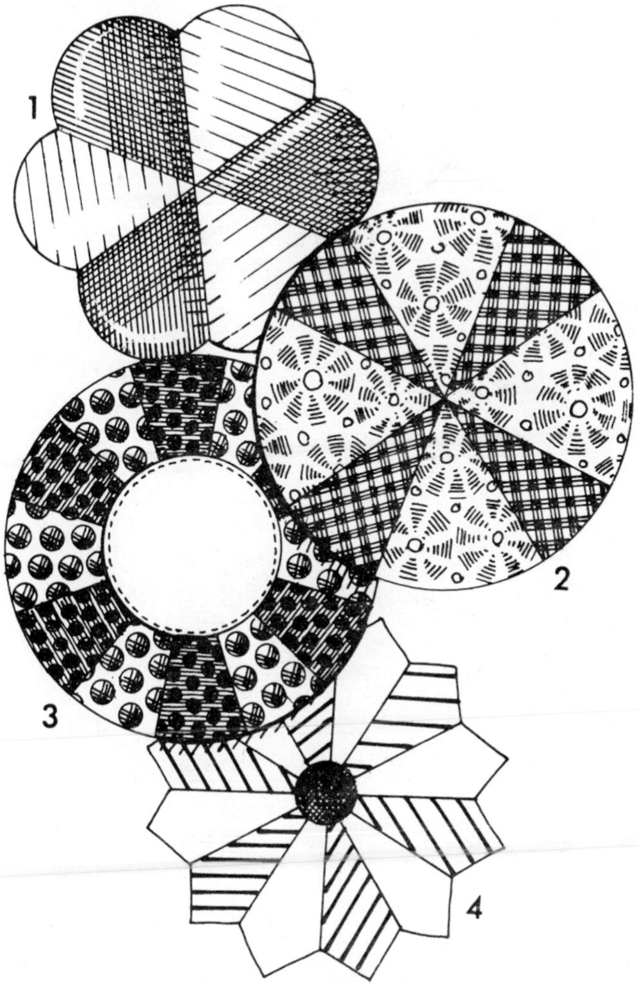

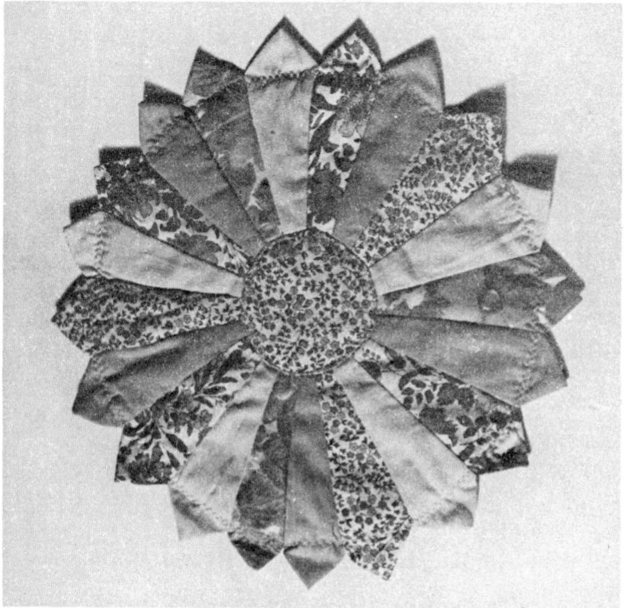

the string taut and describe a circle on the paper with the upright pencil.)

2. Divide the circle into pie-wedge shapes, always cutting through the center point. You can buy a protractor at the five-and-ten or a stationery store to help you draw the interior angles precisely.
3. Cut out the wedges for patterns.
4. Cut wedges from scrap fabric to make the pillow. The fabric pieces must be ¼ inch larger than the patterns on all sides for seams.
5. Sew the fabric wedges together with exact ¼-inch seams to form your circle.
6. If the pillow is to have a center circle on top of the wedges (Figs. 3 and 4), sew it on at this time.
7. The underside of the pillow can be a duplicate of the patchwork on the front or simply a solid piece of fabric.
8. Place the pillow faces together, right sides facing, and sew them ¼ inch in from the edge. Leave about 4 inches of seam unsewn.
9. Turn the cover right-side out and stuff with cotton, chipped foam or polyester.
10. Sew the open seam closed by hand.

The Scalloped Pillow (Fig. 1) has six wedges in alternating colors. When you draw your circle on paper, divide it into six equal parts. Use the compass to draw the outer scallops. (Place the point in the middle of the arc formed by each wedge, and draw a smaller arc to connect the two endpoints of the wedge.)

The Fan Pillow (Fig. 2) has eight wedges, four large and four small. The smaller wedges are made in darker fabric to look like the blades of a fan.

The Big Top Pillow (Fig. 3) has twelve wedges of equal size but alternating colors and fabric. Sew a smaller circle over the center of the joined wedges, tucking under ½ inch of fabric as you sew.

The Star Pillow (Fig. 4) also has twelve wedges of equal size topped with a central circle, but the arcs of each wedge are cut to form points.

PATCHWORK APRONS

Two dramatically different patchwork aprons.

FOR HER

1. A ladies' patchwork apron can be made in any size. Our version uses rows of squares cut 4½ inches on a side. Leave ¼ inch on all sides for seam allowance.
2. Cut out eighteen squares and sew them together in three rows of six squares each.
3. Sew the three rows together, making sure that the squares line up neatly with the squares above and below.

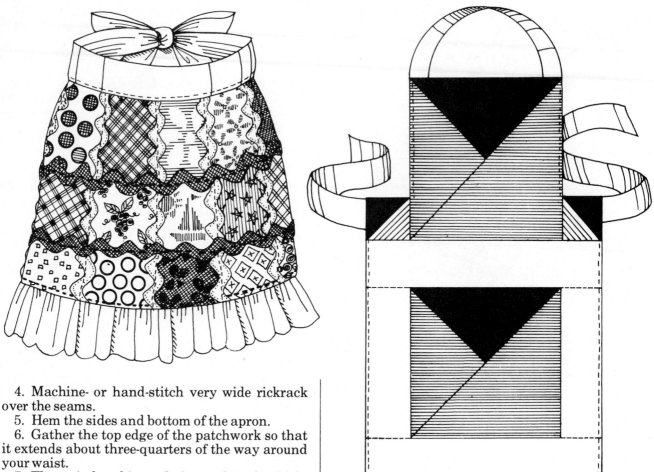

4. Machine- or hand-stitch very wide rickrack over the seams.
5. Hem the sides and bottom of the apron.
6. Gather the top edge of the patchwork so that it extends about three-quarters of the way around your waist.
7. The waistband is made from a length of fabric or a very wide ribbon. Fold the strip in half, tuck the gathered patchwork just inside the fold, and sew down. If you use a band of fabric, you will have to turn the raw edges under before sewing.
8. To make a ruffle for the bottom hem, take a strip of fabric about twice as long as the apron's width and gather it along the top edge.
9. Hem the side and bottom edges of the ruffle.
10. Sew the ruffle to the underside of the apron's hem.

FOR HIM

1. This dramatic apron is designed around two 20½-inch three-quarter diagonal squares in bold colors.
2. To make the bib, sew a 4½-inch diagonal square to each corner of one diagonal three-quarter square.
3. To make the skirt, sew a 4½ x 20½-inch strip to the left and right sides of the other diagonal three-quarter square for a border. Sew 4½ x 28½ inch strips of the same border fabric to the top and bottom edges of the square.
4. Sew the bib and the base together with a ½-inch seam.

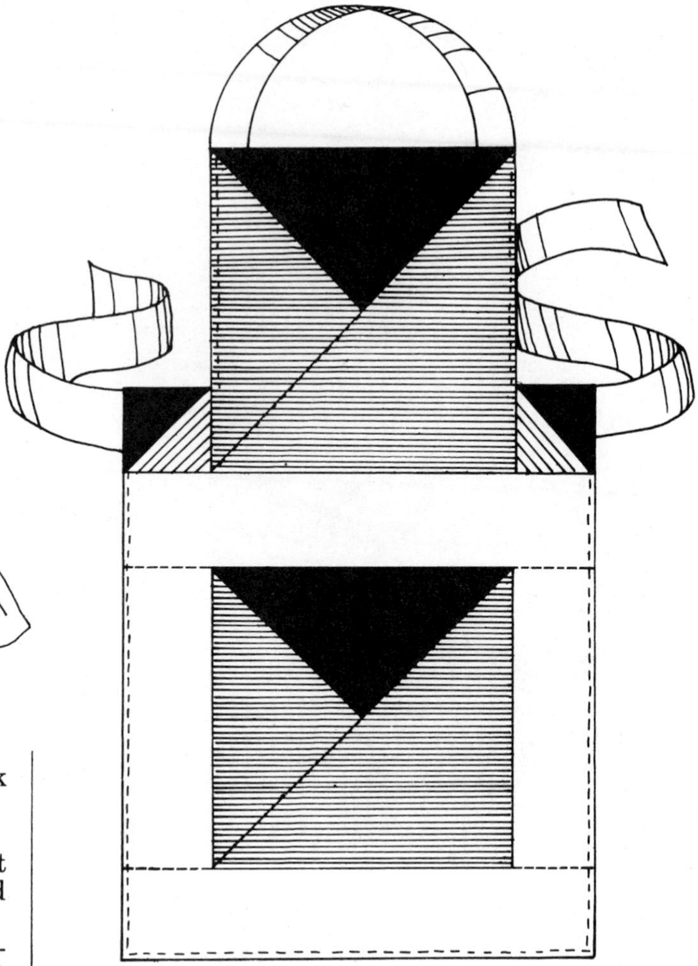

5. Hem the entire apron.
6. Stitch a length of ribbon to the upper corners of the bib to go around the neck. Add two longer ribbons to the smaller diagonal squares at the waist.

GINGHAM ANIMALS

These soft stuffed animals made of gingham patchwork are perfect crib or playpen companions for small children. Patterns for four animals are given here, but the method is so simple you can invent your own.

1. Construct the patchwork front of the animal you choose according to the directions given below. The back of the animal can be either a duplicate patchwork or a solid piece of fabric. When you have completed the patchwork front, use it as a pattern from which to cut the reverse side.
2. Sew or glue on facial features made of felt or fabric. Use black buttons for pupils and embroidery for details.

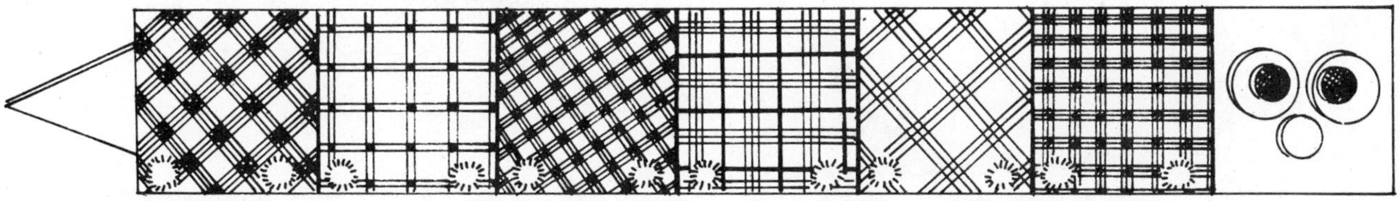

3. Place the two sides of the animal together, right sides facing. Sew the pieces ¼ inch in from the edge, leaving about 3 inches of seam on a side edge unsewn.

4. Turn the animal inside out and stuff firmly with cotton, chipped foam or polyester.

5. Hand-sew the open seam closed.

BEAR

1. The bear's body is a 10-inch diagonal three-quarter square. To make patterns for this section, draw a 10-inch square on a piece of stiff paper. Draw one diagonal line from corner to corner, and then a half-diagonal from a third corner to the midpoint of the first diagonal. Cut out the three triangle shapes. When cutting your fabric; add ¼ inch on all sides to allow for seams. Sew the three pieces together with ¼-inch seams.

2. The head is a 5½-inch square sewn to the top of the body.

3. The arms are 4½-inch diagonal three-quarter square. To make the pattern, draw a 4-inch square on paper and follow the same procedure you used to construct the central body-square. Make two small squares in this way and sew one to each top corner of the body.

4. Each leg consists of a 4½-inch full square

with a half-square beneath. The latter is formed by two 2½ x 4½-inch rectangles sewn together with a ¼-inch seam. Stitch the half-squares to the full squares and sew the legs to the bottom corners of the body.

A suggestion about colors: make the small odd triangles of the three-quarter squares pink, for the bear's hand-paws and tummy. His foot-paws (the lower portions of the horizontal half-squares) could be brown. The face has brown ears, pink nose and cheeks, white eyes and a red mouth, all made of felt.

OWL

1. The owl's body is an 8½-inch square.

CAT

(Shown in color, page 166)

1. The cat's body is a large square, formed by sewing four 5½-inch squares together with ¼-inch seams.
2. The head is another 5½-inch square, sewn to the upper right-hand side of the body.
3. The legs are half-squares made by sewing together two 2½ x 4½-inch rectangles. Sew the legs to the lower corners of the body and embroider toes on the lower half of each one.
4. The tail is made from two 3-inch squares, sewn together with ¼-inch seams and attached to the upper left-hand corner of the body.

Make the lower half of each leg pink, to suggest paws. Sew pink felt ears, nose and cheeks on the face and embroider a red mouth and black whiskers.

CENTIPEDE

1. The head is a 5½-inch square made from solid-color fabric.
2. The body consists of six 5½-inch squares of different ginghams, sewn in a straight line behind the head with ¼-inch seams.
3. Add a tail, eyes and nose in felt, and embroider feet in the lower corners of each body-square.

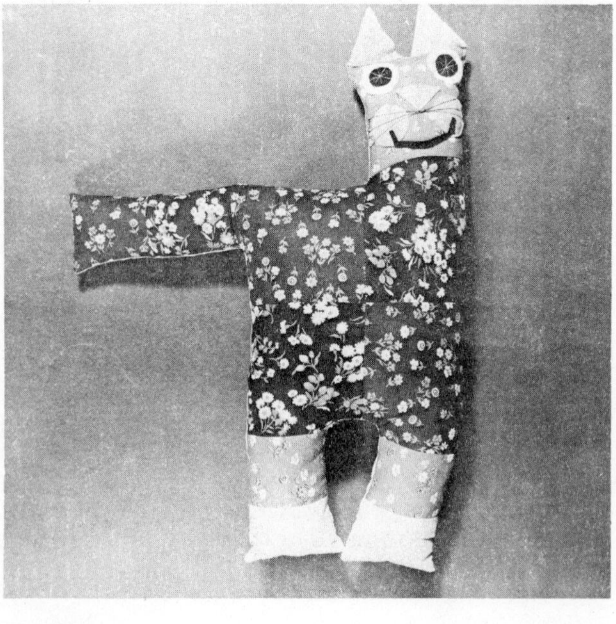

PETAL PILLOW

1. The basic pillow shape is formed by two 17-inch circles cut from felt or another sturdy fabric.
2. The petal shapes are made from 4-, 3½, 3¼, 3- and 2½-inch squares.
3. To form the petal shape, fold each square twice on the diagonal, first from corners x to x and then from y to y (see diagrams).
4. Pin the largest petals in a circle around one pillow shape, one inch in from the edge. Keep all

folded edges facing left and points facing out. Overlap the bottom corners if necessary. When the complete row is set in place, hand- or machine-stitch each petal to the pillow along the bottom edge. Continue to pin and sew each ring to the pillow shape, using progressively smaller petals as you work toward the center.
5. Sew a large circle to the center of the pillow so that it slightly overlaps the innermost row of petals.
6. To construct the pillow, place the petal-covered front and the back together, right sides facing. Sew the two sides together with a ½-inch hem, leaving 4 inches unsewn. Be careful not to sew the petals into the hem.
7. Turn the pillow right-side out and stuff with

cotton or chipped foam. Hand-stitch the open seam closed.

BRAIDED RUG

The classic scrap-fabric rug, still a favorite today, is within reach of anyone who can braid a pigtail. Wool is the most durable material for larger rugs, but small throw rugs can be made from washable fabrics. Even shreds torn from old clothes will do.

1. Cut your fabric into long strips 2 inches wide.
2. Sew three strips together at the top.
3. Fold each strip in half lengthwise, keeping the folded side facing in and the raw edges facing out. First bring the strip on the right (3) over the middle strip (2); then bring strip 1 in over strip 3. The strips of fabric on the outside are always brought over the middle strip in this alternating fashion.
4. Sew additional lengths of fabric to the braid whenever a strand runs out, making ¼-inch seams on the underside of the joined strips.
5. When you have braided several lengths,

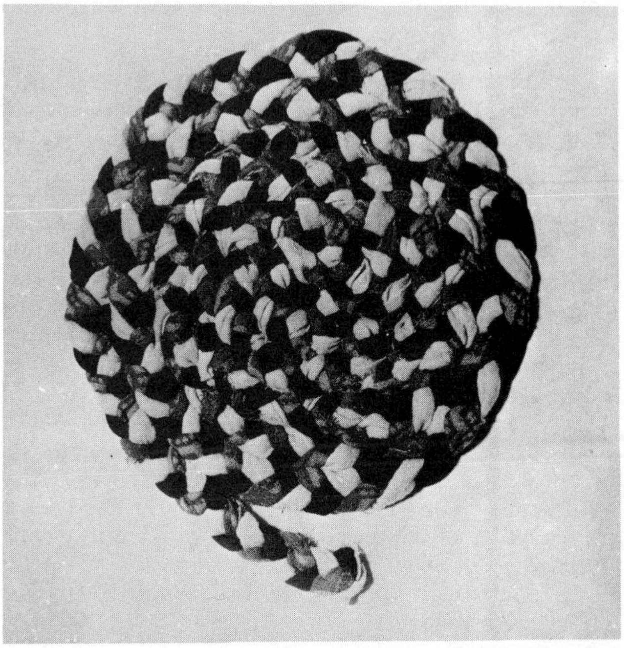

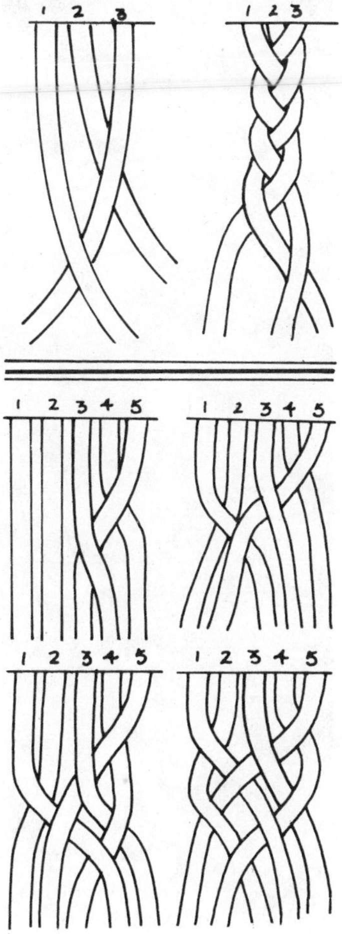

begin to form the rug. Start by twisting the braid in a flat circle around the knot at the top. Sew the winding braid in place with a wide-eyed needle and heavy-duty thread. Be sure that the rug is lying flat as you wind. Sew gently but firmly. (Stitches that are too tight will cause the rug to buckle, while those that are too loose will form ripples in the braided surface.)

6. Continue braiding and sewing until the rug reaches the desired size.
7. To finish the rug, taper the braid gradually toward the edge of the preceding coil and sew the loose ends to the underside.

FIVE-STRAND BRAIDING

1. This variation of the basic rug-braiding technique uses five strands instead of three. The strips have been numbered on the diagram for easier identification. Cut and fold the strips as before, but sew five of them together rather than three.
2. Weave the outside strip on the right (5) over the adjacent strip (4) and under the third one (3).
3. Bring the outside strip on the left (1) over strip 2 and under strip 5.
4. Continue to braid in this way, weaving the outer strip on the left and then the outer strip on the right in toward the center. Proceed with the rug as directed above.

RAG RUG

The rag rug can be made of woolens, synthetic fabrics or cottons. Do not mix different textiles in the same rug; those that can be washed should not be used with those that require dry cleaning.

1. Cut scrap fabric into 2 x 5-inch strips.
2. These strips will be knotted onto two longer base strips of durable fabric. The base strips should be at least 2 inches wide and as long as possible. Try to cut all of them to the same width.
3. Knot two base strips together.
4. To lay the first short strip over the base strips, bring the ends of the short strip down under the base strips and then up between them. Tighten the loop by pulling the loose ends in the direction of the original knot. Repeat with subsequent short strips so that the two base strips become one heavy strand.
5. Sew extensions to the base strips as needed.
6. When you have knotted several feet, begin to sew the rug. Roll the joined base strips in a flat coil around the original knot, and sew the coil in place with a wide-eyed needle and heavy-duty yarn.
7. Continue to knot, wind and sew until the rug is the desired size.
8. To finish, tuck the two base strips under the rug and sew down.

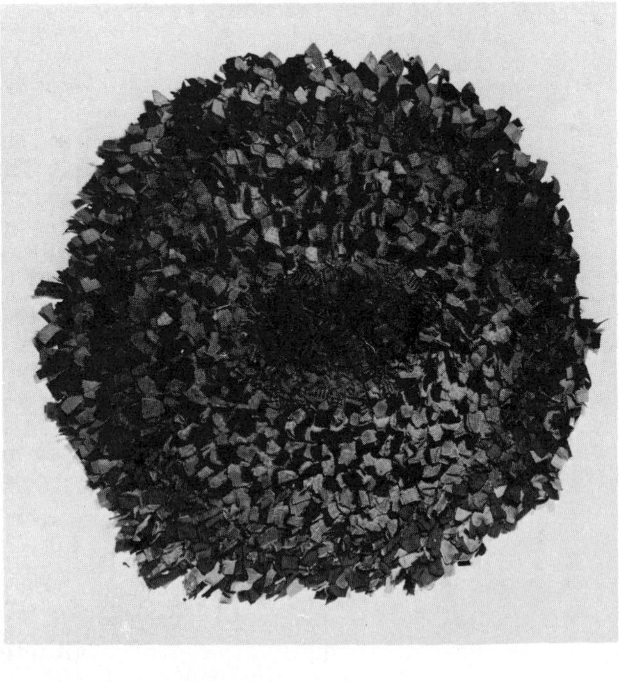

SEWING WITH APPLIQUE

SEWING WITH APPLIQUE

Appliqué can be thought of as the art of collage in cloth. It is a French term that connotes the placing of one material over another. The process was anciently known as Opus Consutum *or "cut work,"* Passementeri *and* Di Commesso. *Of these names, the first is the oldest but as it also described some of the early laces, it came to be replaced by "appliqué," a more specific word derived from the Latin* applicare, *to join or attach, and the French* appliquer, *to put on.* Di Commesso *was a name given to the work by Vasari, who claims the invention of it for Sandro Botticelli, but its existence dates earlier than the two.*

The work was known in India and Persia, and it was here that it was probably invented. Italians, Germans and French have used it largely for household decorations while the English used it more for altar cloths and vestments. The word appliqué has a wide meaning, and many varieties of needlework come under its designation. It embraces every description of work that is cut or stamped out or embroidered and then laid upon another material. Under this broad definition, it is possible to appliqué in almost every known material—feathers, skins of animals, gold and silver, mother of pearl and other substances. The process was originally introduced as an imitation of, and substitute for, raised embroidery, which was so laborious to work. It was an easier form of ornamentation.

In America, appliqué was an offshoot of pieced patchwork. In time, settlers and their offspring were living a little better. A new affluence lessened the burdens of colonial women, gave them the time to enjoy a creative outlet and the money to buy new cloth. They were able to turn from the more economical patchwork quilt to the appliquéd. Their patterns were quite intricate as the technique lends itself to graceful curving lines. There were flowers and foliage, birds and butterflies, many lovely things.

A traditional American appliqué-related custom was the Friendship Medley. This charming custom combined the announcement of a girl's engagement with a shower for her. A mother invited all her daughter's friends, and they would arrive early in the afternoon with quilt blocks in their workbaskets. Each would work one appliqué block and stitch her name or initials on it. It had to be completed by sunset when the young men arrived for the quilting party supper and dance. The quilt would be pieced together and quilted at another quilting bee.

Sons had quilts too—Freedom Quilts, celebrating a male child's twenty-first birthday. A young man's labor belonged to his parents until he was twenty-one. After this age, the boy might leave his parents and work for himself. A rich father might give him a team and wagon. His young lady friends contributed blocks of his quilt.

Appliqué was also used to create family records. As a family takes years to grow, so a family quilt would take years to make. Every block would be a picture, dated and signed by its maker. A large block in the center might picture the homestead with all details included. Smaller blocks set around it would be signed by aunts and cousins. A family record quilt held many memories.

The projects that follow are not nearly as ambitious as the projects that absorbed early American quilters. They take less time and less money in order to see results. In fact, you probably have enough scrap fabric and worn clothing about the house to keep you quilting appliqué for years to come.

TRADITIONAL APPLIQUÉD QUILTS

The applique is the sister of the patchwork, born from the same "mother of necessity" yet very different in nature. Patchwork quilts are made by sewing together many small bits and pieces of cloth to form a larger piece or "top." Appliquéd quilts are made by cutting fabric shapes and sewing them onto a large sheet of cloth. Where patchwork designs are usually geometric, appliqué can be as fanciful as any painting. In fact, you could consider appliqué painting in fabric.

MAKING APPLIQUÉ PATTERNS

The patterns for the appliqué designs shown, all of which are classics, are drawn on grids. To make working patterns, enlarge the grid and design you have chosen on cardboard and cut the patterns out. (See page 13 for detailed directions on how to

400. Mrs. Proper's Oldtime Quilt

IN our editor's home there are many lovely old things. This beautiful quilt has been in the family for three generations. It was made by Mrs. John B. Glisan, in 1855, at Fredericksburg, Maryland. The quilt measures 84 by 90 inches and is made of six large blocks with a border down the center. I wish you could see the tiny stitches taken in appliqueing. This design might be used in any desired colors for your own bedroom.

EARLY American quilt designs are increasingly popular and in good taste. The two blocks shown at right, Nos. 401 and 402, measure 18 inches square, are made of white muslin and have guaranteed fast-colored applique pieces. In No. 401, the basket is of yellow, the leaves of green and the flowers of pink and yellow. In No. 402, the flower is rose with yellow center, the buds are rose with yellow tips and the leaves are green.

No. 2812 design has a hemstitched hem and is a 42-inch sewed case. This may be worked in solid stitch or lazy daisy and is pretty embroidered all in white or in white and yellow.

Nos. 2833 and 2831 are of a nice quality 42-inch pillow tubing. The basket design is embroidered in pastel colors and the pansy design in lavender and yellow with green leaves.

401. Early American quilt block (at left)

402. Early American quilt block (below)

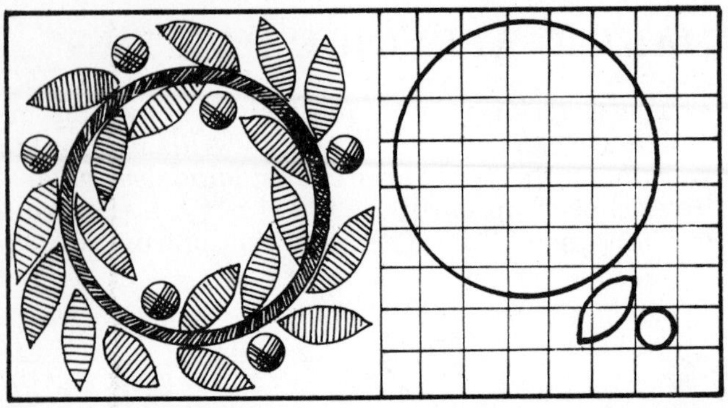

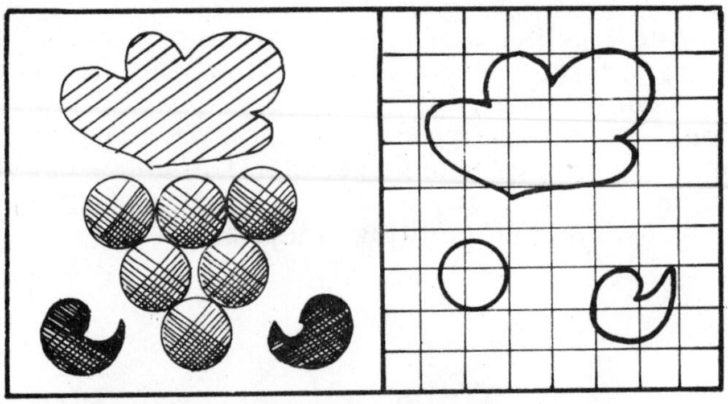

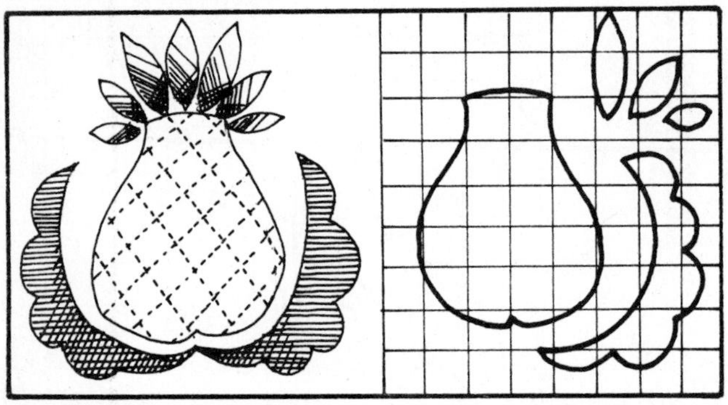

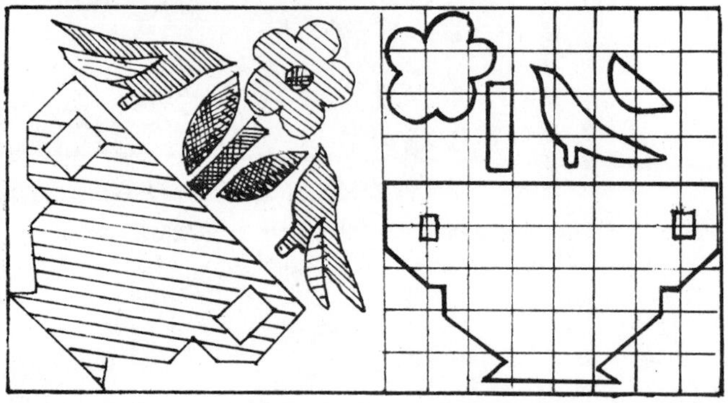

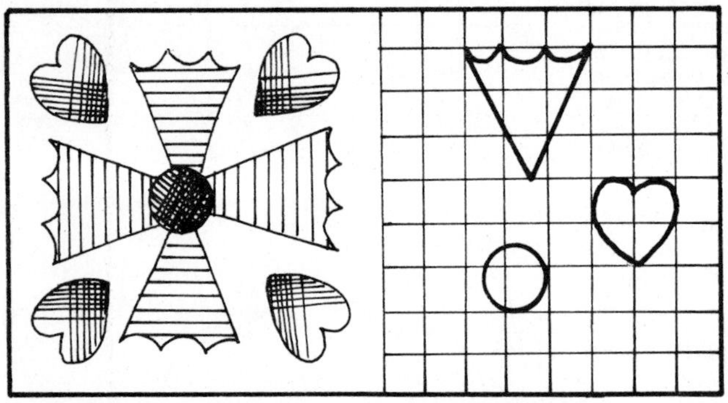

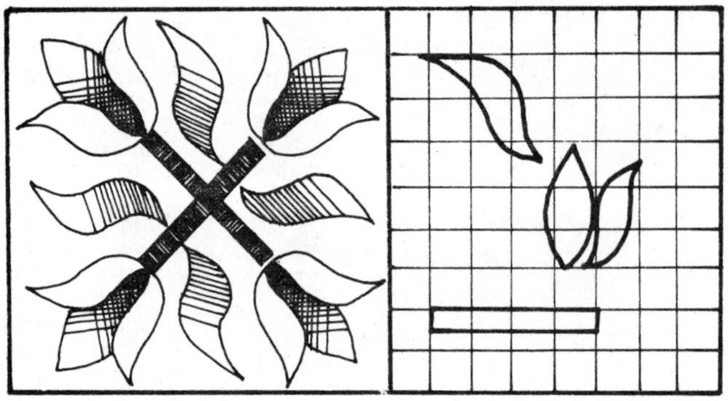

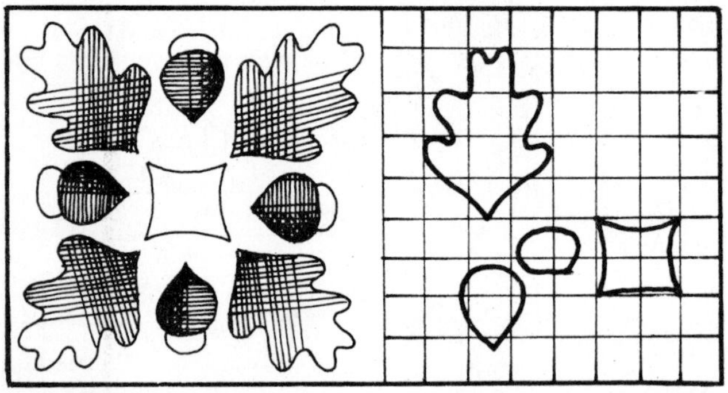

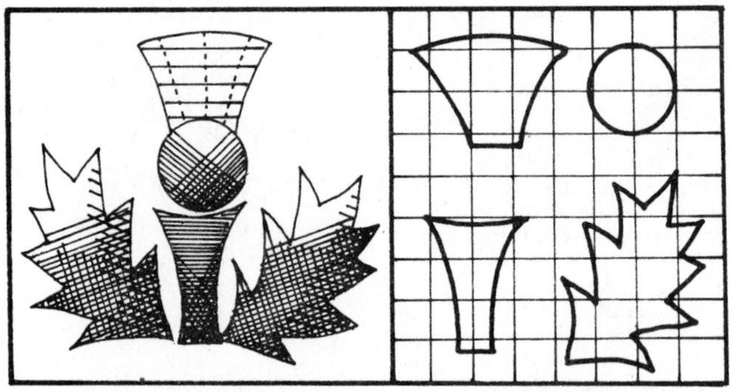

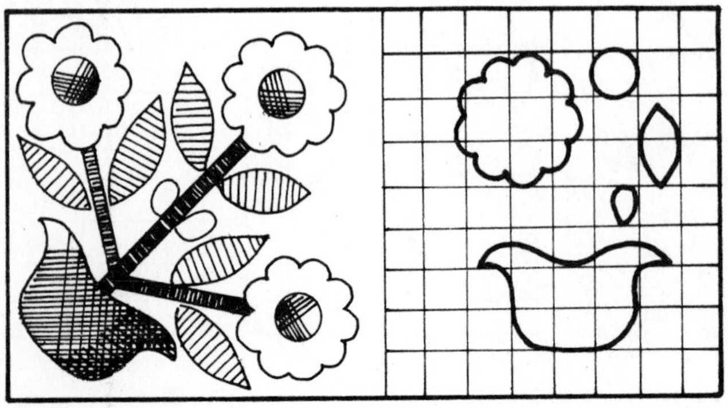

enlarge patterns from a grid.) The first set of designs, from a 1915 magazine, should be drawn on a grid enlarged so that one square equals one inch. The designs that follow are placed on a grid on which one square equals ¾ inch.

Trace each pattern with a pencil onto the wrong side of your fabric. Cut out the appliqués carefully.

SEWING ON THE APPLIQUÉS

(Shown in color, page 167)

Pin all the appliqués for each design unit to the base surface you are using—either a 13-inch square or a single piece of fabric cut to the size of the finished quilt. (A new bed sheet can be used for larger quilts.)

To sew, fold ⅛ inch of the raw edge of an applique under and blind-stitch it to the base fabric along the entire edge. If one appliqué overlaps another, sew on the underpiece first. Individual appliqué pieces can be raised slightly above the base fabric by adding a small wad of cotton or polyester before sewing.

QUILTING AN APPLIQUÉD SURFACE

To make a quilt from 13-inch squares, follow the instructions given in the chapter **The Patchwork Story.** Use ½-inch seams when sewing the appliquéd squares together.

If appliqué designs are sewn on a single piece of fabric, assemble the quilt in three layers (see How to Quilt a Patchwork Spread). On a quilt made with squares, the three layers should be stitched along the squares' seams. The single-fabric appliquéd quilt is quilted together in a predetermined pattern that covers the entire background but skirts the appliqués. The easiest method is to make wavering lines of stitches that cross the quilt one to 3 inches apart. (See illustration.) The dips in these lines can be deep enough to meet the peaks in the lines beneath, creating a connecting pattern. You can also stitch in zigzags or loops or simply in straight lines.

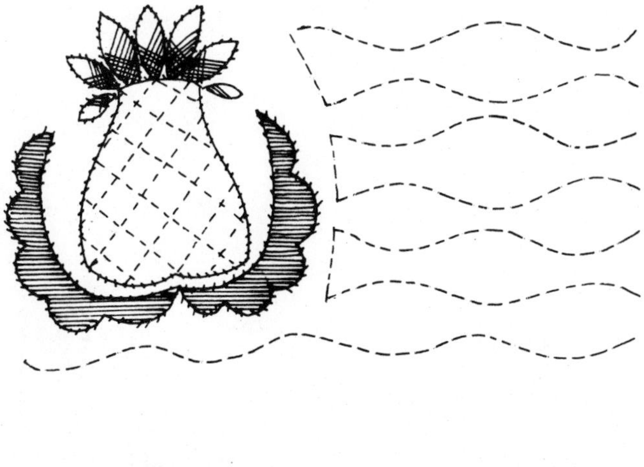

BONNET BABY QUILT

(Shown in color, page 167)

Nothing is cozier than a good old-fashioned comforter. This one employs a popular turn-of-the-century design.

1. To make patterns for the bonnet baby, enlarge the grid on a sheet of cardboard so that one square equals one inch. Draw the four shapes on the enlarged grid and cut them out. (See page 13

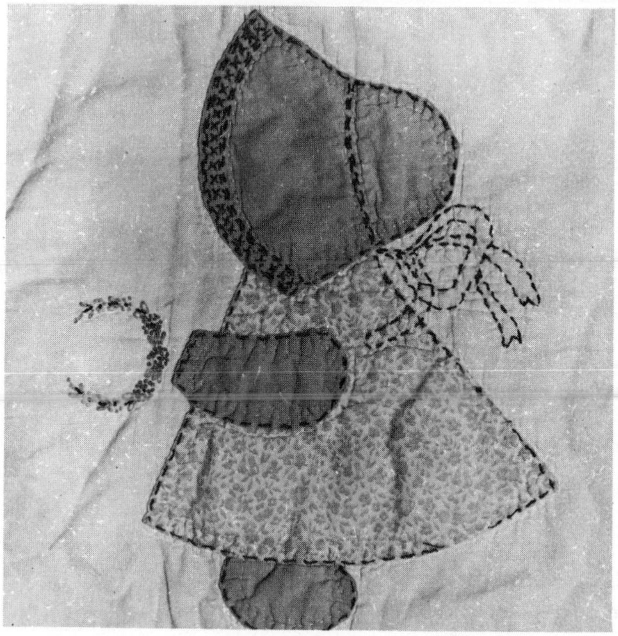

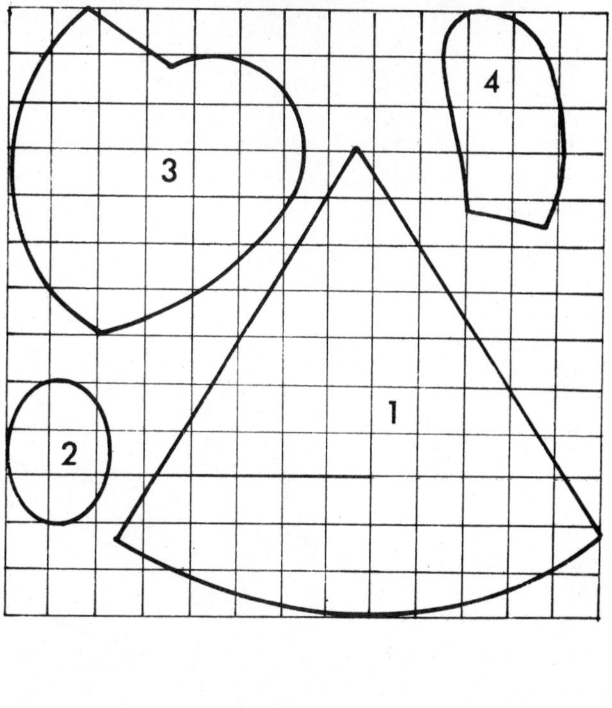

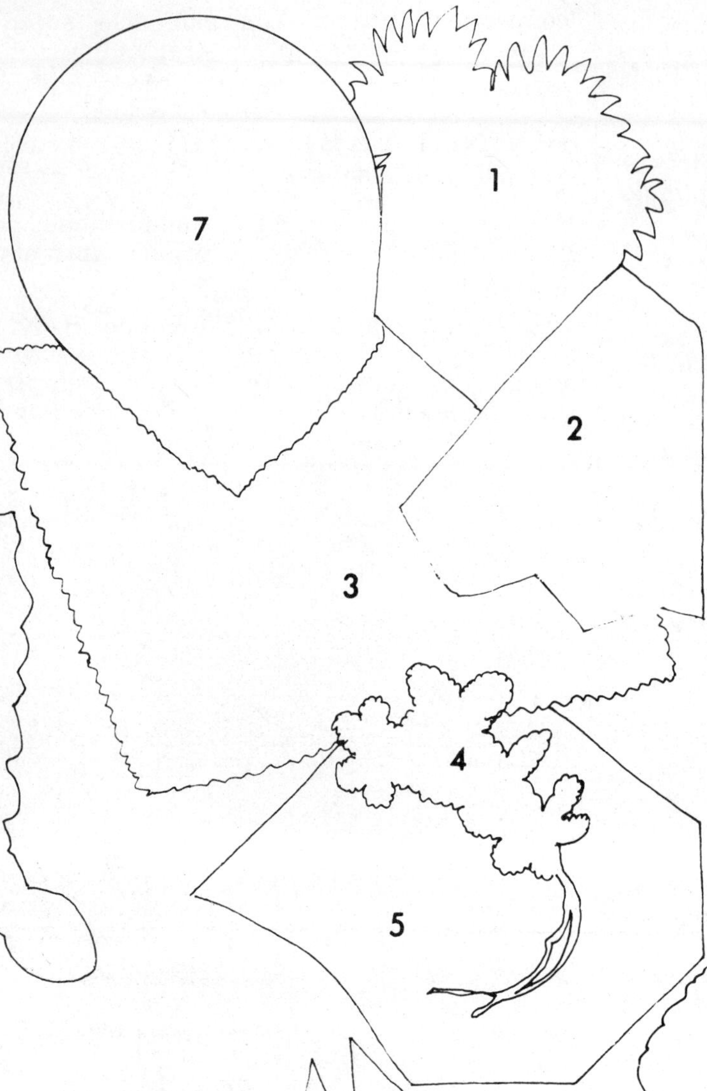

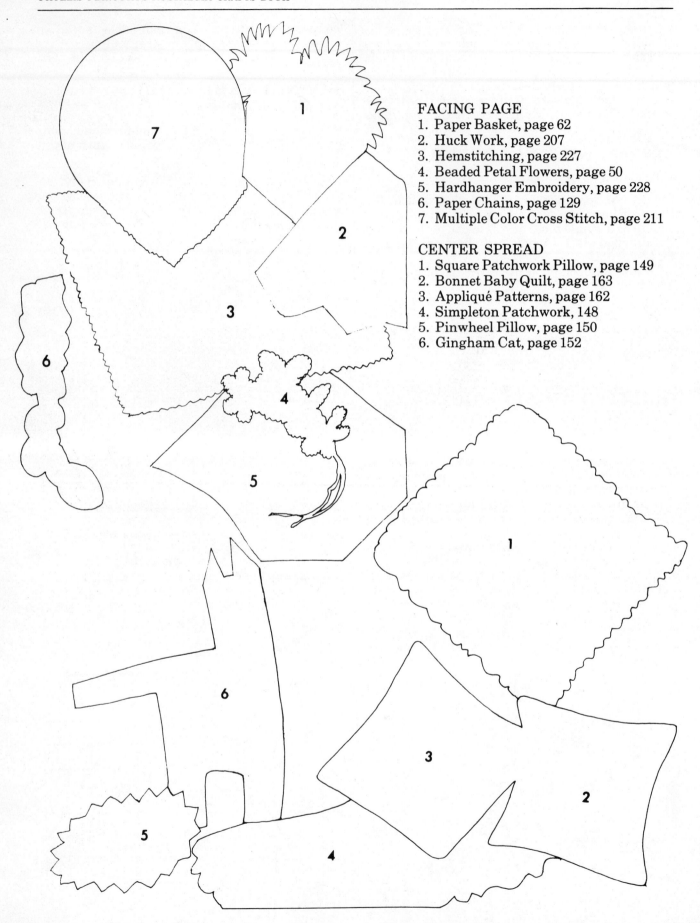

FACING PAGE
1. Paper Basket, page 62
2. Huck Work, page 207
3. Hemstitching, page 227
4. Beaded Petal Flowers, page 50
5. Hardhanger Embroidery, page 228
6. Paper Chains, page 129
7. Multiple Color Cross Stitch, page 211

CENTER SPREAD
1. Square Patchwork Pillow, page 149
2. Bonnet Baby Quilt, page 163
3. Appliqué Patterns, page 162
4. Simpleton Patchwork, 148
5. Pinwheel Pillow, page 150
6. Gingham Cat, page 152

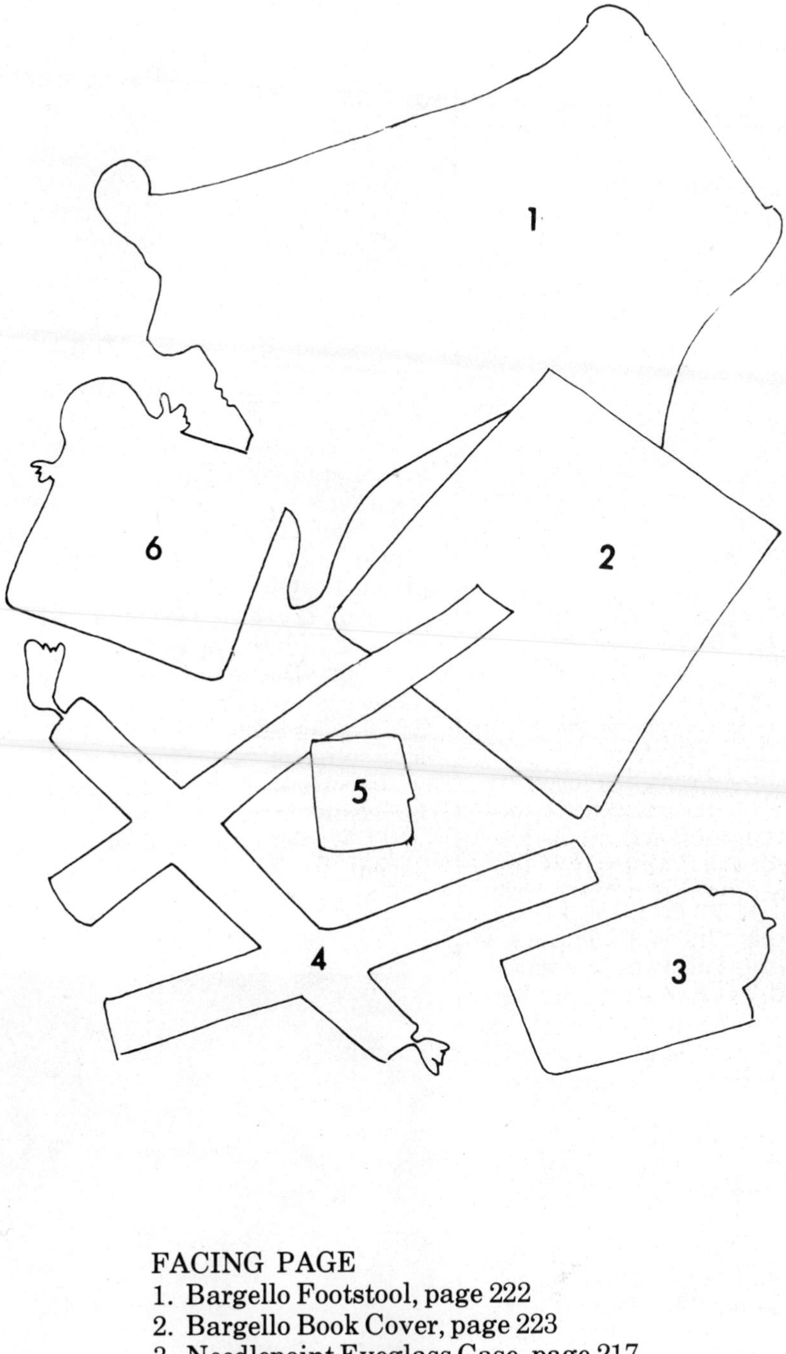

FACING PAGE
1. Bargello Footstool, page 222
2. Bargello Book Cover, page 223
3. Needlepoint Eyeglass Case, page 217
4. Needlepoint Belts, page 215
5. Needlepoint Change Purse, page 214
6. Needlepoint Mirror Frame, page 217

All items on this page were designed by Giavana LaMarca

for detailed directions on how to enlarge patterns from a grid.) Fig. 1 is the dress; Fig. 2, the shoe; Fig. 3, the bonnet and Fig. 4, the sleeve.

2. Trace each part of the motif onto your fabric and cut out.

3. Construct a quilt either in squares or on a single length of fabric, as discussed in Sewing on the Appliqués.

4. For a bonnet baby doll to go with the quilt, see the chapter **You're A Doll.**

JEAN HARLOW QUILT

This sumptuous satin bedspread recalls the era of

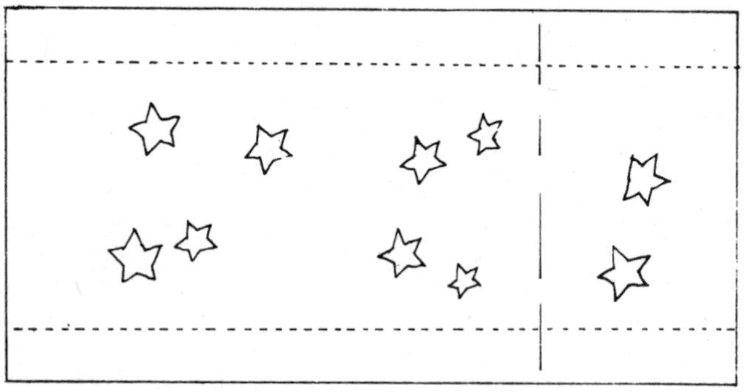

Jean Harlow, the 1930s movie queen adored by men, envied by women. With its companion pillows of shimmering bridal satin it will make you feel that you too are a star in the grand style.

1. The face of the quilt is white bridal satin.
2. The center panel of the quilt is made from a full width of the satin fabric and runs the entire length of the bed. Allow an overlap at the bottom end and extra material at the top for tucking under the pillow. The side panels are each half the width of the fabric and the same length as the center panel.
3. Sew the sides to the center panel.
4. A king-size sheet should fit as a backing. For extra-wide quilts, you may have to add additional fabric to the sheet.
5. Assemble the three layers of the quilt—satin, stuffing and sheet—and baste them together as described in the chapter **The Patchwork Story.**
6. The quilt is made thick and puffy by placing the stitches far apart. Start at one end and sew the three layers together by hand in the following manner. Take two stitches in the same place; then pass the needle between the top and bottom layers of fabric coming out 3 inches away. Again stitch through the three layers with two stitches and pass the needle 3 inches away. Continue across. The second row should be 3 inches away from the first, with the stitches falling midway between the initial stitches. Quilt the entire surface in this

manner—sets of stitches 3 inches away from each other.

7. Turn the edges of the top and bottom layers into the quilt and blind-stitch them together.
8. The stars are cut from silver or gold fabric. Make your patterns from the star given in Old Glory Pillows. By varying the scale of the grid (see page 13), you can make stars of different sizes.
9. Sew the stars to the spread by turning under a ⅛-inch hem and blind-stitching it down. Cut a small slit in the crook of each star point for easier turning. Stuff the star lightly with cotton or polyester before sewing it completely in place.
10. Make matching bed pillows for a dramatic accent.

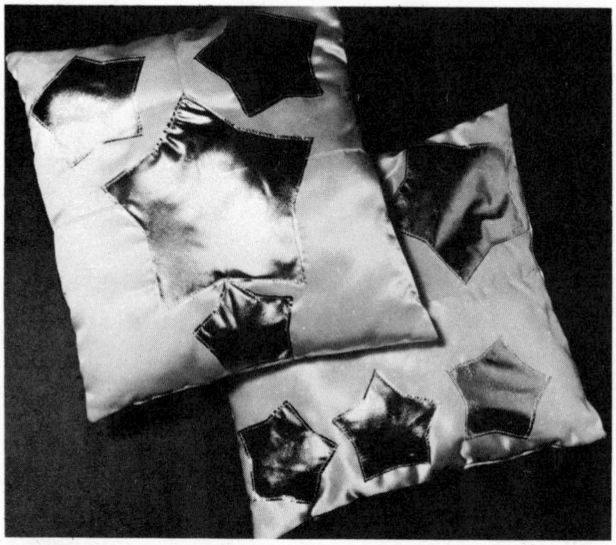

TOYLAND AND PENNSYLVANIA DUTCH FELT QUILTS

The Pennsylvania Dutch Quilt is a folk quilt still

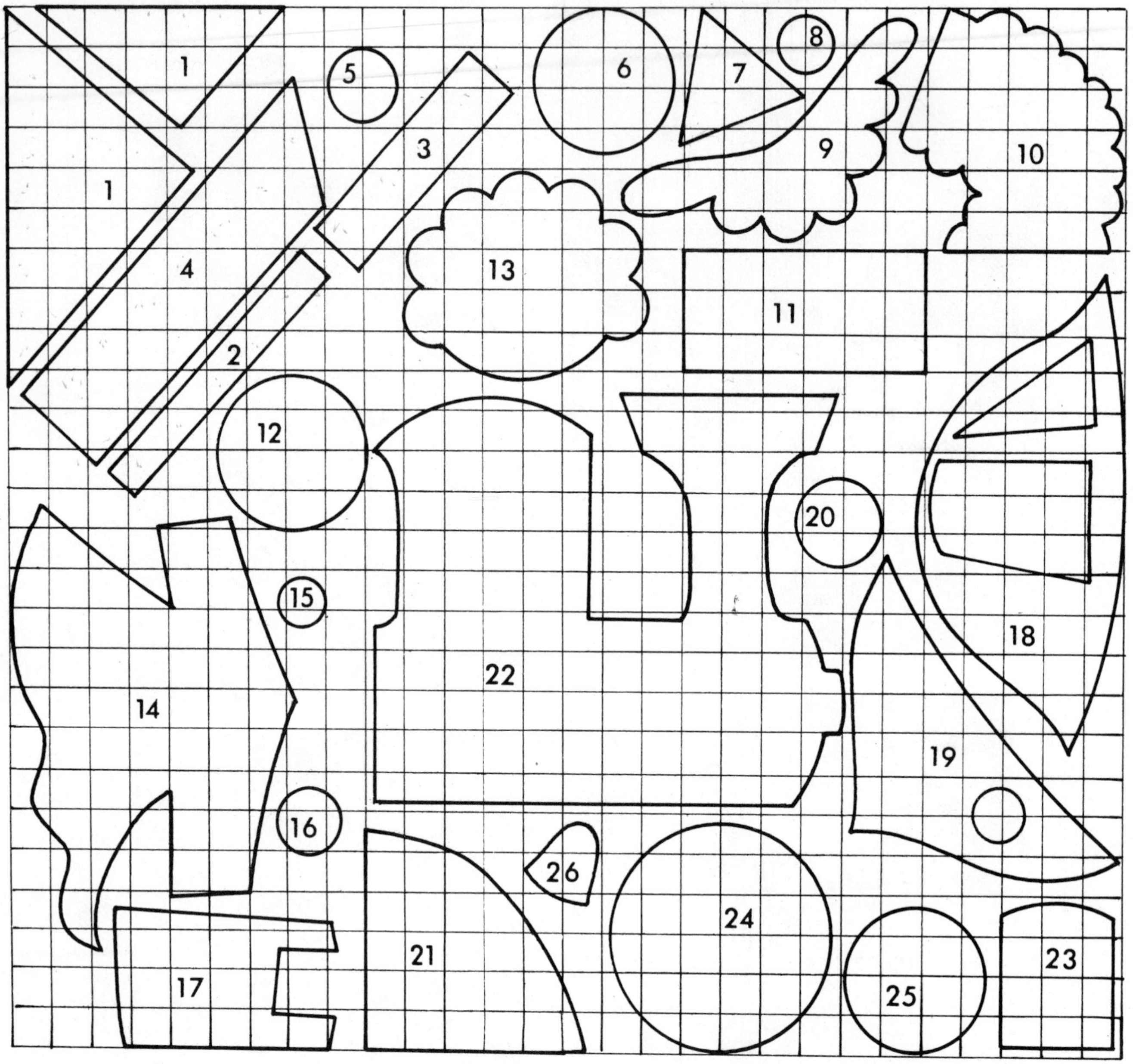

made among the Amish people who were its creators. The Toyland Quilt was inspired by the 1903 Victor Herbert play, *Babes in Toyland.*

1. To make patterns for either quilt, enlarge the grid on a piece of cardboard so that one square equals one inch. Draw the patterns on the enlarged grid and then cut them out. (See page 13 for detailed directions on how to enlarge patterns from a grid.) The appliqué designs should be cut from felt. The base squares can be felt or another fabric.

2. The patterns for the Toyland Quilt are as follows: boat sails (Fig. 1), mast (Fig. 2), cabin (Fig. 3), hull (Fig. 4) and portholes (Fig. 5); Jack-in-the-box face (Fig. 6), hat (Fig. 7), pompon and nose (Fig. 8), collar (Fig. 9), body (Fig. 10) and box (Fig. 11); doll's face (Fig. 12), hair (Fig. 13), dress (Fig. 14), hands and cheeks (Fig. 15), shoes (Fig. 16) and apron (Fig. 17); upper part of top with details (Fig. 18), lower part with details (Fig. 19) and handle (Fig. 20); ball (quarter section of an 11-inch ball, (Fig. 21) and finally the locomotive (Fig. 22) with its window (Fig. 23), back wheel (Fig. 24), front wheel (Fig. 25) and bell (Fig. 26).

3. The pieces for the Pennsylvania Dutch Quilt are as follows: heart (Fig. 1), tulip (Fig. 2), tulip petal (Fig. 3), flower bud (Fig. 4), circles (Fig. 5) and leaves (Fig. 6); basic circle for the three hex signs (Fig. 7); five-pointed star (Fig. 8), inner star (Fig. 9) and outer star (Fig. 10); eight-pointed star (Fig. 11), inner circle (Fig. 12) and inner star (Fig.

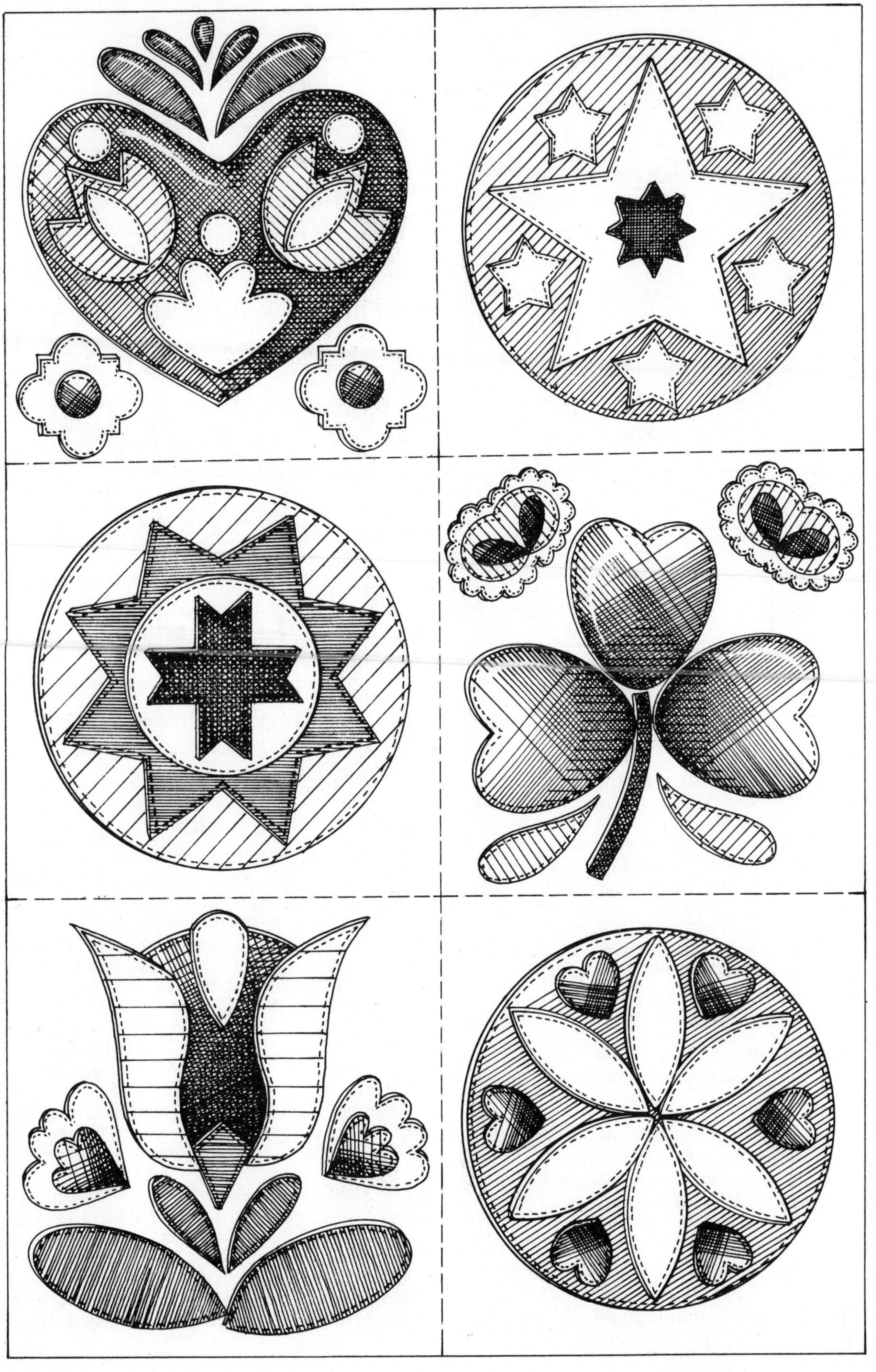

13); clover petal (Fig. 14), stem (Fig. 15), leaf (Fig. 16), outer lace flower (Fig. 17), and inner flower with detail (Fig. 18); Dutch tulip core (Fig. 19), petal (Fig. 20), pistil (Fig. 21), stem (Fig. 22), flower (Fig. 23) and leaves (Figs. 24 and 25); and for the last motif, flower petals (Fig. 26) and hearts (Fig. 27).

4. The base squares for the Toyland Quilt are in bright colors with light and dark alternating. The base squares for the Dutch Quilt are in subtle pastels or all white.

5. Pin all appliqués in place on the base squares.

6. Machine- or hand-stitch the appliqués in place. Felt does not require hemming. If one appliqué overlaps another, sew on the one underneath first.

7. Sew together as many appliqué squares as you need to complete the quilt. Sew with ½-inch seams. (Follow the procedures described in the chapter **The Patchwork Story.**)

Note: felt quilts must be dry-cleaned.

SABRINA

Sabrina is a combination of appliqué and crewel embroidery. The scraps of fabric that make each grape and seed are sewn to the background with wide buttonhole-like stitches.

1. Cut a piece of background cardboard 12 x 14 inches. Cut a piece of velvet one inch larger than the cardboard on all sides.

2. To make patterns for the fruit, enlarge the grid on another piece of cardboard so that one square equals one inch. Draw the fruits on the cardboard and cut them out. (See page 13 for detailed directions on how to enlarge patterns from a grid.) Fig. 1 is the leaf; Fig. 2, the lemon; Fig. 3, the apple; Fig. 4, the pear; Fig. 5, the banana and Fig. 6, the watermelon seed. The watermelon rind is a 6-inch circle, topped with a 4½-inch circle for the pulp. The grapes are 1½-inch circles and the plums 2-inch circles.

3. Cut the fruit from velvet and/or satin in appropriate colors.

4. The basket, also of velvet or satin, is about 10½ inches long and 4 inches high. Curve the top and bottom edges gently and slant the sides inward.

5. Pin the basket to the lower half of the fabric background. Turn the edges under ⅛ inch and sew down with an embroidery stitch (see direc-

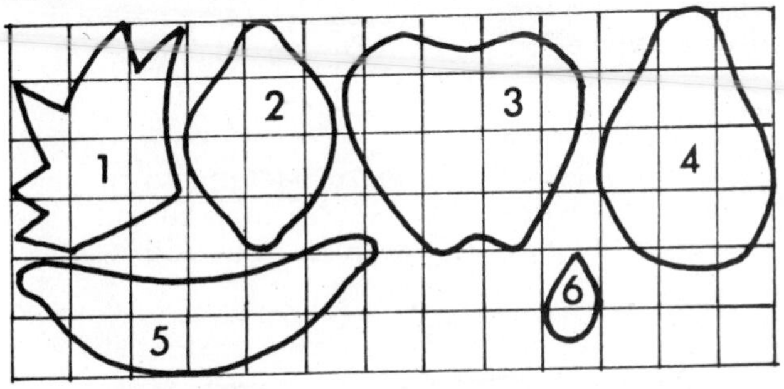

tions in the chapter **A Stitch in Time).** Before you complete the stitching, stuff the basket with a thin layer of cotton or polyester. Sew running stitches in a crisscross pattern on the basket to create the impression of a weave.

6. Sew on the watermelon rind next, stuffing it slightly. Top with the watermelon pulp and the seeds, stuffing both these layers as well.

7. Arrange the other fruits around the melon, sewing and stuffing as above. The apple and pear should overlap the melon.

8. Stretch the fabric on the cardboard, giving the overlap to the back.

FELT FLORAL APPLIQUÉS

Here's a three dimensional daisy floral for a wall or bureau top.

1. The patterns for the flowers are given here in actual size. Trace the daisies (Figs. 1 and 2), the half daisy (Fig. 3), the flower core (Fig. 4), the daisy bud (Fig. 5) and the leaf (Fig. 6) on tracing paper.

2. Use the tracings to make cardboard patterns.

3. Cut out the floral appliqués from colored felt or flannel. Note that the petals should be cut along the dotted lines. Also cut out a free-form vase.

4. The background for the floral arrangement is a piece of cardboard cut to the size of the frame you intend to use. Cover the cardboard in black

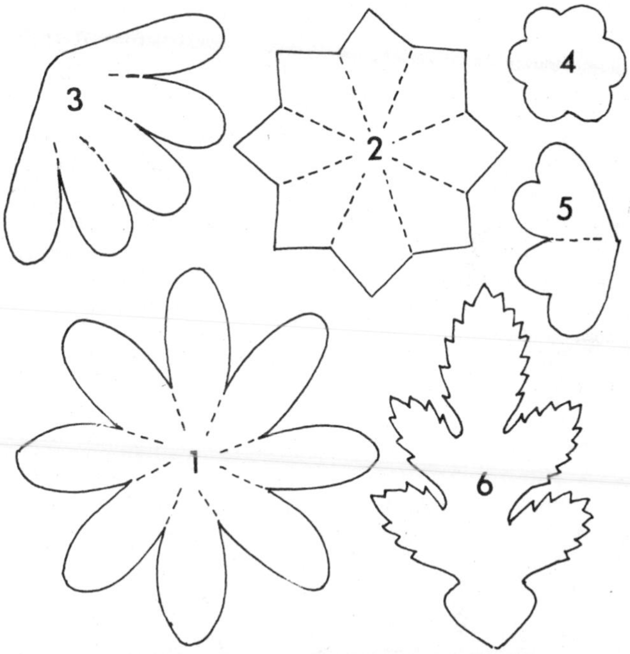

felt (see Brocade Mats in the chapter **Ribbons and Old Lace.)**

5. Arrange all the appliqués on the felt background.

6. Brush liquid white glue on the back of the appliqués and glue them in place one by one. Be careful to keep the glue ⅛ inch away from the edges of the appliqués to prevent any excess from spreading onto the background.

SQUARE POTHOLDERS

The appliqués on these potholders represent pots and utensils found in the typical colonial kitchen.

1. To make patterns for the appliqués, enlarge the grid on a piece of cardboard so that one square equals one inch. Draw the four shapes on the enlarged grid and cut them out. (See page 13 for detailed directions on how to enlarge patterns from a grid.) Fig. 1 is an iron; Fig. 2, a preserve jar; Fig. 3, a tea kettle and Fig. 4, a water pitcher.
2. Using the patterns, cut the appliqués from felt.
3. Machine- or hand-stitch the appliqués onto 8-inch felt squares.
4. Sew a small tab of felt to the underside of each square in the upper right-hand corner.
5. Pin a felt square to the back of the appliquéd one with a generous layer of stuffing in between.
6. Sew the squares together, ¼ inch in from the edge.

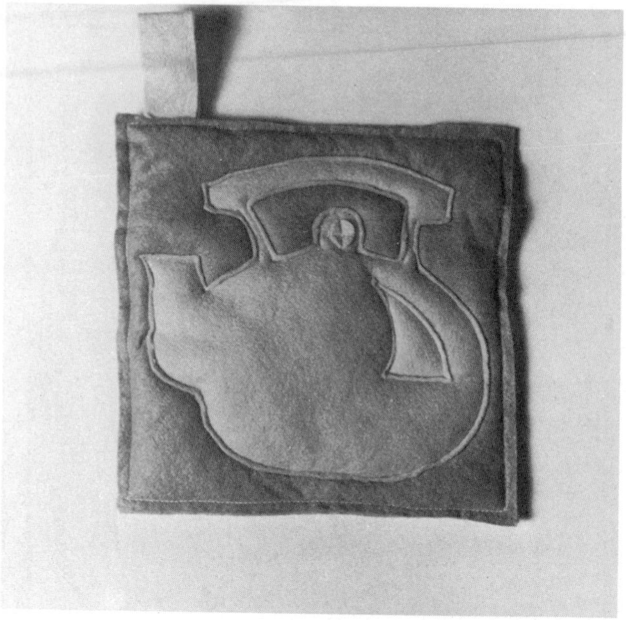

CALICO PAINTINGS

Something colonial women were particularly adept at was creating paintings from cloth.

PICTURES

1. Cut a piece of cardboard backing to fit your frame, and cover it with a solid color fabric. (See lace frames in chapter **Ribbons and Old Lace.)**

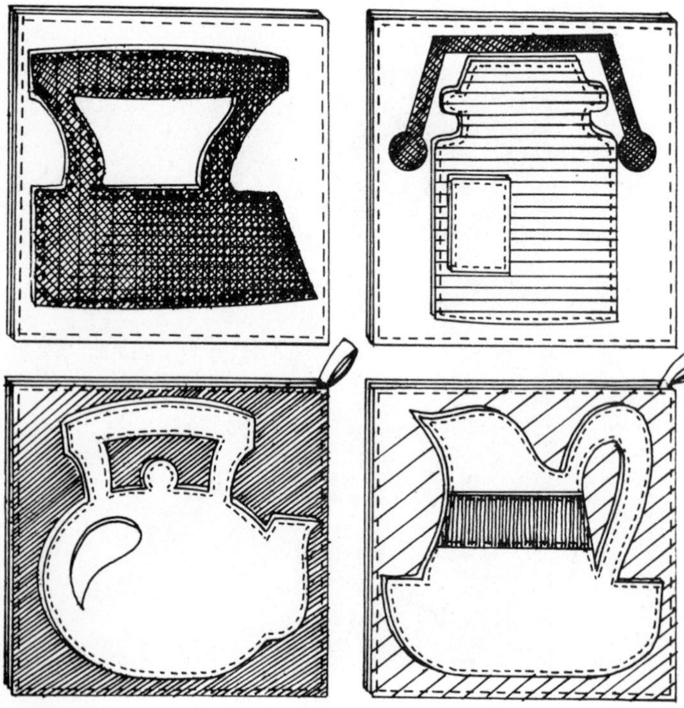

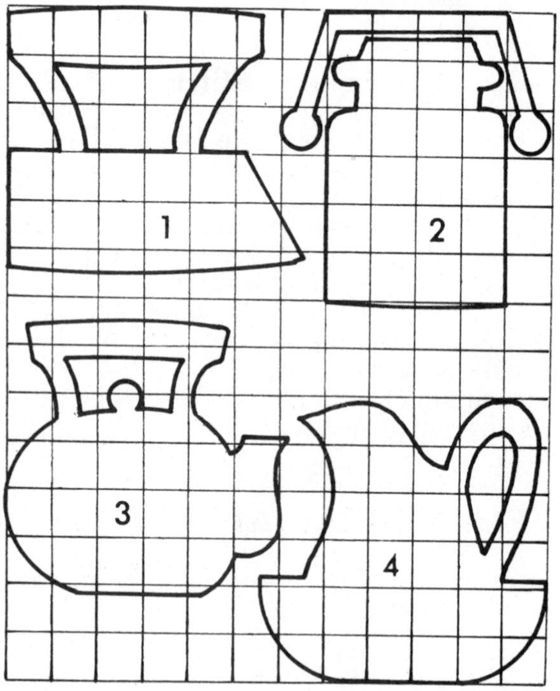

2. Dig into your scrap pile for interesting fabrics, preferably ones with small prints.

3. Cut out simple shapes to create landscapes like the one shown here or still-life or floral designs. Choose fabrics that fall into the color range of the objects you are making—a predominantly green print for a tree and so on.

4. Brush a thin layer of white glue on the underside of the appliqués and start to assemble your collage, overlapping the fabric pieces where necessary.

5. Calico paintings can also be machine-stitched or embroidered in place. Use decorative embroidery stitches to add details—veins in the leaves, for instance, or shingles on the roof.

GREETING CARDS

1. Cut colored construction paper into cards that will fit standard-size envelopes.

2. Create simple designs with calico scraps and glue them carefully to the cards.

3. Trim the outer edges of the cards with rickrack or ribbon.

PLACE CARDS

1. Fold a 3 x 4-inch piece of paper in half lengthwise.

2. Glue simple calico shapes to the left side of the cards just beneath the fold.

3. Write the name of your guest on the right side of the card.

CHAIR PILLOWS

A Tiffany lampshade cushion to soften a colonial wooden chair.

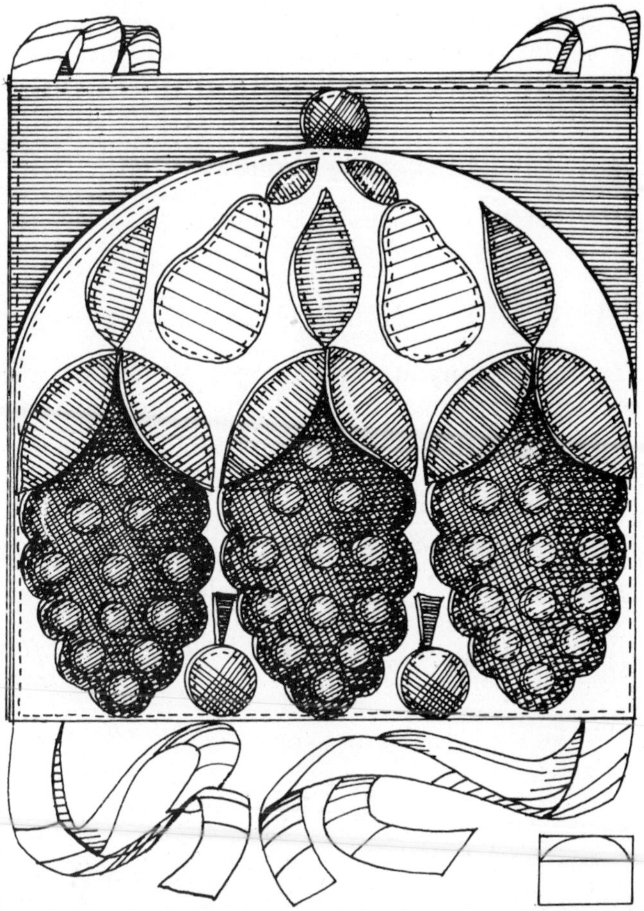

1. To make patterns for the fruit, enlarge the grid on a piece of cardboard so that one square equals ¾ inch. Draw the fruit on the enlarged grid, cut them out and trace their shapes on pieces of felt. (See page 13 for detailed directions on how to enlarge patterns from a grid.) Fig. 1 is the grape cluster; Fig. 2, the leaves; Fig. 3, the pears; Fig. 4, pear leaves and Fig. 5, the cherries. Cut smaller circles for individual grapes.

2. To plot the lampshade dome on felt, mark off a rectangle 12½ inches high and 14 inches long. Measure 4½ inches down from the top and draw a line across. Draw a curved line in the upper 4½-inch area, reaching to the top of the rectangle. Cut the dome from beige felt.

3. Cut two 14-inch squares from blue felt for the pillow.

4. Sew the lampshade dome to one base pillow shape.

5. Pin all appliqués on the dome as shown. Sew

them down ¼ inch in from the edges of each piece.

6. Sew two lengths of ribbon to each corner of the second pillow shape, on the underside.

7. Sew the two pillow shapes together, right sides facing *out,* on three and one-half sides. Stuff with cotton or polyester and sew the open seam closed.

8. Tie the pillows to the legs of the chair and, if possible, to the back as well.

SUNSUIT APPLIQUÉS

These charming appliqués are taken from a 1915 mail-order catalog ad for children's sunsuits.

1. To make patterns for the appliqués, enlarge the grid on a piece of cardboard so that one square equals ¾ inch. Draw the designs on the enlarged grid and cut them out. (See page 13 for detailed directions on how to enlarge patterns from a grid.) Fig. 1 is the sun's halo and Fig. 2 the sun's face. Figs. 3 and 4 are the morning glories. Fig. 5 is the bunny's body, Fig. 6, its head, Fig. 7, its ears; Fig. 8, its hands and Fig. 9, its feet. Figs. 10 and 11 are the bluebells and Fig. 12 is a leaf.

2. Trace the patterns on your fabric and cut them out. Use washable scrap fabric.

3. Pin the appliqué pieces on the playsuit or frock.

4. Turn the edges ⅛ inch under and machine- or hand-stitch the assembled appliqué in place.

HAPPY VEGETABLE APPLIQUÉS

These vegetable designs were popular in the 1940s. They were a favorite on aprons but occasionally showed up on pillows and children's clothes.

1. To make patterns for the vegetables, draw them on a grid that's been enlarged or reduced in size to make the patterns fit the item you intend to appliqué. Use cardboard for the grid. (See page 13 for detailed directions on how to enlarge patterns from a grid.) The vegetables are as follows: carrot (Fig. 1), carrot top (Fig. 2), radish (Fig. 3),

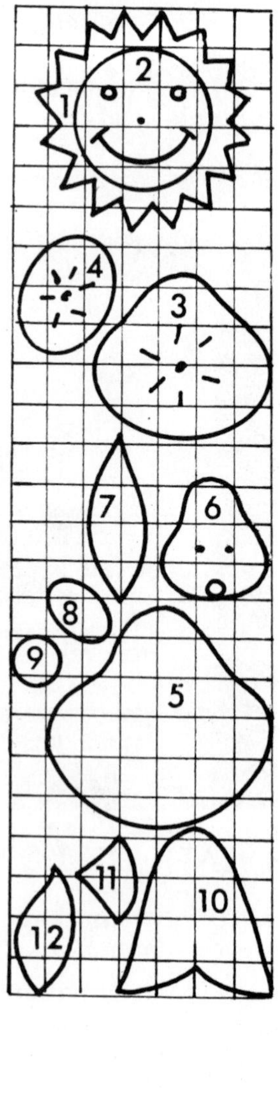

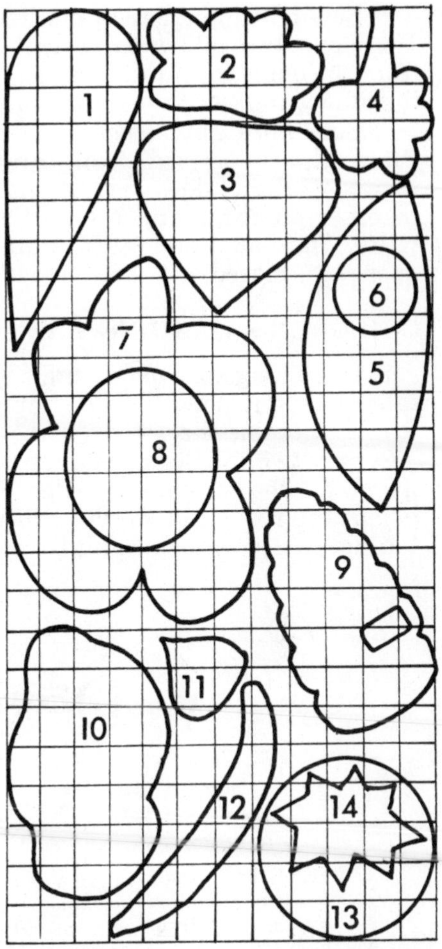

radish top (Fig. 4), peapod (Fig. 5), pea (Fig. 6), cabbage leaves (Fig. 7), cabbage head (Fig. 8), corn (Fig. 9), potato (Fig. 10), pearl onion (Fig. 11), string bean (Fig. 12), tomato (Fig. 13) and tomato leaf (Fig. 14).

2. Draw the vegetables on the grid, cut them out and trace their shapes on the fabric. Choose cotton or synthetic blends for appliqués on items that will be washed. You can use felt for non-washable items such as pillows. Cut out the appliqués.

3. To sew fabric appliqués, tuck the edges under 1/8 inch and stitch to the selected surface, either by hand or machine.

4. Felt requires no hemming; simply sew the appliqués to the underlying surface 1/8 inch in from the edge.

5. Sew round white eyes on the face of each vegetable. Make pupils with black French knots or buttons for all but the corn, which should have golden eyes to match its kernels. Embroider a grin onto each face.

APRONS

1. Sew or buy a full or half apron.
2. Decorate with washable appliqués.

PLACEMATS, NAPKINS AND TABLECLOTHS

1. For placemats, make 1/2-inch hems around 13 x 17-inch pieces of durable material. Sew fabric appliqués along the left side of each mat.

2. For napkins, make 1/4-inch hems around 12-inch fabric squares. Stitch a vegetable appliqué to one corner of each napkin.

3. For a tablecloth, take the dimensions of your table, allowing for an overlap of 8 inches on each side. Buy fabric by the yard. If you need to sew lengths of fabric together, plan to have the seam fall along an edge of the table. Make a one-inch hem all around the cloth and appliqué a border just above.

APPLIQUÉ QUILT

Follow the directions for the Toyland Quilt given earlier in this chapter, substituting the vegetable patterns for toys.

PILLOWS

1. The pillow covers are made from 12-inch squares of felt or 13-inch squares of any other fabric.

2. Sew felt appliqués to one felt pillow shape. Then sew two pillow faces together, ¼ inch in from the edge, on three and one-half sides. Stuff the pillow and sew the open seams closed.

3. Sew fabric appliqués to a fabric pillow cover. Place the appliqued front and back fabrics together, right sides facing, and sew the two together on three and one-half sides. Turn the pillow right-side out, stuff it and hand-sew the open seam closed.

CHILDREN'S HANGING BANNER

1. Cut a long strip of felt and appliqué felt vegetables along its length. Add simple arms and legs to the vegetable shapes.

2. Sew two tabs large enough to accommodate a dowel to the banner's top edge. Slip the dowel or a curtain rod through the tabs and hang the banner on a wall in your child's room.

OLD GLORY PILLOWS

The American flag is basically a creation in patchwork, but it lends itself nicely to appliqué.

1. From satin fabric cut a 7½ x 9-inch blue rectangle, four 1½ x 10-inch red strips, three 1½ x 10-inch white strips and six 1½ x 18½-inch strips, three in red and three in white.

2. Sew the seven 1½ x 10-inch strips together, alternating the colors, ¼ inch in from the edge.

3. Press open the seams.

4. Sew the assembled strips to the right-hand side of the blue field, right sides facing, with a ¼-inch seam.

5. Sew the remaining strips together with ¼-inch seams, again alternating the colors.

6. Press open the seams.

7. Sew the longer strips to the assembled top section with a ¼-inch seam.

New Designs for Sofa Cushions

THERE are fashions in sofa pillows as well as in other kinds of household belongings; perhaps they cause even greater cry for novelty, but whether new or old in design, the potent fact remains that they are one of the furnishings of which it is practically impossible to have too many. Cushions for the parlor may be strictly decorative, and

No. 1113—SILK AMERICAN FLAG CUSHION COVER

those for the piazza adapted to the rougher kinds of service, but the good, all-around, general utility cushion finds its place in the living-room, and there should be an abundant supply of all sorts and sizes. Every schoolboy can tell us how old is the design of the first cushion cover shown here, and it is particularly well suited for a boy's room, or for the place of honor in any room.

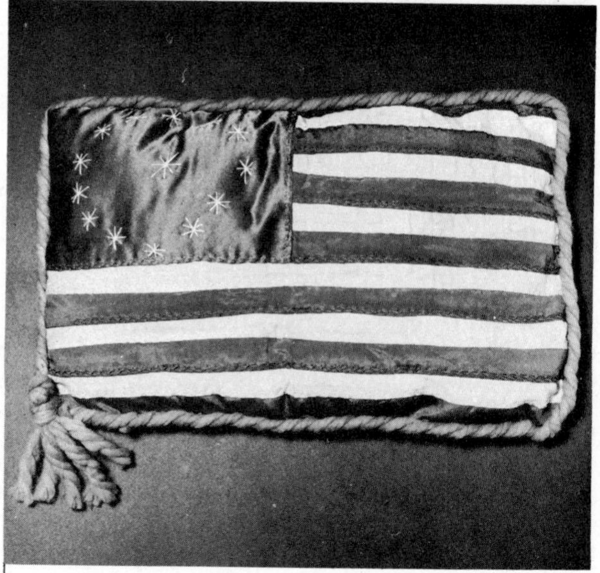

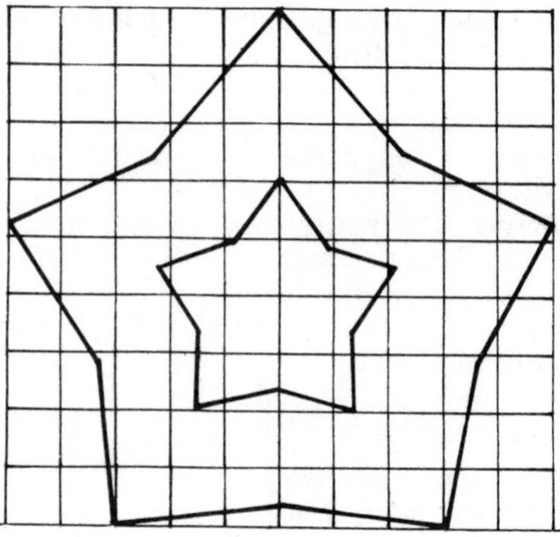

8. The two stars on the grid are shown in actual size. The larger one is for the colonial pattern of thirteen stars in a circle. The smaller one is for a fifty star flag. If you prefer a single large star centered on the blue field, enlarge the pattern as described on page 13.

9. Trace the star you choose on cardboard to establish your pattern. Transfer to white satin and cut out as many stars as you need.

10. Pin the star or stars in place on the blue field, fold under a narrow hem, and sew down with embroidery or blind stitches. Make a tiny slit in the crook of each star's points when turning under. The stars can also be machine-hemmed before you stitch them in place. [*Note:* if you prefer the entire star can be done in embroidery instead of appliqué.]

11. The back side of the pillow is cut from red, white or blue fabric.

12. Sew the two pillow shapes together, right sides facing, ¼ inch in from the edge. Leave 3 inches unsewn on one side.

13. Turn the pillow inside out, stuff with cotton or polyester and blind-stitch the open seam closed.

14. Add a decorative cord and tassel for a finishing touch.

THE PATIO PILLOW

In 1910, when this illustration was drawn, wicker and bamboo furniture for the patio or porch was as fashionable as it has again become today. The vintage pillow design given here recalls the long summer days at Newport or Marblehead before the First World War.

1. Cut out four 5-inch [light-colored] squares of fabric, one 11-inch square of the same fabric, and four black 5 x 11-inch rectangles.

2. Sew the rectangles to the top and bottom sides of the center square with ½-inch seams.

3. Sew the four small squares to the ends of the two remaining black rectangles.

4. Press all the seams open.

5. Pin the side strips to the sides of the assembled center. If the corners don't match, adjust the seams at this time.

6. Sew the patchwork together with ½-inch seams. Press the seams open.

7. The appliqués are circles of different sizes and two leaf shapes. Sew the circles inside the center and side squares in overlapping designs. Turn the edges under ⅛ inch and hand- or machine-stitch down the individual pieces.

8. Cut the back of the pillow to match the size of the front.

9. Place the two pillow sides together, right sides facing, and sew them on three and one-half sides, ½ inch in from the edge.

10. Turn the pillow right-side out, stuff it firmly and blind-stitch the open seam closed.

BOLSTER PILLOWS

Bolster pillows were popular in Victorian parlors where they eased the repose of many an afternoon tea guest. Though Victorian sofas were upholstered, many still had arms of unbuffered wood.

LONG BOLSTER

1. The long bolster is a patchwork of several lengths of fabric. The central piece is 24 x 38 inches. Two strips in a constrasting color, measuring 6 x 38 inches, should be sewn to the ends of the first. Strips in yet a third color, measuring 7 x 38 inches, should then be added at each end (see

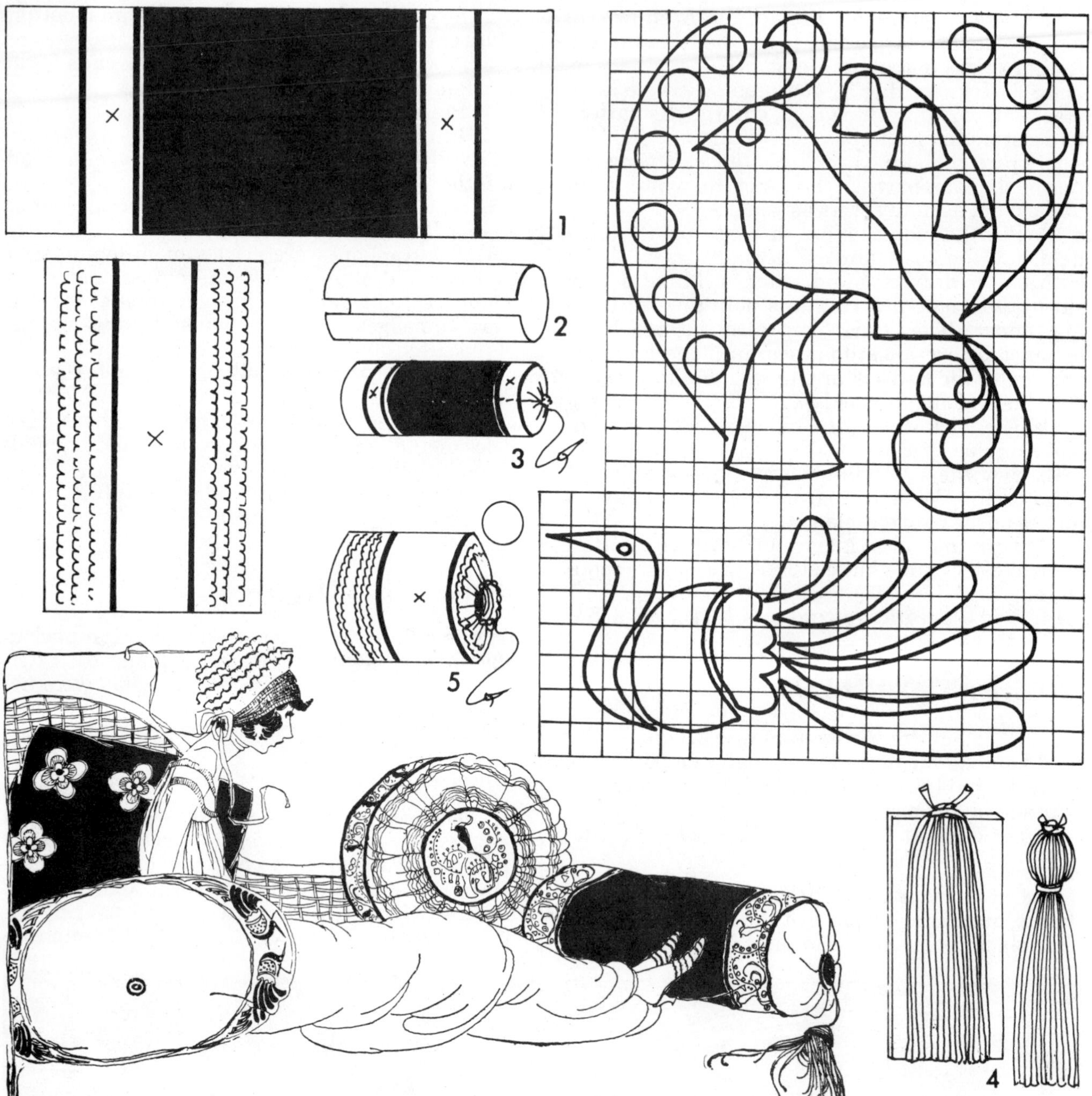

Fig. 1). Sew all the pieces together with ½-inch seams.

2. Press seams open.

3. Sew decorative ribbon or cord along the seams between the second and third strips and just outside the seams between the second strips and the center panel.

4. To make patterns for the Bird in a Tree appliqué, enlarge the grid on a piece of cardboard so that one square equals ½ inch. Draw the appliqués on the enlarged grid and cut them out. (See page 13 for detailed directions on how to enlarge patterns from a grid.)

5. Trace several appliqué units on the felt and cut them out.

6. Sew them along the panels marked X in Fig. 1, stitching ¼ inch in from the edges of the felt. Embroider the fine curves with a decorative stitch.

7. Roll the fabric lengthwise into a sausage with right sides facing (Fig. 2). Sew the sides together ½ inch in from the edge.

8. Turn the cover inside out.

9. Gather the edges at one end of the cover (Fig. 3) and sew tightly. Before sewing up the second end, fill the bolster with chip foam.

10. Cover the gathered fabric at each end with a large button.

11. To make a tassel (Fig. 4), wrap yarn or silk cord around a long piece of cardboard. Tie all the yarn together at the top of the cardboard, and cut the yarn along the bottom edge. Remove from the cardboard and gather the hanging yarn in a second tie one inch below the top knot. Make two tassels in this way and tie one around each button.

WHEEL BOLSTER

1. The wheel bolster is made with three lengths of fabric, each 13 x 62 inches, that are sewn together along the long sides. Make the middle panel a different color than the other two. Sew rickrack along the outer panels.

2. Roll the fabric into a fat sausage, right sides facing, and sew the widths together, leaving 5 inches of the seam open in the center. Turn the fabric right-side out.

3. Cut two 9-inch circles from felt or fabric.

4. Enlarge the Lone Peacock design on a grid on which one square equals ½ inch and cut two sets of appliqués from felt. (See page 13 for detailed directions on how to enlarge patterns from a grid.)

5. Sew one peacock design onto each circle.

6. Gather the edges of the fabric at both ends of the pillow to form an opening smaller than the felt circle (Fig. 5), and sew firmly.

7. Baste the felt circle over the end openings, spreading the gathered fabric evenly under the circle.

8. Stitch the circles in place and sew decorative cord over the raw edges.

9. Stuff the bolster firmly with cotton or chipped foam through the 5 inches of seam left open in the center.

10. Hand-stitch the open seam closed.

INTERLOCKING PLACEMATS

Originally, the placemats in this 1910 design were sewn together to form a single tablecloth; in our adaptation, the pieces are separate but interlocking.

1. Make the patterns for the placemats (Fig. 1) and center mat (Fig. 2) on brown wrapping paper or draw them directly on the wrong side of your fabric. Draw the rose (Fig. 3) and the leaf design (Fig. 4) on cardboard. If you want to make mat patterns, enlarge the grid so that one square equals 2½ inches. To make the appliqué patterns, enlarge the grid so that one square equals ½ inch. (See page 13 for detailed directions on how to enlarge patterns from a grid.)

2. Cut out the patterns and trace their shapes onto a washable fabric.

3. Cut four placemats and one center mat.

4. Sew a ½-inch hem along all sides. (Slit the corners at the base of the circular extension on the placemats for easier hemming.)

5. Embroider around the hemmed edges with a stitch of your choice (see the section on embroidery in **A Stitch in Time**).

6. Sew the rose and leaf appliqués to the mats. They stem out from a center circle made with running stitches (see illustration). To sew on the appliqués, turn the edges under ⅛ inch and blind-

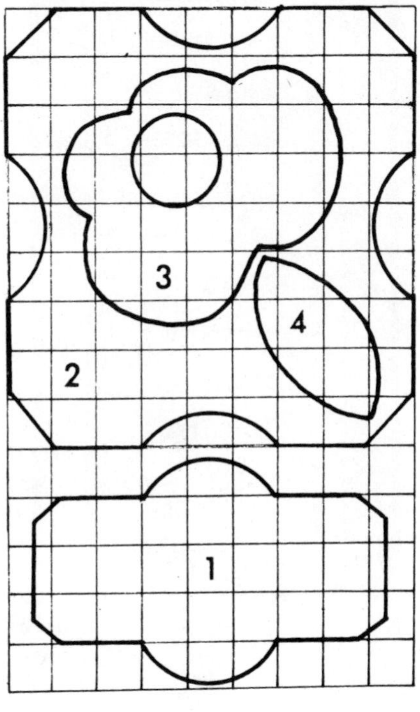

stitch or embroider them in place.

7. The arrangement of mats given here is for a square card table. If your table calls for more place settings along the sides, add extra center mats placed end to end. Each added center mat will give you two more settings, one on each side of the table.

FLATWARE SLEEVES

To keep silverware from tarnishing and getting scratched, knives, forks and spoons were gently coddled in soft cloth.

1. The base shape of the flatware sleeve is a 12 x 18-inch rectangle, extended with a curved flap that protrudes 5 inches beyond the rectangle. Cut two base shapes from felt.
2. The heart appliqué is given in actual size. Trace the heart on tracing paper and then transfer it to cardboard to make a pattern.
3. Cut hearts from red and pink felt.
4. Sew the heart appliqués, alternating color and direction, along the lengths of the outside base shape (see illustration).
5. Pin two heavy ribbons 15 inches long to the inside base shape, running parallel to each other 5 inches apart.
6. Tack the ribbon to the base at 1¼-inch intervals to hold the flatware pieces in place. Slack the ribbon slightly as you sew.
7. Sew the two base shapes together, right sides facing out, along the dotted line.
8. Now finish by wrapping bias tape around all raw edges and sewing in place. Add ribbon ties to the tip of the tab.
9. Insert twelve pieces of flatware, fold the appliquéd side over, roll and tie.

NAPKINS IN A BLANKET

Elegance in domestic appointments was the mark of the rich around the turn of the century. A lady of means made it a point of displaying the fine Irish or Belgian or Italian linens she had brought back from her last Continental tour. Bring a little Edwardian luxury to your table with this set of fine napkins, complete with a matching napkin blanket for storage.

NAPKINS

1. Cut twelve 17-inch squares of washable fabric.
2. Hem each napkin by folding the raw edges under twice, ½ inch each time, and stitching down the folds. The hemmed napkin will thus be 16 inches on a side.
3. Fold the napkins in four.

NAPKIN BLANKET

1. The blanket is made from two 9½ x 17-inch

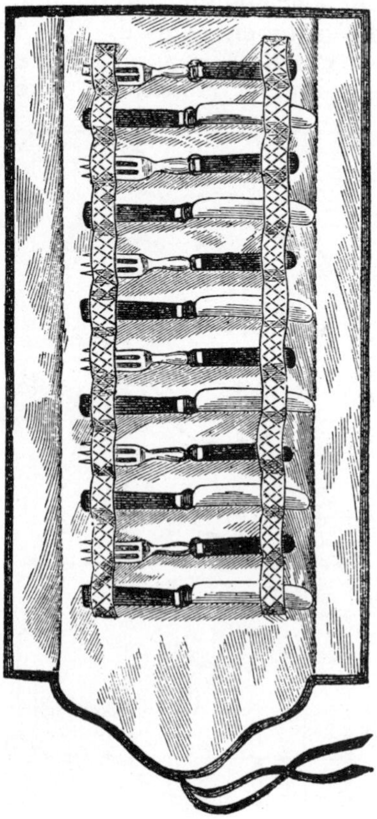

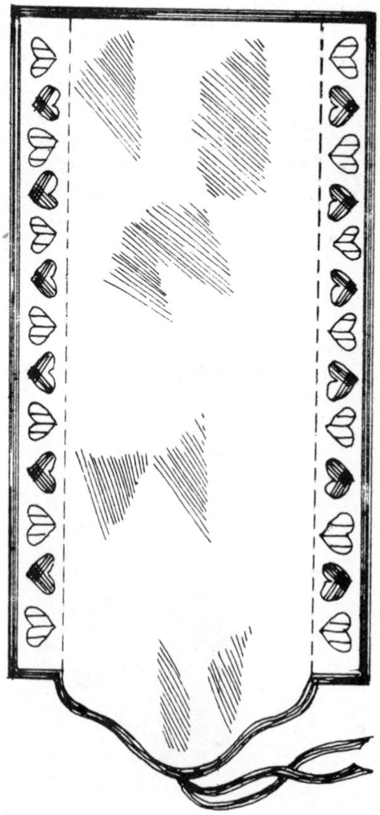

strips of fabric hemmed in the same manner as the napkins.

2. Place one fabric length across the center of the other (see Fig. 1), with the wrong sides of both pieces facing up. Place the napkins on the center of the blanket.

3. Fold the ends of the fabric strips over the napkins.

4. Attach thin ribbons to the upper corners where the ends fold over the napkins. Tie in bows to keep the blanket in a box shape (Fig. 2).

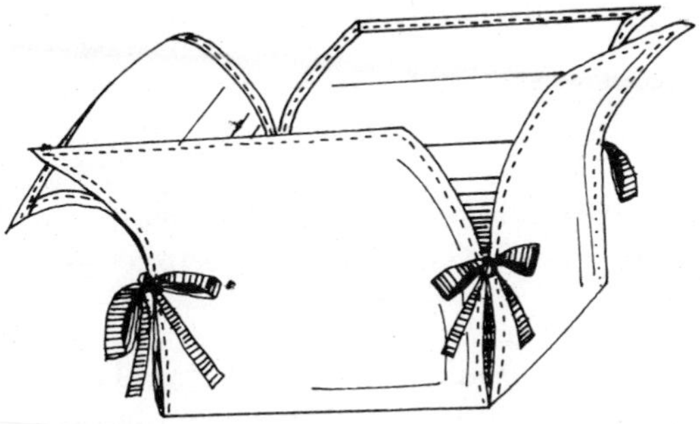

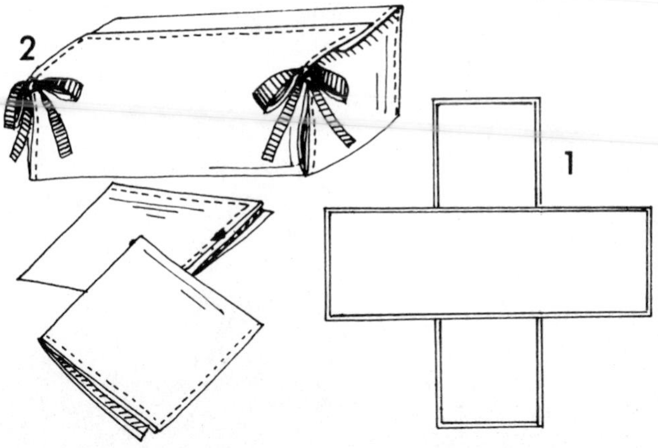

TEAPOT COZY

Good tea—the mainstay of a centuries-old, Anglo-American social ritual—must be hot. A tea cozy is to insulate the teapot and keep the tea warm.

1. Measure the height of your teapot and add 4 inches; then measure the circumference, including the handle and the spout, and add 5 inches.

2. Cut a piece of calico or felt to fit the above measurements.

3. Hem the bottom edge if you're using calico. (Turn the hem up one inch.) Felt requires no hemming.

4. To make a pattern for the teacup appliqué, enlarge the grid on a sheet of cardboard so that one square equals ½ inch. Draw the two shapes on the enlarged grid and cut them out. (See page 13 for detailed directions on how to enlarge patterns from a grid.) The doughnut is a 5-inch circle with a one-inch hole cut out of its center. Cut the cup and doughnut from felt.

5. Sew the appliqués to the center of the fabric.

6. Sew the cozy together, right sides facing, along the width, with a ½-inch seam. Turn the fabric right-side out.

7. Hem the top edge of the cozy with a 2-inch hem. (Place your stitches a little less than 2 inches down from the top.) Run a second line of stitching around the top of the cozy, one inch below the upper edge. (See the dotted lines in the insert.)

8. Make a small slit between these two stitched lines.

9. Insert a narrow ribbon through the slit and feed it all they way around the cozy, exiting in the same slit. Keep a tail of the ribbon hanging from the slit. (If you tie a paper clip to the ribbon end it will make threading it through the fabric easier.)

10. Discard the paper clip, pull the ribbon tightly and make a bow with the two ends.

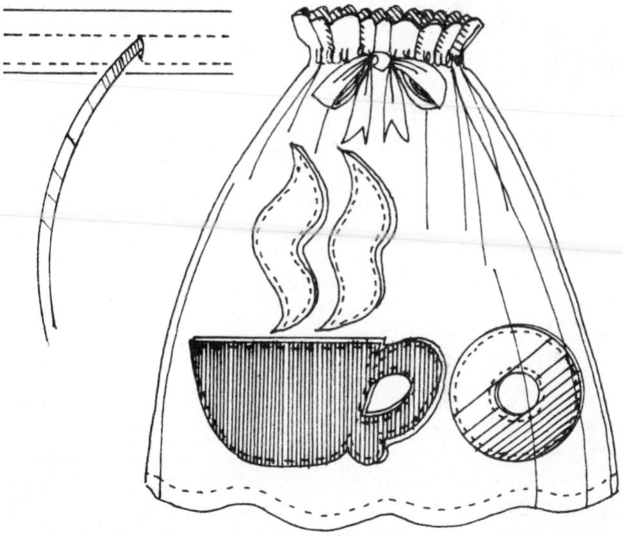

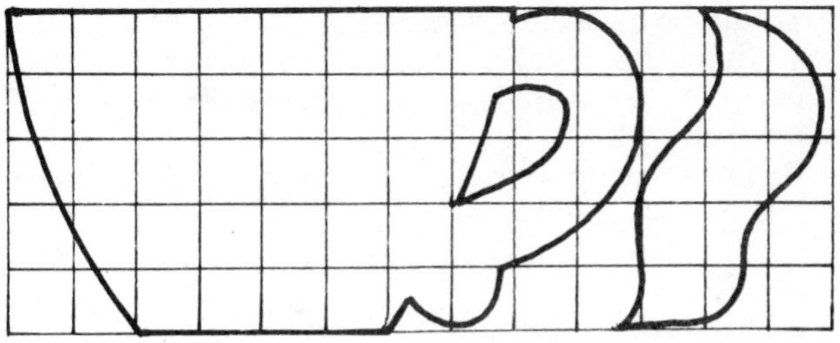

PHOTO CASE

A sturdy and portable felt photo case with the charm of the old leather-bound albums that once were.

1. The base fabric is a piece of felt 4 x 12½ inches. Extend the rectangle at one end by adding a 2-inch curved flap and center a circular protrusion on the flap. This is your final base shape.

Cut two of them as two layers give more body.

2. The photos are placed behind 4-inch felt squares. Cut out three squares and cut out windows from each. The windows should be slightly rounded at the top.

3. Sew a colored felt circle over the circular tab on the flap of one base shape. Sew half of a snap to the tab on the other base shape.

4. Place the base shapes together, right sides facing out, and place the windows on top of the two layers. Pin the windows in place leaving a little space between them.

5. Sew the three layers of the case together along the top and bottom edges ¼ inch in and along one side of each window.

6. Fold the case up and position the rest of the snap. Sew it in place.

7. Slip the photos in place through the open side of each window.

8. Embroider designs for added detail.

SEWING CADDY

This Victorian catchall will put your sewing paraphernalia at your fingertips. Its construction is simple and it can hang almost anywhere.

1. Cut a diamond shape with rounded corners from heavy cardboard.

2. Use pinking shears to cut two felt shapes ½ inch larger than the cardboard one on all sides.

3. Sew the two felt shapes together so that they encase the cardboard.

4. Cut a felt pocket that is slightly more than half the height of the backing. The width of the pocket fans out from the bottom point, as shown in the diagram.

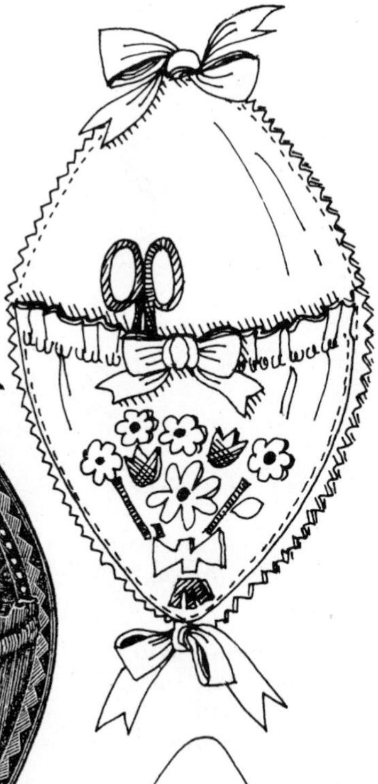

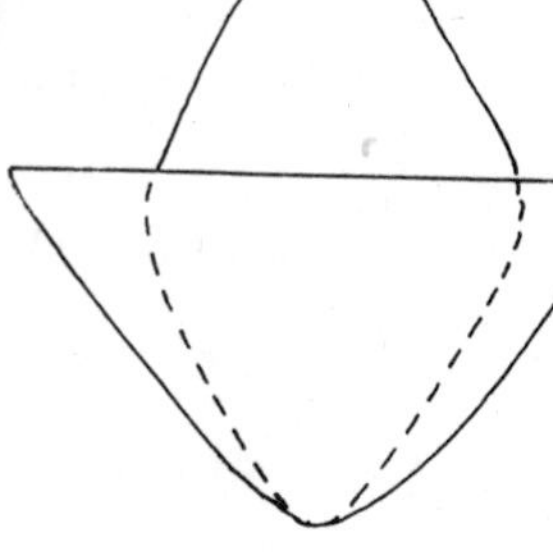

5. Sew a simple bouquet of flowers and a bow cut from scrap felt to the face of the pocket.
6. Sew elastic tape to the upper edge of the pocket, gathering the fabric so that the pouch is just a little wider than the backing.
7. Sew the sides of the pocket to the backing.
8. Add small bows to the top and bottom of the backing and to the center of the gathered pocket. You can also add rickrack around the edge of the caddy.

PURSE ORGANIZER

A handy purse organizer in which you can store almost anything.

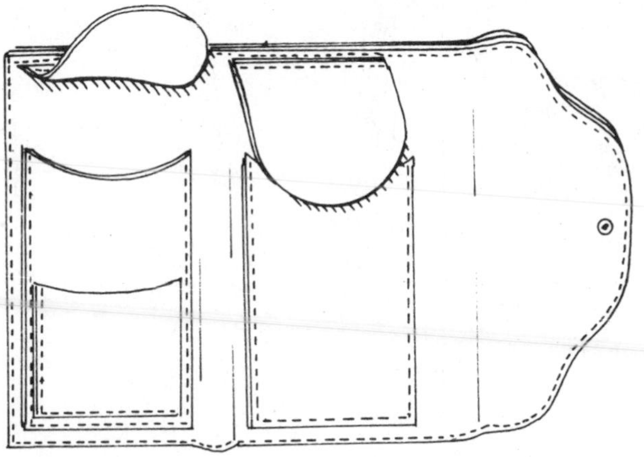

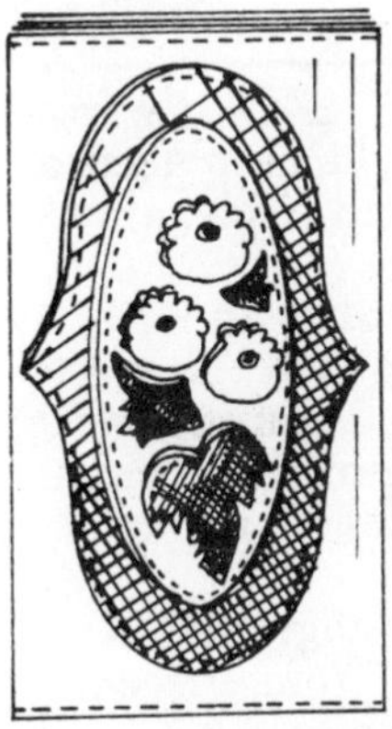

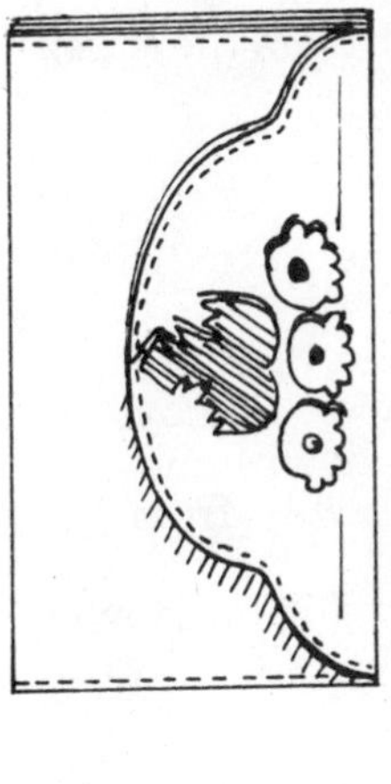

1. The base shape of the organizer is an 8 x 12-inch rectangle. Add a curved flap (the exact shape is up to you) extending 4 inches beyond one end of the rectangle. Cut two base shapes from felt.
2. To make patterns for the cameo appliqués, enlarge the grid on a piece of cardboard so that one square equals ½ inch. Draw the designs on the enlarged grid and cut them out. (See page 13 for detailed directions on how to enlarge patterns from a grid.) The flowers are Fig. 1, the leaves are Fig. 2, the inner oval; Fig. 3 and the outer frame, Fig. 4.
3. Trace the appliqués onto pastel shades of felt and cut them out.
4. Center the outer frame of the cameo appliqué on one base shape and sew in place. Finish the appliqué work.
5. Sew flowers and a leaf to the 4-inch tab (see illustration).
6. Cut two 4 x 6-inch pockets from felt. Make the top of each pocket slightly concave. Cut a third pocket 3 x 3 inches, also curving one end.
7. Top one pocket with the smaller pocket.
8. Stitching ¼ inch in from the edges of each piece, sew the pockets to the second base shape. Leave 1½ inches between pockets to allow for folding.
9. Cut two 4 x 4-inch felt squares for flaps. Round them off at one end.
10. Sew the flaps to the top of the base fabric so they fall directly over the pockets.
11. Sew a snap to the underside of the flap on the pocketed shape and to the corresponding point on the lower half of the appliquéd shape.
12. Place the two base shapes together, right sides facing out, and sew around all sides, ¼ inch in from the edge. Fold the organizer and snap it closed.

KNICKERS

It was a happy day when a young man traded in his knickers for his first pair of long pants. (Notwithstanding the fact that it was considered quite stylish for his father to appear in them on the golf course.)

1. Any old slacks or men's trousers can be cut down to make knickers. Cut off the slacks at a point 2½ inches below the knee.
2. Sew decorative ribbon along the side seam of one or both legs and around the waistband.
3. Sew a 1½-inch hem on both legs.
4. Cut enough one-inch elastic tape to fit around each leg at the base of the knee, and add one extra inch per strip.
5. Sew the tape to the underside of the hem,

Made From Men's Suits, Too,

Were These Smart Tailor-Mades

HAVE you a brother or a husband who has just discarded his uniform and tried to get into the suits he wore before he sailed away, only to find they were several sizes too small? Well, here are two ways in which you can use them in making dresses for yourself; and if you are as skillful at conniving as the two women who made the dresses illustrated here, even the former owners will be slightly incredulous of your achievement.

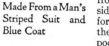

Made From a Man's Striped Suit and Blue Coat

The good-looking tailored dress on the left was made by combining a man's blue coat with a dark-gray-and-white-striped suit, and the result more than justified the use of the striped suit, which was in a fairly good condition, so that the striped material was used on the right side. The trousers were utilized for the skirt panels, front and back, and the side fronts of the coat for the side sections of the skirt, with the patch pockets at the top.

To make the trim-fitting bodice, the vest itself was used, and an extra buttonhole and button were sewed in between each of the original ones, to give a smarter finish.

A PORTION of the fronts of the blue coat was cut in a wide band and fitted in a square outline, and striped material inserted for the underarm section of the front of the bodice, extending up into the shoulder, and the sleeves of the striped coat were used, refitted closely. Striped material was used for the back of the waist and blue cuffs were added to the sleeves.

In making the skirt the striped trousers and coat fronts were used in conjunction with the fronts and a portion of the back of the plain blue coat, which formed a knee-length panel front and back, and a deep yoke around to the center back gore was made of the striped material.

A yard of plaid material, in dull harmonizing colors, which would intensify the color of the brown cheviot of the man's suit, was chosen for the extra fabric required to complete the dress illustrated below. The material was washed in warm soapsuds and pressed under heavy canvas, so as to avoid the slick look pressed woolens so often have. The cut-in pockets of the jacket were obviated by the use of darts ending in embroidered arrowheads. Additional buttonholes were made and new buttons added. The sleeves were refitted snugly, and narrow turn-back cuffs of the plaid and buttons and buttonholes gave a nice finish at the wrists.

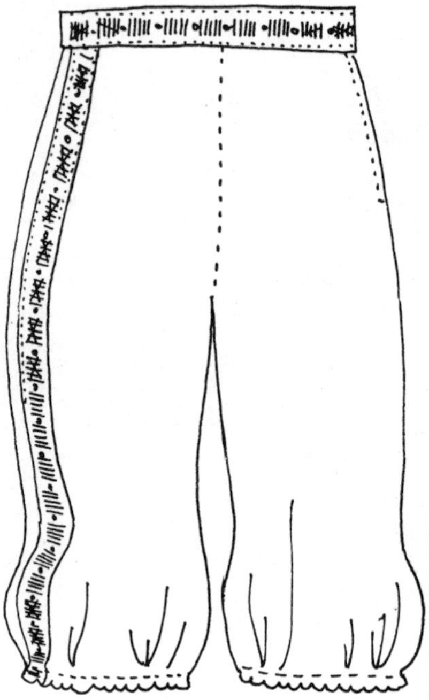

pulling the tape as you sew so that all the material is gathered underneath it.

TOTE BAGS

In the thirties, when all women wore shoulder bags, there was a dissident, fashionable clique that took to the tote.

ROUND TOTE

1. Cut two 12-inch circles (you can use a large pot to draw the outline) from fabric or felt. Remember that felt bags are sturdy but not washable.
2. Cut a slit in one circle up to the center point.
3. If you are using fabric, finish off the raw edges of the slit with bias tape.
4. The cherry appliqués are composed of simple triangles, circles and leaf shapes. Cut the shapes from fabric or felt.
5. Pin the triangle stem and the leaves at four equally-spaced points on the slit circle, ¾ inch in from the edge. The cherries should be placed at corresponding points on the second circle, also ¾ inch in from the edge.
6. To sew on fabric appliqués, turn under a ⅛-inch hem and blind- or machine-stitch the pieces in place. Felt appliqués require no hemming.
7. Sew a handle of folded ribbon at the center of the slit circle and a tassel at the center of the other circle.
8. Place the two fabric circles together, right sides facing, and sew ½ inch in from the edge. Turn right-side out. A felt bag can be sewn with the right sides facing out, ¼ inch in from the edge.

CYLINDER TOTE

1. Cut two 7-inch circles and one 12 x 21-inch rectangle from felt.
2. Sew a 12-inch zipper along the 12-inch sides of the rectangle. To attach the zipper, fold over ½ inch of the fabric (right side folds down) and sew the zipper to each fold, a ¼ inch away from the actual fold.
3. The felt appliqué is a 3-inch circle placed over a 5-inch wedged circle that has been cut into a

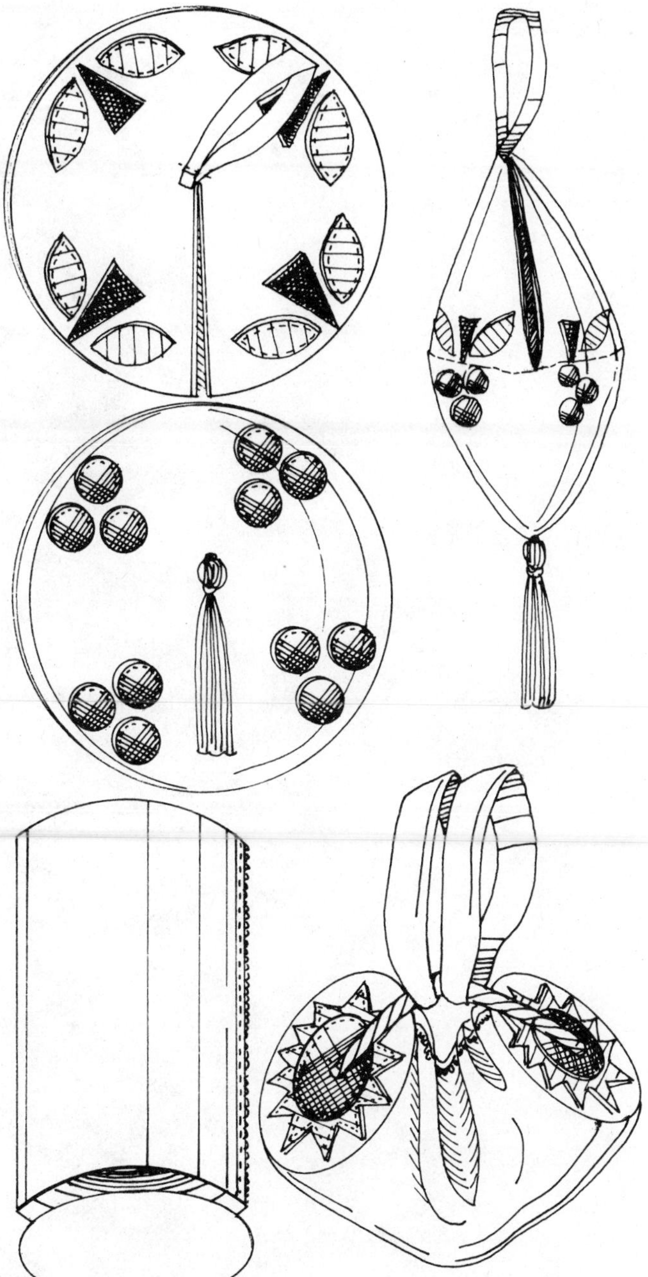

sun design. Pin and sew one appliqué to each circle.

4. Pin one circle at each end of the zippered rectangle, right sides facing, and sew with ½-inch seams.

5. Turn the bag right-side out through the zipper.

6. Cut a thick cord three-quarters the length of the bag and sew one end to the center of each sun appliqué.

7. The handles are made from two 5½ x 22-inch strips of felt.

8. Fold the strips in half lengthwise, right sides facing, and sew with a ¼-inch seam. Turn right-side out. Press each strip flat with the seam on the underside.

9. Slip the handles under the center cord on the bag. Tuck the raw edges of each end into the handle and blind-stitch the ends together with heavy thread.

PIONEER BONNET

The pioneer bonnet is a relic from covered wagon days and a perfect gift for a little girl who loves make believe.

1. To make patterns for the bonnet, enlarge the grid on a sheet of paper so that one square equals ½ inch. Draw the two shapes on the enlarged grid and cut them out. (See page 13 for detailed directions on how to enlarge patterns from a grid.)

2. Trace onto the fabric of your choice one bonnet cap (Fig. 1) and two brims (Fig. 2). Trace a third brim on a stiff interfacing fabric.

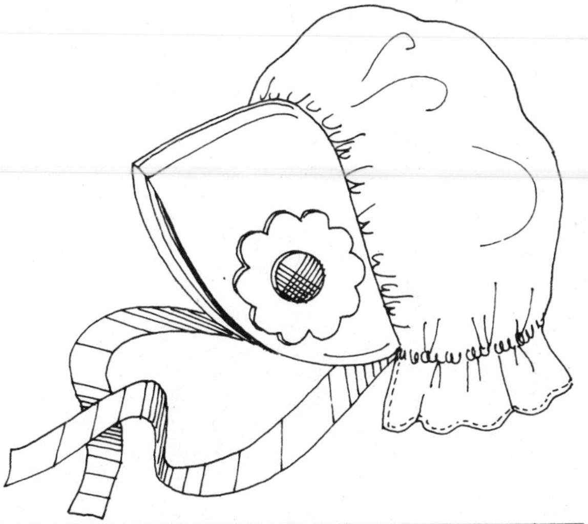

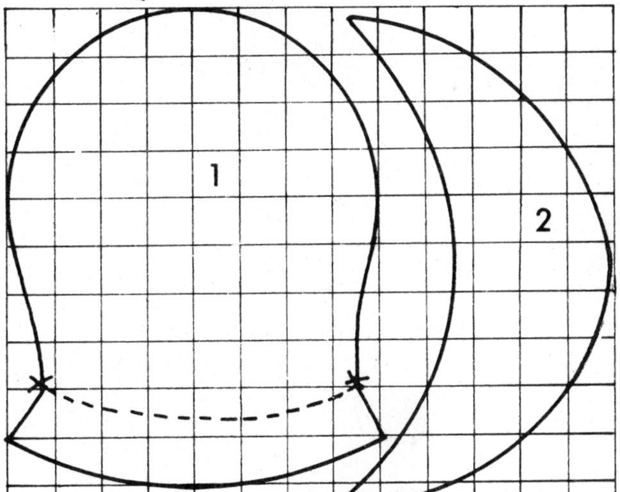

3. Place the two fabric brim shapes together, right sides facing. Place the interfacing on top of the two brims.
4. Sew the three brim shapes together around the outer curve with a ¼-inch seam.
5. Run basting stitches all the way around the curve of the cap between the points marked X.
6. Pull the basting thread to gather the cap to the same width as the brim.
7. Baste the gathered side of the cap to the interfacing and one brim shape, right sides facing.
8. When the cap and brim sections are in place, sew them together.
9. Turn the brim right-side out.
10. Turn the unsewn edge of the second brim section under ½ inch and sew it down under the cap.
11. Hem the extending bottom edge of the bonnet with a ¼-inch hem.
12. Sew 8 inches of elastic tape to the base of the cap (see the dotted line) gathering in all the fabric.
13. Sew a simple flower shape to each side of the brim.
14. Sew on ribbon ties or ties made from the same fabric as the bonnet.

A Stitch in Time

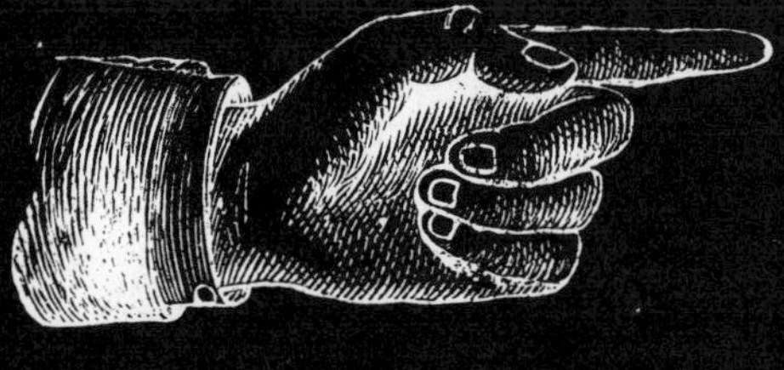

A Stitch in Time

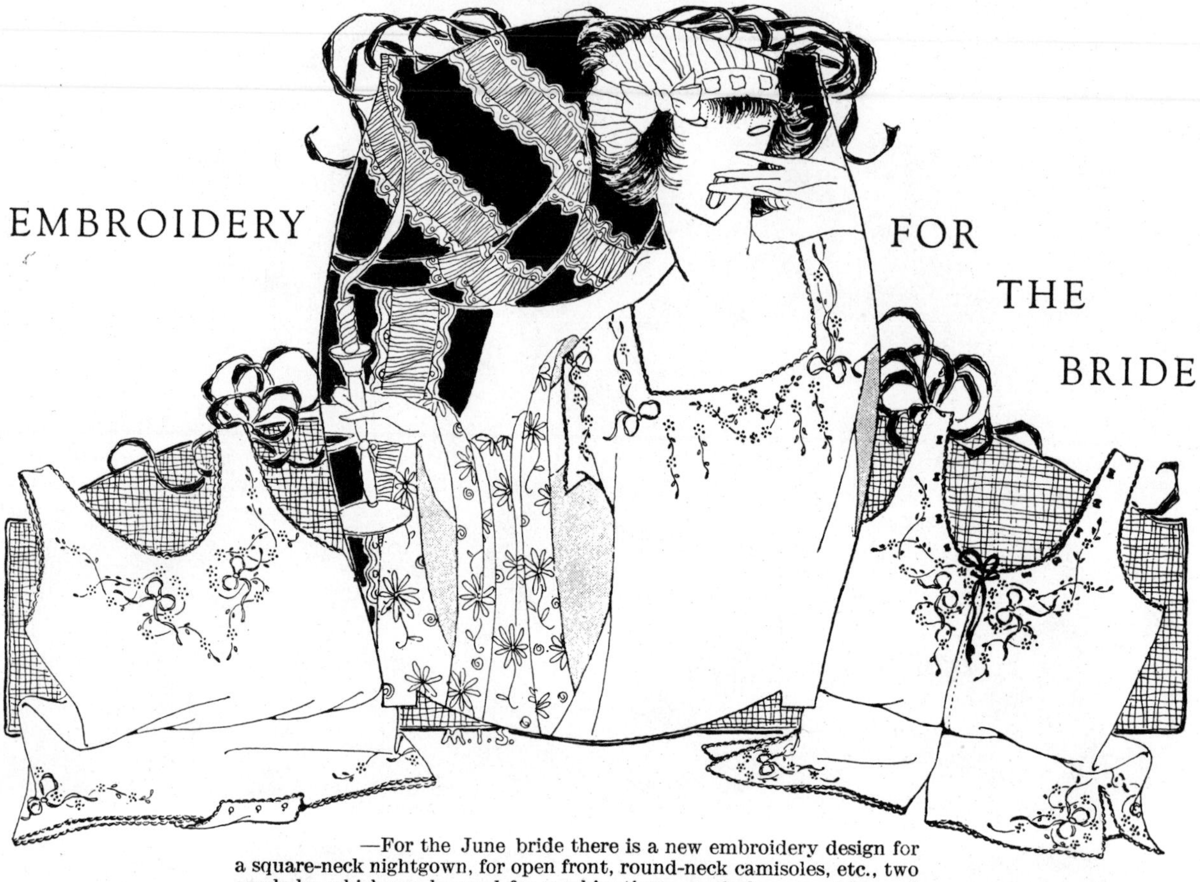

—For the June bride there is a new embroidery design for a square-neck nightgown, for open front, round-neck camisoles, etc., two armholes which can be used for combinations, camisoles, etc., 1⅝ yard scallops, two long motifs and 4 corners. The design can be worked in a combination of outline and French-knot embroidery.

If you study American needlework you'll discover some interesting and singular things about it. It is different from the work of other countries. Most everywhere else you'll find that there are two kinds of needlework—usually there's an indigenous peasant needle art and a wealthier, more formal needle art. In this country we have neither extreme. American needlework is neither crude nor formal. It has a new and unique spirit and may be more truly American than our painting, sculpture or music.

American needlework designs are airy and loose. Old World needlework has always been somewhat rigid. Each detail is essential to the whole and no part can stand alone. The backgrounds are solid, the patterns are formal, the borders are considered essential. Although early American women rebelled against this tight and constraining design, many of the European needle arts remained popular up to and including the present.

There are hundreds of techniques to work with needle and thread—from smocking to stitching samplers, from hemstitching to huckwork. Some particularly interesting designs and techniques follow.

BASIC EMBROIDERY

ENLARGING EMBROIDERY DESIGNS

The designs in this chapter are drawn the actual size called for in most of the projects. If you wish to enlarge a design, trace the design on tracing paper or wrapping tissue. Draw a grid over the tracing forming ¼-inch boxes. Once your designs are on the grid, see page 13 for detailed directions on how to enlarge patterns from a grid.

TRANSFERRING A DESIGN

Whether you are using a design that is exact size or a design you have enlarged on a grid, the first step is to trace it on tracing paper or wrapping tissue. Pin the tracing to the intended fabric. Use an embroidery hoop if the design is small enough. When embroidering, sew through the fabric and the tracing. When the embroidery is completed, tear away the tracing.

To transfer the design directly to the fabric, place a sheet of carbon paper on the fabric, carbon side facing down. Note: to avoid smudging the fabric, do not move the carbon paper once it is on the fabric. Place your tracing over the carbon and punch holes along the traced lines with a straight pin. The design will transfer to the fabric in dots.

MATERIALS

Embroidery threads are best for embroidery work. They are sold in small skeins and come in a wide variety of colors. Embroidery thread can be split easily if you wish to work in very fine lines. Other threads and yarns can be used, but then you are really doing crewel work, which is discussed later on in this chapter.

Needles should be short and wide-eyed. A needle threader is a must.

Fabric choice is optional and can range from a fine silk to a coarse burlap to a velvet. For items that will require heavy wear, choose a washable fabric.

An embroidery hoop is composed of two rings, one fitting inside the other. Force the area of the fabric to be embroidered between the two hooped circles.

SIMPLE EMBROIDERY DESIGNS

Practice the three simple designs on scrap fabric to try your hand at embroidery. The original designs embellished children's hats in the early 1900s. First try the designs in different outline stitches and then use more elaborate stitches. You might try it on an old knitted winter hat.

BASIC EMBROIDERY STITCHES

The following stitches are popular time-tested favorites. Stitches fall into three categories: outline, filler and decorative. The numbers correspond to the illustration.

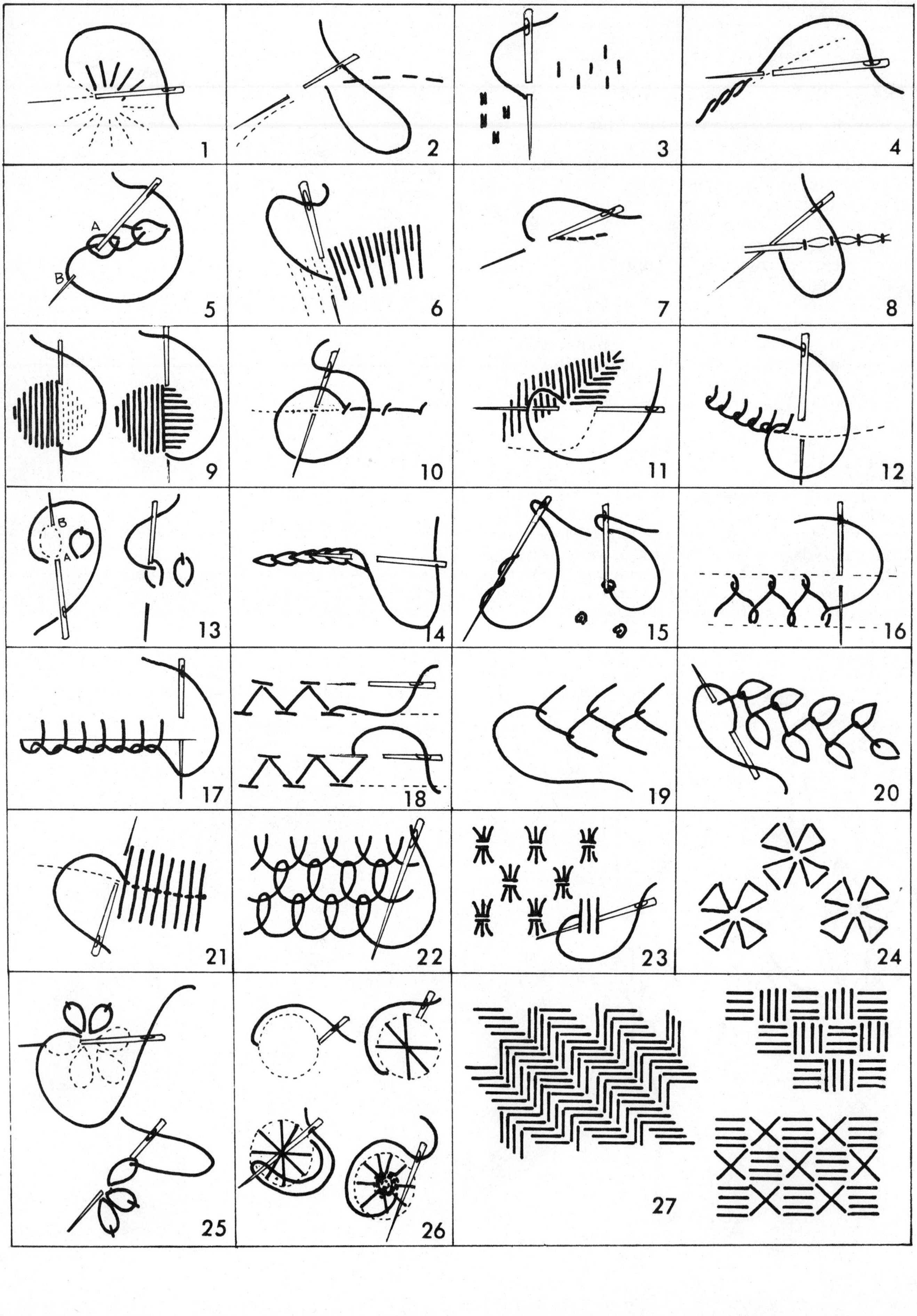
1
2
3
4
5
6
7
8
9
10
11
12
13
14
15
16
17
18
19
20
21
22
23
24
25
26
27
A
B

1. **Straight Stitch.** Bring the needle up and then under the fabric in small or long stitches.
2. **Running Stitch.** A straight stitch in a line.
3. **Seeding Stitch.** Short straight scattered stitches, equally spaced.
4. **Outline Stitch.** Worked left to right inserting the needle a short distance to the right. Bring the needle to the left at a slight angle.
5. **Chain Stitch.** Bring the needle up at A, holding the thread down with your thumb. Insert the needle back down at A and then up at B.
6. **Kensington Stitch.** Stagger long and short straight stitches. Alternate long and short in the second row. This is a good stitch for filling in large areas.
7. **Back Stitch.** Worked from right to left.
8. **Couching.** Place the thread along the intended line and tack it down with small even stitches.
9. **Satin Stitch.** Bring needle up at one edge and down at the opposite edge. Return to the starting edge, bringing the needle under the fabric. Use this stitch for filling in small areas.
10. **Coral Stitch.** The needle is inserted into the fabric on the line, going under and then through the loop. Stitches should be equidistant.
11. **Satin Stitch Leaf.** Work stitches from the outer edges into an imaginary center line. The stitches get larger as you work downward.
12. **Buttonhole Stitch.** Work the needle in and out of the fabric. Bring it through a loop. Work from left to right.
13. **Lazy Daisy.** Bring the needle up at A. Hold the thread down with your thumb. Insert the needle back at A, under and up at B. Tack down the loop by inserting the needle back under the fabric.
14. **Split Stitch.** Work the thread from left to right, passing the needle through the thread.
15. **French Knot.** Bring the needle up through the fabric. Twist the thread twice or more around the needle. Insert the needle back into the fabric a thread away from the extending thread.
16. **Cretan Stitch.** Bring the needle up on the bottom line, working from left to right. Work the needle up to the top line, keeping the needle straight up and down, making a small stitch, as the needle moves over the base thread.
17. **Blanket Stitch.** This is a buttonhole stitch worked on the edge of the fabric.
18. **Chevron Stitch.** The stitch is worked from left to right. Sew a small stitch on the top line which forms the diagonal center line. Bring the needle back and make a second stitch a little to the right of the first stitch, emerging to the left of the newly formed horizontal line on the diagonal. Follow the same procedure working down to the bottom row.
19. **Feather Stitch.** Form a short loop. Bring the needle back up through the fabric, emerging through the fabric at the center of the loop. Form a second short loop and proceed as above.
20. **Feather Chain.** The feather stitch is worked in a closed loop rather than an open loop.
21. **Roman Stitch.** Make a long straight stitch. Bring the needle out and over the center of the stitch. Insert the needle into the fabric tacking down the stitch. Bring the needle under and out at the left of the first stitch. Continue with a long straight stitch.
22. **Open Buttonhole.** Make a row of looped stitches. The needle enters the fabric at the beginning and end of each row. The stitches in the following rows are detached loops, each connected to the loop directly above each.
23. **Sheaf Filling.** Group three or four equal Satin Stitches. The needle emerges at the center of the left stitch and goes over and under at the right stitch. Pull and work a second stitch.
24. **Back Stitch Star.** Three short Back Stitches form a triangle. Make four triangles.
25. **Lazy Daisy Flower.** Group six lazy daisy stitches in a circle. Add a French knot to the center.
26. **Spider Web.** Make four crisscrossing stitches equally spaced on a circle. Bring the needle back through the dotted imaginary line and under the center point of the crossed stitches. Bring the needle through the looped thread and pull, securing the crossed threads. Slide the needle under two threads. Go back and slide the needle under the last thread plus a new thread. Continue going back one and forward under two threads.
27. **Background Fillers.** Three different designs using short stitches in fixed patterns are used to fill in large background areas.

EARLY AMERICAN FLORAL DESIGNS

The flowers illustrated here come from a crewel coverlet that was handmade sometime in the mid-eighteenth century.

QUILT

1. Enlarge one design to fit a pillow-size recric that have been cut to your desired size. Rectangles should be exactly the same size.
2. Make as many embroidered rectangles as needed to complete the quilt. You can make it as large or as small as you desire.
3. Follow the directions for constructing a quilt given in the chapter **The Patchwork Story.**

PILLOW

1. Enlarge one design to fit a pillow-size rec-

tangle. Embroider your chosen floral on the rectangle.

2. Cut a back for the pillow the same size as the embroidered front.

3. Sew the two sides together, right sides facing, with ½-inch seams on three and one-half sides.

4. Turn inside out, stuff with cotton or polyester, and hand-sew the open seam closed with a blind stitch.

5. Trim the edges of the pillow with fringe or decorative cord.

PICTURES

1. Enlarge the design to fit a piece of fabric that has been cut one inch larger on all sides than the intended frame.

2. Cut a piece of cardboard to fit the frame.

3. Place the embroidered floral over the cardboard and fold over the extra one inch, wrapping it around the cardboard. Glue it to the underside.

4. Frame the floral when dry.

BELL PULL

1. Use the designs the same size as shown.

2. The base of the bell pull is 5 inches wide and as long as you desire. Cut the bottom edge to a point. Cut two pull shapes.

3. Embroider the floral designs down the center of the pull.

4. Place the embroidered pull shape together with the back pull shape, right sides facing.

5. Sew the two pull shapes together along the sides and the bottom point.

6. Turn inside out and blind stitch the top edge closed, tucking in the edges ½ inch.

7. Press the edges flat and hang on a narrow wall.

OTHER IDEAS

Use the florals for chair seat or footstool covers; to border the bottom edge of curtains; on clothing, shawls, scarves and on felt or straw hats.

LACE FRINGED PILLOWS

In the early 1900s there wasn't an overwhelming demand for scatter pillows. What was available was quite expensive and complemented imported furniture. For the woman with an all American decor, handmade pillows were the only answer to this problem. With available fabric, make a pillow and an embroidered pillowcase. The pillowcase was often embroidered or crocheted with beautiful designs to match the interior decorations.

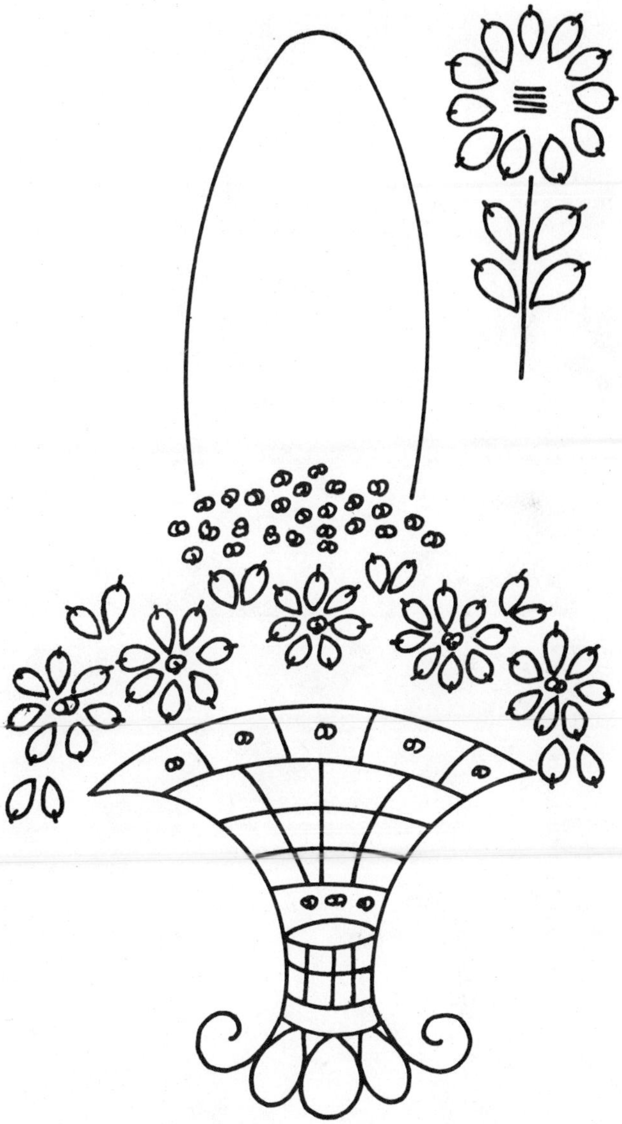

1. For the front and back of the pillowcase use a sheer beige fabric. Construct the pillow itself from a heavier beige fabric.

2. For the square pillow, cut four 12-inch squares, two from the sheer fabric and two from the heavier fabric. For the heart-shaped pillow, cut four 13 x 14-inch heart shapes from the same materials.

3. For the square pillow, crochet the basket design (given in actual size) to the center of one square. Cut off the corners with a curved embroidered line. Fill in the corners with three rows of decorative motifs. A second curved line of French Knots connects all the corners. Add three flowers in each corner.

4. For the heart-shaped pillow, sew a thin lace ribbon cutting off the top curves and the bottom point. Fill in these areas with Lazy Daisy Flowers and leaves.

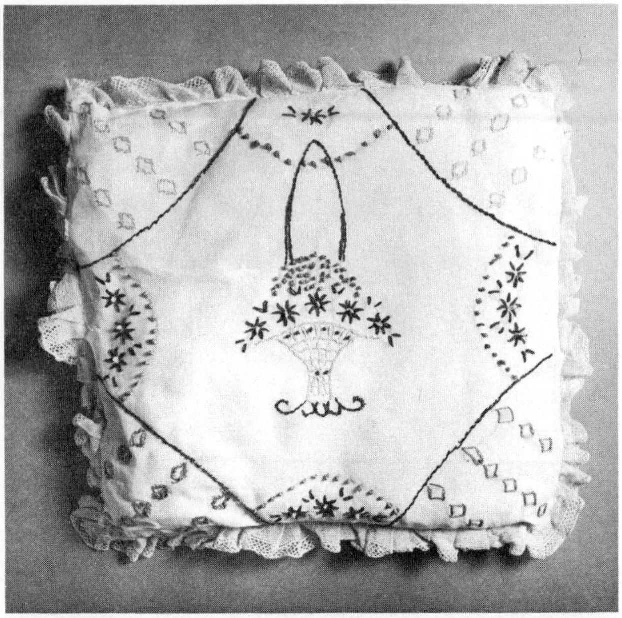

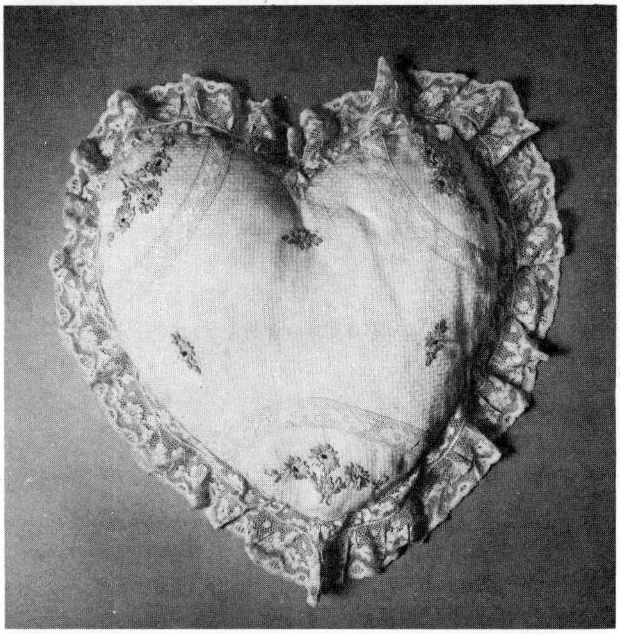

5. Pin, gather and sew lace around the embroidered side of the pillowcase, right sides facing. Place the two pillowcase shapes together, right sides facing, with the lace tucked inside, and sew together on three sides. Leave the upper part of the heart unsewn.

6. Turn the pillowcases right-side out.

7. Place the two inner pillow shapes together, right sides facing. Sew all but 4 inches of the hem.

8. Turn right-side out, stuff with cotton or polyester, and hand-sew the open seam closed.

9. Slip the pillows into the pillowcases and hand-sew the open ends closed with a blind stitch.

PULLED BURLAP EMBROIDERY

Burlap was primarily used for packaging produce until the 1950s when designers started using it for curtains, wallpaper, any number of household applications. Fabric companies started manufacturing it in decorative colors and weights, and now it's available all over. If you haven't yet discovered burlap, it's now time.

1. Cut a piece of burlap to the size desired.

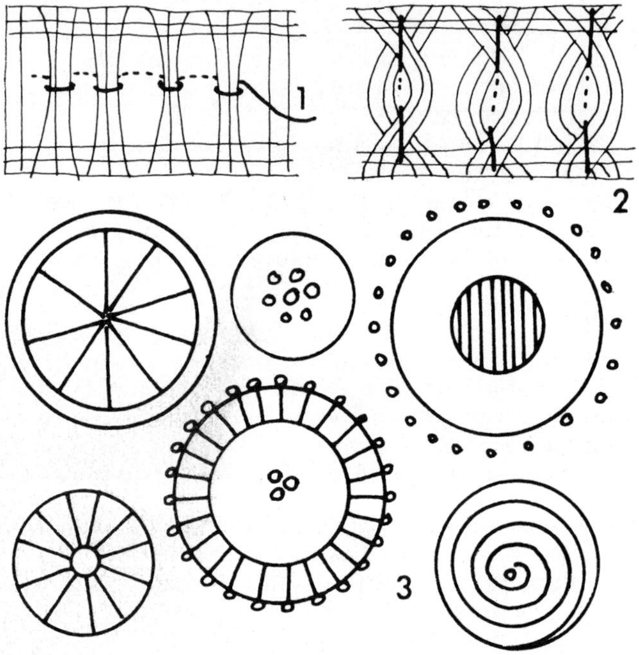

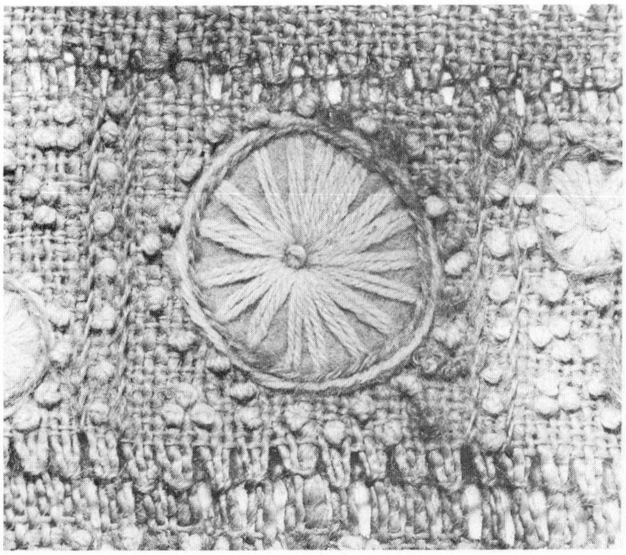

2. Pull sections of horizontal threads out of the burlap at the right side, forming single vertical bands across the fabric. How high these bands are depends on the number of threads you pull.
3. The Sheath: gather every three threads in the pulled thread band and tie together with yarn. Move to the next three strands with the yarn, gather and tie. Continue working across (Fig. 1).
4. The Double Twist: gather every six threads in the pulled thread band. Pull the three left threads and the three right threads to the opposite sides, crossing at the center. Sew at the top and bottom point where the threads cross (Fig. 2).
5. Cut felt circles and embroider them to the burlap. Some of the design possibilities are shown in Fig. 3.
6. Fill in the remaining burlap with French Knots and embroidery stitches.
7. Use as a hanging, throw pillow, placemat or as café curtains.

COVERED COAT HANGERS

With some fabric and embroidery thread, wire coat hangers take on a frilly face.

1. To make a pattern for the rose design, enlarge the grid on a sheet of tracing paper so that one square equals one inch. Draw the design on the enlarged tracing. (See page 13 for detailed directions on how to enlarge patterns from a grid.)
2. To plot the size of the hanger cover, place a wire coat hanger on the chosen fabric and cut ½ inch larger than the hanger on all sides. Cut two shapes for each hanger.
3. Pin the tracing to one base shape and embroider the design. Remove the tracing when through.
4. Place the two base shapes together, right sides facing, and sew together along the sides. Leave a ¼ inch of the seam unsewn on the top to accommodate the hook of the hanger. Also leave the bottom edge unsewn.
5. Turn the hanger cover inside out.
6. Slip the hook into the ¼ inch left unsewn at the top and fit the hanger into the cover.
7. Stuff the hanger cover with cotton or polyester.
8. Hand sew the bottom edge closed by tucking the edges inward and blind stitching.
9. Hand sew a thin lace around the outer edges.

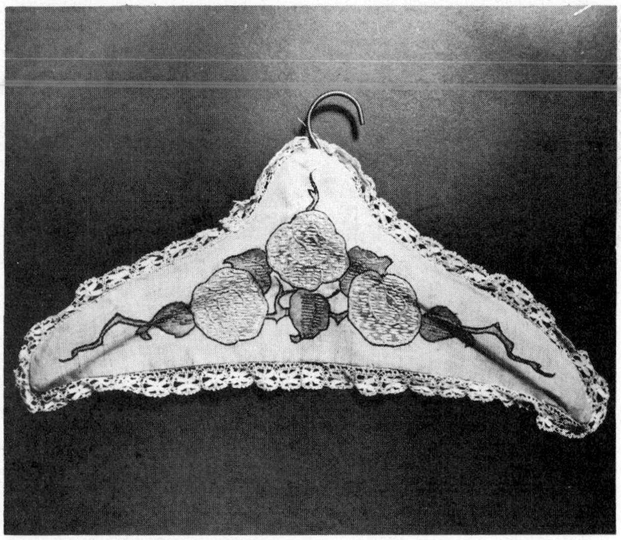

EMBROIDERED TABLE LINENS

The showpiece for fine embroidery has always been the tablecloth. Instructions follow for not only a tablecloth, but matching napkins and placemats. The design is adapted from a 1918 original.

TABLECLOTH

1. The design given is in actual size. Measure your table to establish the size of the tablecloth. Plot the seams when sewing two or more lengths of fabric together so that they fall on the edges of the table. To make a circular tablecloth, the width of the fabric falls on the center of the table. Additional fabric is added equally on both sides.
2. The design should fall just below the edges of the table. Embroider the designs around the entire tablecloth.
3. Hem the bottom edge with a ½-inch hem.
4. Sew lace to the bottom edge of the cloth.

PLACEMATS

1. The placemats are made from 13 x 19-inch pieces of fabric. If you are going to use them over the tablecloth, pick fabric in a contrasting or harmonizing color.
2. Hem with a ¼-inch hem that is turned under twice.
3. Embroider the design down the left side of the placemat.

NAPKINS

1. The napkins are 13-inch squares. Hem ¼ inch on all sides.
2. Embroider one design element in a corner of each napkin.

MONOGRAMS

As far back as ancient Egypt, people have monogrammed fine clothing and linens. It adds a feel of ownership and personal distinction to your wardrobe and is not nearly as difficult as it might appear.

1. The monograms drawn are in actual size. You can enlarge or reduce them to fit your needs.
2. The widest part of each letter is worked in the Satin Stitch either straight across (horizontally) or upward at an angle.
3. The thinnest part of the letter is worked in the Outline Stitch.
4. When embroidering a three letter monogram, there are two ways to design the motif: a large center initial flanked on both sides with

smaller initials, or if the letters are the same size, raise the middle letter higher than the outer two.

5. Some ideas for monograms: bathroom towels and washcloths, placemats and napkins, men's ties, scarves, blouses, bed linen, canvas handbags and sleepware.

SIMPLE EMBROIDERED SAMPLERS

No young lady's education during the eighteenth and nineteenth centuries was considered complete until she had embroidered in silks and gold thread.

1. Both of these designs come from turn-of-the century postcards. To make a pattern for either of them, enlarge the grid on a sheet of tracing paper so that one square equals one inch. Draw the design and lettering on the enlarged grid. (See page 13 for detailed directions on how to enlarge patterns from a grid.)

2. Cut the fabric larger than the design to allow room for framing.

3. Pin the tracing to the design.

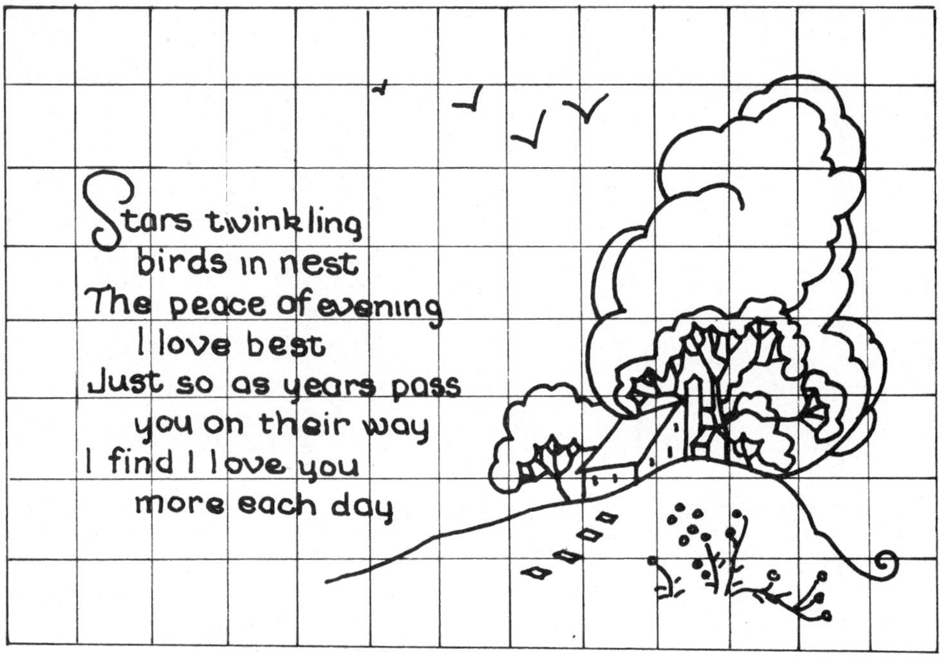

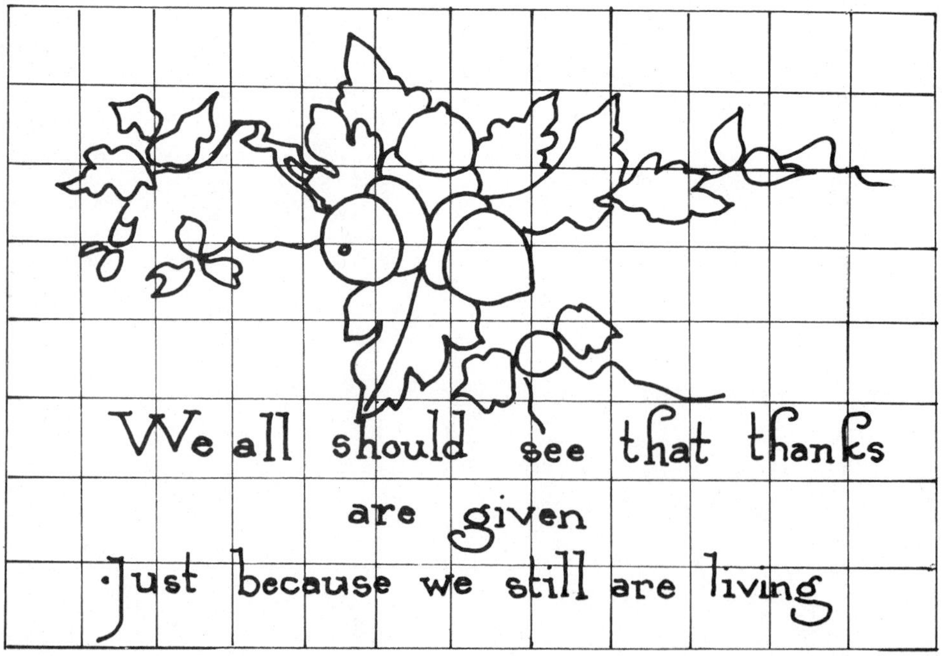

Stars twinkling
birds in nest
The peace of evening
I love best
Just so as years pass
you on their way
I find I love you
more each day

Stars twinkling
birds in nest
The peace of evening
I love best
Just so, as years pass
you on their way
I find I love you
more each day

We all should see that thanks
are given
Just because we still are living

4. The sentiment is worked in an Outline Stitch and the design is filled in with the stitches of your choice. Discard the tracing when you have completed the stitching.
5. Cut a piece of cardboard to fit the intended frame.
6. Place the embroidered sampler on the cardboard and fold under the edges. To keep the sampler from shifting, glue the edges to the cardboard.

DESIGNS FOR TINY TOTS

These sweet and innocent animal designs were popular on children's clothes in the 1950s. Follow the directions for enlarging and transferring designs in Basic Embroidery. Crochet clothing, baby blankets, bibs, pillow covers, or work the designs into a nursery picture.

CREWEL PAINTING

Indigo was about the only dye available in colonial times and that's why early examples of American crewel work are invariably worked in blue yarn on bleached white linen. Crewel takes its name from a type of two-ply wool. The most traditional crewel design is the tree of life. If you can baste a collar neatly in place or smoothly darn a sock you can work intricate crewel. Think of it as painting—in embroidery stitches—with yarn.

1. Use the design in the size shown or enlarge, as you prefer. (The squares on an enlarged grid could be ½ inch or one inch. See page 13 for detailed directions on how to enlarge patterns from a grid.) Draw the grid and the design directly on the fabric with a soft pencil.
2. The main difference between crewel and embroidery is that crewel uses yarn rather than thread and that the background behind the design is filled in completely. Choose stitches that are solid rather than open. None of the background should show in crewel work.
3. Cut the fabric to be worked with fabric to spare.
4. Work the design to the size of the intended frame.
5. Cut a piece of heavy cardboard to fit the frame.
6. Place the completed crewel design over the

cardboard, turning under the unembroidered edges. Glue the edges down and frame.

HUCK WORK

(Shown in color, page 165)

Huck work, a very old art, is a simple but quite stunning type of embroidery done on the surface of huckaback toweling. Huckaback is a coarse linen cloth, made with small knots taken at close and regular intervals that form a rough face. This cloth is the surface to be darned on it. Choose the side of the fabric where the threads of the raised dots run up and down and parallel with the selvage. This is actually the wrong side of the fabric. Huckaback towels are sold in five-and-dime stores.

1. The embroidery is worked on the side where the raised threads run parallel with the selvage. Choose a blunt needle and six-strand embroidery thread.
2. Sew through each raised stitch in a straight line across the toweling, starting near one edge.
3. At predetermined intervals along the line, connect three stitches deep with a twisting stitch shown in Fig. 1.
4. The second row of stitches follows along the base line, up to the twisting stitches.
5. The vertical stitches skip two sets of huckaback dots before it picks up the third. Turn, stitch, and turn, again skipping two stitches to get back to the base line (Fig. 2). Continue stitching straight until you reach the next group of twisted stitches on the base line.
6. Sew a second line following the first. Repeat

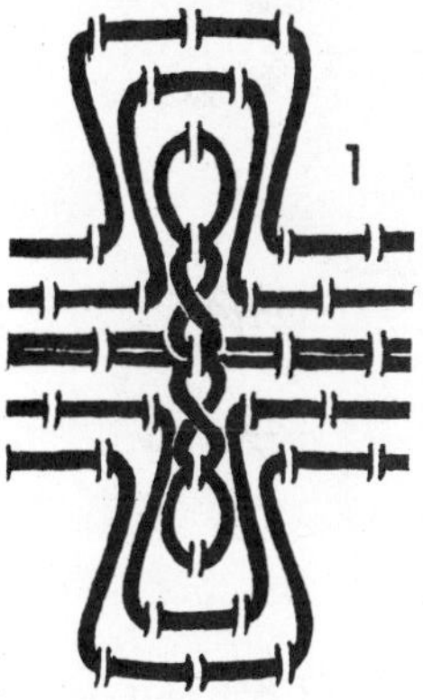
1

2

3

these lines on the other side of the base line.

7. The next two lines on both sides of the base line are stitched like the two previous lines, allowing for the twisting stitches, though, in fact, there are none there.
8. The exact stitch count is given in Fig. 3. When sewing through the huckaback stitches, do not stitch through the fabric. Changing colors creates dramatic design. The down (or up) thread that skips stitches on the fabric gives the designs the appearance of being in relief.

BASIC CROSS STITCH

The Cross Stitch is exactly what its name implies: two equal diagonal stitches crossing each other at the center. The stitch looks like the letter X.

Cross Stitches should follow the weave of the fabric. Following the weave will give you uniform stitches in straight rows.

Gingham is an excellent fabric to experiment with because its design is composed of equally spaced boxes.

If you are working tiny Cross Stitches, split the embroidery thread in half and use three strands rather than the full six.

CROSS STITCH BORDERS

Here's an assortment of Cross-Stitch borders from a 1920s women's magazine. All you have to do is work out the initial design, then keep repeating it, linking or joining designs together in a

EMBROIDERY

CROSS STITCH

YOKE AND FRONT BAND FOR WAIST.

THE realistic style of embroidery which, under the name of South Kensington, enjoyed great vogue has been quite superseded in the past few years by the revival of conventional designs, ecclesiastical embroidery, and the fine stitches which have been handed down through many centuries, and were in common use when Matilda of Normandy and her handmaidens wrought the famous piece of needle-work which is known as the Bayeux tapestry. The foundation of the stitches for wrought tapestry (tapestry is usually woven on a loom) of the intricate Persian patterns, and the chair seats, hangings, etc., which are to be found all over Italy and Spain, and even decorate the Pope's apartments in the Vatican, is the simple cross stitch which any child can learn with a thread and a piece of canvas.

The worsted, silk, or linen used is carried from left to right across the mesh of the canvas for the under row of stitches, ⁄, and crossed in the opposite direction, making an exact square, ×; and most intricate patterns can be copied without stamping, as it is only necessary to keep count of the squares.

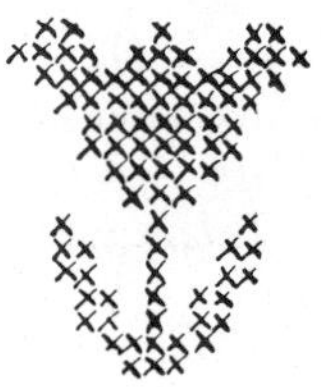

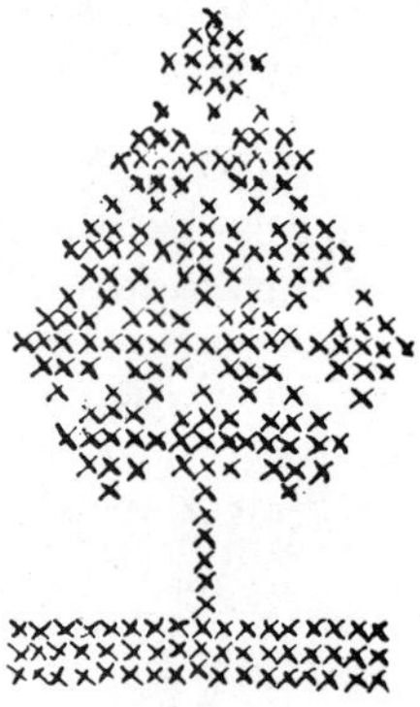

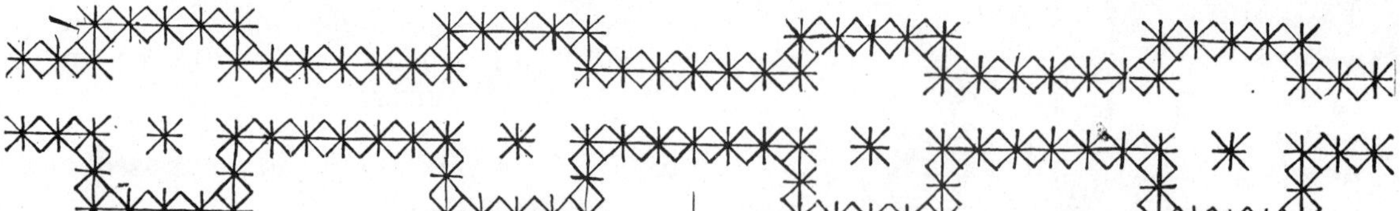

straight line. The yoke shows how dramatic an all-over border design can be.

SIMPLE CROSS STITCH DESIGNS

Practice working a few of the motifs until you feel fairly adept at it. Then try putting them together in a sampler.

The designs are of fruit, flowers and other traditional subjects. The girl and boy can be worked in a long row for borders. The designs are actual size. Count the stitches and duplicate them on your fabric, sewing the Cross Stitches into the weave of the fabric.

Other places to work up these are on clothing, table linens, afghans, kitchen curtains, pot holders, aprons and toaster covers.

Silhouettes
in Cross-Stitch

CROSS STITCH SILHOUETTES

Cross Stitch silhouettes are worked in black thread. The designs shown are from the 1920s. Follow the designs by counting stitches on your fabric. Each black square equals one stitch.

CROSS STITCH LETTERS

A display of lettering is a traditional and essential part of any sampler. Work family names or interesting sayings in the Cross Stitch.

BLOCK LETTERS

The alphabet shown is formed with single lines of Cross Stitches. For a thicker letter, double each line.

OLD ENGLISH LETTERS

These letters are more ornate in design and use single, double and triple lines of Cross Stitch. Use these letters for monogramming.

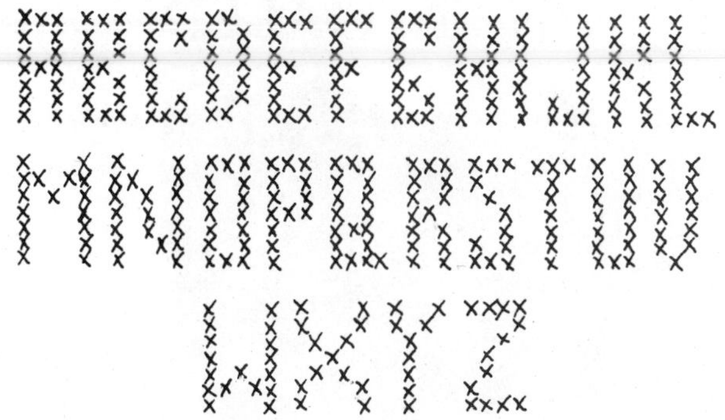

MULTIPLE COLOR CROSS STITCH

(Shown in color, page 165)

The designs shown are from a turn-of-the-century runner. The finished product has a sort of Oriental look, a style popular up until the 1920s. You will be surprised by what happens when you combine many colors.

1. Work the designs on both ends of a 9 x 15-inch piece of coarsely woven fabric.
2. Color key: solid circles, black; Cross Stitches, pink; hearts, red; triangles, green; stars, blue; squares, a second shade of blue; diamonds and lines, brown.

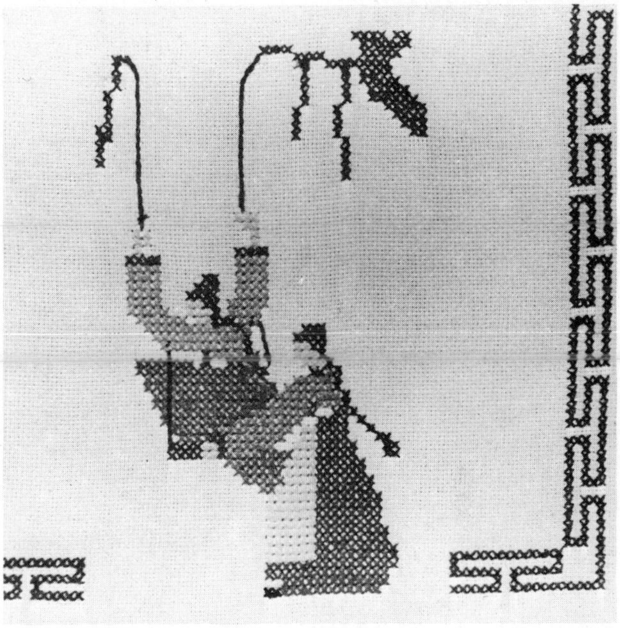

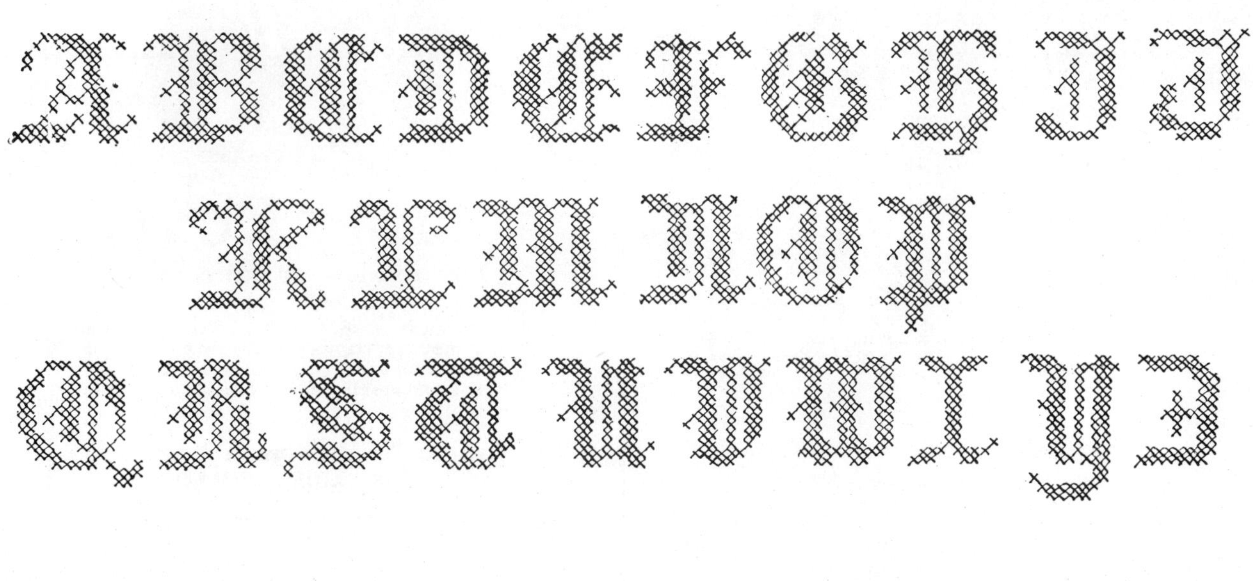

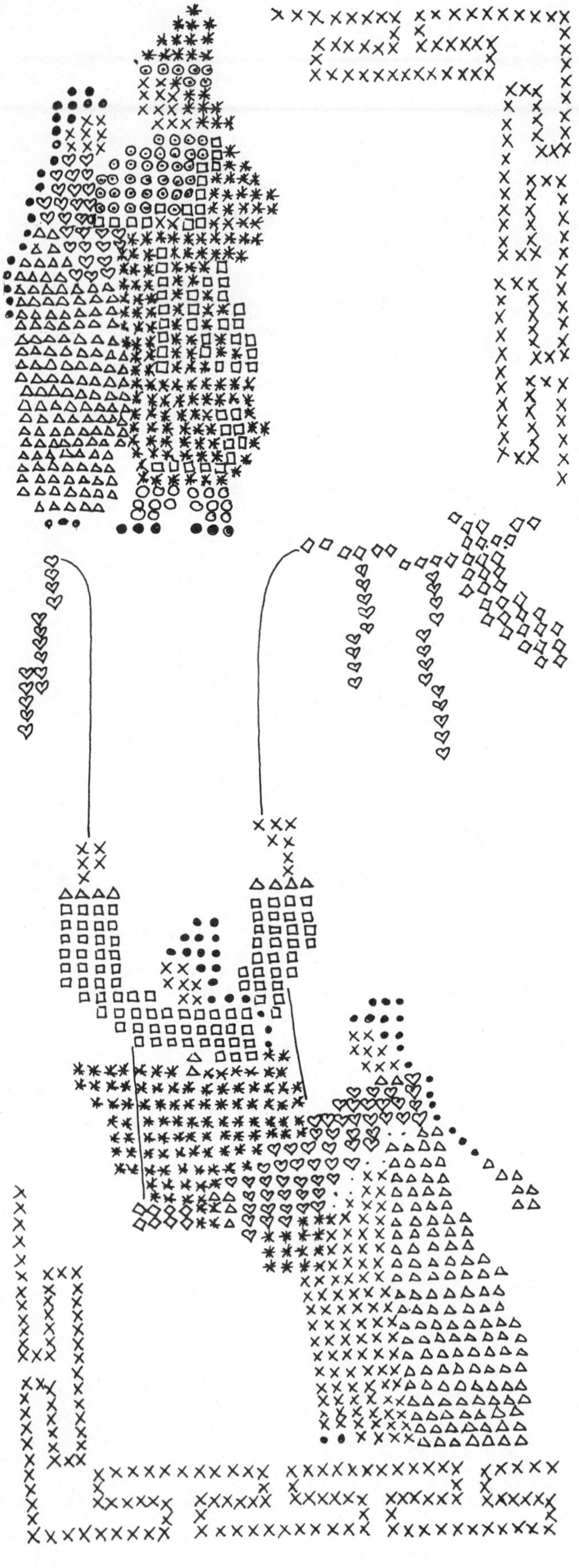

3. Always work cross stitches in straight rows.
4. Pull the threads along the edges for a fringe.

CROSS STITCH SAMPLERS

Little girls were obliged to repress any rebellious instincts. When they finished their daily stint of stitching, *then* they could go out to play. Times may have changed but the beauty of a sampler hasn't.

1. Your sampler can use all or some of the designs shown. The designs are given in actual size.
2. The center box is for cross stitching the family name. Eliminate some of the designs on the top or bottom for a favorite sentiment or proverb.
3. You can expand the sampler by adding some of the designs on the proceeding pages.
4. Trace and embroider the Cross Stitch sampler following the instructions in Basic Embroidery.

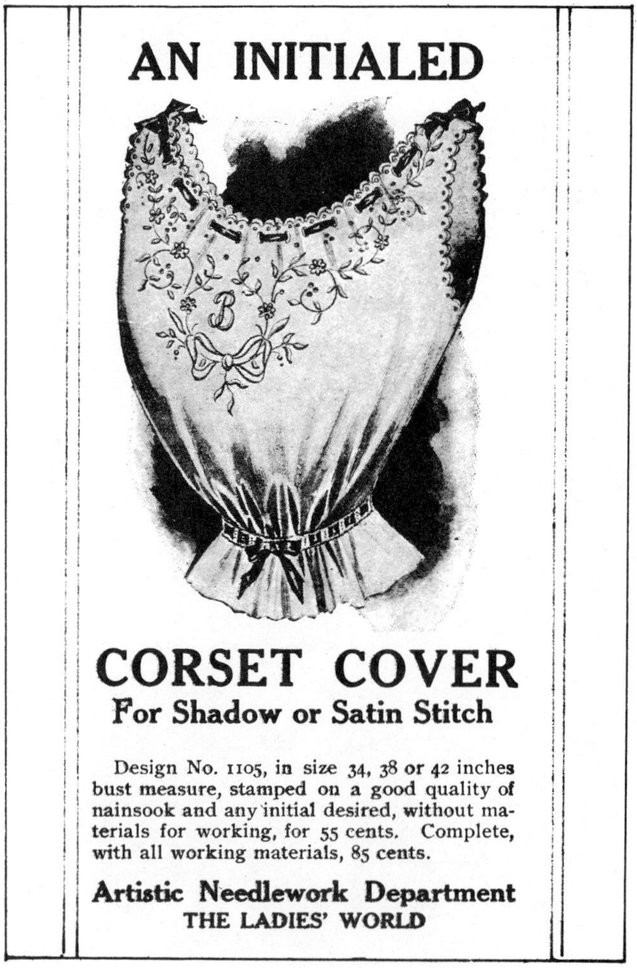

BASIC NEEDLEPOINT

There are two types of needlepoint canvas: the single mesh and the double mesh. Canvas also comes in different sizes which are determined by the number of mesh to the inch. The more mesh to the inch, the smaller the stitches, the longer it takes to complete the design. The fewer mesh to the inch, the larger the stitches, and the easier the piece is to work up.

Use sturdy yarns and a tapestry needle which is a blunt needle with an elongated large eye. The needle should be able to pass through the canvas quite easily.

Always add an extra inch of canvas on all sides of the design for turning under a frame. When making small items, allow a few extra stitches for shrinkage.

Work in one direction as opposed to turning the work around and going back in the opposite direction. This will provide a smoother finish. Do not pull the thread too tightly or the canvas may buckle or shift in one direction. Do a little every day.

There are many stitches that are worked on a canvas backing. We are giving you the two simplest stitches. The Continental Stitch (Fig. 1) is worked from right to left. The needle moves diagonally, passing under the canvas at the cross point where the left bottom corner of the upper square meets the top right corner of the lower square. The Half Cross Stitch (Fig. 2) is worked from left to right with the needle held vertically. In both cases, the stitches will be diagonal on the

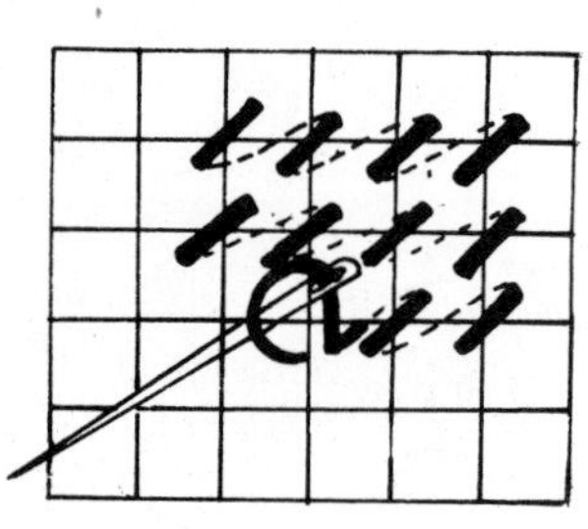
1

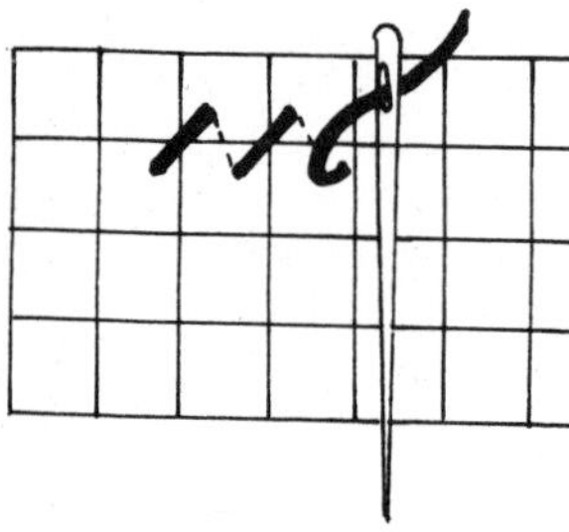
2

front side of the canvas. The look of the stitches will vary on the back of the canvas.

Note: needlepoint canvas can be blocked by dipping the finished work in cold water and pinning the wet canvas on heavy cardboard, pulling it taut. Blot all excess water with paper towels, and allow the finished work to dry thoroughly before removing it from the cardboard.

CREATING YOUR OWN DESIGNS

1. The rose design shown on the small change purse was first designed on graph paper. Graph

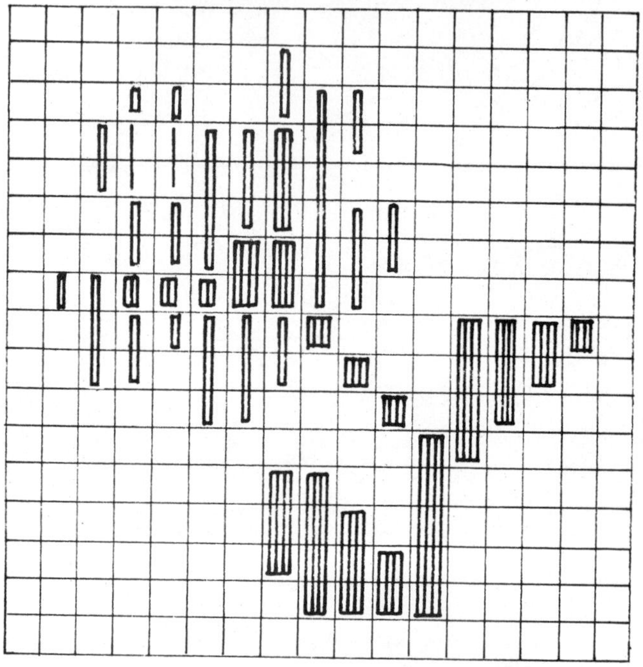

paper is lined with equidistant horizontal and vertical lines forming a boxed network. You can buy graph paper in stationery stores or at stationery counters.

2. The number of lines crossing the boxes in-

dicate color. One line is pink; two lines, red; three lines, maroon; and 4 lines, green. Each box on the graph represents a stitch on the needlepoint canvas.

3. To work out your own designs, color in the boxes on the graph paper with crayons or colored pencils. Designs can be simple in one color, or they can be elaborate with intricate color detail. Work the design onto the canvas, box to box.

4. Work your designs into small purses, cases, pillows, belts or even jewelry. The change purse is stitched together with matching yarn and is lined with a lightweight fabric.

THE LONG STITCH

The Long Stitch covers larger areas of canvas in little time. It looks most impressive when worked in geometric designs and is a good filler stitch.

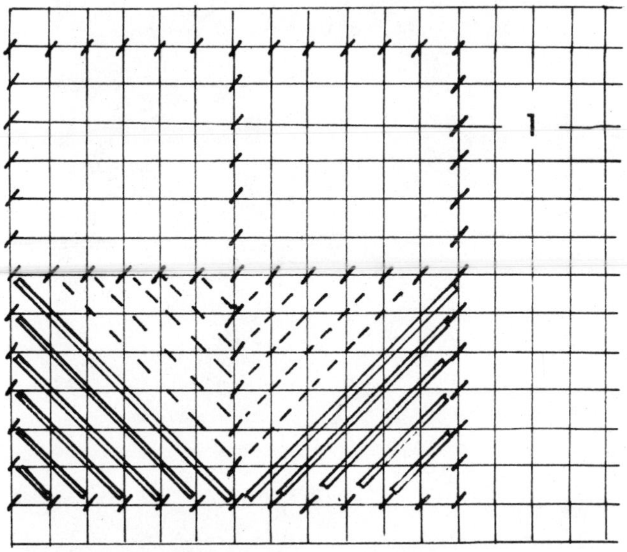

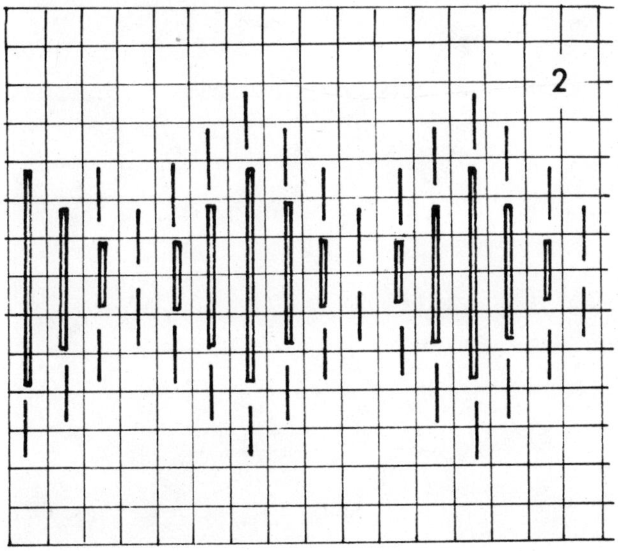

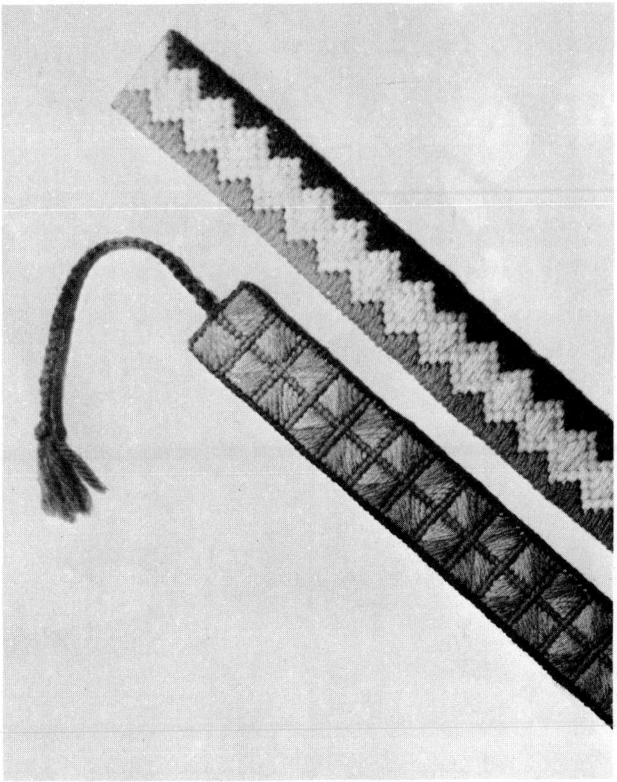

1. The Long Stitch extends over two or more spaces on the canvas.

2. The neckbands are made to fit around your neck minus one inch. Fold ½ inch of the unstitched edges under and stitch down. Use wide ribbon as an underlining. Add a thin braided tie to each end of the neckband.

3. Neckband 1 uses the basic Continental Stitch with the Long Stitch. Start in an outer square with the Continental Stitch. Long diagonal stitches are worked toward the center, shifting colors halfway. The square ends in a second Continental Stitch.

4. Neckband 2 uses only the Long Stitch. Stitch a diamond starting with a six-space stitch (goes over 5 canvas threads) centered top and bottom. Make a four- and then a two-space stitch on both sides of the center stitch. Two-space stitches border a line of diamonds. Fill in the background with Long Stitches.

5. Try the Long Stitch on belts, headbands and bell pulls.

LONG STITCH WEAVING

The Long Stitch worked in rows gives the canvas the look of a woven fabric.

1. The Long Stitch is worked vertically over five spaces on the canvas. The horizontal rows of

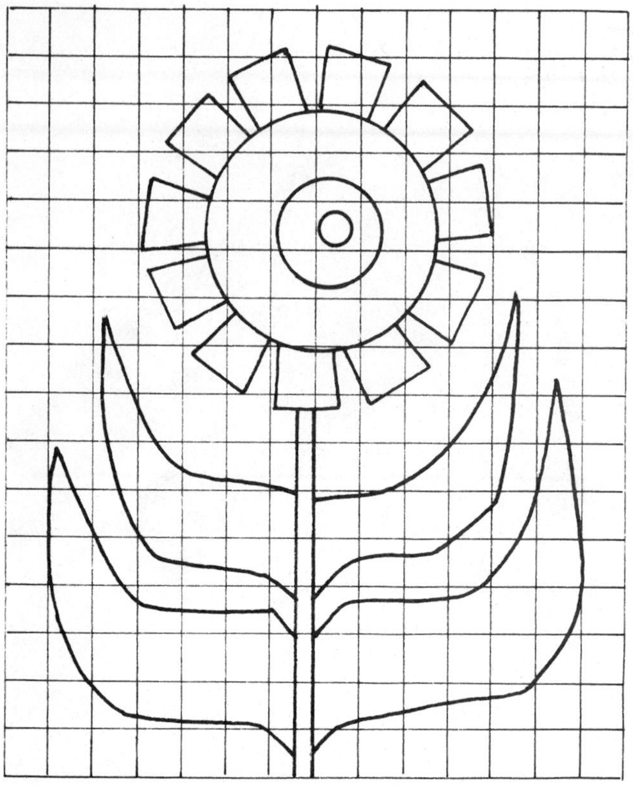

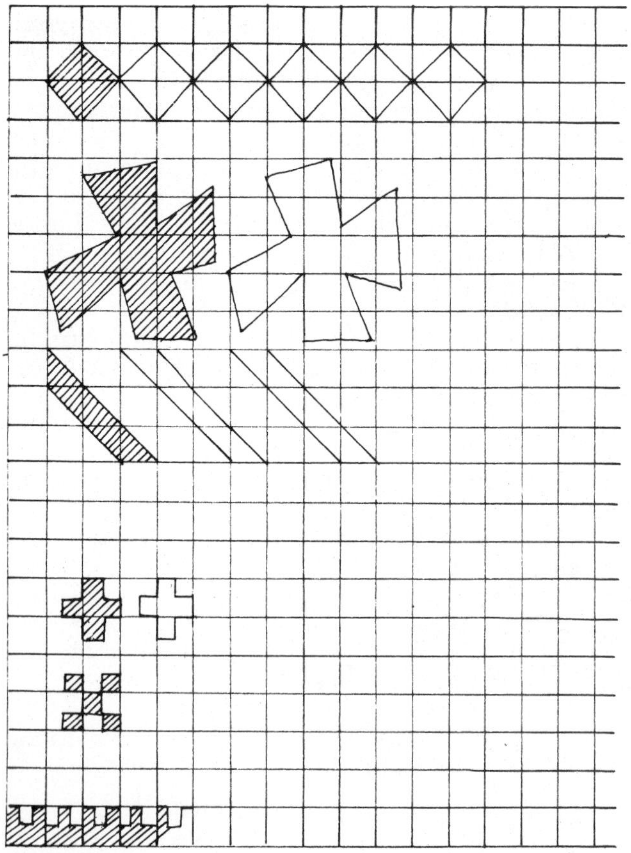

uniform stitches create the look of a weave.

2. Enlarge the grid and the flower design directly on the needle-point canvas. For the designs illustrated here, make one square equal one inch. (See page 13 for detailed directions on how to enlarge patterns from a grid.)

3. The Long Stitches, five spaces long, are worked back and forth across the canvas. The stitches may be broken when nearing an area of the design that shifts color. For instance, the background could be three spaces deep then shift to a petal color that takes up the remaining two spaces. No matter how many colors may fall in a

given stitch, the stitch must still add up to five spaces. This five space pattern creates definite horizontal lines moving across the needlepoint.

4. On the geometric design, one square represents five spaces on the canvas. You do not have to draw your design on the canvas. Instead, follow the design, counting stitches.

5. The designs can be worked into a sampler picture, or handbag.

SCULPTURED DIAMONDS

If you enjoy working the Long Stitch, try this simple motif taken from an Italian fabric design.

1. The Long Stitches are worked from corner to corner. The diagram shows in numbers the direction and order the stitches are worked.

2. The first stitch is worked from the top left corner to the bottom right. The second stitch goes up to the top right and down to the bottom left corner, see Fig. 1.

3. The second set of stitches starts a stitch away from the bottom right corner, crossing to the opposite stitch on the top left. The second stitch is worked from the next stitch on the bottom left, crossing over to the opposite stitch on the top right, see Fig. 2.

4. The third set of stitches follows the same pattern, see Fig. 3.

5. Stitches are always worked in a counter-clockwise direction, moving inward. Sculptured diamonds can vary in size. The number of stitches on the canvas must be worked in even numbers.

6. Continue to work the same pattern of stitches inward, filling in all stitches.

EYEGLASS CASE

(Shown in color, page 168)

1. Work the case 3 sculptured diamonds wide

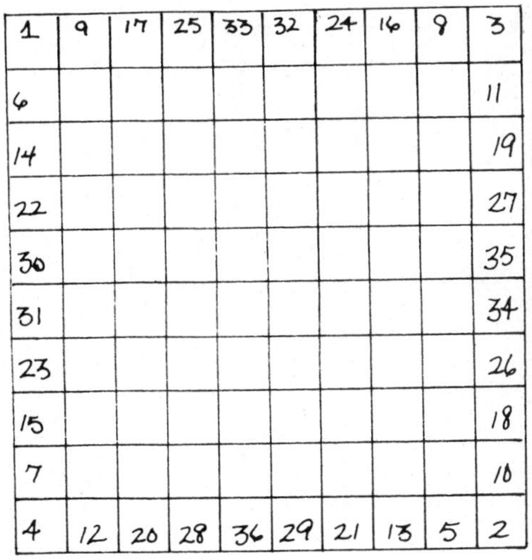

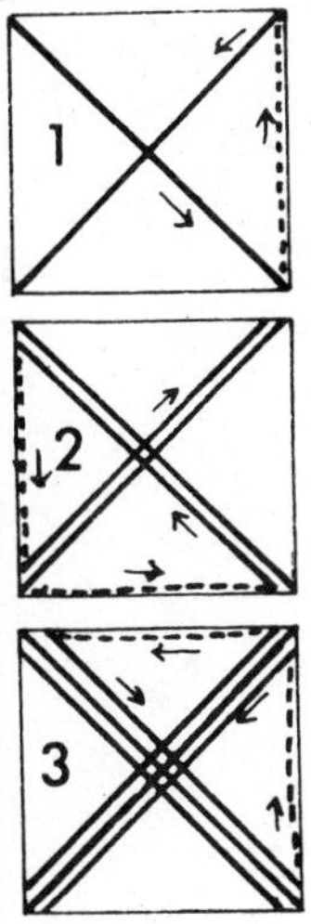

and 12 diamonds deep. Shift to a second color halfway through each diamond motif.

2. Fold ½ inch of the unstitched hem under and stitch down.

3. Hand-stitch a lining to the underside of the needlepoint, tucking the edges under ¼ inch. Sew the lining a little in from the outer edge.

4. Fold the needlepoint in half and whip stitch the sides together.

MIRROR FRAME

(Shown in color, page 168)

1. Measure the mirror of your choice. Cut a piece of canvas one inch larger than the mirror on all sides. Cut out the inside window. First figure how much of the mirror you want to frame, then cut the opening ½ smaller on all sides. (See Bargello Frame.)

2. Work three sculptured diamonds into each corner one inch in from all edges.

3. Fill the remaining areas with stitches in geometric designs.

4. When the needlepoint is finished, slit the inside corners of the unworked canvas.

5. Turn under the four canvas flaps and stitch down.

6. Place the needlework over the mirror. Fold the outside unworked edges under and glue them to the underside of the mirror with white glue. *Note:* do not use a bond cement.

7. Sew or glue a piece of felt cut to the size of the back of the mirror. Hang.

NEEDLEPOINT PICTURES

Needlepoint came to America with the first Virginia colonists. They worked traditional six-

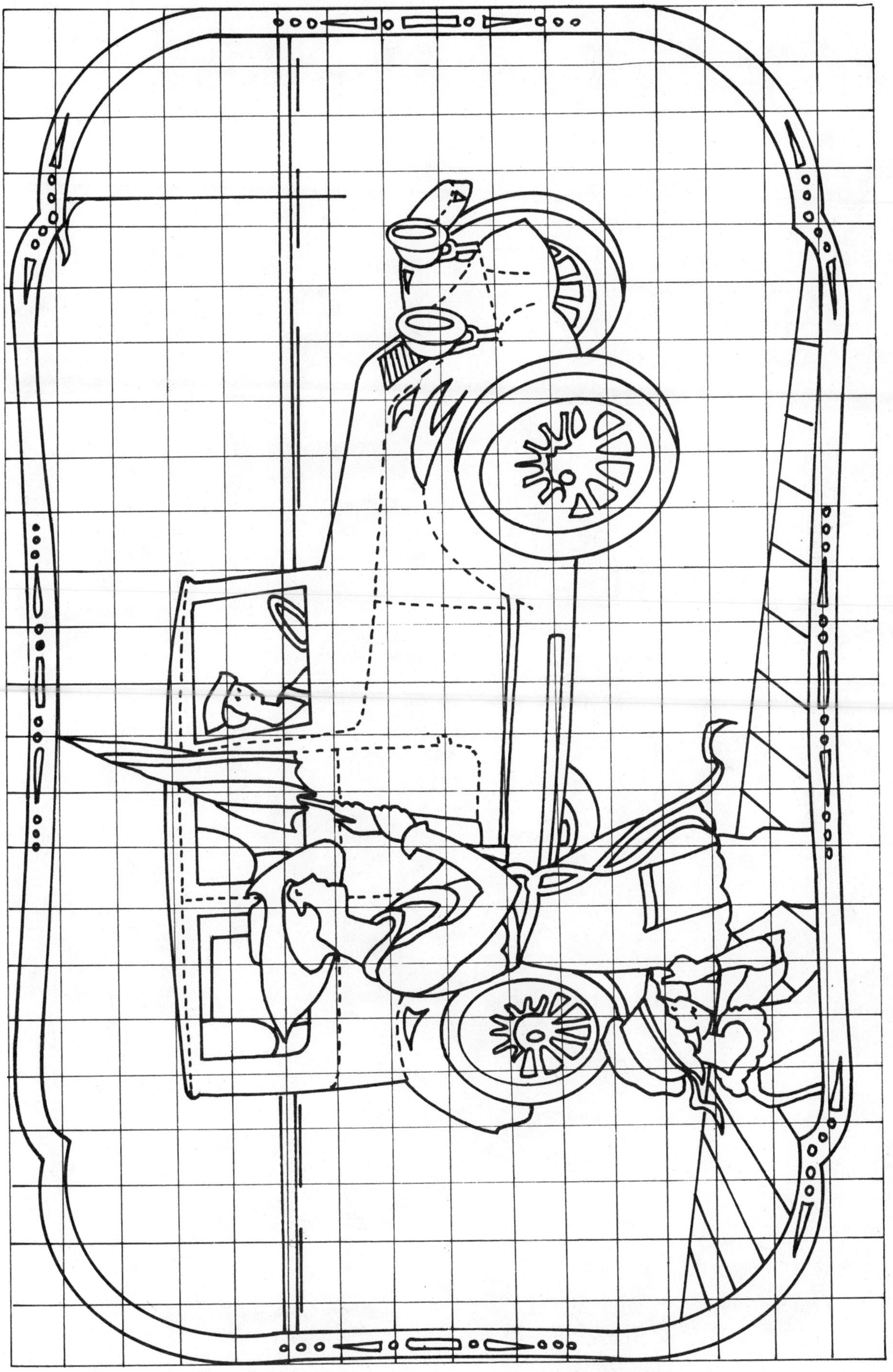

A
APPLE
PIE

A
APPLE
PIE

teenth-century English designs which were to remain in vogue for generations. It is only in this last century that American needlepoint designs have come into their own.

1. Draw the grid and the design—the Kate Greenway apple pie or the car advertisement—directly on the canvas. You can draw it the same size or enlarge it slightly. (See page 13 for how to enlarge patterns from a grid.) If you enlarge the grid so that one space equals ½ inch, the design will become 12 inches long.

2. The Kate Greenway design should be worked in soft pastel shades. The car ad is worked in bolder colors. Make the car black or red. The car highlights are given in dotted lines.

3. The completed design can be framed or can be made into a throw pillow.

BASIC BARGELLO

The Bargello, or Florentine, stitch is a long vertical stitch that covers from two to ten spaces of the canvas.

The designs of Bargello are precise geometric patterns. The first line of the design establishes the general pattern. Start this line in the middle of the canvas. Work the first line of stitches up and down in a pattern.

This first line can be worked with a single stitch or to as many stitches thick as you desire. The thickness can also vary as the line moves up and down. The only rule is that the design is consistent as it moves up and down.

A second color is used above or below the first line. Align this line with the first line of stitches and follow precisely the first row pattern as you move across the canvas.

Bargello is most effective worked in colors that fall in the same color range and gradually shift in shades.

As with all needlepoint projects, leave at least one inch of canvas unworked on all sides.

BARGELLO FOOTSTOOL

(Shown in color, page 168)

Examples of Bargello date back to the late thirteenth century. Though the stitch is also known as the Florentine stitch, its origin is not Italian but Hungarian. It was traditionally used to cover furniture. These instructions are for a simplified version of the turn-of-the-century footstool shown in color.

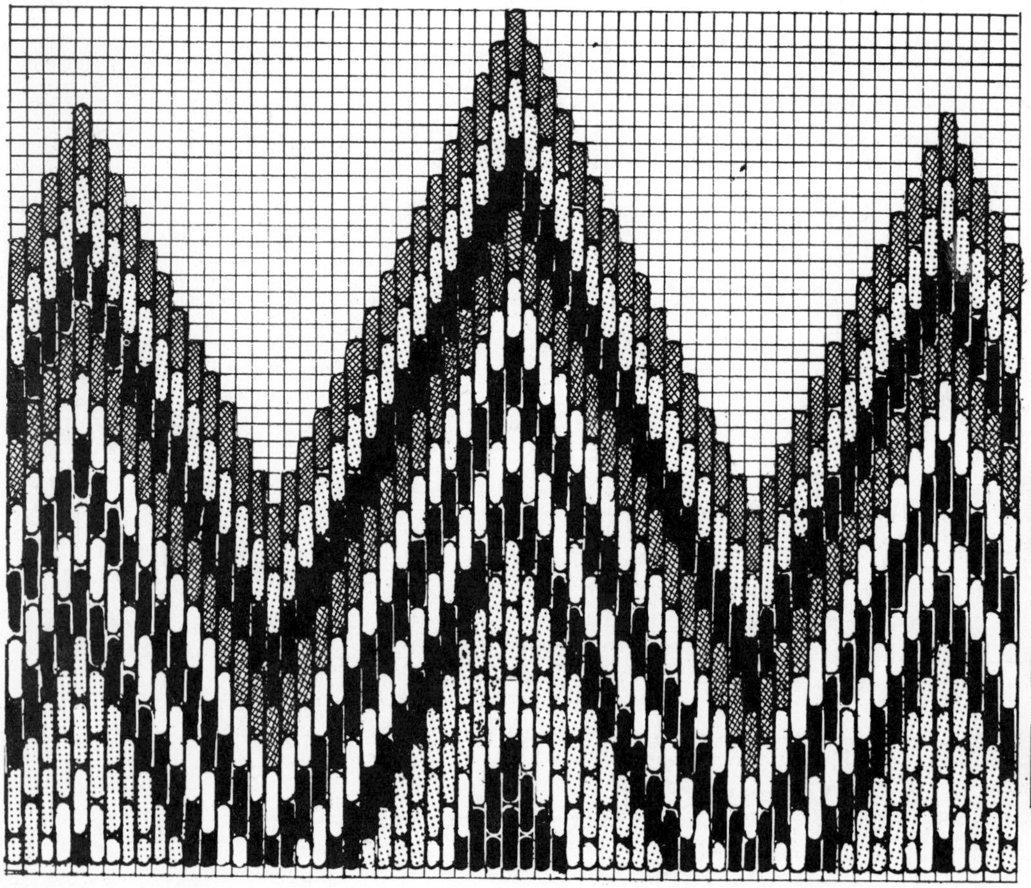

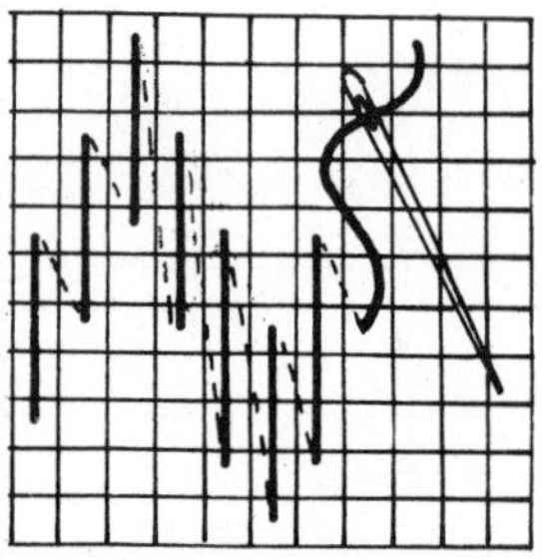

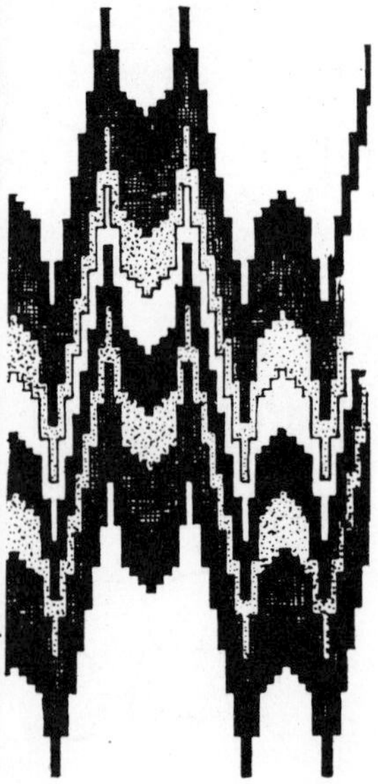

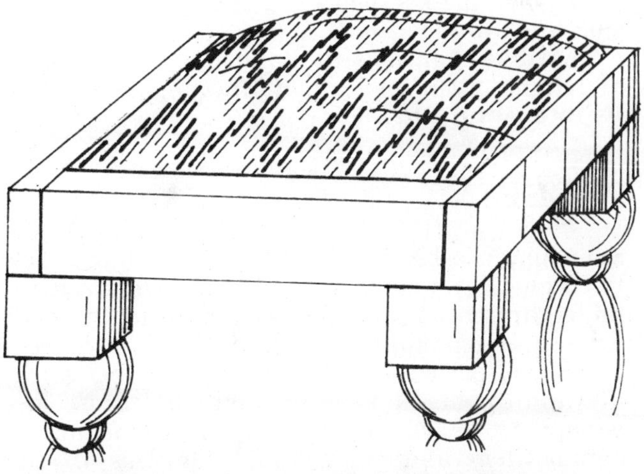

1. Cut one-inch scrap lumber to the intended size of the footstool.
2. Make a Bargello needlepoint leaving 2 inches of canvas unworked on all sides.
3. Pad the top of the scrap wood with stuffing cotton and place the finished Bargello over the padding.
4. Turn the wood over and tack the canvas edges to the underside of the padded wood with carpenter tacks.
5. Cut 1 x 4-inch lumber to fit the width of the padded top. Cut two pieces, one for each side.
6. Sand raw edges and stain or paint the wood.
7. Hammer the finished sides to the padded top.
8. Accurately measure the length of the seat including the attached sides. Cut two pieces of one x 4, one for each side.
9. Sand the cut side ends until smooth. Finish the lengths as you did the widths.
10. Hammer the lengths to the seat.
11. Buy attachable wooden legs sold in hardware or lumber centers. Finish as above and attach a leg to each corner on the underside of the seat with the clamps sold along with the legs.
12. The assembled footstool can be varnished.

BARGELLO TELEPHONE BOOK COVER

(Shown in color, page 168)

What a lovely way to camouflage that necessary reference guide, the telephone book.

1. Measure a closed telephone book from top to bottom and from front cover to back cover including the binding. Add one inch to all sides.
2. Work a Bargello design to the telephone book's measurements allowing for an extra one inch of unworked canvas on all sides.
3. Fold over the edges of the completed Bargello and stitch it down to the underside of the canvas.
4. Cut a piece of fabric to the size of the cover and add ½ inch on all sides.
5. Tuck in ½ inch of the fabric toward the underside of the Bargello and hand-sew both lining and Bargello together. Use a blind stitch.
6. Ribbon sleeves hold the cover to the book. Place a length of grosgrain three inches in from each edge on the lining side and sew in place at top and bottom. Tuck under the ends of the ribbon as you sew.
7. Attach the Bargello to the telephone book by slipping the covers of the book into the ribbon sleeves.

BARGELLO FRAME

(Shown in color on cover)

An elegant way to display a favorite photo, print or painting is to frame it in Bargello.

1. Center the picture on a sheet of cardboard and glue in place. Trim the cardboard if the area

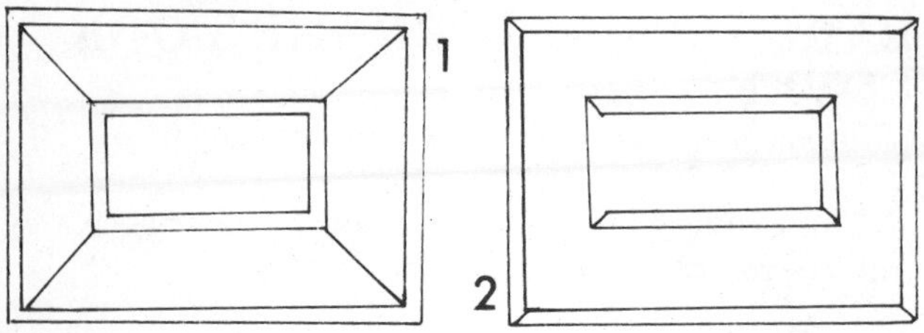

around the picture, which is the area to be framed, seems too large.

2. Cut needlepoint canvas one inch larger than the cardboard on all sides.

3. To determine the size of the window, measure the picture itself and add ¼ inch on all sides. (The extra ¼ inch is added to the needle-point area so the frame will overlap the photo slightly.) Plot this measurement in the center of the canvas and draw with a felt-tipped marker. Draw lines ½ inch in from the four sides. (This extra ½ inch is allowance for hems.)

4. Cut out the window along the second set of lines just drawn.

5. Draw diagonal lines bisecting the corners. These stitching guides establish where to turn corners (Fig. 1).

6. Work two opposite sides in the same Bargello design up to the diagonal lines. Work the Bargello on the other two sides making the design butt at the corners. It should look as though the design were turning a sharp corner.

7. When the needlepoint is finished, cut slits on all the outside and inside corners of the unworked canvas. Turn the tabs of the inside opening under and stitch to the underside of the canvas (Fig. 2).

8. Place the needlepoint over the cardboard. Turn the unworked outer edges under and glue them to the back of the cardboard.

9. Glue felt or decorative paper to the back of

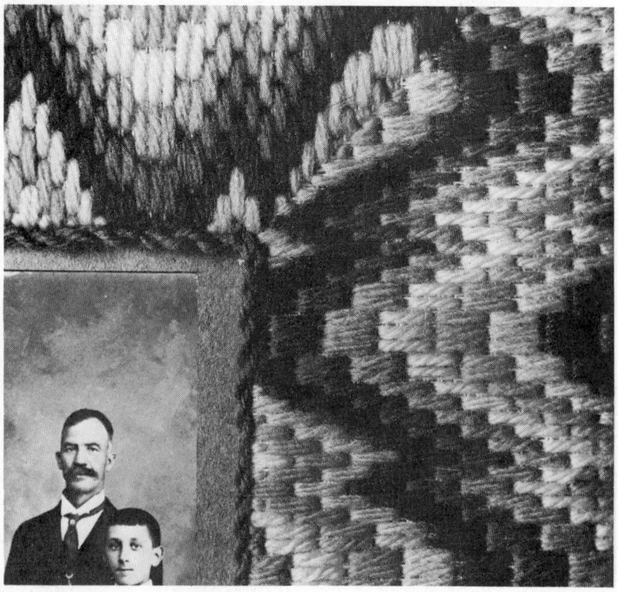

the framed picture. Cut the felt or paper slightly smaller than the frame.

10. Make a cardboard stand following the instructions given for Ribbon Mats in the chapter **Ribbons and Old Lace.**

SMOCKING

Smocking is a beautiful old art which dates back to Anglo-Saxon times when women wore a loose undergarment called the smock beneath wool dresses. It gradually became the fashion to decorate the upper part of the smock with fine stitching and to cut the neck of the actual dress low enough to display the handwork. Smocking is symmetrical and elastic, and limitless in the colorful designs that can be achieved.

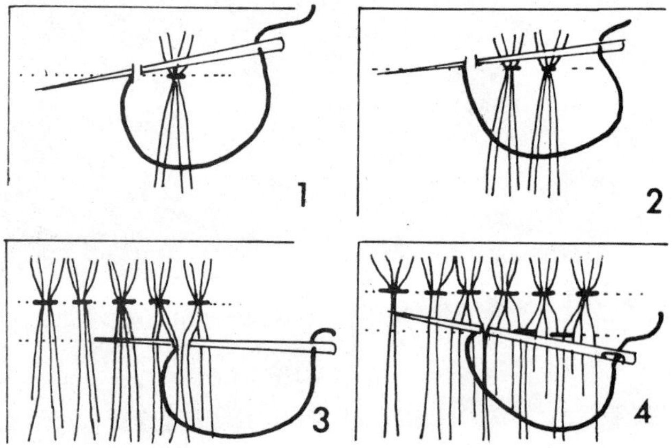

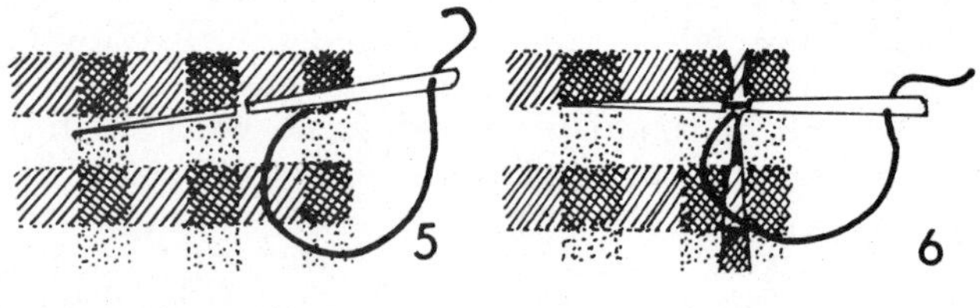

1. Pass the needle from under the fabric on an imaginary or lightly penciled line.

2. Make a ¼-inch stitch. Pull tightly. Sew the stitch a second time.

3. As you complete the second stitch, pass the needle under the fabric ¼ to one inch away depending on the desired size of the smocking.

4. Exit the needle on the line and proceed with a double stitch (Fig. 1).

5. Continue the same stitch procedure across the desired area (Fig. 2).

6. Begin the second row by exiting the needle exactly between the two top stitches. Make the double stitches the same distance apart as the stitches in the first row (Fig. 3).

7. Continue across on a straight line (Fig. 4).

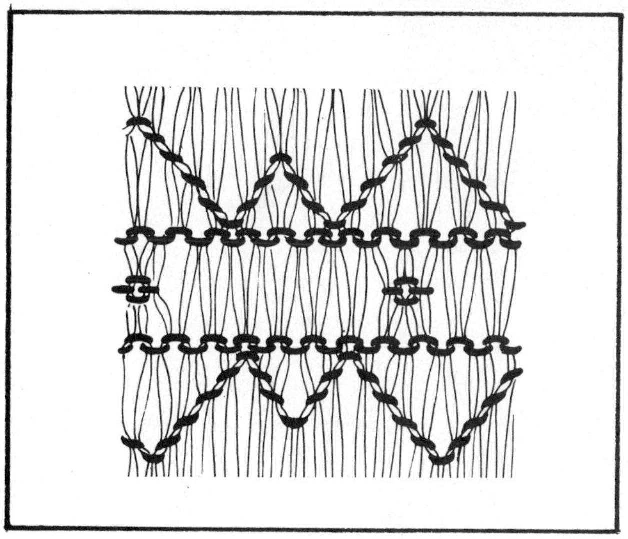

This basic smocking design creates diamonds.

8. Smocking is fun to work on gingham because the basic smocking points are already established for you. Bring every other square together on the first line (Figs. 5 and 6). Shift one square to the left in the second line and again bring every other square together. The third line is an exact repeat of the first.

9. Smocking patterns can be quite elaborate—note some of the patterns illustrated.

10. If you are creating an outfit, the smocking should be worked before you cut your patterns as smocking shrinks fabric considerably.

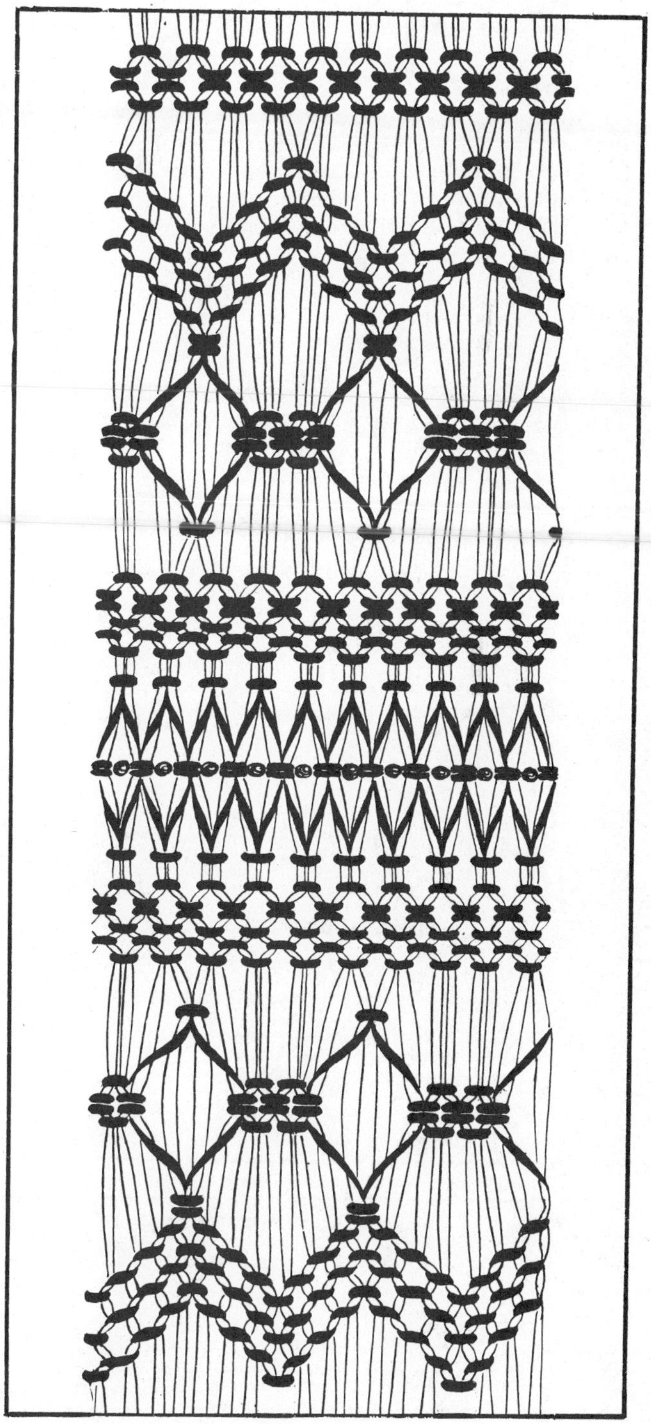

TRAPUNTO

Trapunto is a needle art that originated in Italy. Delicate designs—small flowers and leaves—were drawn on fine white linen and quilted with outline stitching to a lining. The fabric was then turned over, and from the back bits of cotton were

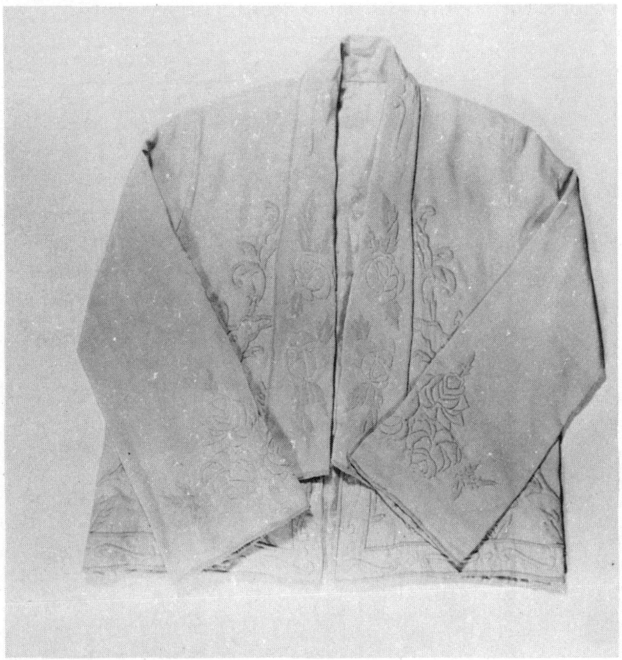

pushed through the weave to pad each leaf and petal. Our version of Trapunto is a little different from the traditional.

1. The rose and border designs are shown in actual size. Trace them on tracing paper or wrapping tissue.
2. Pin the tracing to two layers of fabric.
3. Work the border first. Make a tight running

stitch along the lines.

4. When the border stitching is completed, tear away the tracing.

5. Thread wool yarn (double thickness) on a wide-eyed needle.

6. Insert the needle through the underside of the fabric between the two layers at a key point. For instance, at the point marked X on the border design.

7. Pass the needle and yarn between the two layers and between the rows of stitches.

8. Exit the needle at another key point in the design through the underside and snip off excess yarn. The idea is to fill all the channels made by the stitched lines with yarn for a raised effect.

9. Trace the rose design as you did the border and pin it in place. Stitch along all the lines and remove the tracing when through.

10. Because the rose design has larger areas, fill in by sewing in rows of yarn in tight lines. Snip off the excess yarn up to the fabric. Another method is to cut small slits in each area on the underside of the fabric and force yarn or cotton into the areas with a small crochet hook. Sew the slits closed.

11. If the top fabric is sheer, colored yarns will show through.

12. Line trapunto designs.

13. Use trapunto on evening skirts, jackets, shawls and bedspreads.

HEMSTITCHING

(Shown in color, page 165)

Hemstitching—a technique that came from Italy several centuries ago—is a method of sewing a hem in place and incorporating it into a decorative border. The border is made by pulling out horizontal threads to form vertical thread bands. The vertical threads are then drawn into neat little groups.

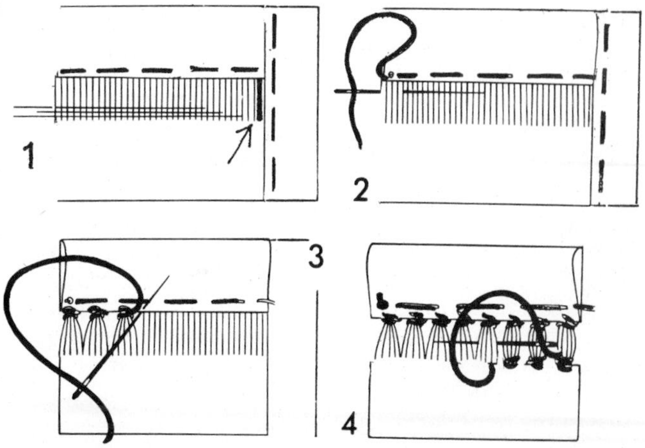

1. Choose a moderately loose woven fabric from which threads can be pulled easily. Whether you are making a handkerchief, placemat, runner or any other item, turn all sides under and hem with a ¼ to ½-inch hem on all sides.

2. Cut one ¾ inch vertical slit (see arrow, Fig. 1) where two hemmed sides meet.

3. Cut a second slit, same size, on the opposite corner.

4. Pull out all horizontal threads between the slits. If you want the border to go all the way around the piece, make pulled thread bands along the other three sides by cutting slits and proceeding as above.

5. Thread a needle with whatever thread you want to use. Gather a group of vertical threads with the needle (Fig. 2) and stitch tightly together at least twice. Stitch close to the hemline.

6. Move to the next group of threads and gather in the same way (Fig. 3). Complete the gather-

ing around the entire hemline and around any other side from which you have pulled threads.

7. Stitch together the groups at the other end of the shaft (Fig. 4).

DRAWN WORK

Drawn work is one of the earliest forms of open work embroidery and the precursor of lace. It was known all over Europe under different names, and was used largely for ecclesiastical purposes and for the ornamentation of shrouds. Specimens of drawn work have been traced back to the 1200s and are of such fine material you need a magnifying glass to observe the detailed work.

1. Drawn work is an elaborate form of hemstitching. Start with a hemstitched item—a handkerchief, doily or rectangular runner.
2. The design shown has a second row of hemstitching about ½ inch from the first hemstitched row.
3. A third row of pulled threads, one-inch wide, is formed ½ inch away from the second hemstitched row.
4. Form another hemstitched row ½ inch away from the one-inch row and sew as you did the two bottom rows.
5. The one-inch pulled thread row is worked after the rows above and below are hemstitched. Gather every two groups of threads at their centers. Sew or knot as you did in the hemstitched areas or use the twist design shown in the insert.
6. Finish corner threads by twisting yarn around them.

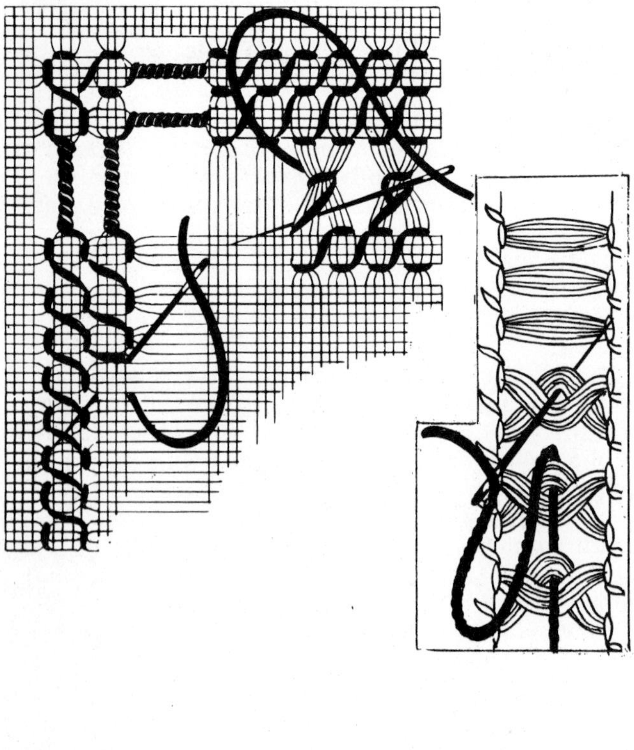

EMBROIDERED DRAWN WORK CORNERS

The following designs are worked in the corners of large pulled bands, where squares are automatically formed by the very process of pulling threads. Gather all pulled bands before you begin to embroider the corners.

CIRCLE MOTIF

1. Sew embroidery thread from corner to corner (from X to X).
2. Sew embroidery thread in and out of the pulled bands (see threads marked Z). Z threads crisscross each other at the corner squares and form, with the X threads, an eight-arm start. The needle, threaded with embroidery thread, passes under and then over each arm as it moves to the following arm.
3. Continue to weave around the arms, forming a circle. Make the circle as large as you like, filling in some or all of the area, as desired.

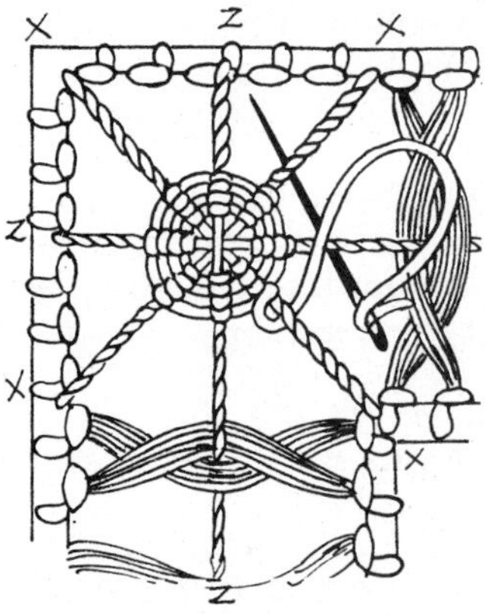

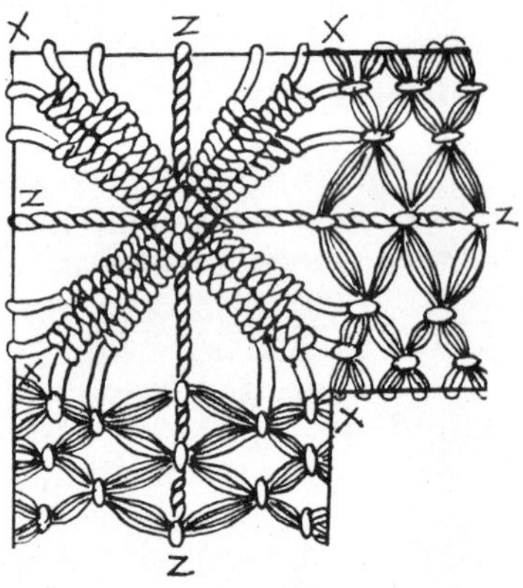

CROSS MOTIF

1. Sew embroidery thread along the center of the pulled bands (from Z to Z). Z threads crisscross each other at the corner squares.
2. Sew four strands of embroidery thread from corner to corner (from X to X). Some threads are sewn to the sides and some to the gatherings on the side bands.
3. Sew a small circle in the center of the cross as you did in the Circle Motif.
4. Each arm of the cross is worked separately by sewing in and out of the four threads. Extend the sewn threads on the two inner threads.

HARDANGER EMBROIDERY

(Shown in color, page 165)

Hardanger embroidery comes from a district with the same name in west Norway. The embroidery

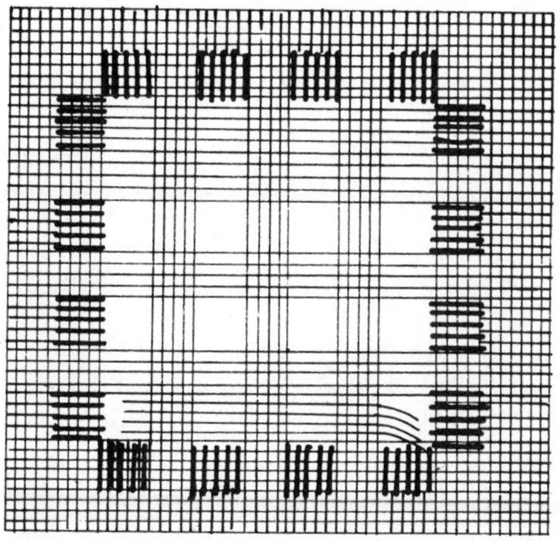

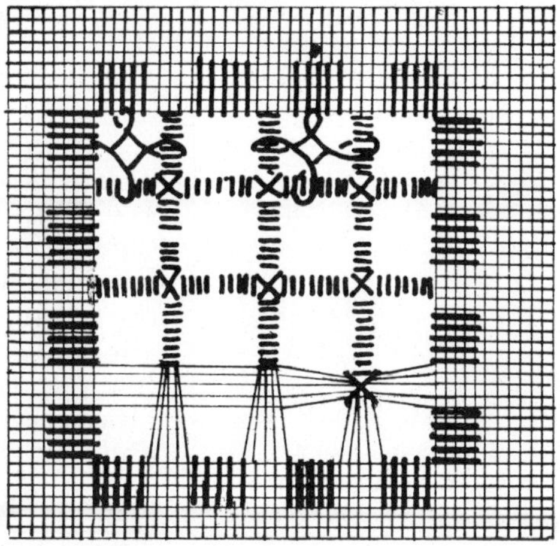

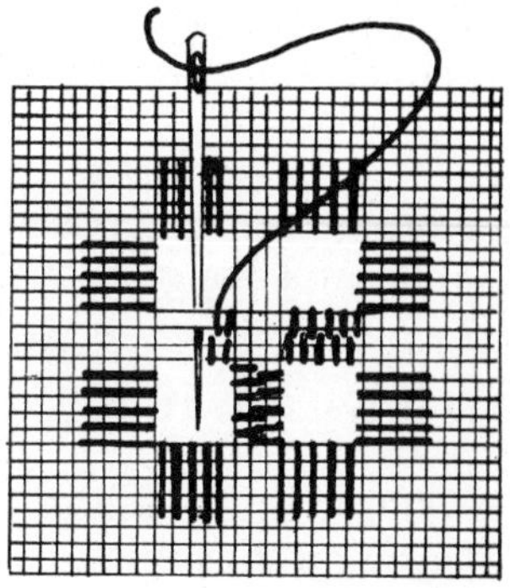

was traditionally worked in white thread on white fabric, but today's modern designs have introduced color. It is basically a drawn thread technique that is used to decorate household linens and articles of clothing. The work requires that you accurately count threads.

1. Starting one inch in from hemstitched or drawn sides and corners, cut equidistant vertical and horizontal pulled bands by slitting the fabric and pulling threads as discussed in Hemstiching.
2. To keep the fabric from shifting, sew long stitches with embroidery thread into the areas where threads have been pulled away (note the heavy lines, Fig. 1).
3. In the center area of the fabric (bottom row, Fig. 2) tie all points where the vertical and horizontal threads cross.
4. Wrap each band of threads in a rope-like fashion. (The insert, Fig. 3, shows a method of stitching the bands rather than wrapping them. You sew in and out of the threads forming a flat weave.)
5. Sew a looped diamond with embroidery thread in each open square of the center design.

CUTWORK

Cutwork is more correctly called Richelieu embroidery, named after the cardinal who was Minister to Louis XIII of France. Richelieu, eager to develop industry in France, arranged for skilled Venetian lace workers to set up schools and workshops to train native craftsmen.

1. Draw a design on the intended surface with a soft pencil. Flower designs were given earlier in this chapter. You can transfer a design with tracing or carbon paper. Cutwork designs are also available on stamped linen ready to be worked.
2. The lines of the entire design are worked in a narrow buttonhole stitch. The pearl of the buttonhole stitch must fall on the edge to be cut away.
3. For a raised buttonhole stitch, sew a running stitch along the lines before you begin to embroider.
4. Lock the completed design in a border which

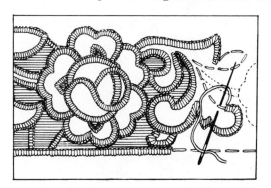

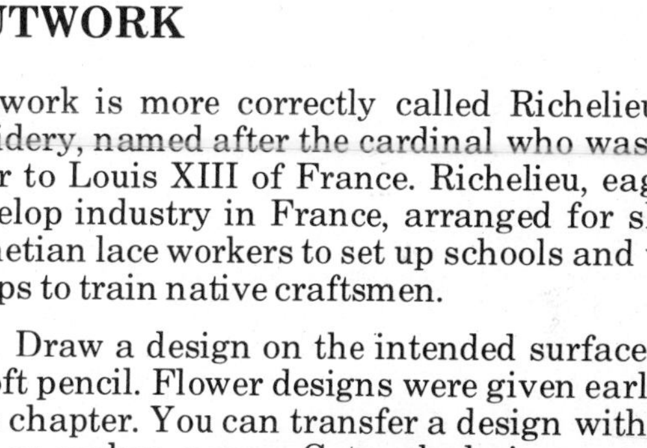

is either circular or straight and which abuts the design at random points. Buttonhole the border with the pearl of the stitch facing the design (inward).

5. Cut away areas of fabric with a pointed scissor. Cut close to the stitching. The stitching on the border and on the design that abuts it holds the cutwork design to the fabric.

CANDLEWICKING

Candlewicking is as American as apple pie, emerging about the time this country became an independent Republic. It is a combination of weaving and embroidery. Today it is mass-produced and called chenille. It is seen most often on bedspreads.

1. Candlewicking should be worked on muslin.

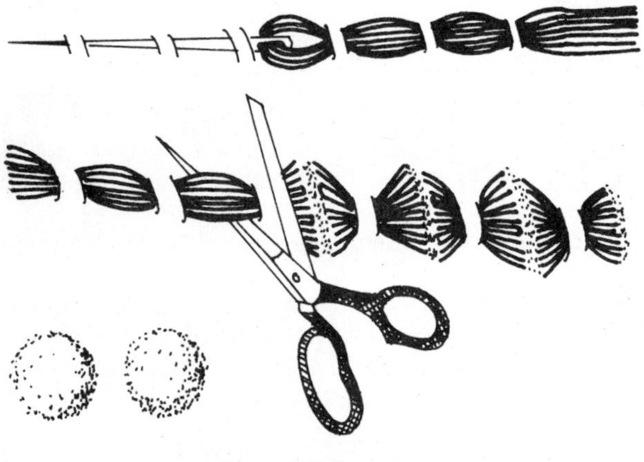

Use a heavy soft thread composed of many strands and which has little or no twist. There is a product called candlewicking thread; if you can find it, use that.

2. Thread a long length of yarn on a large needle. Double the yarn for larger tuff balls.

3. The stitch is a straight running stitch, picking up 1/8 inch of fabric with 3/4 inch between stitches. Do not draw the thread tightly through the fabric.

4. Cut each stitch in half with a scissors.

5. Submerge the muslin in water to shrink the fabric. Shrinking holds the stitches in place. Dry and do not iron.

6. When dry, brush the cut stitches into ball tuffs.

CORD WORK

Cord work is drawing on fabric using yarn or cord.

1. Cord work can be done with knitting yarn, decorative cord, braiding or any other sturdy, narrow trim.

2. The stitching resembles Couching which is explained in the section Basic Embroidery Stitches. Lay the cord in a design on the intended fabric and stitch down at close intervals with your chosen thread. Use nylon thread for invisble stitches or colored embroidery thread for a more dramatic look.

3. The needle passes under the fabric, exiting close to the cord. Pass the needle closely over the cord and back down under the fabric.

FAGOTING

Fagoting is simply a way of joining two pieces of fabric (edges, seams or tapes) with decorative stitches. The stitches form an openwork lacy pattern. It was last fashionable in the early 1920s.

1. Fold over the two sides of the fabric to be stitched.
2. Insert the needle from under the right top fold.
3. Work the needle over to the left side, a little down from the right stitch.
4. Insert the needle from under the fabric and then out. Bring the needle under the diagonal.
5. Place the stitch a little lower than the last and continue crisscrossing back and forth.
6. To insure perfectly parallel fabric sides and stitches, pin or baste a piece of scrap fabric to the underside of the surfaces being fagoted. Remove the under fabric when the stitching is completed.
7. Fagoting can be used on blouses, bed and table linens and on any two surfaces that can be joined together.

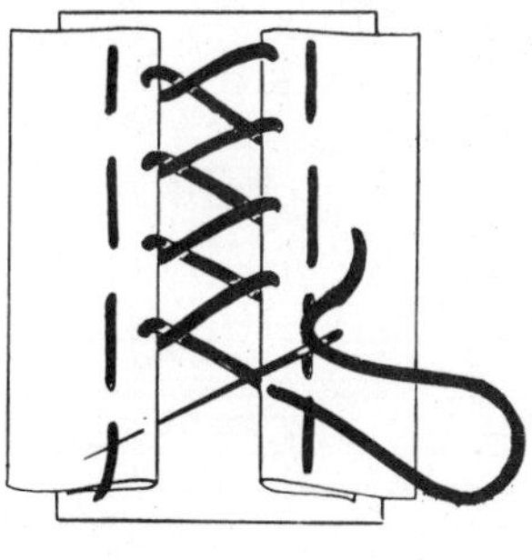

MOCK FILET WORK

Filet work is an intricate lacy embroidery worked on netting. Our version is a mock filet because we work it on store-bought netting whereas colonial craftsmen created their own. Filet work reached the height of its popularity in America in the 1920s.

1. Buy netting for filet work.
2. The object in mock filet work is to fill in the individual squares with stitches to form a design.
3. Use thread for stitching. The stitch fills in a given square by going back and forth over the two opposite sides. The thread passes over the left side and then under the right side.
4. To fill in large areas, alternate the direction of stitches in each square and each row. For example, in the insert the top box has stitches going from top to bottom. The box directly under has stitches linking the left and right sides.
5. Any design can be worked on netting. The two animals given here are examples. For those with a hand at crochet, try the crocheted and netted yoke used in a 1910 camisole.

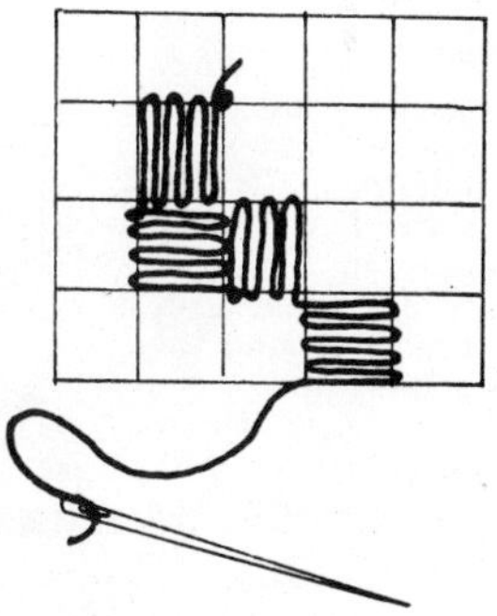

ONE HEARS OF THE YOKE SEEN UNDER SUMMER FROCKS

THE DAINTY SPIDER-WEB MOTIF AND A NEW DESIGN IN FILET CROCHET

FILET CAMISOLE YOKE

NO. 50 crochet cotton, No. 10 steel crochet hook. One-quarter of the yoke is shown in this diagram. The edge on the neck and armhole are worked on after the yoke is completed. Begin at the first row of diagram 1, ch. 39. Skip 8 sts. next the hook, 1 d. c. into next st. to form 1 o. 10 more o. 5 ch. turn.

Second row—10 o. 1 s. Now follow the diagram, working 1 o. for every white square and 1 s. for every black square. When the 14th row is reached make 1 less o. on the armhole edge. In the next 5 rows add 1 o. on the armhole edge of each row. Continue to follow the diagram to the end. When the end is reached count back 12 rows, begin at the next row and follow every row of diagram back to the first row. Make the back in the same manner. Work 2 ch. between each square on the curved part of the neck and armhole. Work a row of filet squares around armhole.

Beading—2 tr. c. * 2 ch. skip 2 sts. 2 tr. c. Repeat from * all the way around neck. Work a row of open squares.

Edge—* Work 4 s. c. into each of next 4 o. of previous row. 4 ch. turn. Sl. st. into fourth single crochet from hook. Turn. Cover this loop with 5 s. c. Repeat from * all around neck and armhole.

CAMISOLE YOKE SPIDER-WEBS

THE yoke was made of white, the drawn work of color—Use No. 50 crochet cotton white, No. 40 crochet cotton pink. No. 12 steel crochet hook.

Diagram 2 shows one half the yoke. Work the small squares first. Begin at the first row of diagram 2, with white, ch. 30. Skip 8 sts. next the hook, 1 d. c. into next st. to form the first o. 7 more o. 5 ch. turn. Continue to follow the diagram, making 1 o. for every small white square and leaving spaces for the spider-web. When the end of the diagram is reached work back 20 rows of o. Following each row back to the first row. Join thread at top of point and work the shoulder-straps of large open squares as follows. * 9 ch. skip 1 d. c. of previous row, 1 d. tr. c. (thread three times around the hook) into the next d. c. 5 ch. skip 1 d. c., 1 d. tr. c. into the next d. c. Turn. Repeat from * for 9 inches. Join to back. Work large square across lower edge and across front and underarm as illustrated in diagram 2.

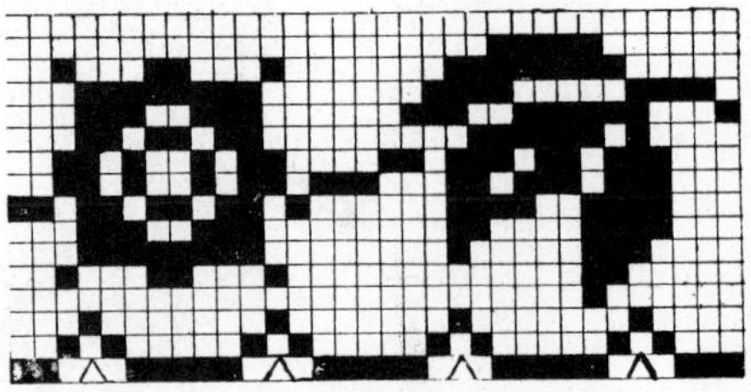

Edge — With white work the following edge all around the neck and armhole. 5 s. c. into every large square, 3 ch. p. over every d. c. Continue this edge up the triangles working 3 s. c. into every small square. With color work s. c. close together all around the open oblong space in the front and the triangles.

Spider Webs—Baste the yoke flat on a piece of cardboard. Thread colored thread in a sewing needle. Join it on A in diagram 3, pass it across to B, overcast up edge to C, cross to D, overcast to E. Continue in this way until J is reached. Fasten thread securely and break it. Join again at K, pass to center and weave the thread around and around, passing the needle under one thread and over the next until the center is ¼ inch in diameter.

In the center front and back join the thread at A in diagram 4, pass across to B, overcast to C, pass across to D. Continue to follow letters all the way across. When end is reached at A, pass to center of next crossing of threads, weave it around, passing the needle over one thread and under the next. * When the circle is one-quarter inch in diameter pass the thread to the next crossing of threads and weave it. Repeat from * all the way across ending the thread off at S.

These crochet yokes are lovely for use on lingerie. The filet crochet yoke is made in a new design and is very effective. The spider-web effect of the other yoke is something both unusual and dainty. The combining of a color and white is very pretty. These yokes, though fine in effect, launder beautifully and are very durable.

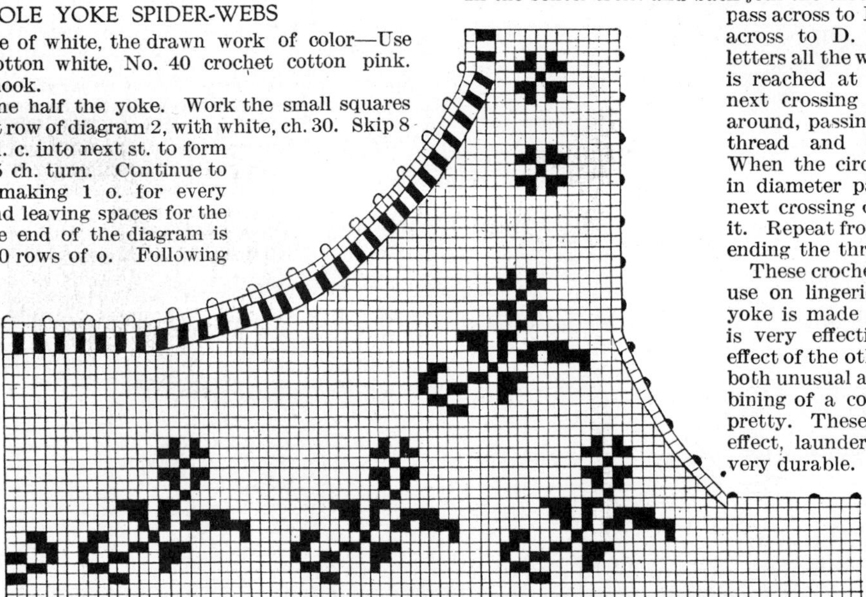

Diagram 1

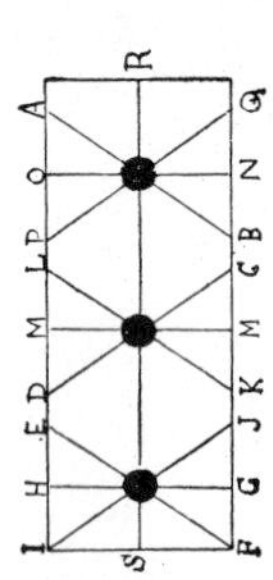

Diagram 4

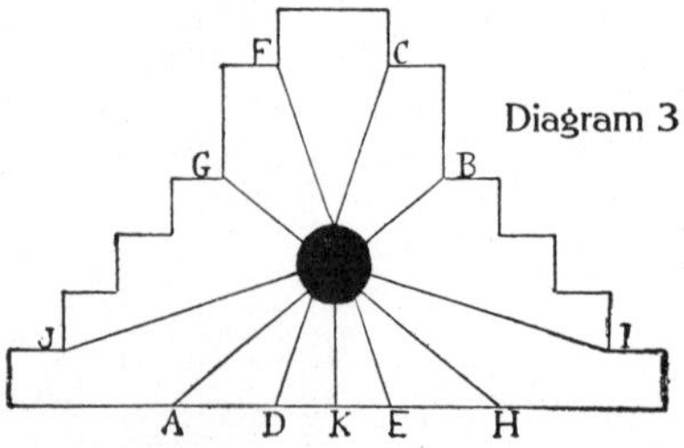

Diagram 3

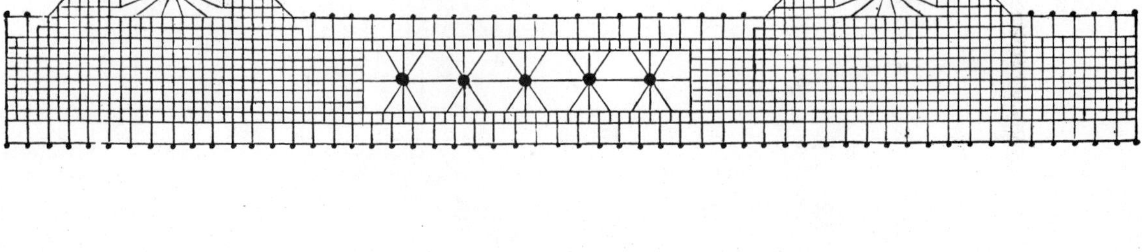

Diagram 2